首斬り朝

SAMURAI 首斬り
EXECUTIONER 朝

Punished is not the man himself,
but the evil that resides in him.

story
KAZUO KOIKE

art
GOSEKI KOJIMA

DARK HORSE MANGA™

translation
DANA LEWIS and **MARK MIYAKE**

lettering & retouch
SNO CONE STUDIOS

publisher
MIKE RICHARDSON

editor
TIM ERVIN

assistant editor
PHILIP SIMON

book design
DARIN FABRICK

art director
LIA RIBACCHI

Dark Horse Comics, Inc.
10956 SE Main Street, Milwaukie, OR 97222
www.darkhorse.com

First edition: December 2004
ISBN: 1-59307-208-2

1 3 5 7 9 10 8 6 4 2

Printed in Canada

To find a comics shop in your area, call the
Comic Shop Locator Service toll-free at 1-888-266-4226.

首斬り朝

TWO BODIES, TWO MINDS

**By KAZUO KOIKE
& GOSEKI KOJIMA**

VOLUME
2

A NOTE TO READERS

Samurai Executioner is a carefully researched re-creation of Edo-Period Japan. To preserve the flavor of the work, we have chosen to retain many Edo-Period terms that have no direct equivalents in English. Japanese is written in a mix of Chinese ideograms and a syllabic writing system, resulting in numerous synonyms. In the glossary, you may encounter words with multiple meanings. These are words written with Chinese ideograms that are pronounced the same but carry different meanings. A Japanese reader seeing the different ideograms would know instantly which meaning it is, but these synonyms can cause confusion when Japanese is spelled out in our alphabet. *O-yurushi o* (please forgive us)!

SAMURAI 首斬り朝
EXECUTIONER

TABLE OF CONTENTS

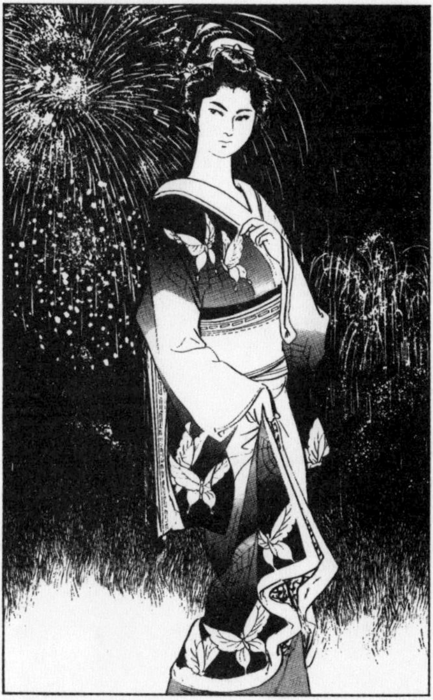

SIXTH CUT

O-TSUYA'S BROOM

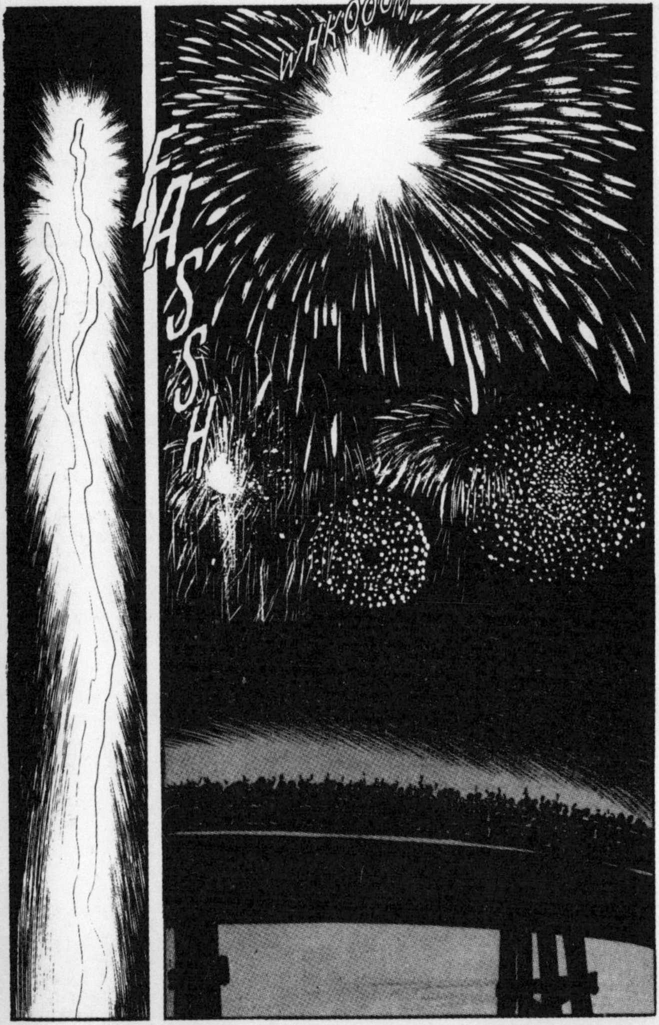
FASSH
WHKOOOM

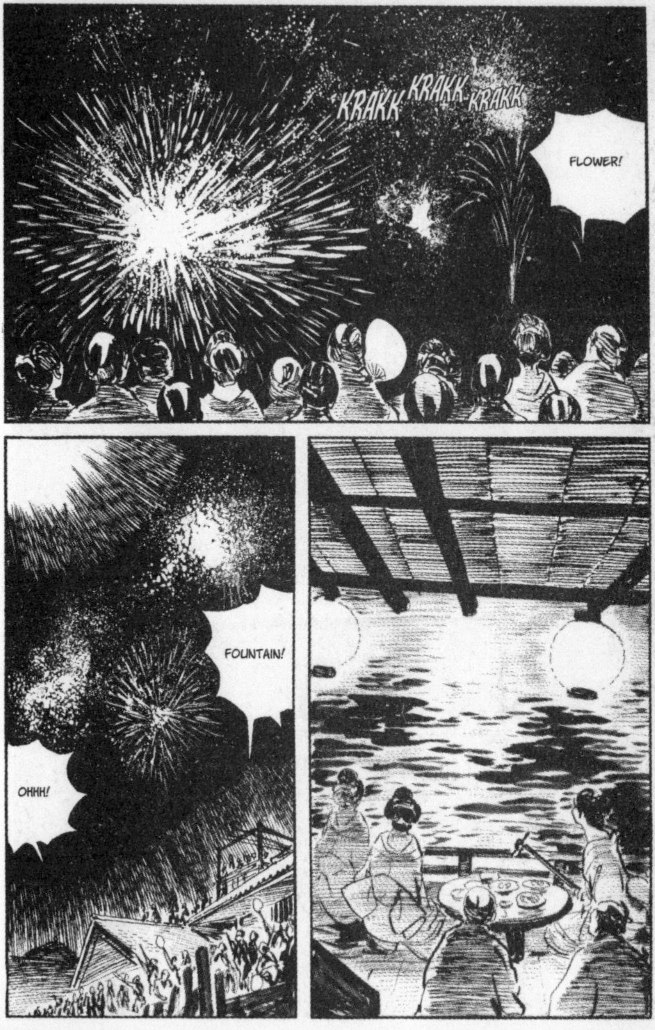
KRAKK KRAKK KRAKK
FLOWER!
FOUNTAIN!
OHHH!

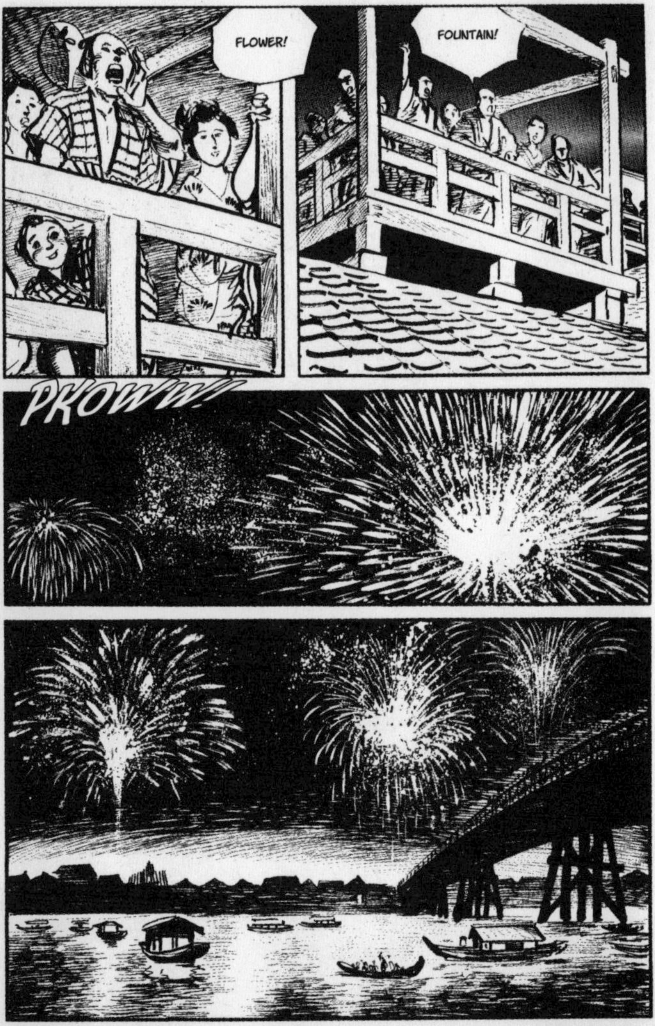
FLOWER!
FOUNTAIN!
PKOWW!!

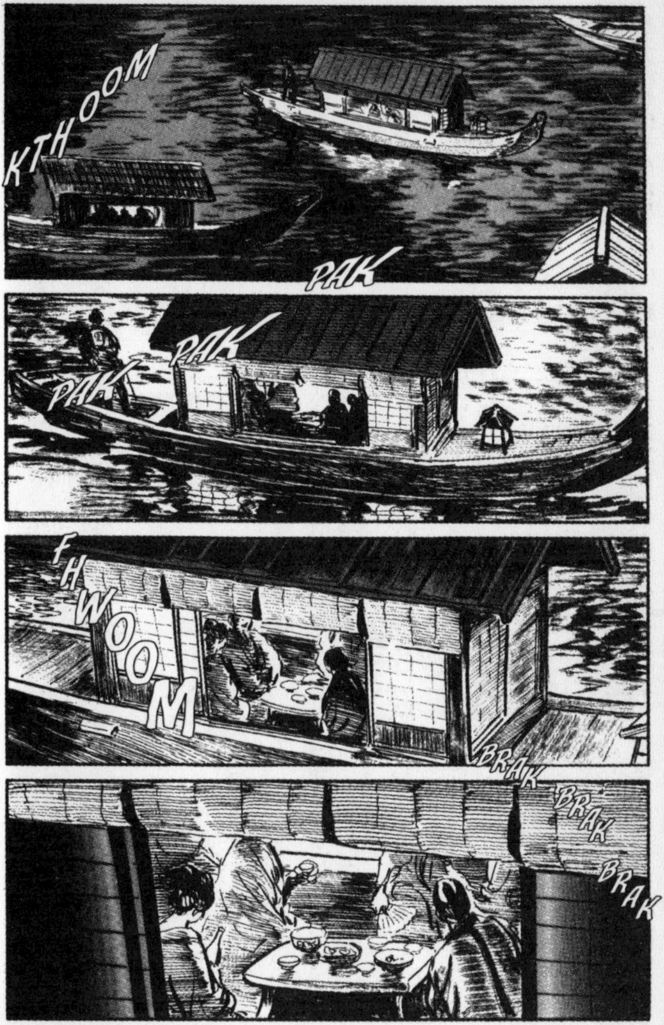
KTHOOM
PAK
PAK
PAK
FHWOOM
BRAK
BRAK
BRAK
!

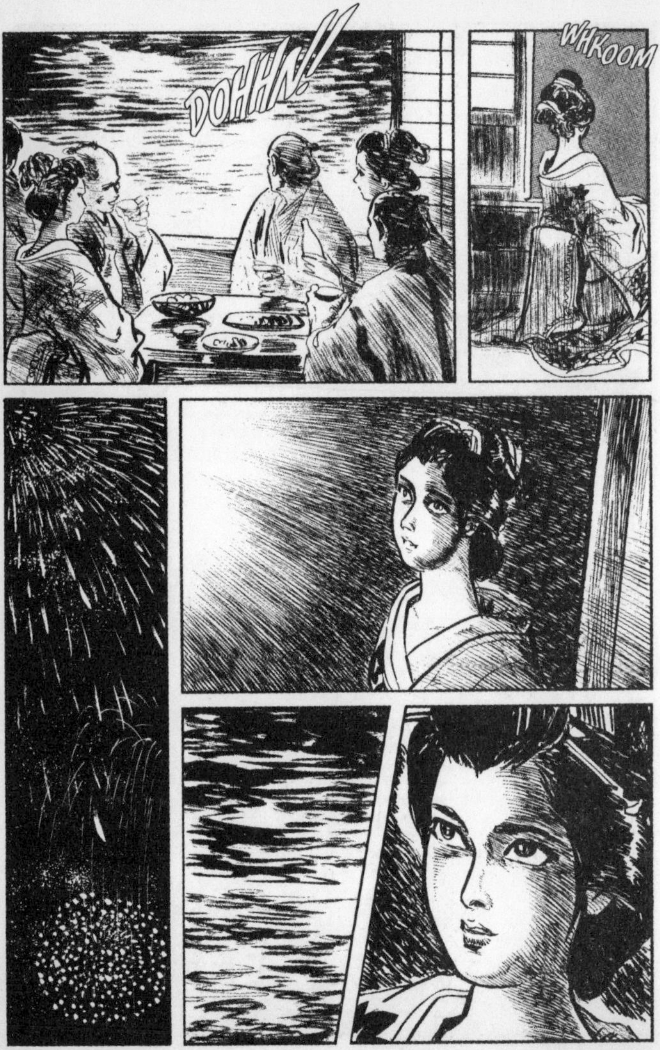
DOHHN!!
WHKOOM

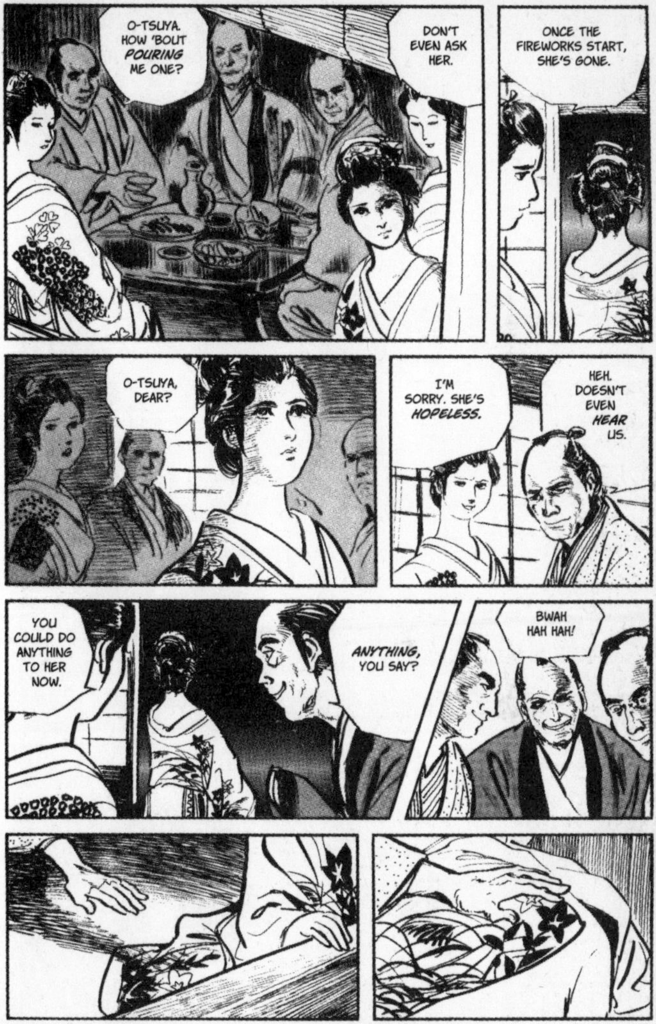
O-TSUYA. HOW 'BOUT POURING ME ONE?
DON'T EVEN ASK HER.
ONCE THE FIREWORKS START, SHE'S GONE.
O-TSUYA, DEAR?
I'M SORRY. SHE'S HOPELESS.
HEH. DOESN'T EVEN HEAR US.
YOU COULD DO ANYTHING TO HER NOW.
ANYTHING, YOU SAY?
BWAH HAH HAH!

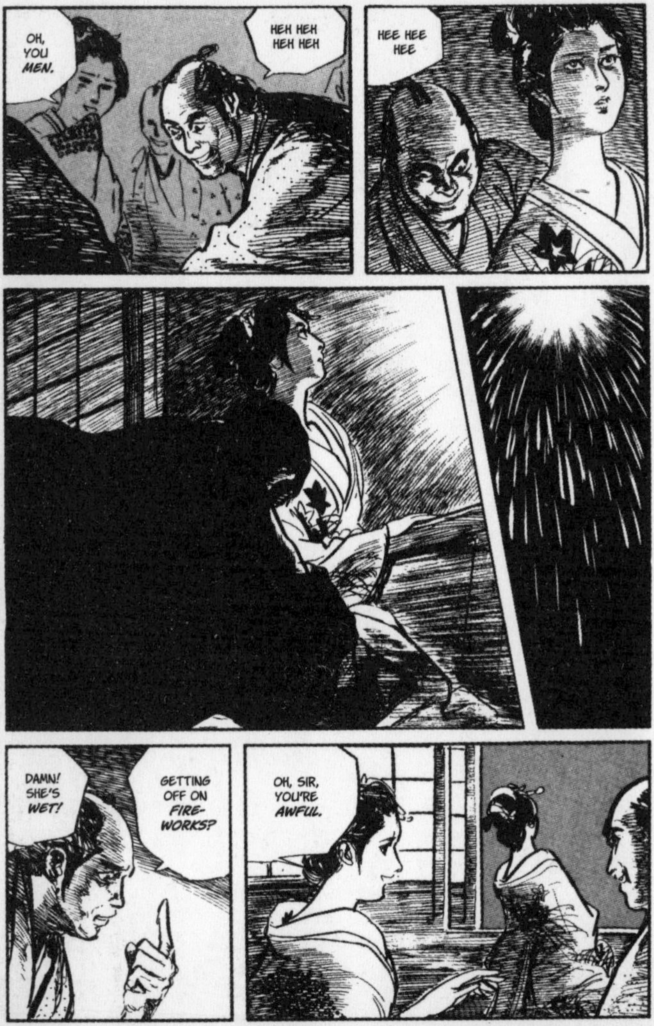
OH, YOU *MEN.*
HEH HEH HEH HEH
HEE HEE HEE
DAMN! SHE'S *WET!*
GETTING OFF ON *FIRE-WORKS?*
OH, SIR, YOU'RE *AWFUL.*

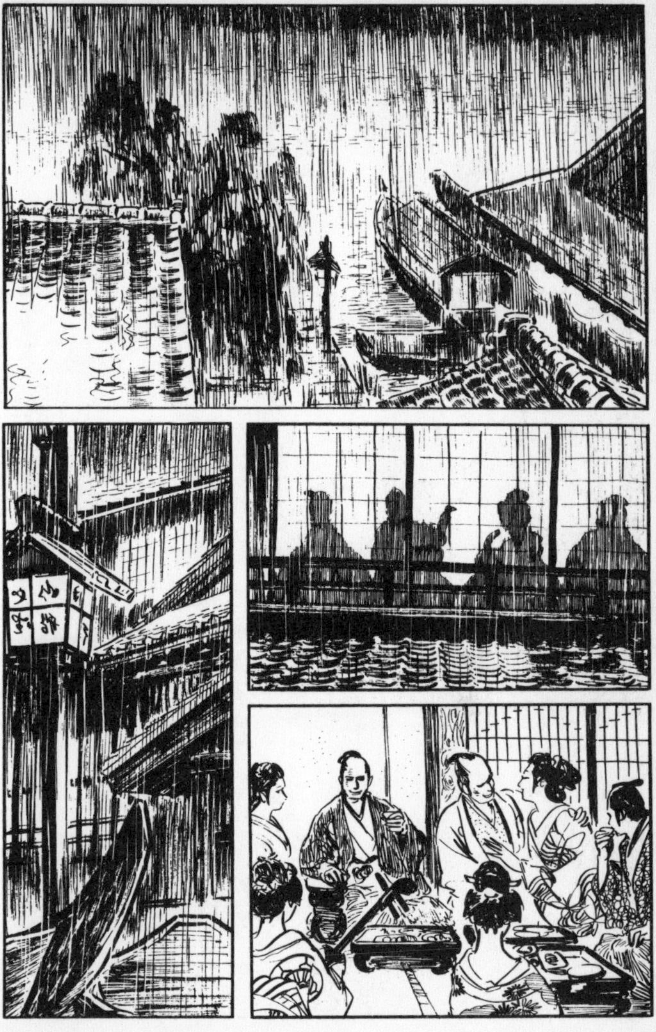

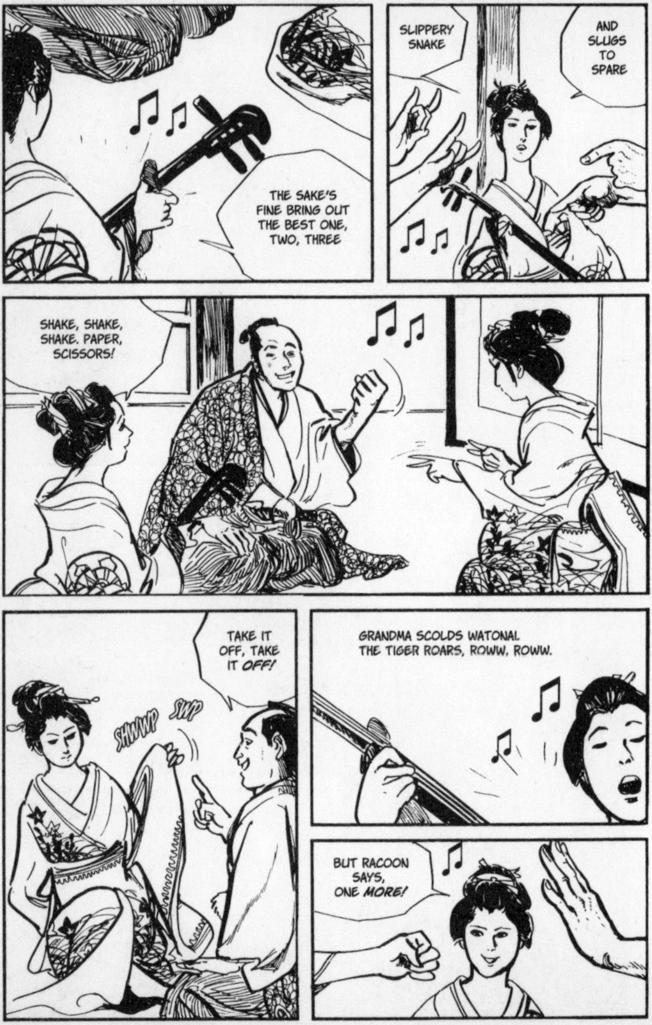
THE SAKE'S FINE BRING OUT THE BEST ONE, TWO, THREE
SLIPPERY SNAKE
AND SLUGS TO SPARE
SHAKE, SHAKE, SHAKE. PAPER, SCISSORS!
TAKE IT OFF, TAKE IT *OFF!*
SHWWP
SWP
GRANDMA SCOLDS WATONAI. THE TIGER ROARS, ROWW, ROWW.
BUT RACOON SAYS, ONE *MORE!*

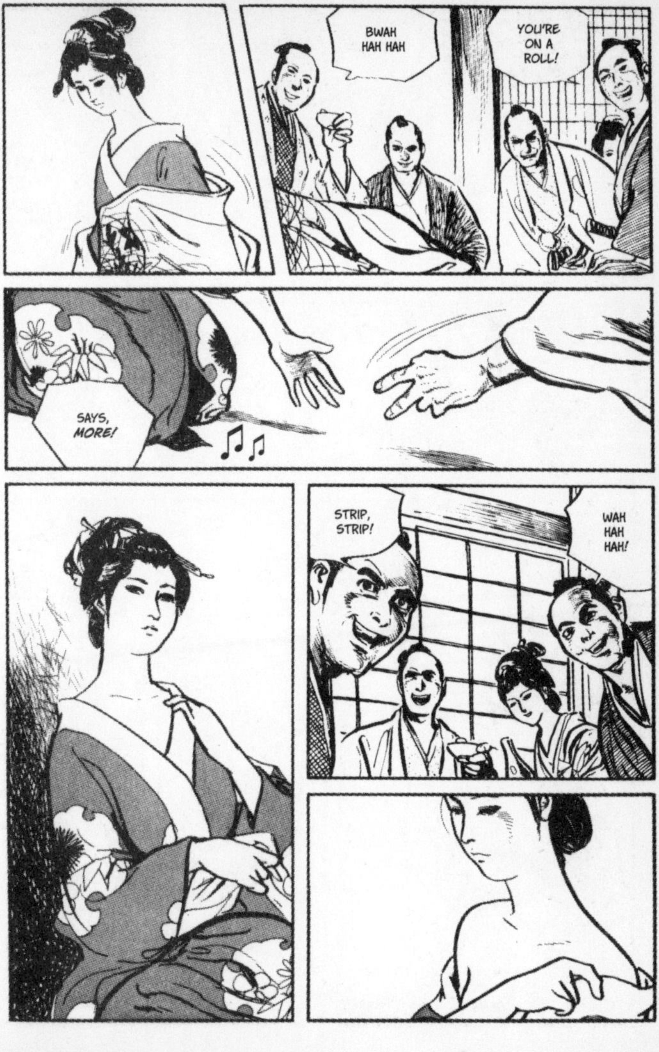
BWAH HAH HAH
YOU'RE ON A ROLL!
SAYS, MORE!
♫♫
STRIP, STRIP!
WAH HAH HAH!

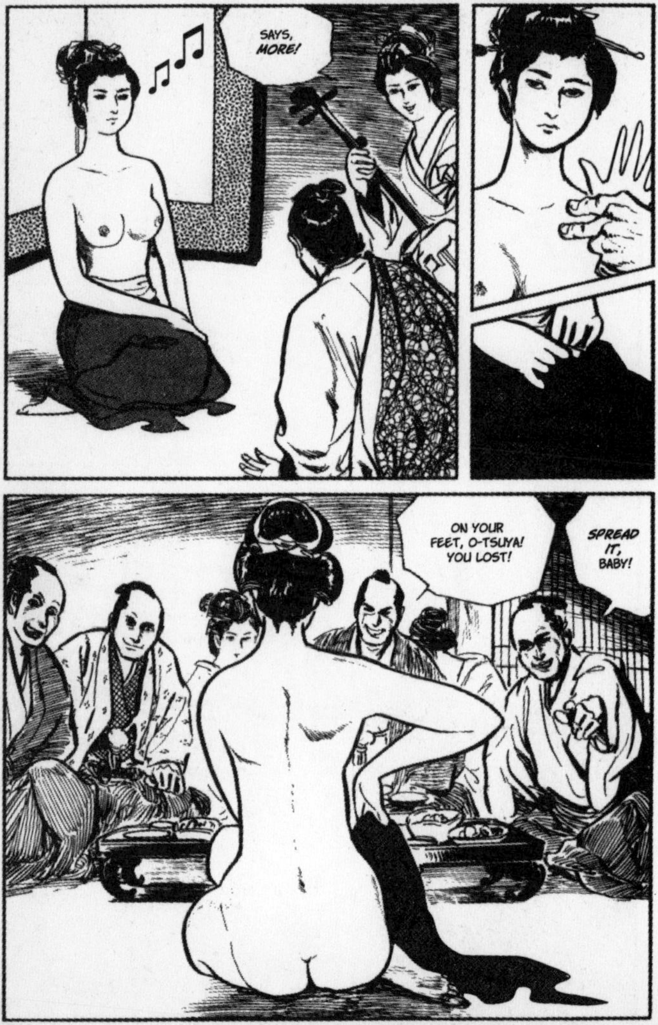
SAYS, MORE!
ON YOUR FEET, O-TSUYA! YOU LOST!
SPREAD IT, BABY!

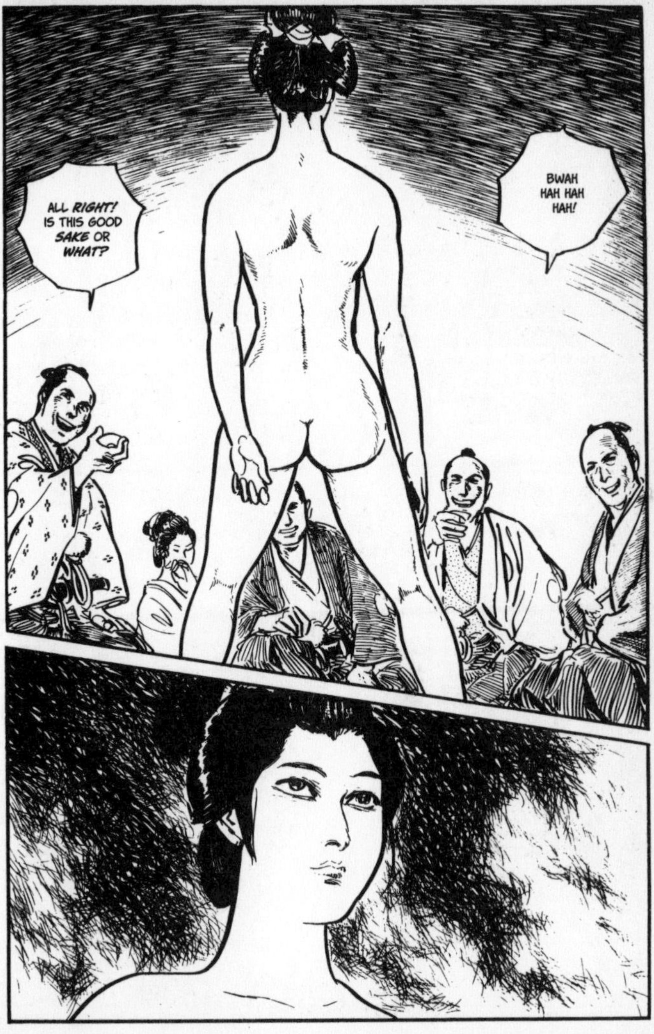
ALL RIGHT! IS THIS GOOD SAKE OR WHAT?
BWAH HAH HAH HAH!

HAH HAHH
HHF HAHH

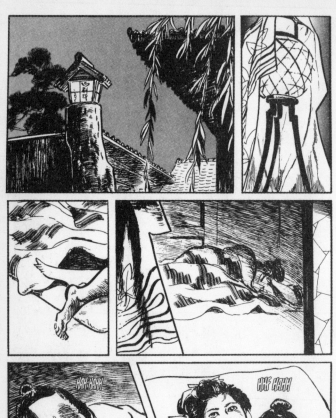

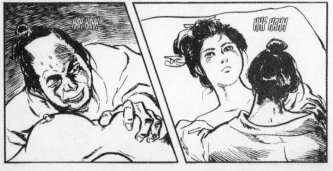

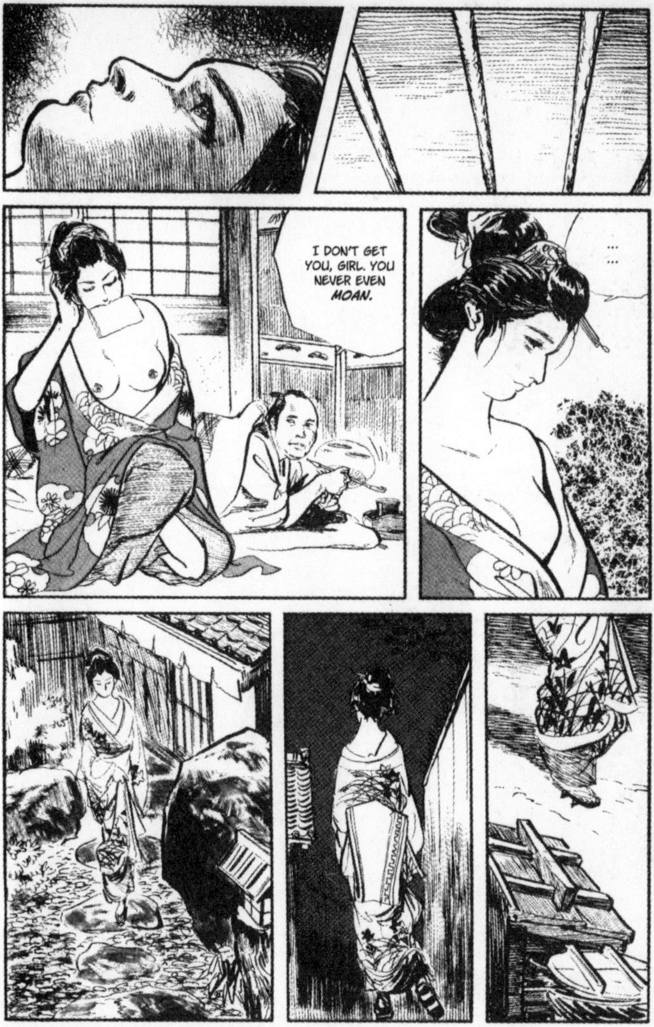
I DON'T GET YOU, GIRL. YOU NEVER EVEN *MOAN.*
...
...

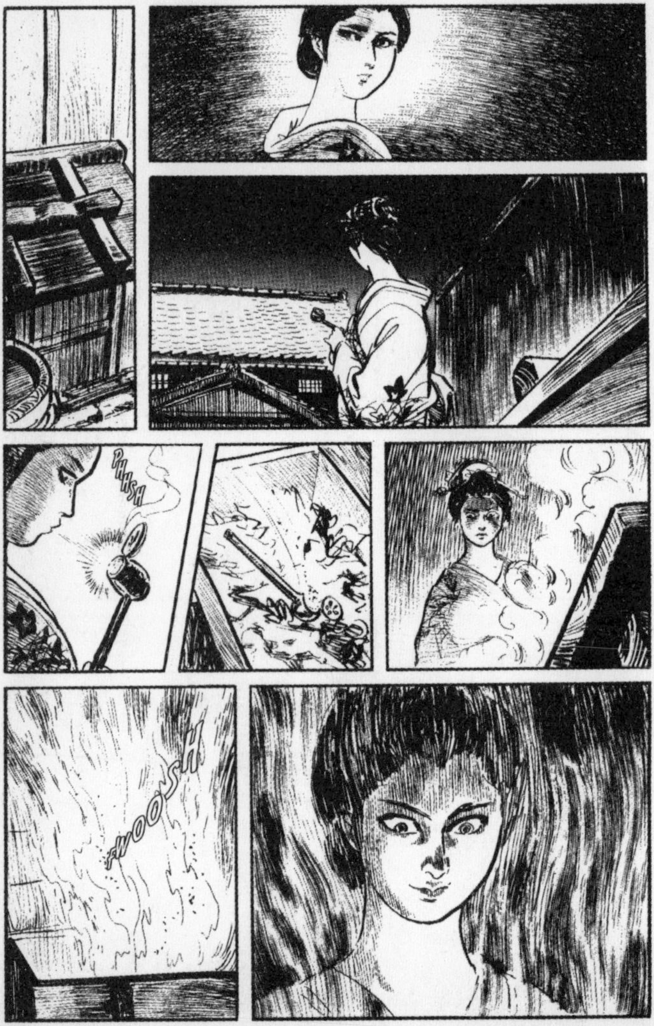
PHHSH
FWOOSH

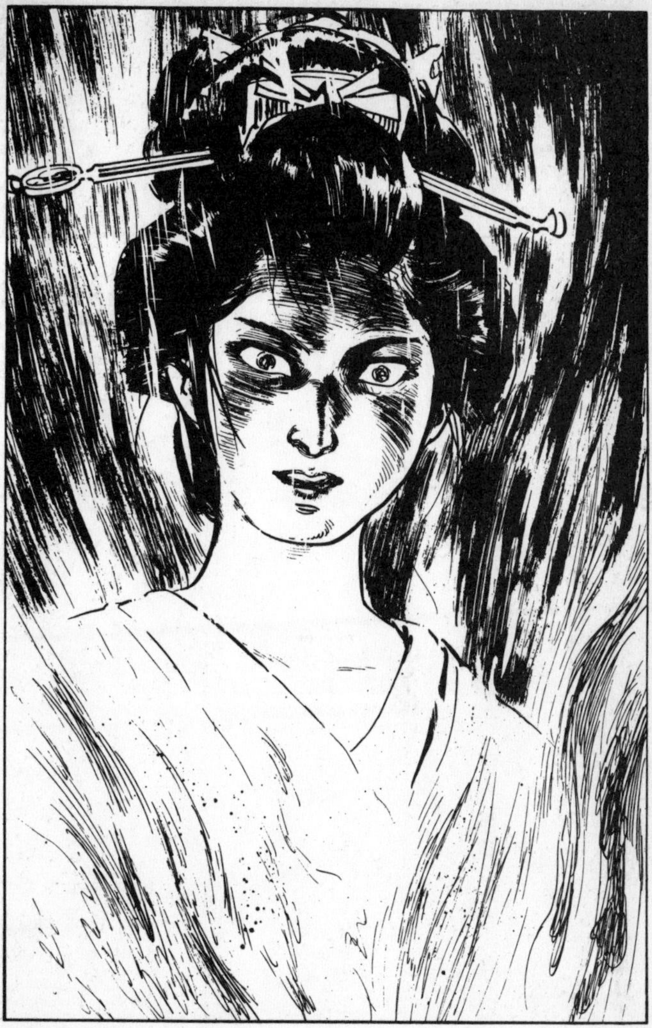

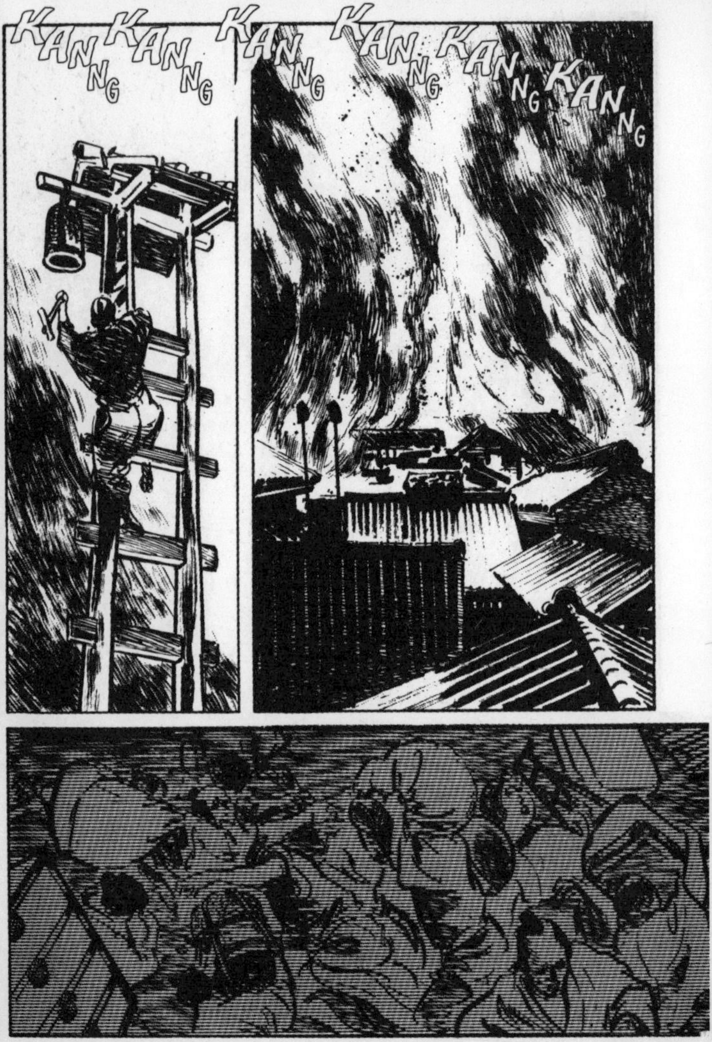
KANNG
KANNG
KANNG
KANNG
KANNG
KANNG

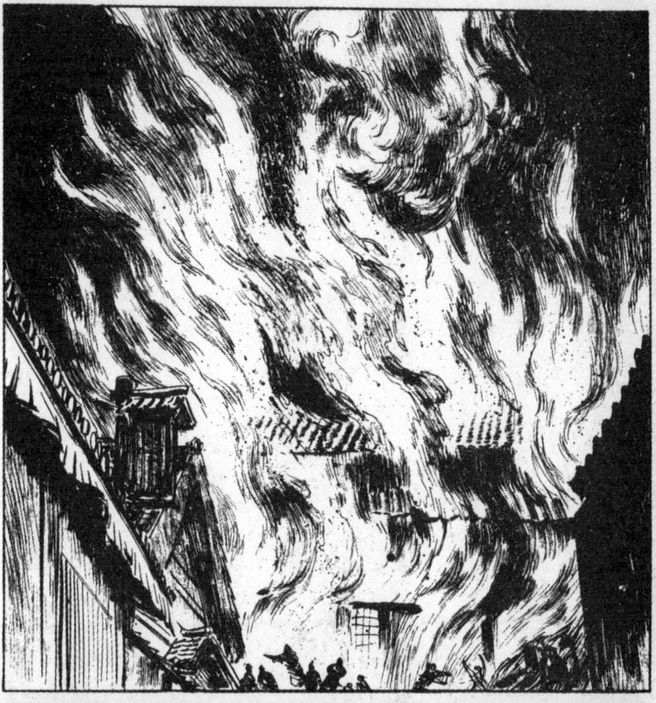
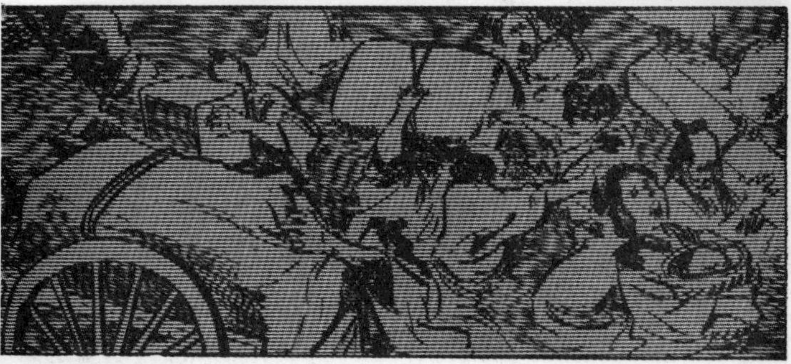

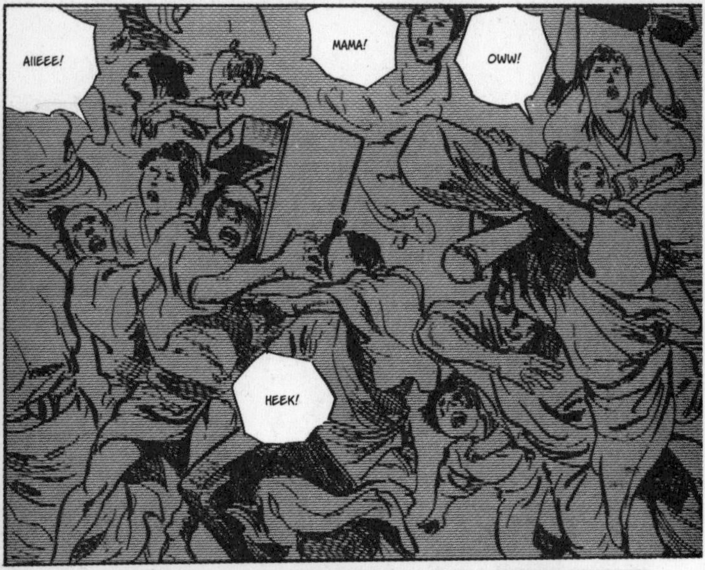
AIIEEE!
MAMA!
OWW!
HEEK!

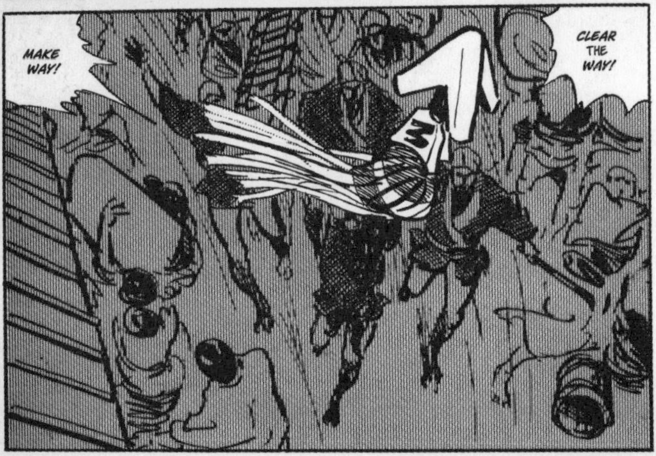
MAKE WAY!
CLEAR THE WAY!

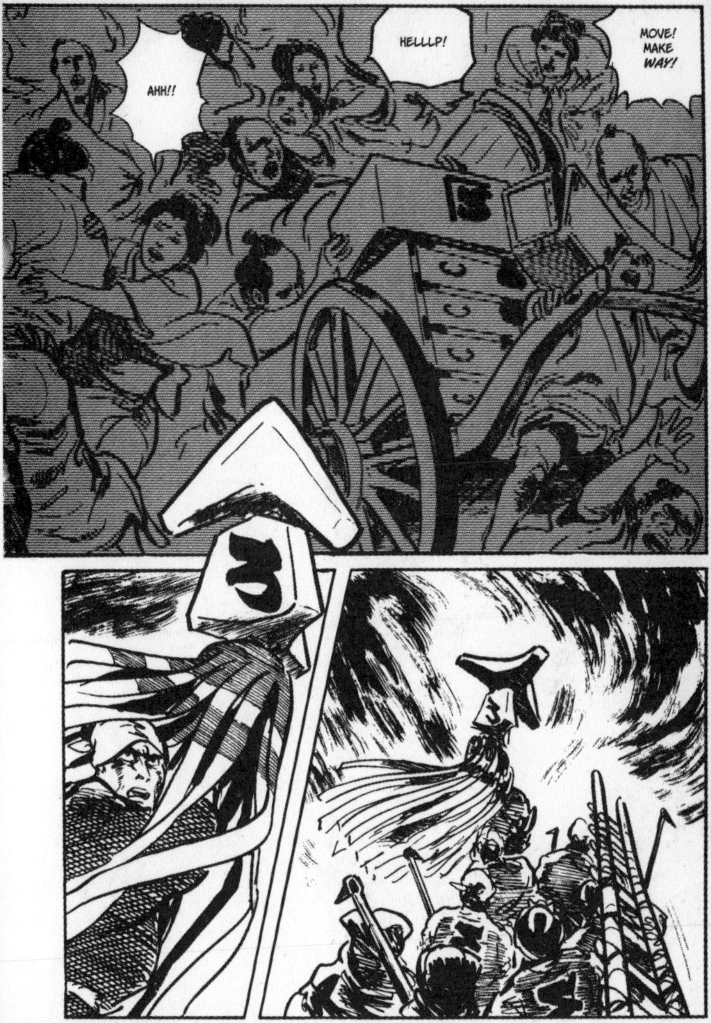
AHH!!
HELLLP!
MOVE! MAKE WAY!

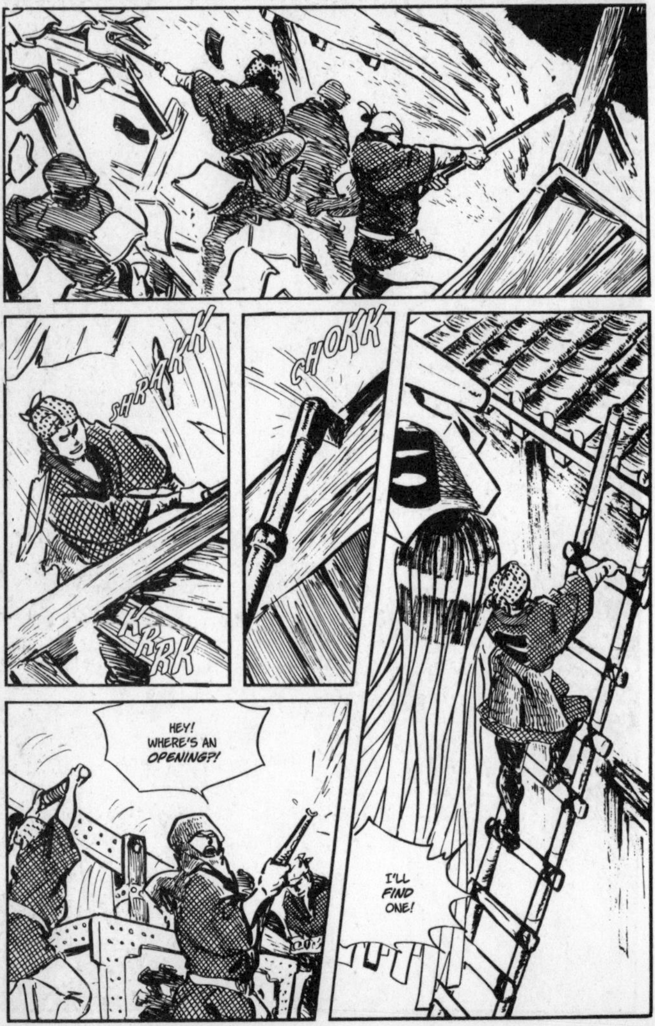
SHRAKKK
KRRK
CHOKK
HEY! WHERE'S AN OPENING?!
I'LL FIND ONE!

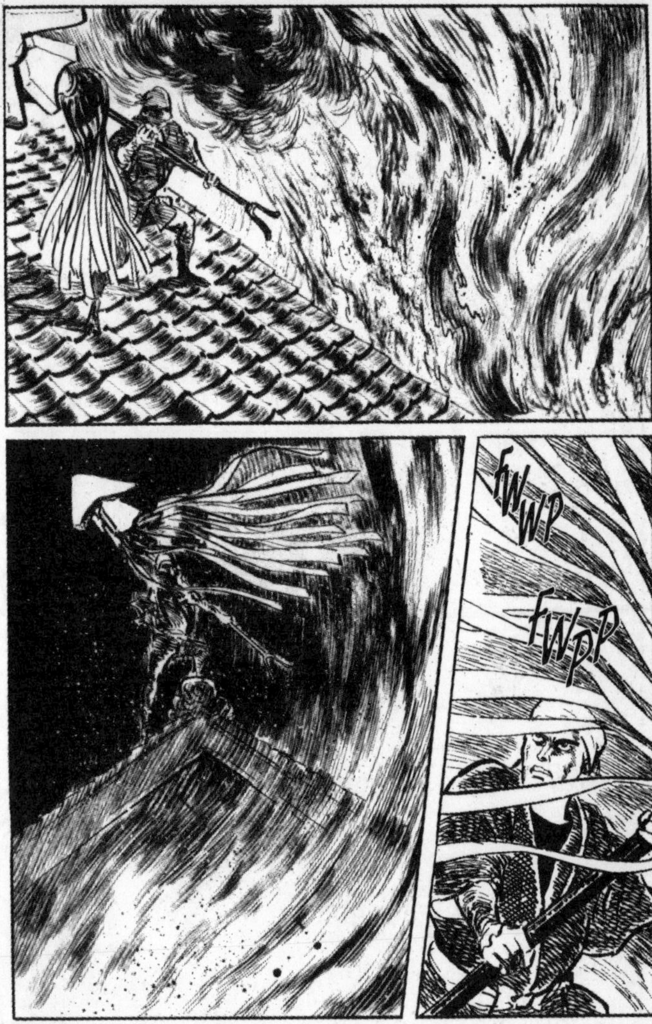
FWWP
FWPP

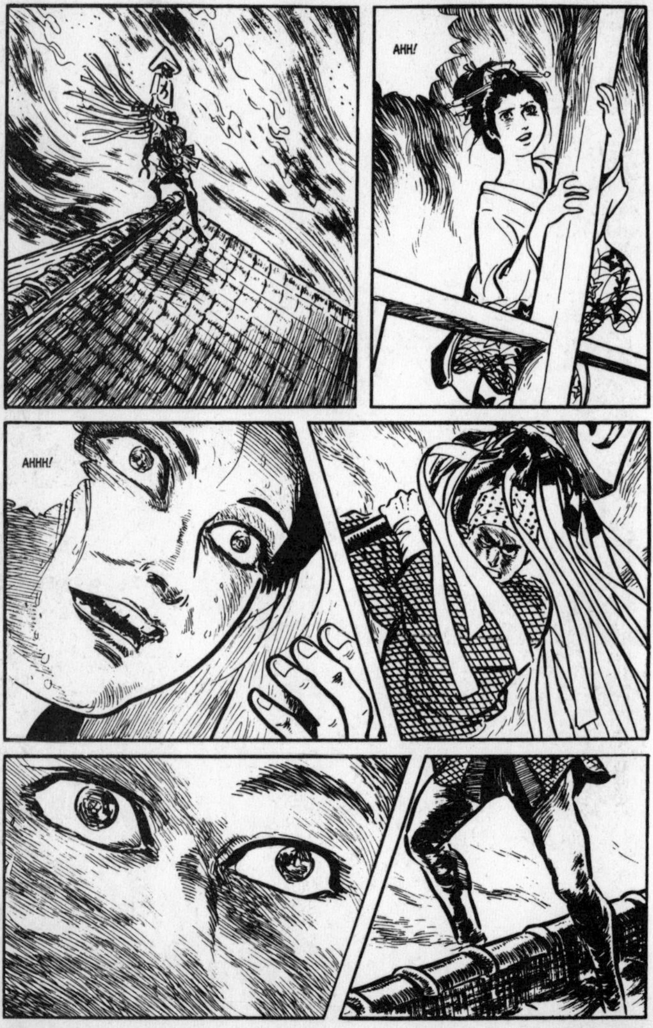
AHH!
AHHH!

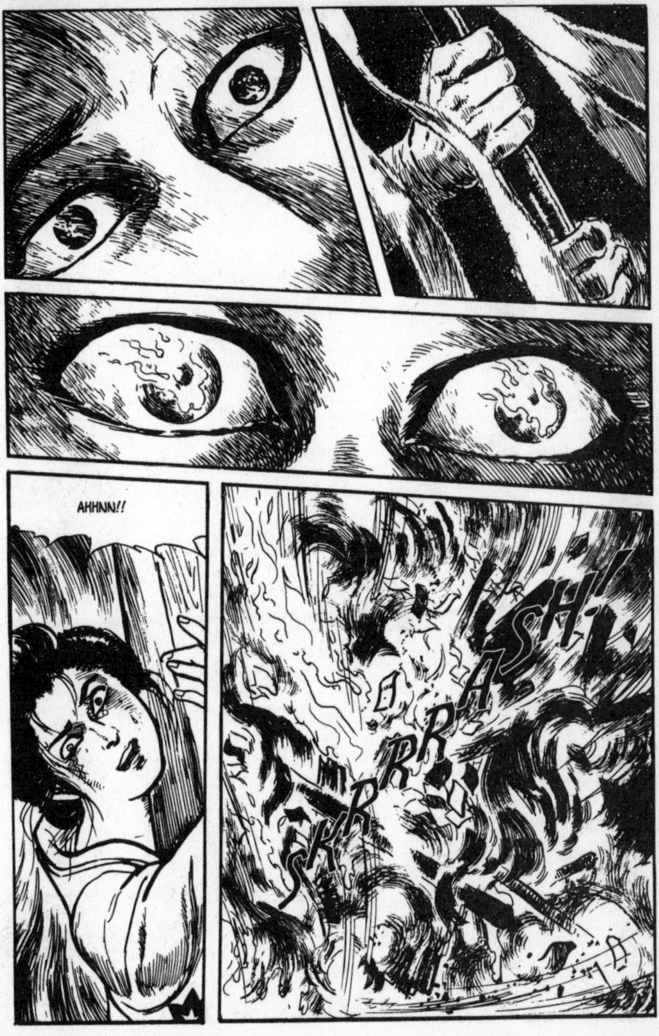
AHHNN!!
SKRRRRASH!

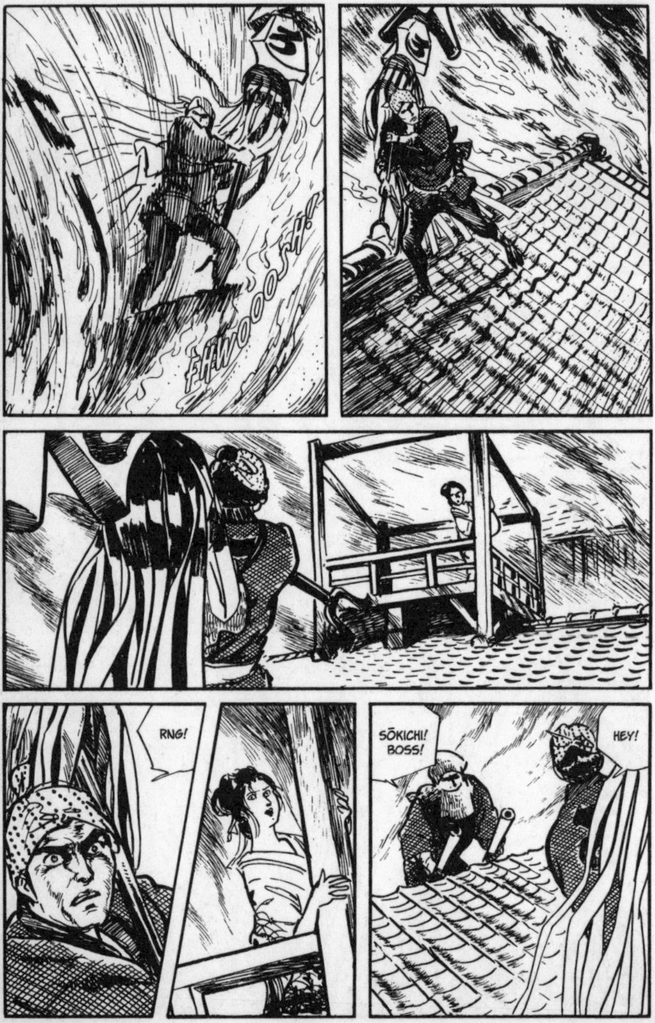
FHWOOOSH!
RNG!
SŌKICHI! BOSS!
HEY!

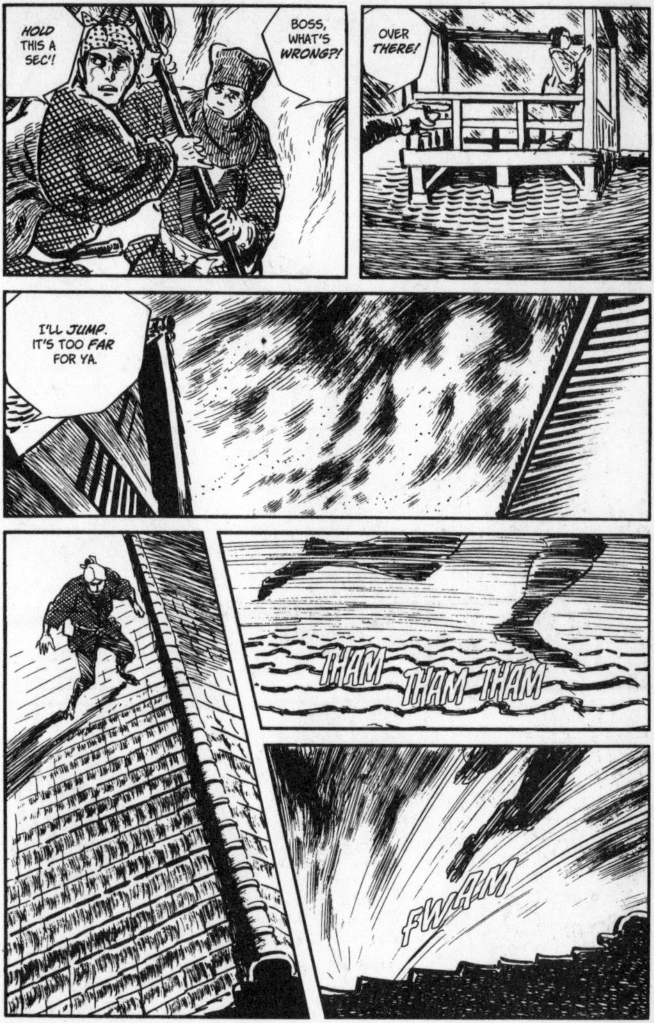
HOLD THIS A SEC'!
BOSS, WHAT'S WRONG?!
OVER THERE!
I'LL JUMP. IT'S TOO FAR FOR YA.
THAM THAM THAM
FWAM

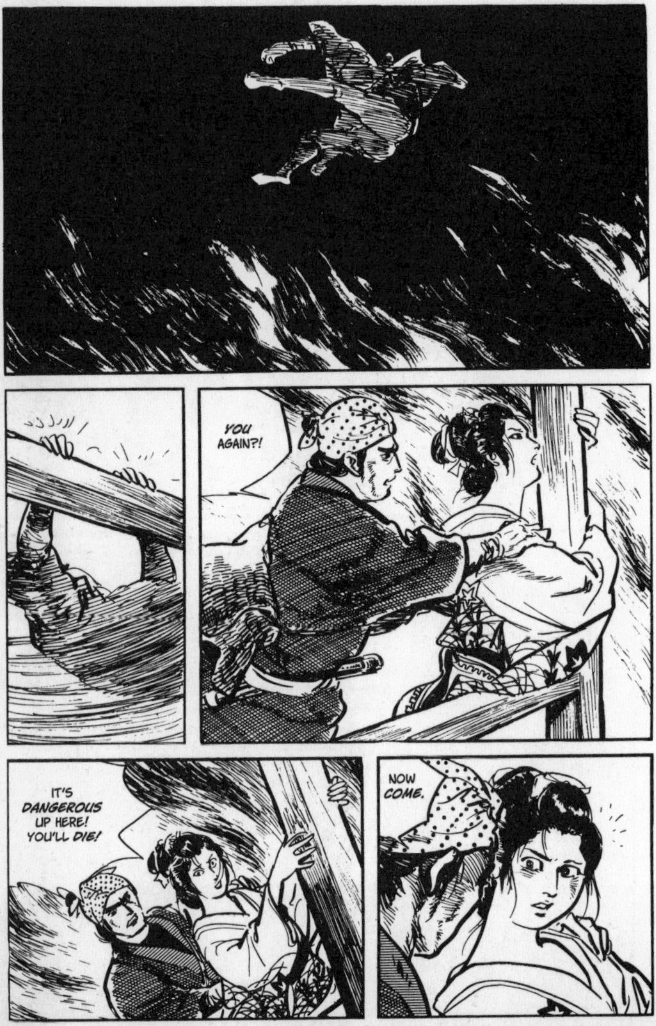
YOU AGAIN?!
IT'S DANGEROUS UP HERE! YOU'LL DIE!
NOW COME.

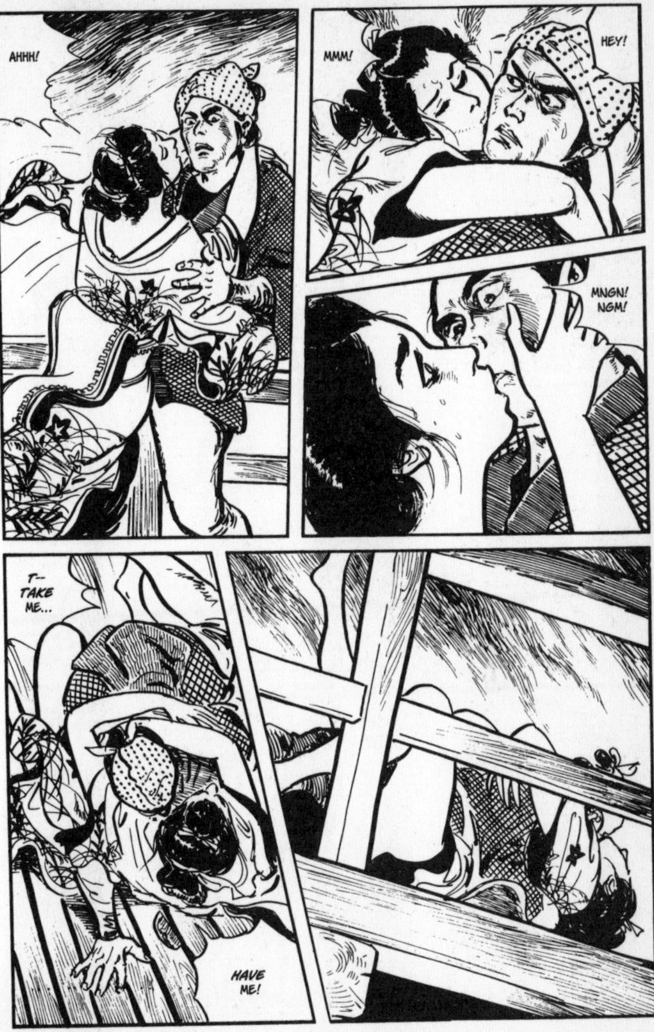
AHHH!
MMM!
HEY!
MNGN! NGM!
T-- TAKE ME...
HAVE ME!

QUICKLY! NOW!
SUCK THEM..!
AH... MISS...
WE'RE GETTIN' YOU OUT!
AHNN!
SPAKK

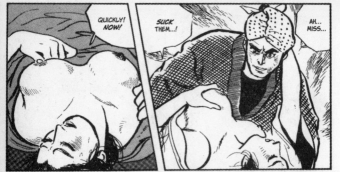

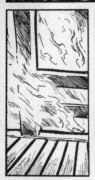

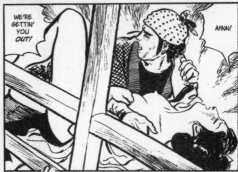

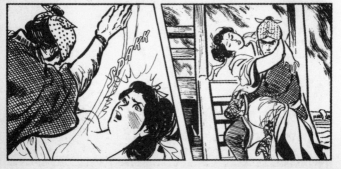

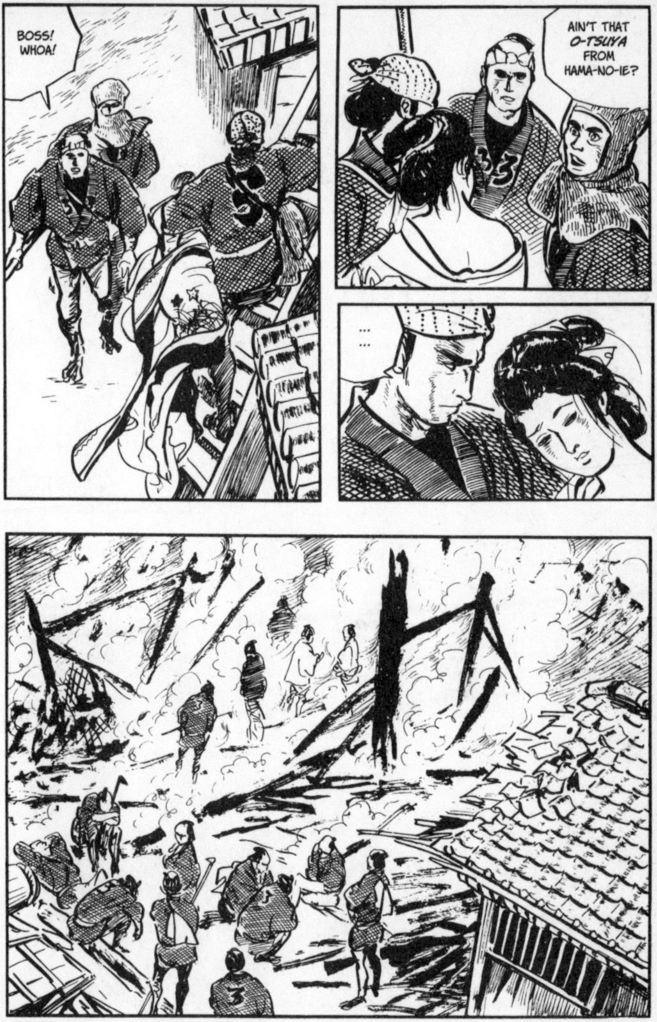
BOSS! WHOA!
AIN'T THAT *O-TSUYA* FROM HAMA-NO-IE?
...
...

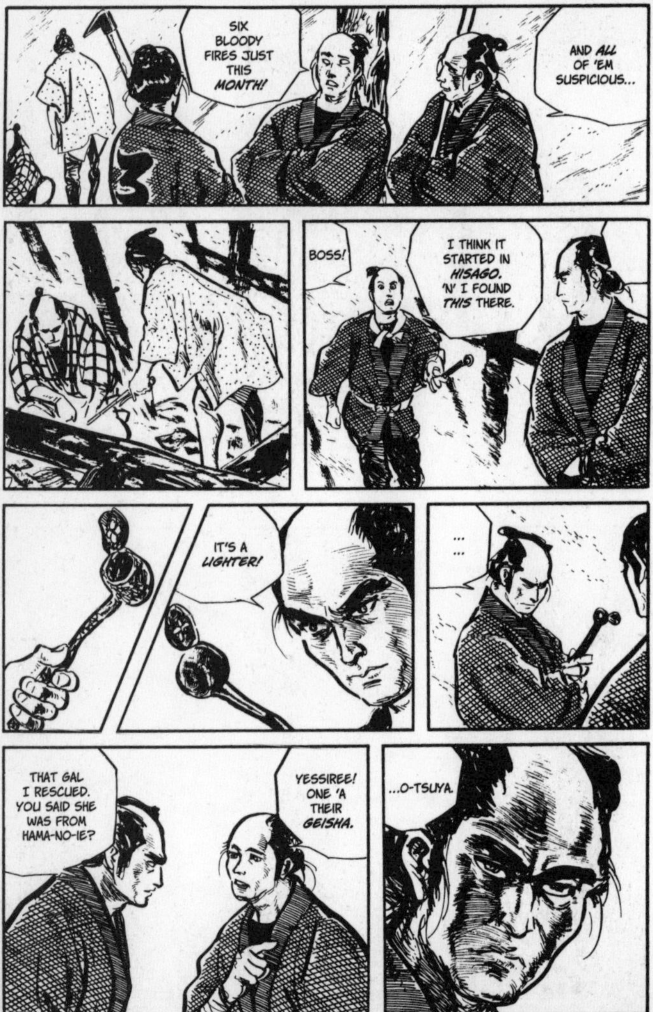
SIX BLOODY FIRES JUST THIS MONTH!
AND ALL OF 'EM SUSPICIOUS...
BOSS!
I THINK IT STARTED IN HISAGO. 'N' I FOUND THIS THERE.
IT'S A LIGHTER!
... ...
THAT GAL I RESCUED. YOU SAID SHE WAS FROM HAMA-NO-IE?
YESSIREE! ONE 'A THEIR GEISHA.
...O-TSUYA.

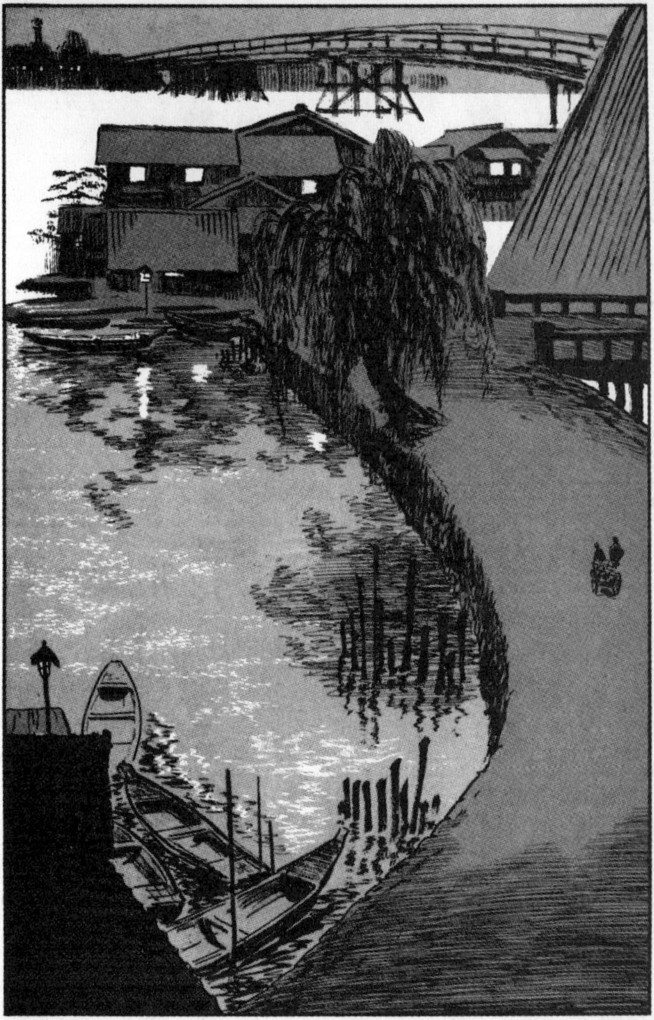

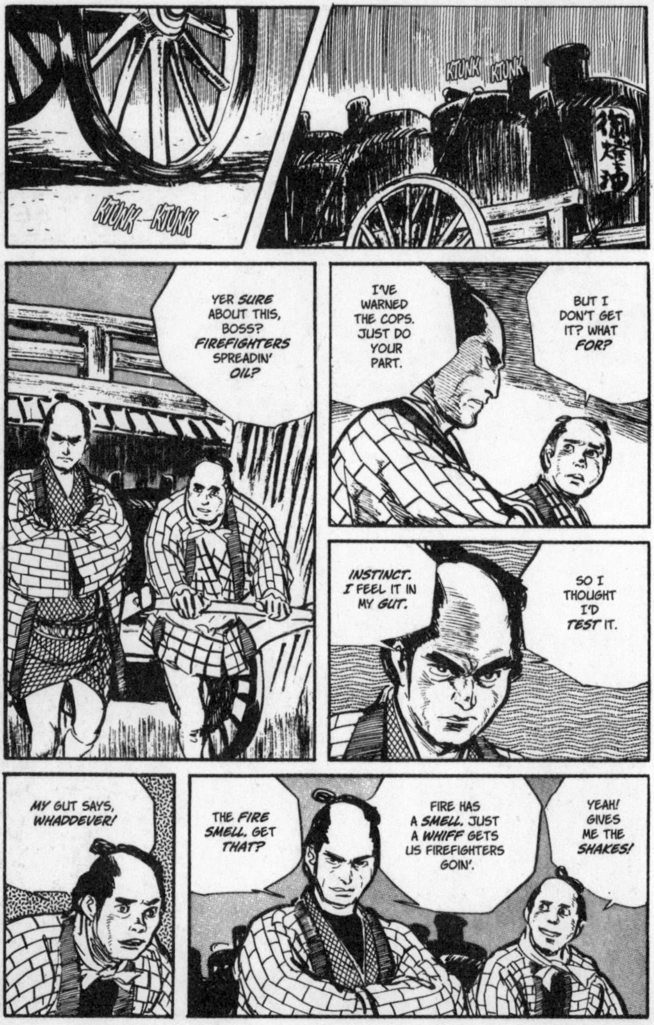
KTUNK KTUNK
KTUNK KTUNK
YER SURE ABOUT THIS, BOSS? FIREFIGHTERS SPREADIN' OIL?
I'VE WARNED THE COPS. JUST DO YOUR PART.
BUT I DON'T GET IT? WHAT FOR?
INSTINCT. I FEEL IT IN MY GUT.
SO I THOUGHT I'D TEST IT.
MY GUT SAYS, WHADDEVER!
THE FIRE SMELL. GET THAT?
FIRE HAS A SMELL. JUST A WHIFF GETS US FIREFIGHTERS GOIN'.
YEAH! GIVES ME THE SHAKES!

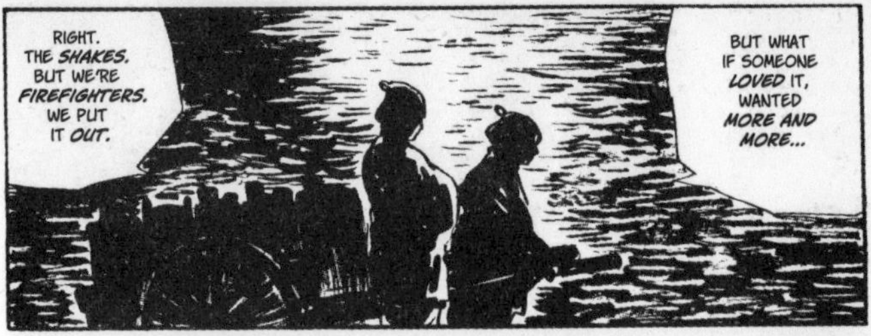
RIGHT. THE *SHAKES.* BUT WE'RE *FIREFIGHTERS.* WE PUT IT *OUT.*
BUT WHAT IF SOMEONE *LOVED* IT, WANTED *MORE AND MORE...*

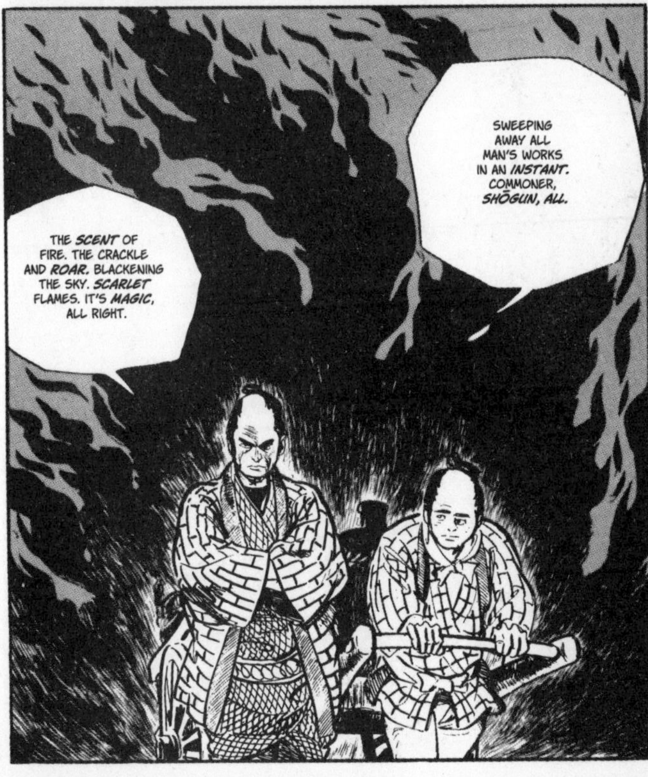
THE *SCENT* OF FIRE. THE CRACKLE AND *ROAR.* BLACKENING THE SKY. *SCARLET* FLAMES. IT'S *MAGIC,* ALL RIGHT.
SWEEPING AWAY ALL MAN'S WORKS IN AN *INSTANT.* COMMONER, *SHŌGUN, ALL.*

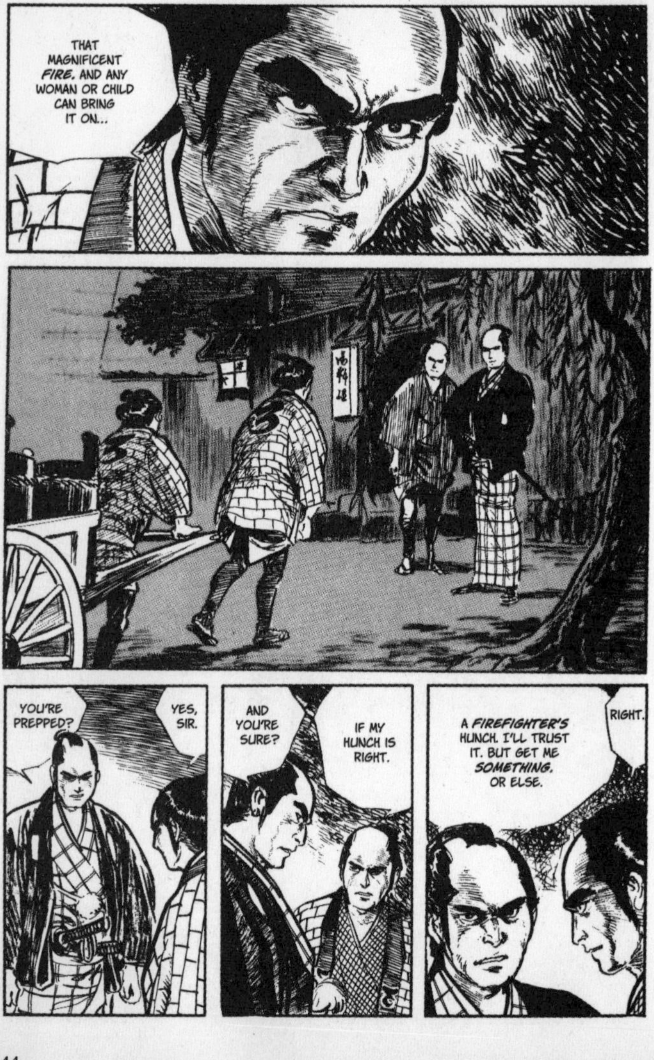

THAT MAGNIFICENT *FIRE.* AND ANY WOMAN OR CHILD CAN BRING IT ON...
YOU'RE PREPPED?
YES, SIR.
AND YOU'RE SURE?
IF MY HUNCH IS RIGHT.
A *FIREFIGHTER'S* HUNCH. I'LL TRUST IT. BUT GET ME *SOMETHING.* OR ELSE.
RIGHT.

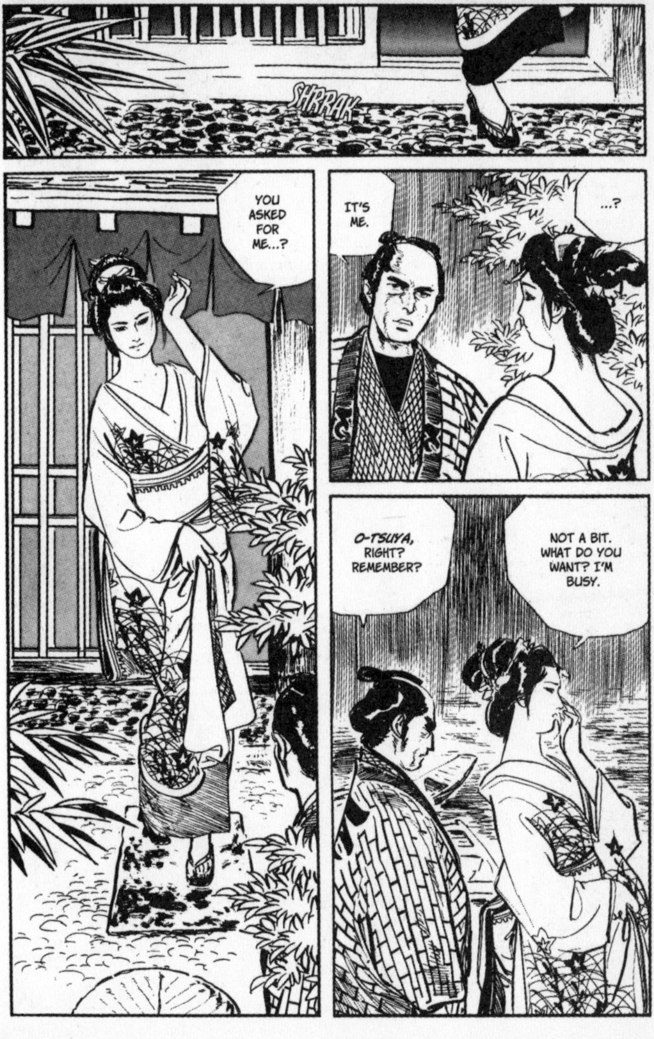
SHRRAK
YOU ASKED FOR ME...?
IT'S ME.
...?
O-TSUYA, RIGHT? REMEMBER?
NOT A BIT. WHAT DO YOU WANT? I'M BUSY.

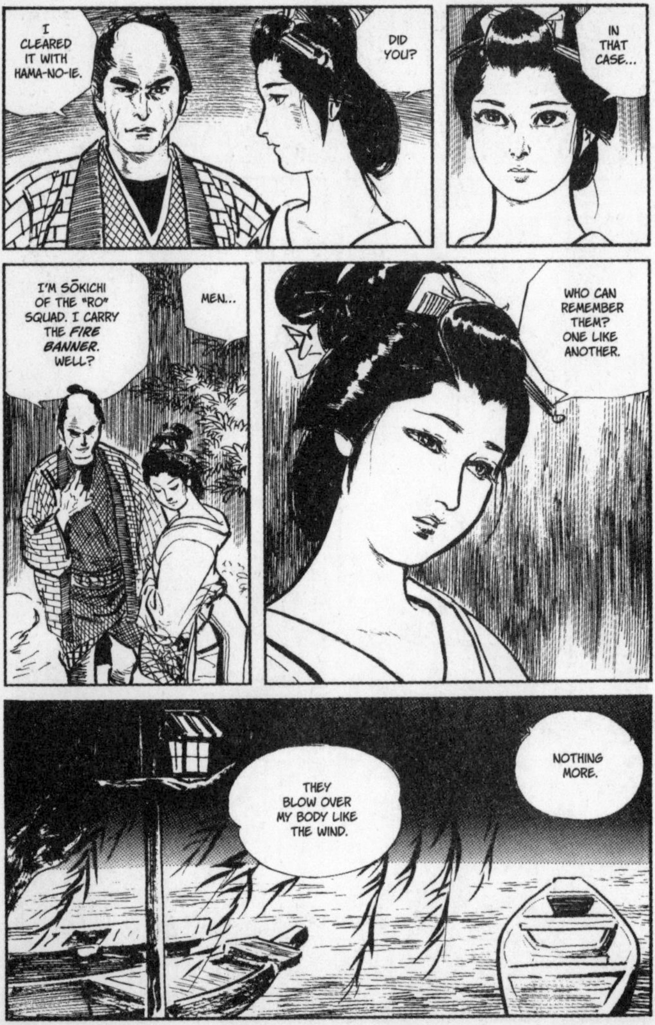
I CLEARED IT WITH HAMA-NO-IE.
DID YOU?
IN THAT CASE...
I'M SŌKICHI OF THE "RO" SQUAD. I CARRY THE *FIRE BANNER*. WELL?
MEN...
WHO CAN REMEMBER THEM? ONE LIKE ANOTHER.
THEY BLOW OVER MY BODY LIKE THE WIND.
NOTHING MORE.

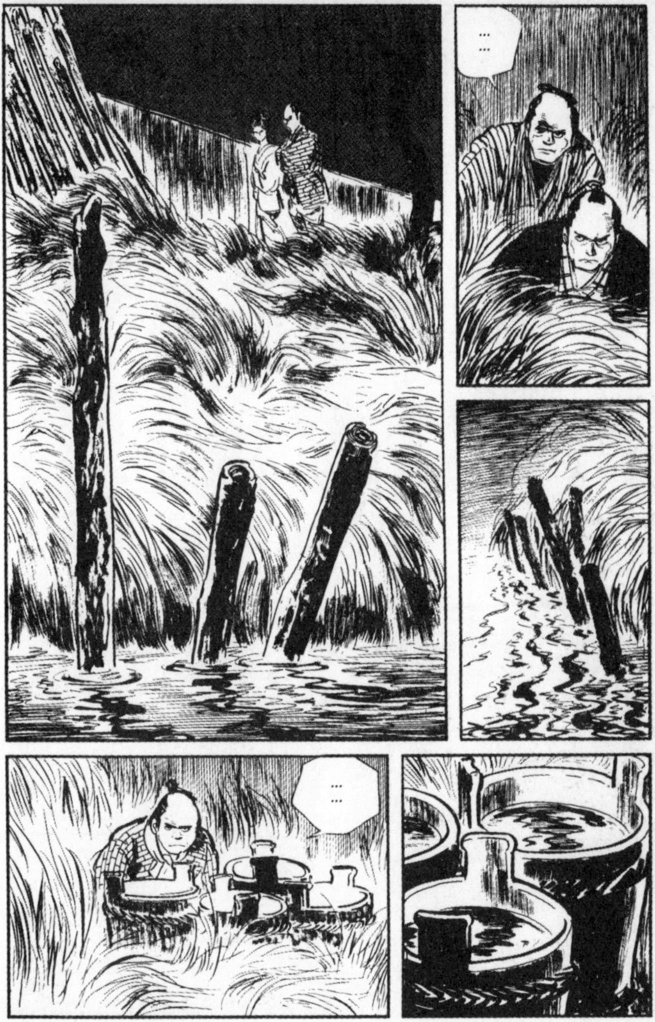
......
......

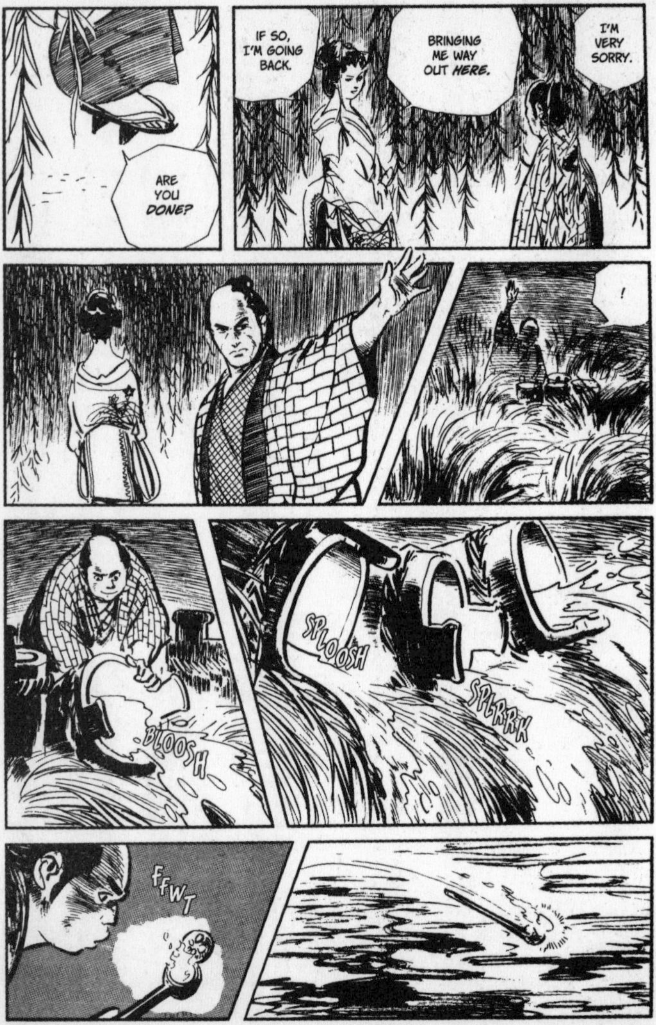
ARE YOU *DONE?*
IF SO, I'M GOING BACK.
BRINGING ME WAY OUT *HERE.*
I'M VERY SORRY.
!
BLOOSH
SPLOOSH
SPLRRRK
FFWT

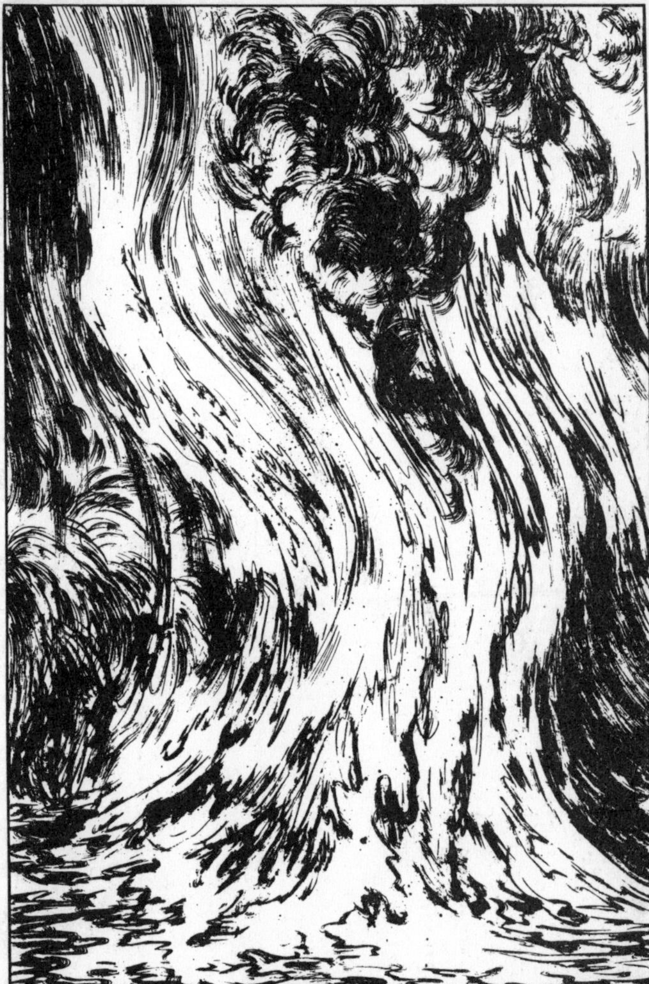

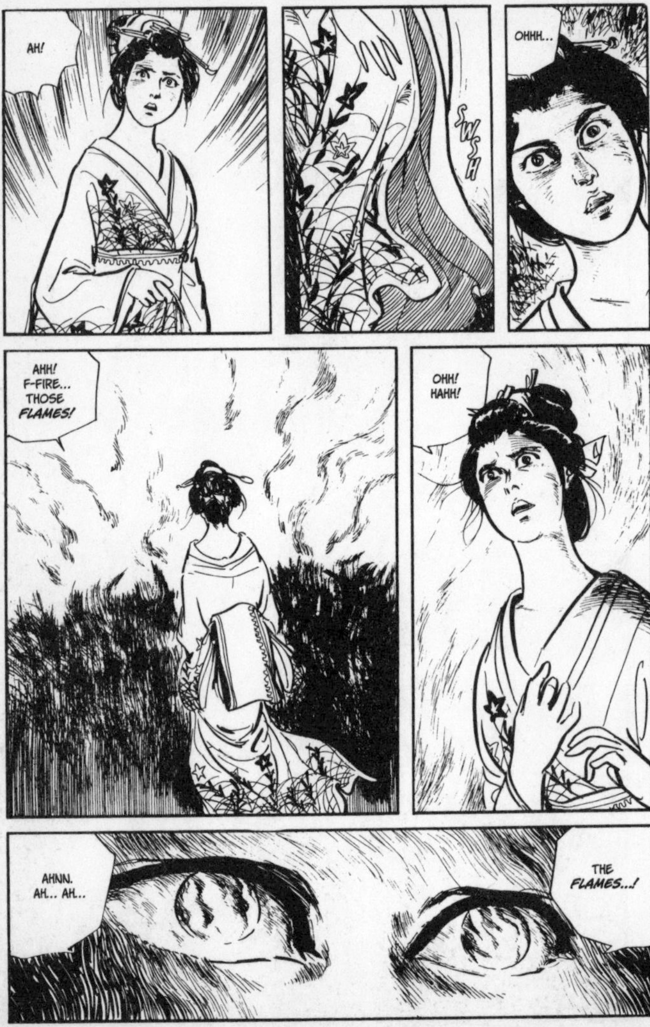
AH!
SWSH
OHHH...
AHH! F-FIRE... THOSE *FLAMES!*
OHH! HAHH!
AHNN. AH... AH...
THE *FLAMES...!*

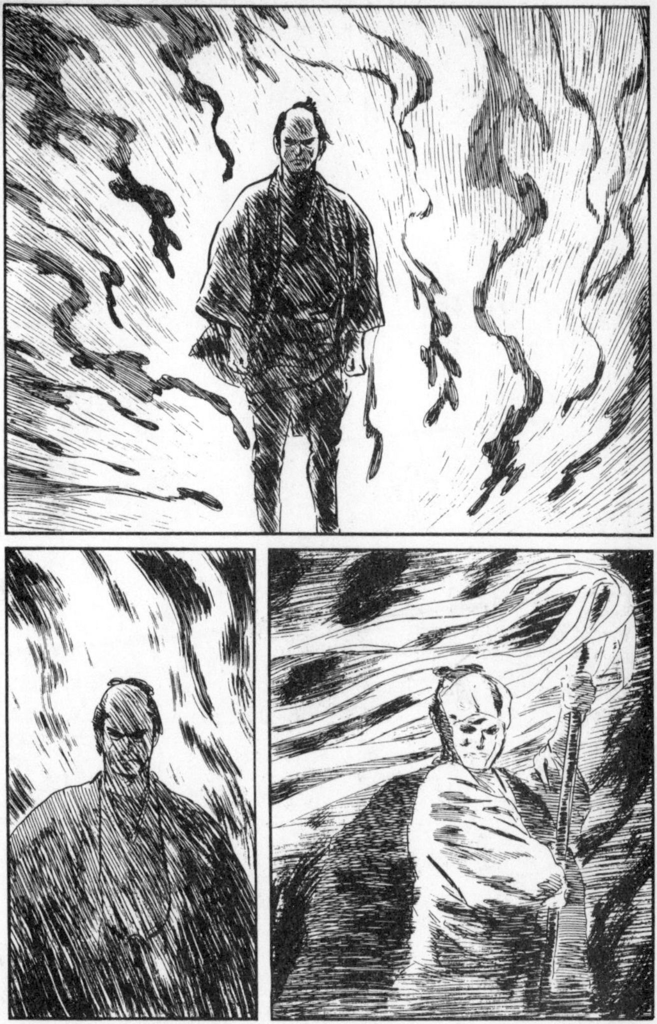

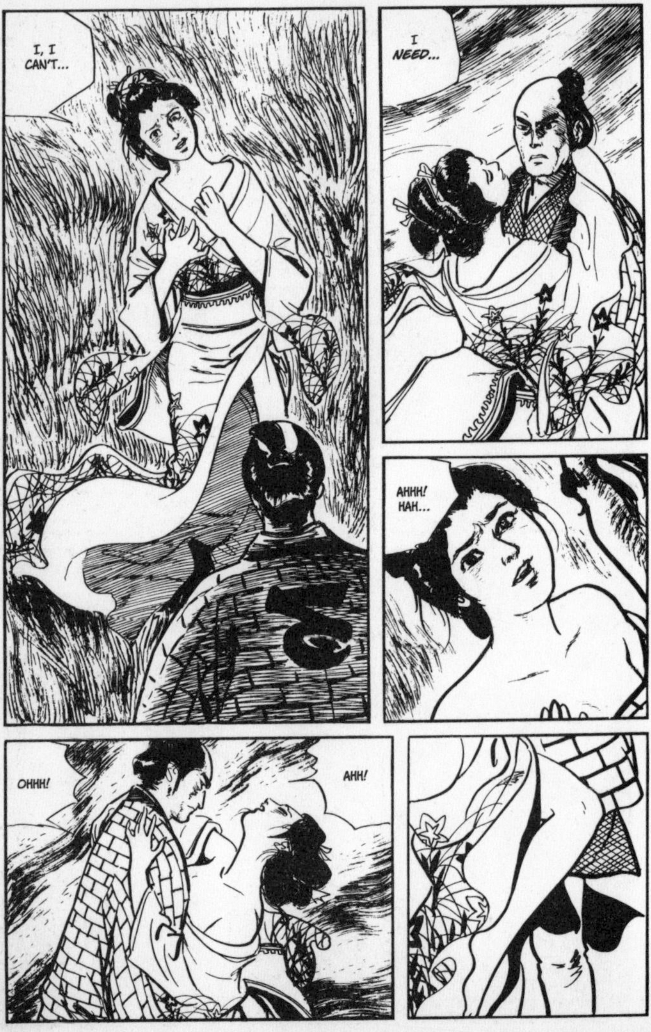
I, I CAN'T...
I NEED...
AHHH! HAH...
OHHH!
AHH!

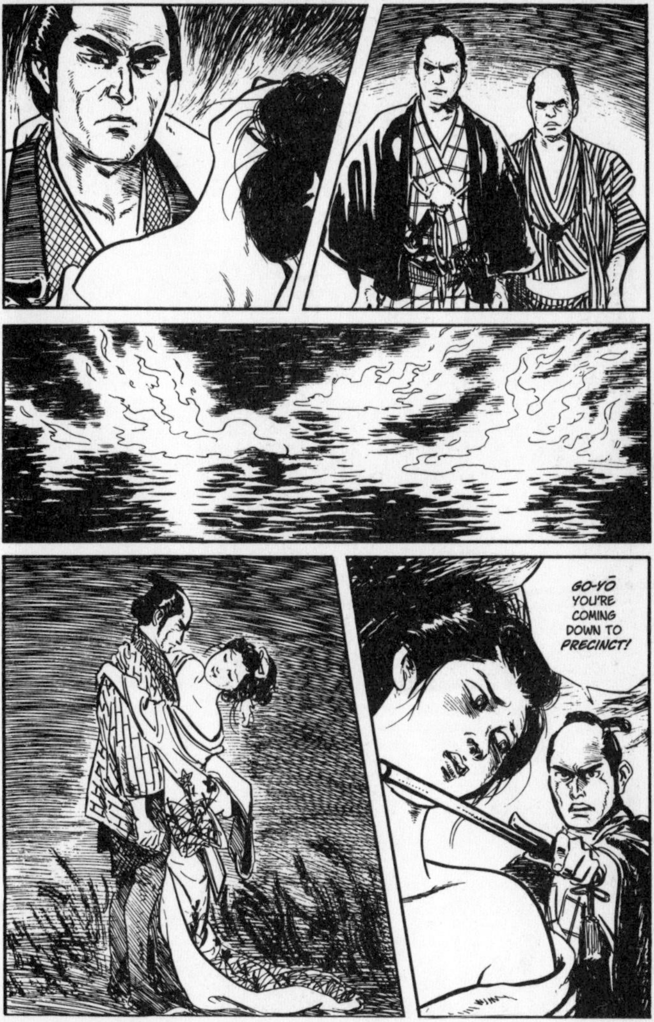
GO-YŌ
YOU'RE
COMING
DOWN TO
PRECINCT!

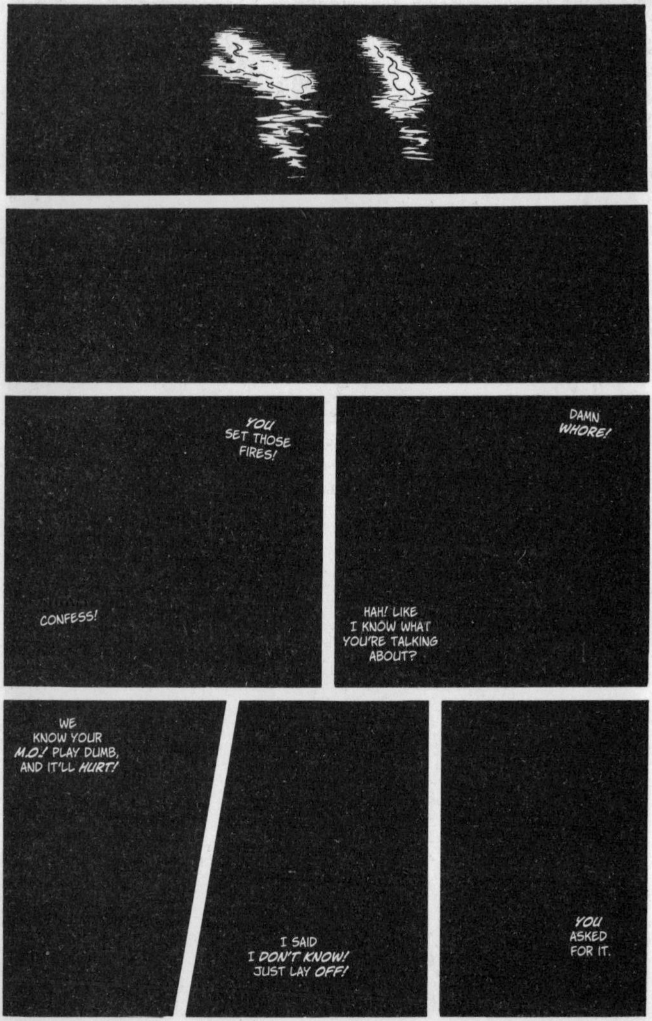
YOU SET THOSE FIRES!
CONFESS!
DAMN WHORE!
HAH! LIKE I KNOW WHAT YOU'RE TALKING ABOUT?
WE KNOW YOUR M.O.! PLAY DUMB, AND IT'LL HURT!
I SAID I DON'T KNOW! JUST LAY OFF!
YOU ASKED FOR IT.

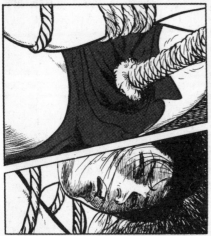

WE CALL THIS ONE *EBIZUME*. LIKE IT?

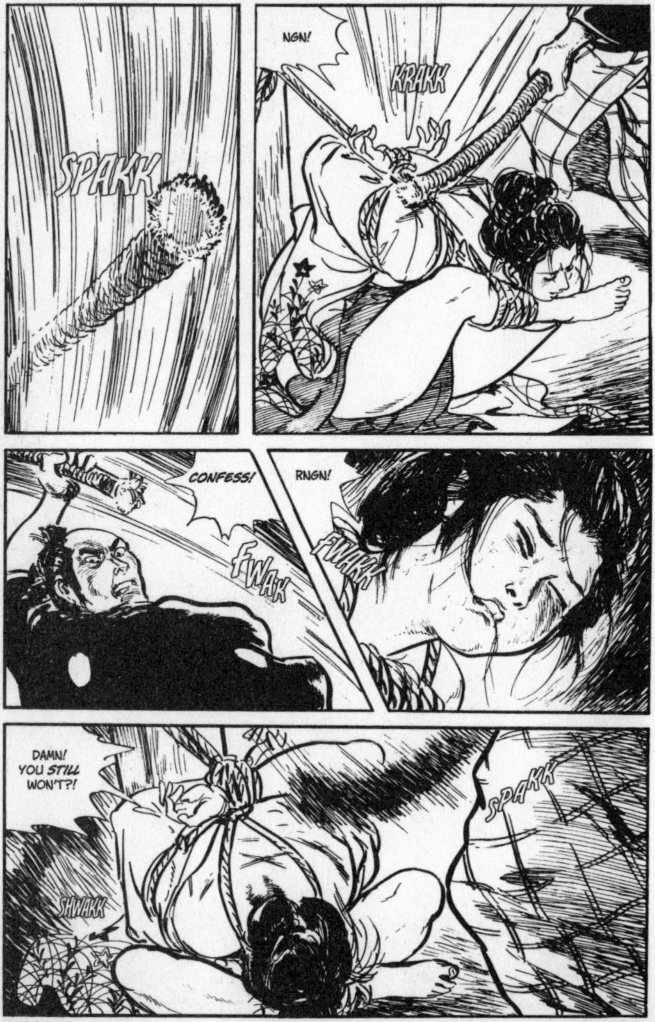
SPAKK
NGN!
KRAKK
CONFESS!
FWAK
RNGN!
FWAKK
DAMN! YOU STILL WON'T?!
SHWAKK
SPAKK

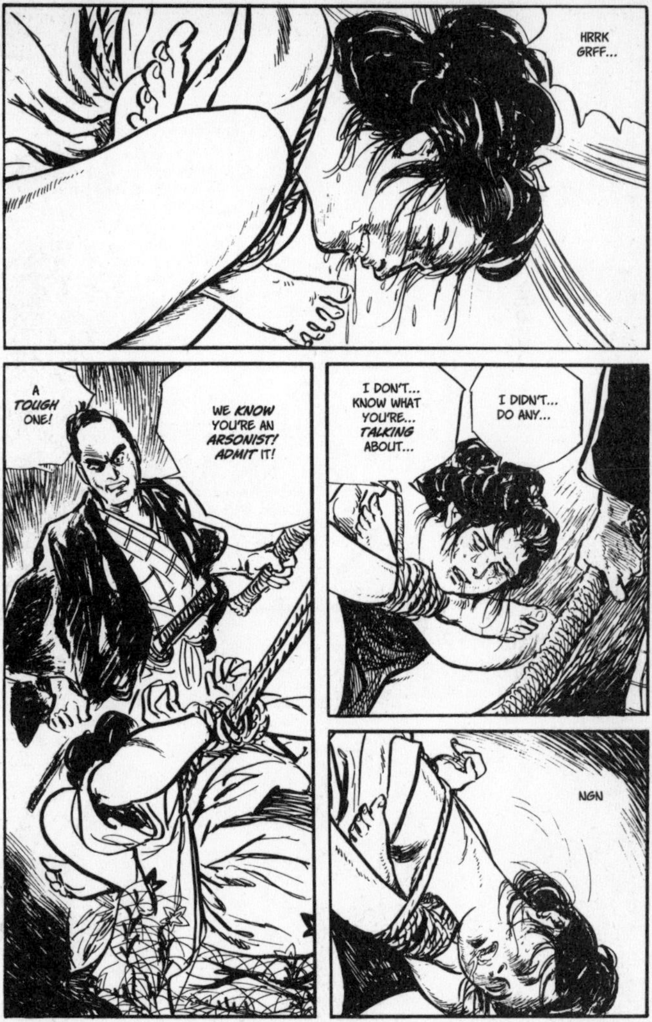
HRRK GRFF...
A *TOUGH* ONE!
WE *KNOW* YOU'RE AN *ARSONIST!* *ADMIT* IT!
I DON'T... KNOW WHAT YOU'RE... *TALKING* ABOUT...
I DIDN'T... DO ANY...
NGN

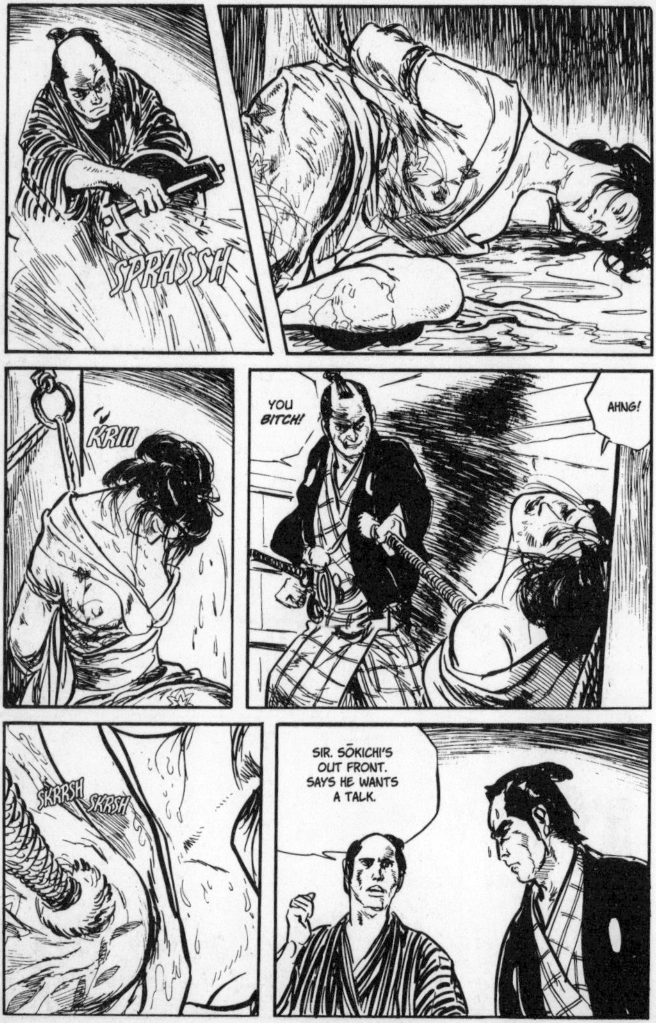
SPRASSH
KRIII
YOU BITCH!
AHNG!
SKRSH SKRSH
SIR. SŌKICHI'S OUT FRONT. SAYS HE WANTS A TALK.

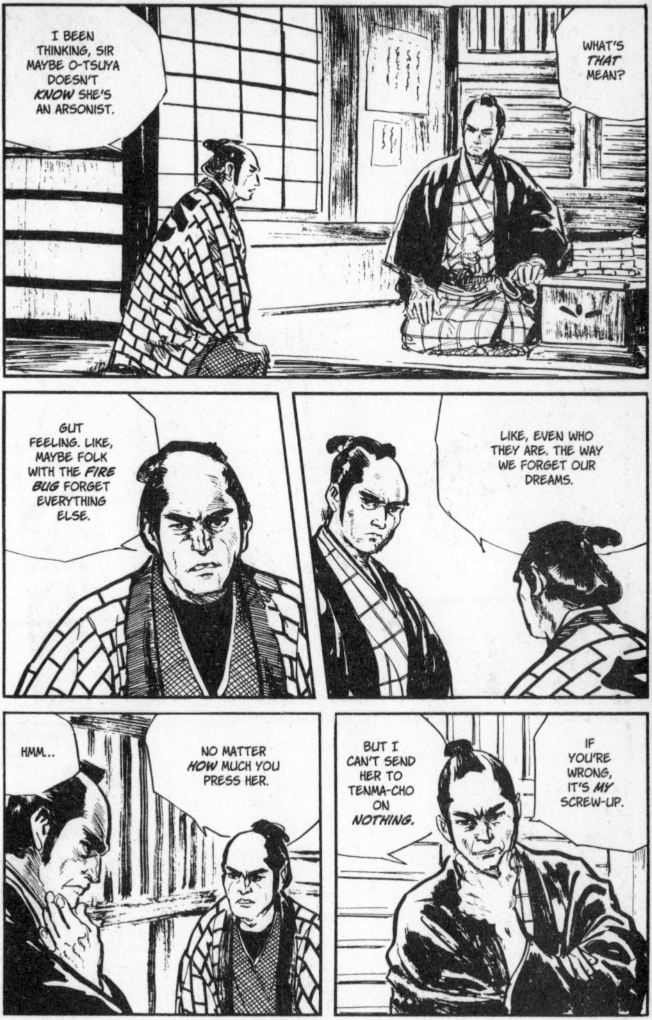
I BEEN THINKING, SIR MAYBE O-TSUYA DOESN'T *KNOW* SHE'S AN ARSONIST.
WHAT'S *THAT* MEAN?
GUT FEELING. LIKE, MAYBE FOLK WITH THE *FIRE BUG* FORGET EVERYTHING ELSE.
LIKE, EVEN WHO THEY ARE. THE WAY WE FORGET OUR DREAMS.
HMM...
NO MATTER *HOW* MUCH YOU PRESS HER.
BUT I CAN'T SEND HER TO TENMA-CHO ON *NOTHING*.
IF YOU'RE WRONG, IT'S *MY* SCREW-UP.

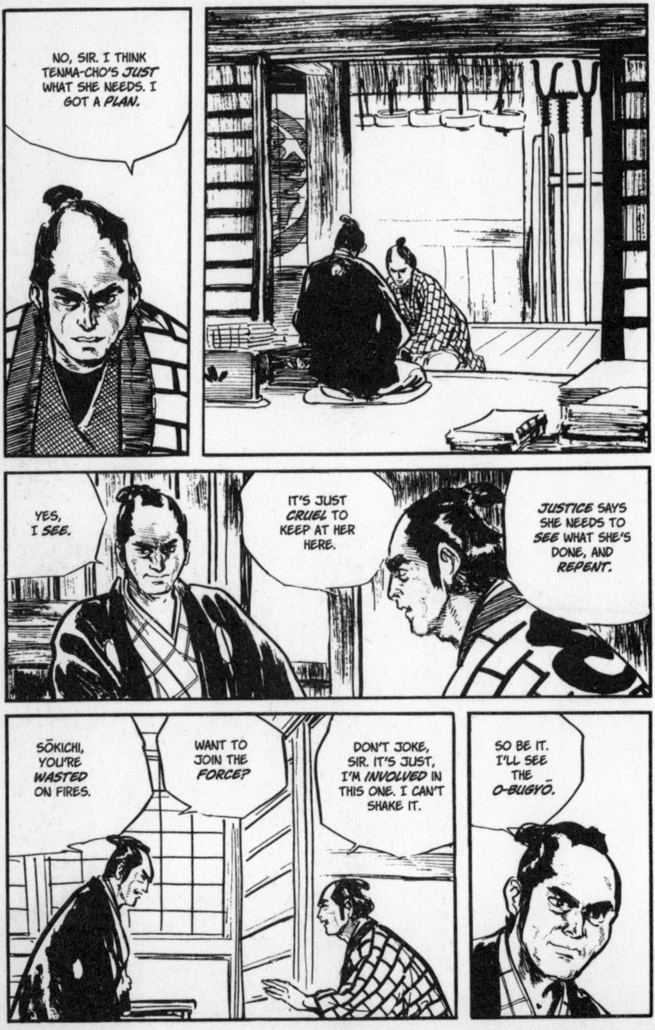
NO, SIR. I THINK TENMA-CHO'S *JUST* WHAT SHE NEEDS. I GOT A *PLAN.*
YES, I *SEE.*
IT'S JUST *CRUEL* TO KEEP AT HER HERE.
JUSTICE SAYS SHE NEEDS TO *SEE* WHAT SHE'S DONE, AND *REPENT.*
SŌKICHI, YOU'RE *WASTED* ON FIRES.
WANT TO JOIN THE *FORCE?*
DON'T JOKE, SIR. IT'S JUST, I'M *INVOLVED* IN THIS ONE. I CAN'T SHAKE IT.
SO BE IT. I'LL SEE THE *O-BUGYŌ.*

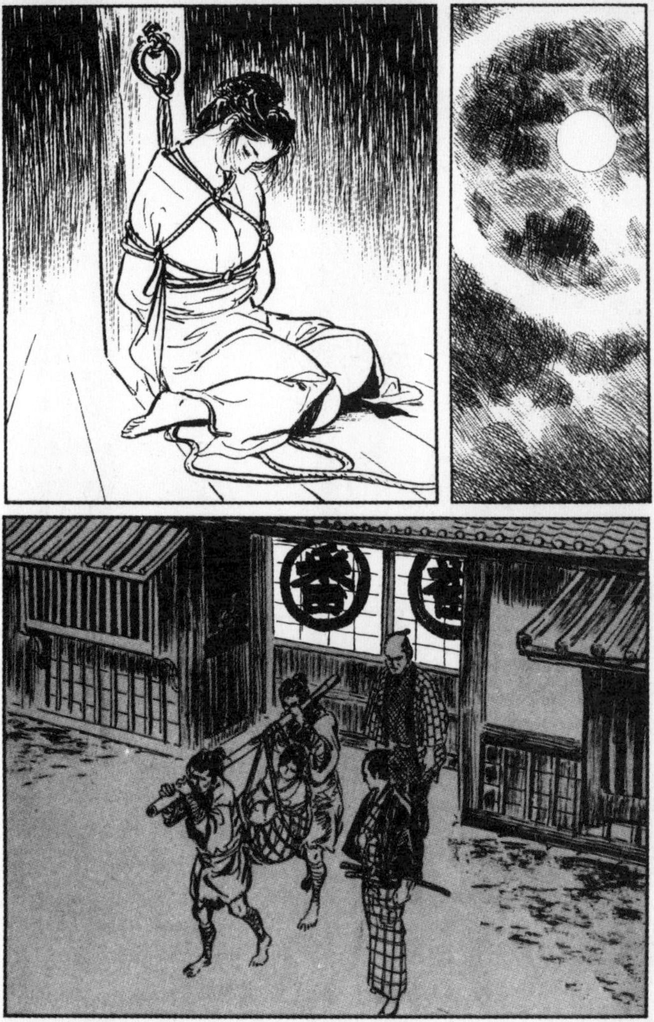

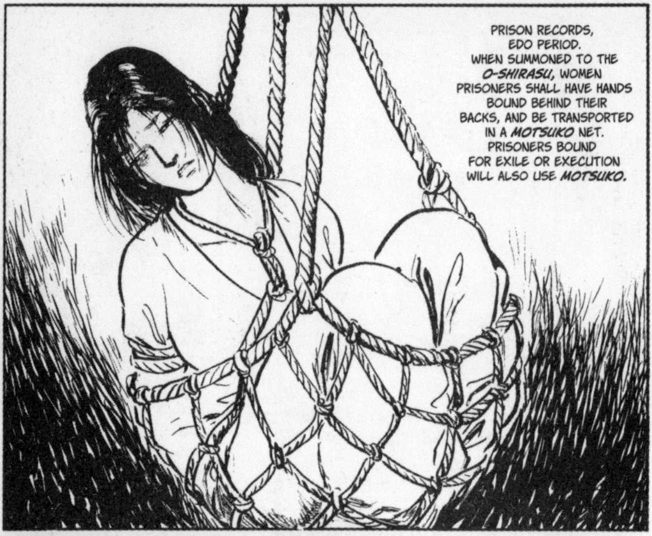
PRISON RECORDS, EDO PERIOD.
WHEN SUMMONED TO THE *O-SHIRASU,* WOMEN PRISONERS SHALL HAVE HANDS BOUND BEHIND THEIR BACKS, AND BE TRANSPORTED IN A *MOTSUKO* NET.
PRISONERS BOUND FOR EXILE OR EXECUTION WILL ALSO USE *MOTSUKO.*

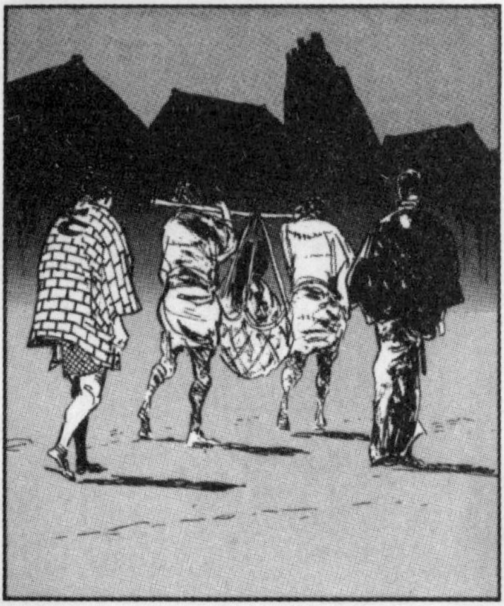

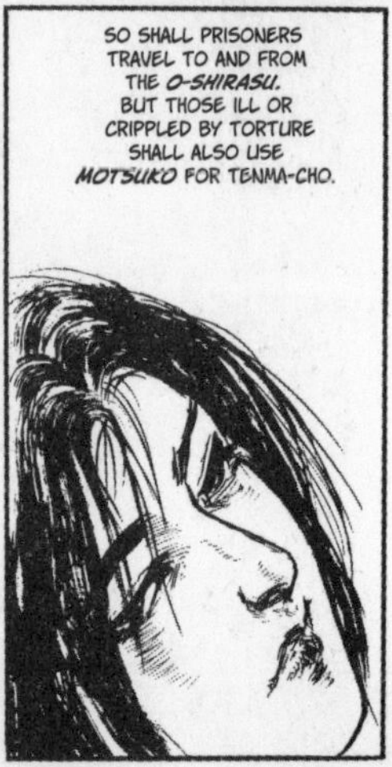
SO SHALL PRISONERS TRAVEL TO AND FROM THE *O-SHIRASU.*
BUT THOSE ILL OR CRIPPLED BY TORTURE SHALL ALSO USE *MOTSUKO* FOR TENMA-CHO.

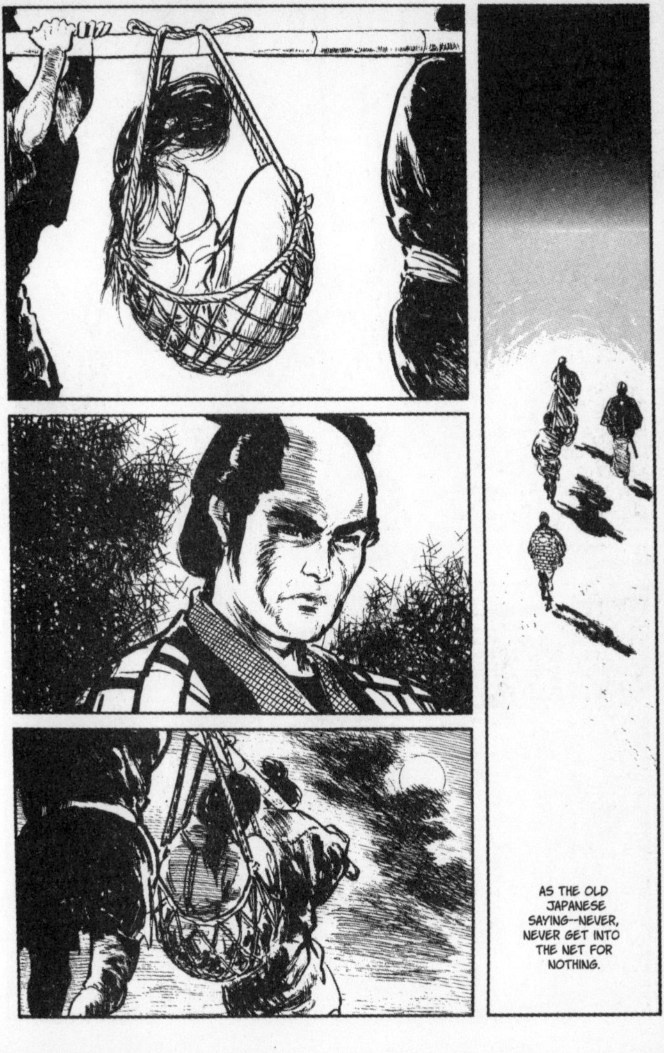
AS THE OLD JAPANESE SAYING--NEVER, NEVER GET INTO THE NET FOR NOTHING.

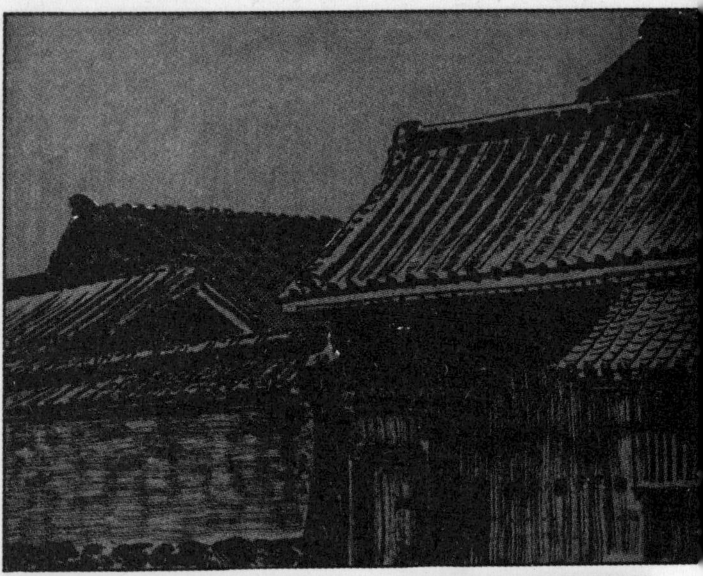
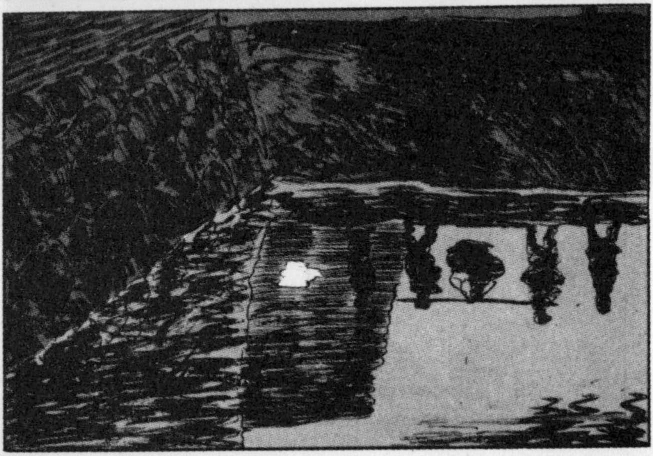

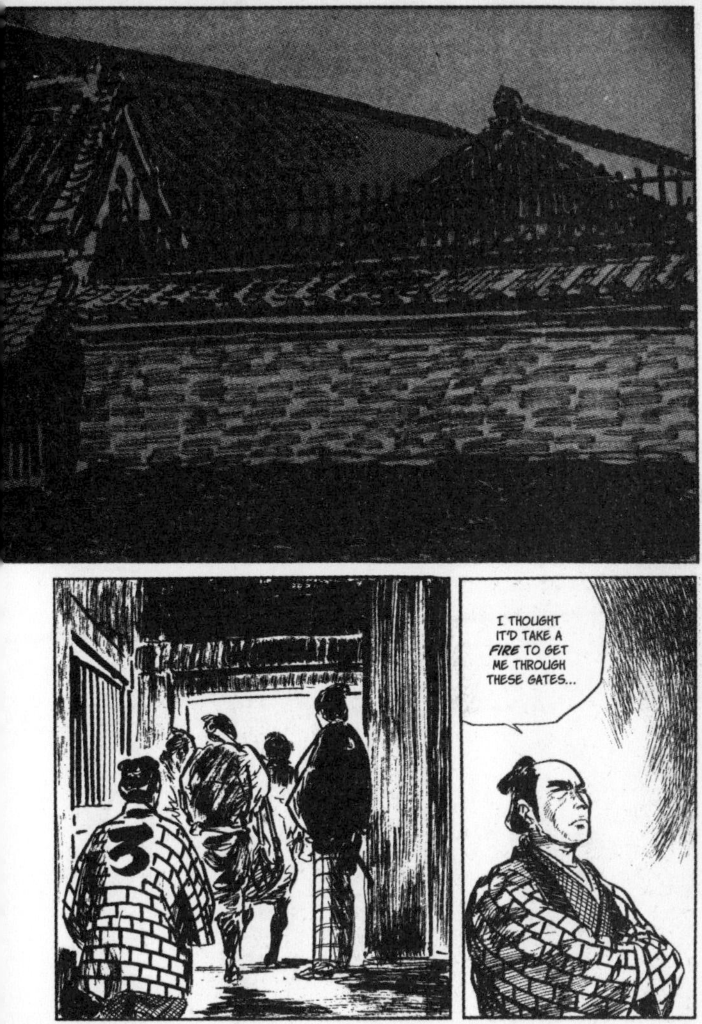
I THOUGHT IT'D TAKE A FIRE TO GET ME THROUGH THESE GATES...

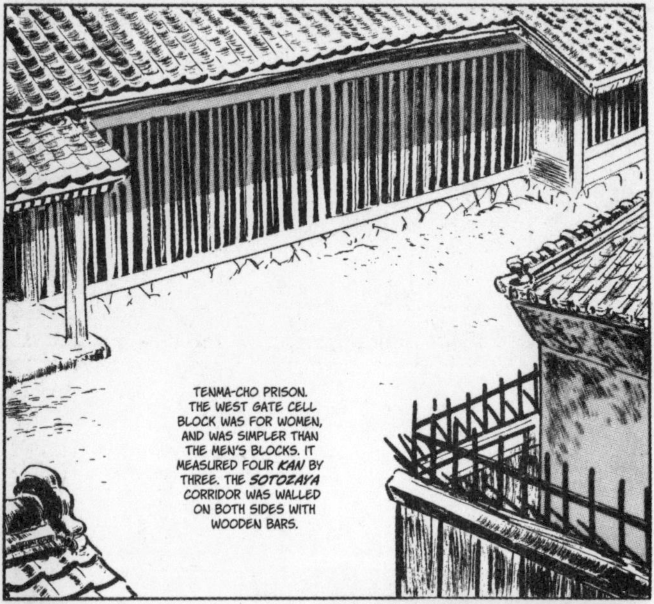
TENMA-CHO PRISON. THE WEST GATE CELL BLOCK WAS FOR WOMEN, AND WAS SIMPLER THAN THE MEN'S BLOCKS. IT MEASURED FOUR *KAN* BY THREE. THE *SOTOZAYA* CORRIDOR WAS WALLED ON BOTH SIDES WITH WOODEN BARS.
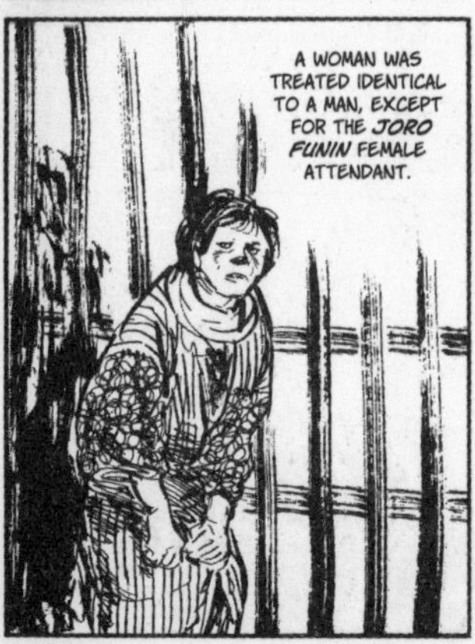
A WOMAN WAS TREATED IDENTICAL TO A MAN, EXCEPT FOR THE *JORO FUNIN* FEMALE ATTENDANT.
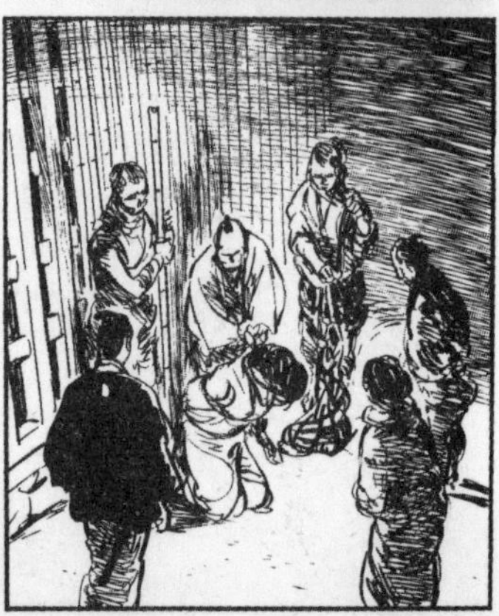

THE *JORO FUNIN* INSPECTED THE PRISONER, AND CHECKED HER CLOTHES.

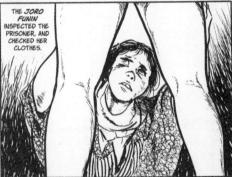

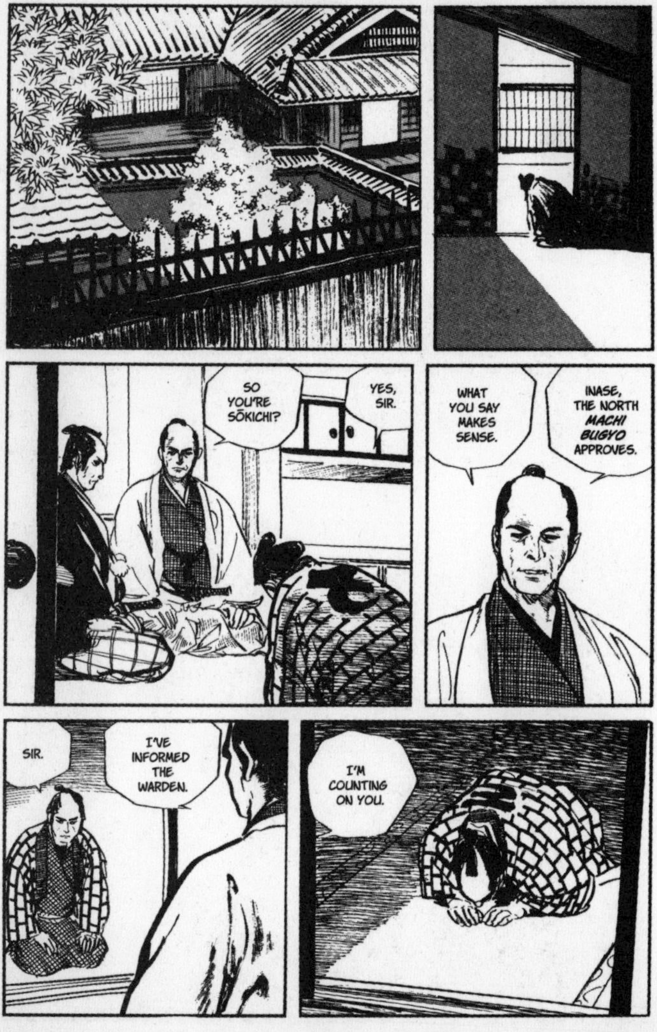

SO YOU'RE SŌKICHI?
YES, SIR.
WHAT YOU SAY MAKES SENSE.
INASE, THE NORTH *MACHI BUGYO* APPROVES.
SIR.
I'VE INFORMED THE WARDEN.
I'M COUNTING ON YOU.

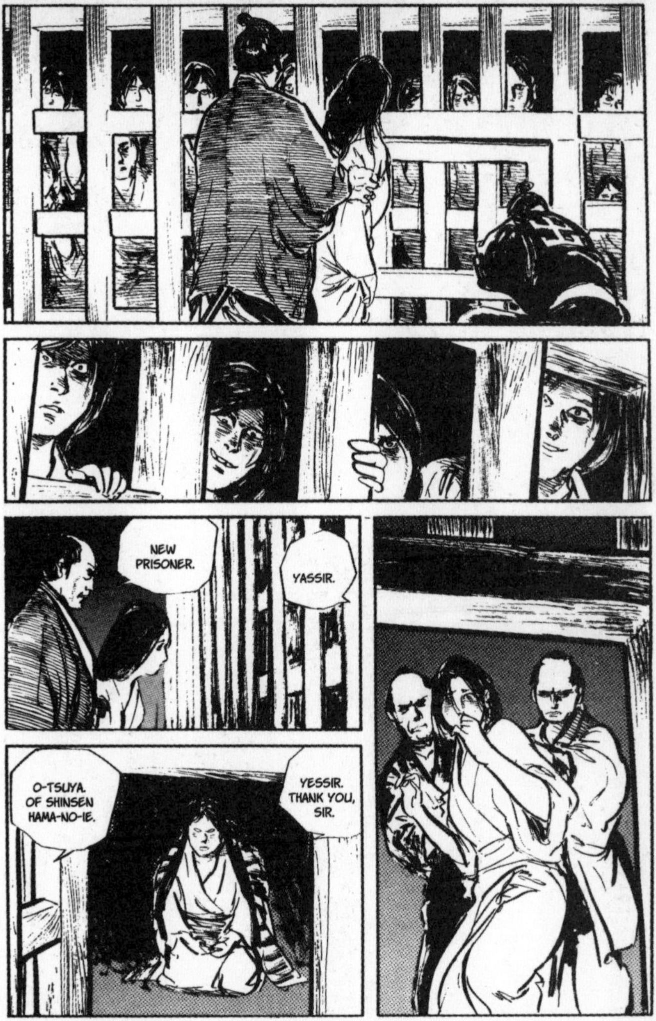
NEW PRISONER.
YASSIR.
O-TSUYA. OF SHINSEN HAMA-NO-IE.
YESSIR. THANK YOU, SIR.

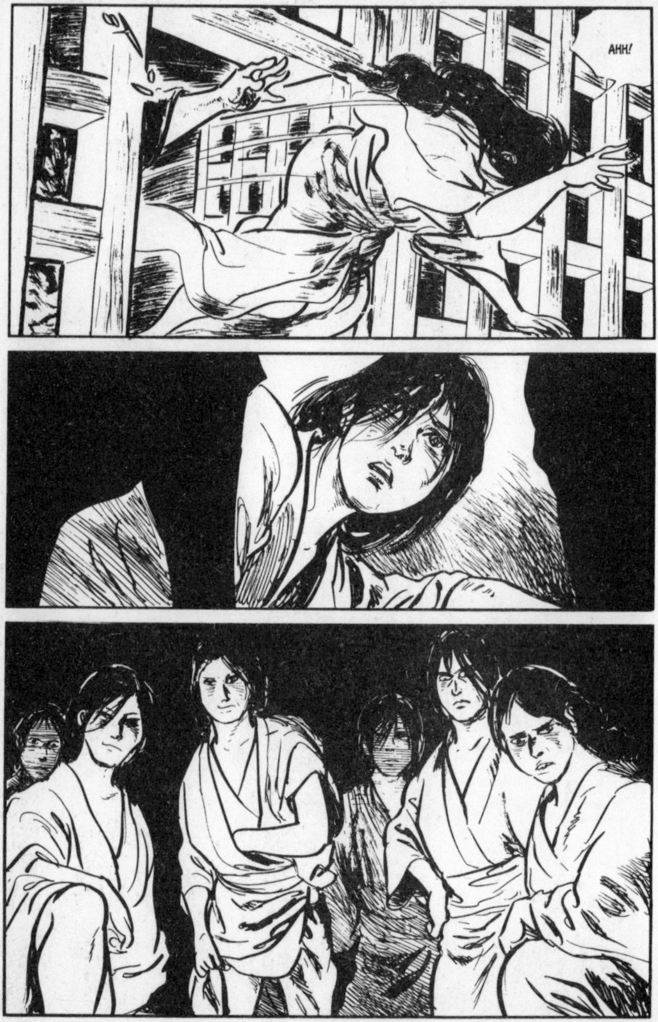
AHH!

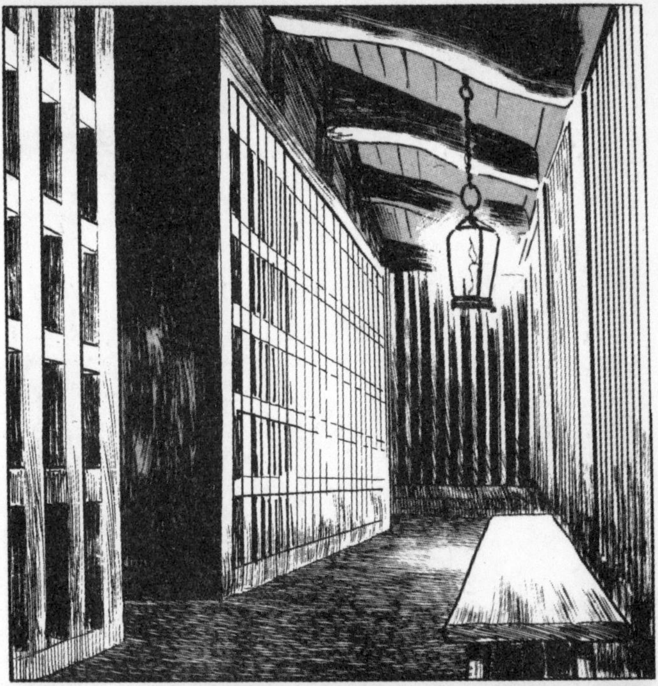

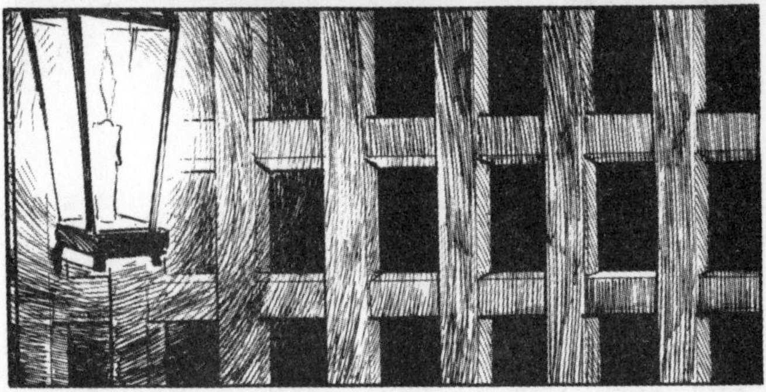

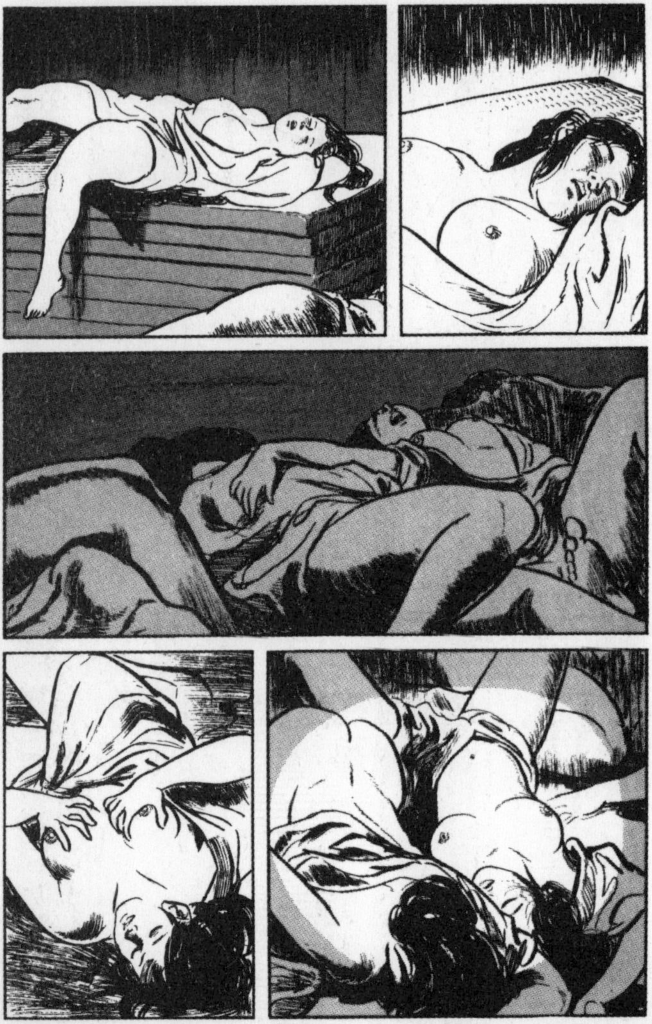

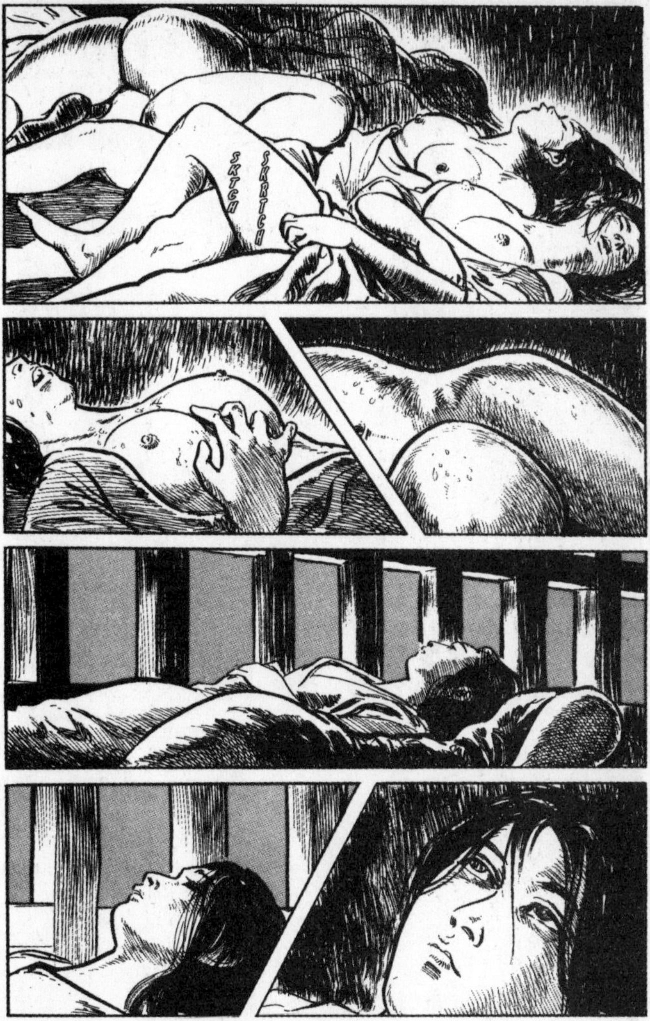
SKRTCH
SKRRTCH

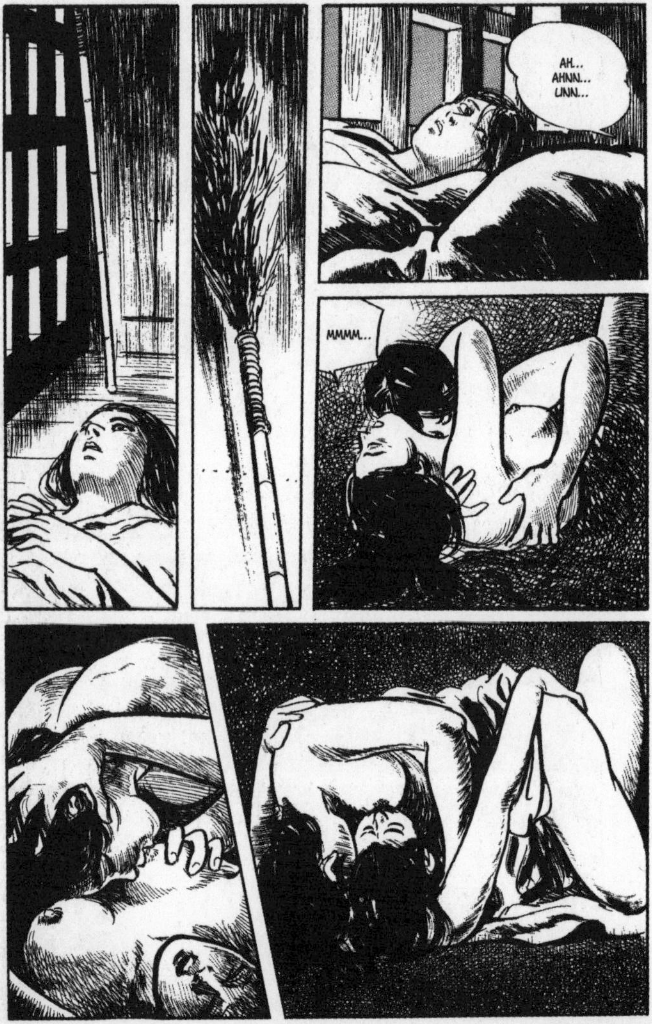
AH... AHNN... UNN...
MMMM...

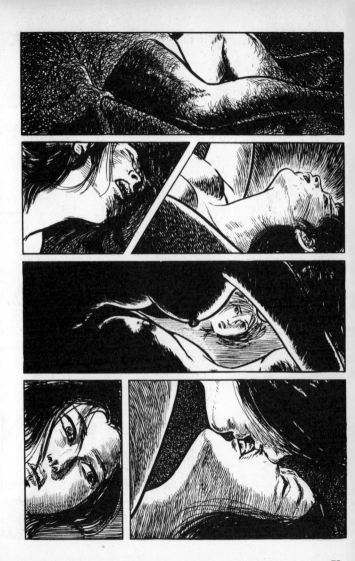

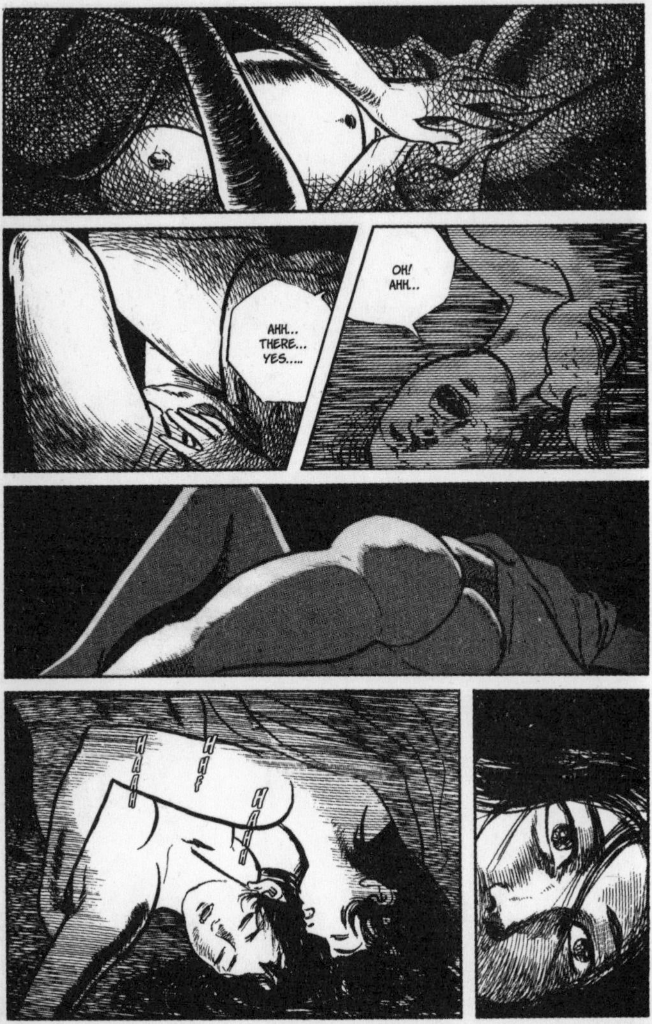
AHH... THERE... YES.....
OH! AHH...
HAAH
HHF
HAHH

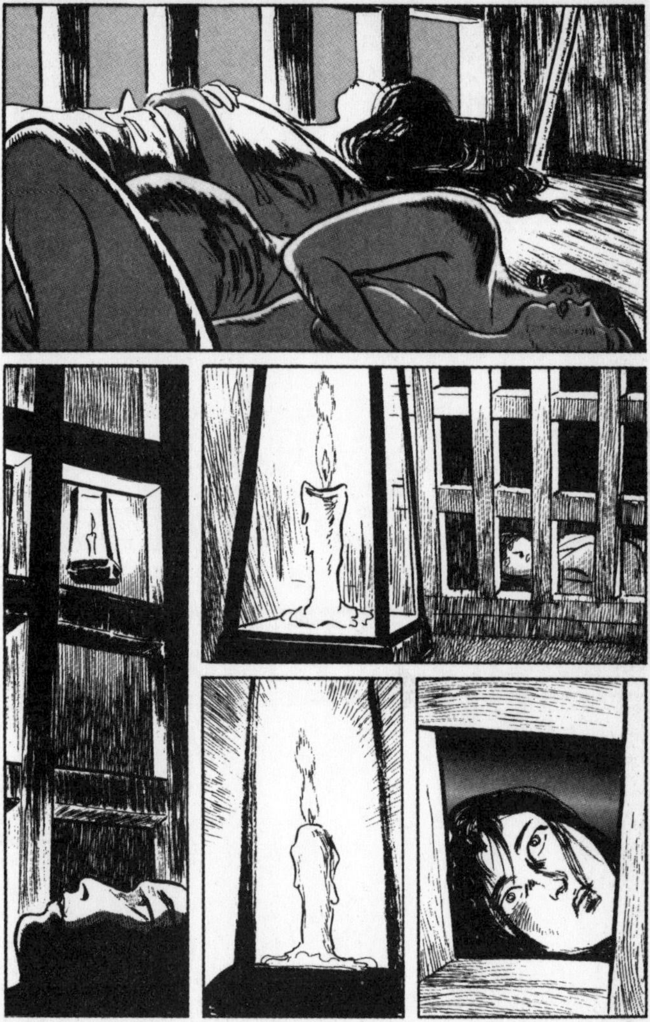

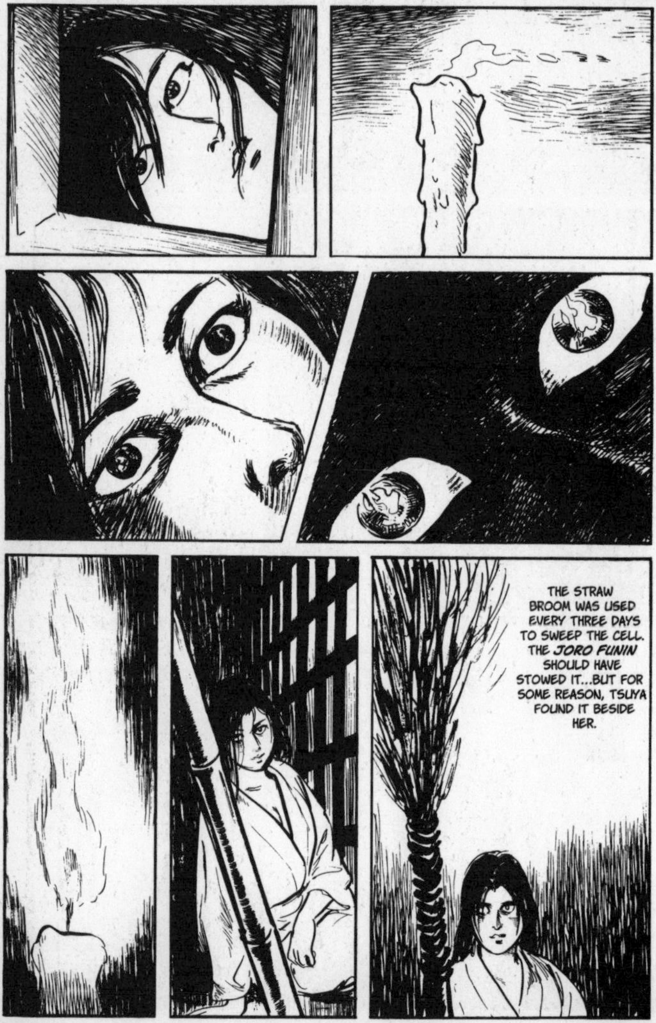
THE STRAW BROOM WAS USED EVERY THREE DAYS TO SWEEP THE CELL. THE *JORO FUNIN* SHOULD HAVE STOWED IT...BUT FOR SOME REASON, TSUYA FOUND IT BESIDE HER.

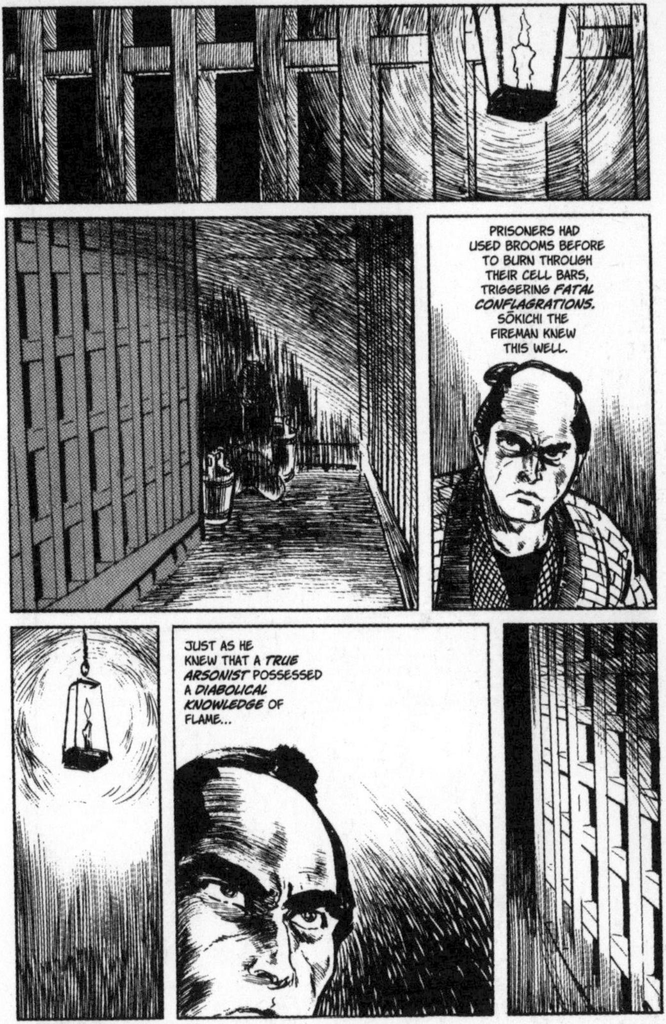
PRISONERS HAD USED BROOMS BEFORE TO BURN THROUGH THEIR CELL BARS, TRIGGERING FATAL CONFLAGRATIONS. SŌKICHI THE FIREMAN KNEW THIS WELL.
JUST AS HE KNEW THAT A TRUE ARSONIST POSSESSED A DIABOLICAL KNOWLEDGE OF FLAME...

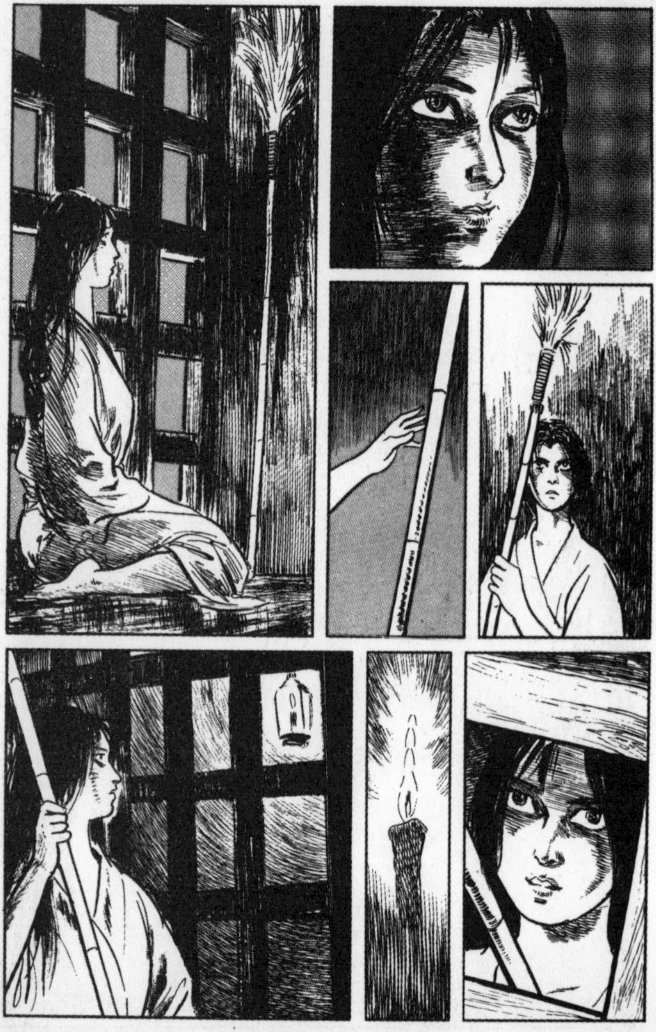

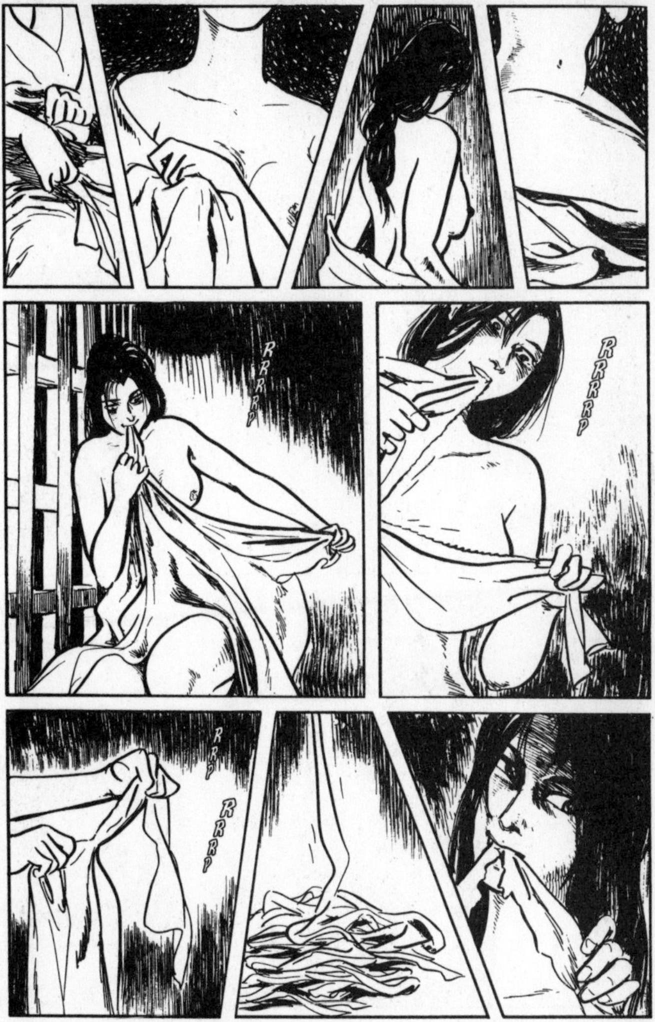
RRRRP
RRRRP
RRP
RRRP

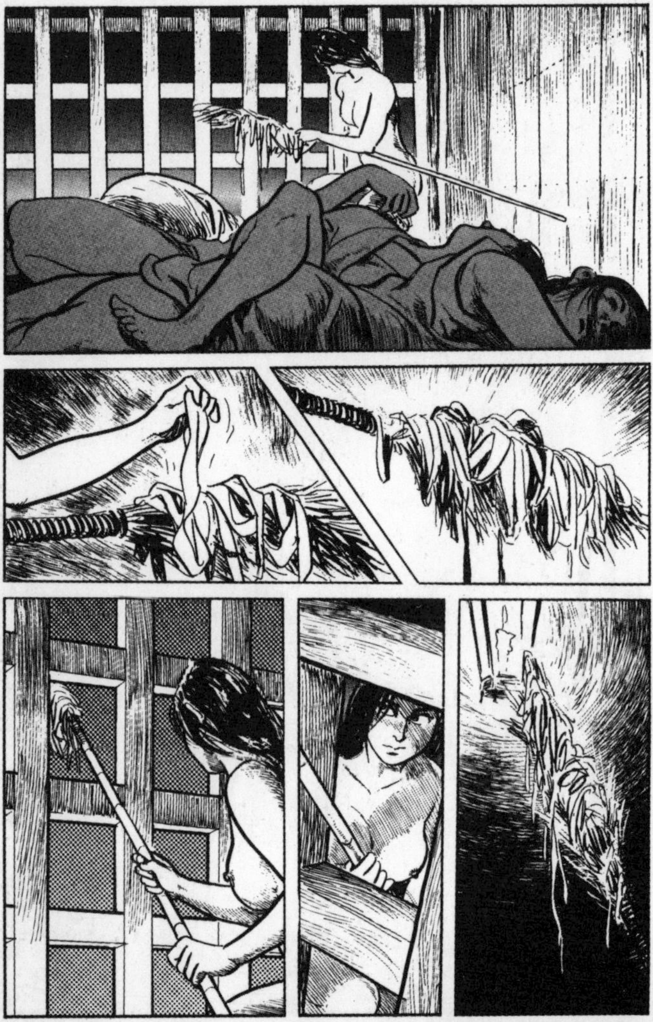

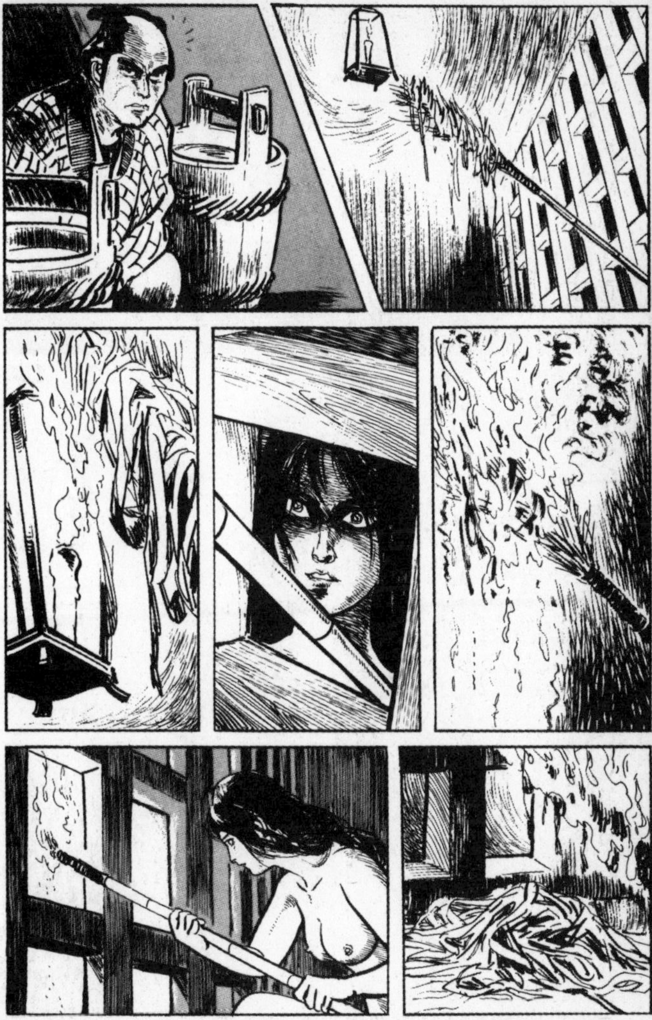

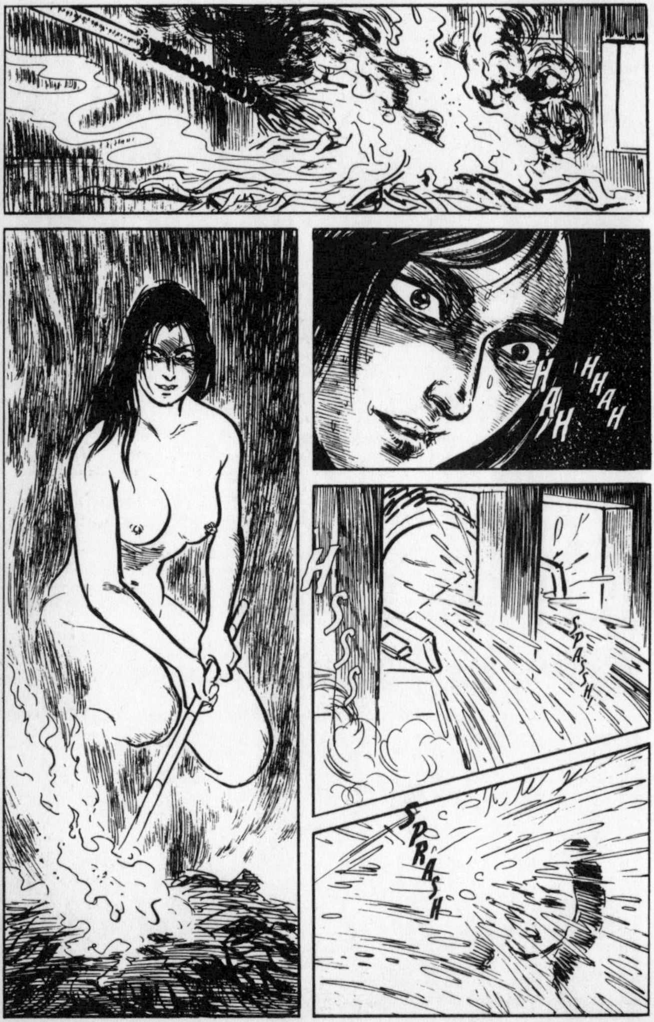
HAH
HHAH
HSSSS
SPASSH!
SPRASH

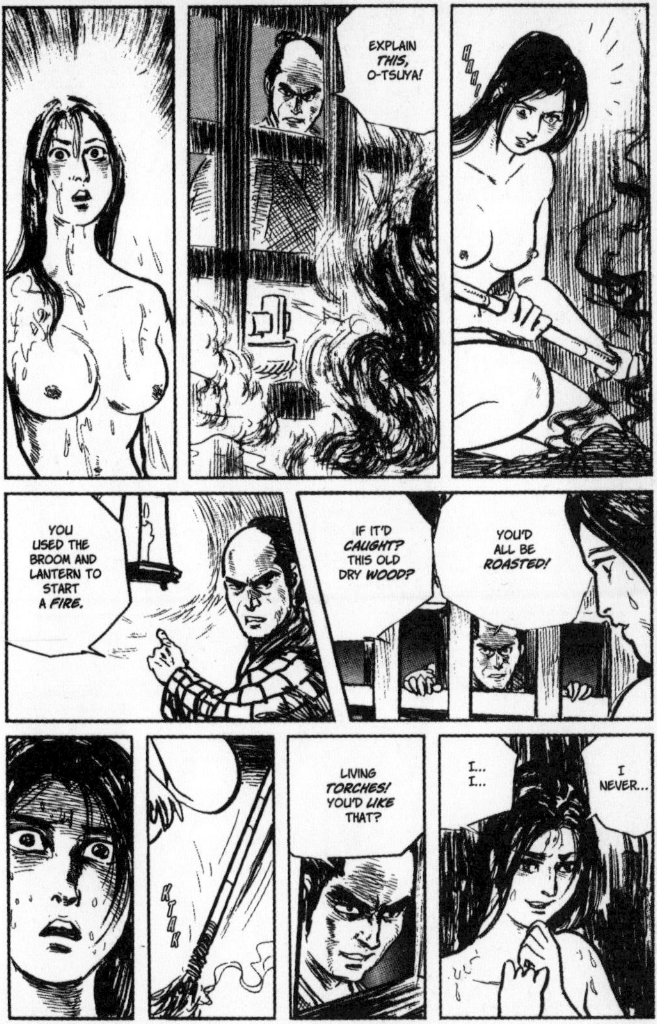
EXPLAIN THIS, O-TSUYA!
HAH!
YOU USED THE BROOM AND LANTERN TO START A FIRE.
IF IT'D CAUGHT? THIS OLD DRY WOOD?
YOU'D ALL BE ROASTED!
KTAK
LIVING TORCHES! YOU'D LIKE THAT?
I... I...
I NEVER...

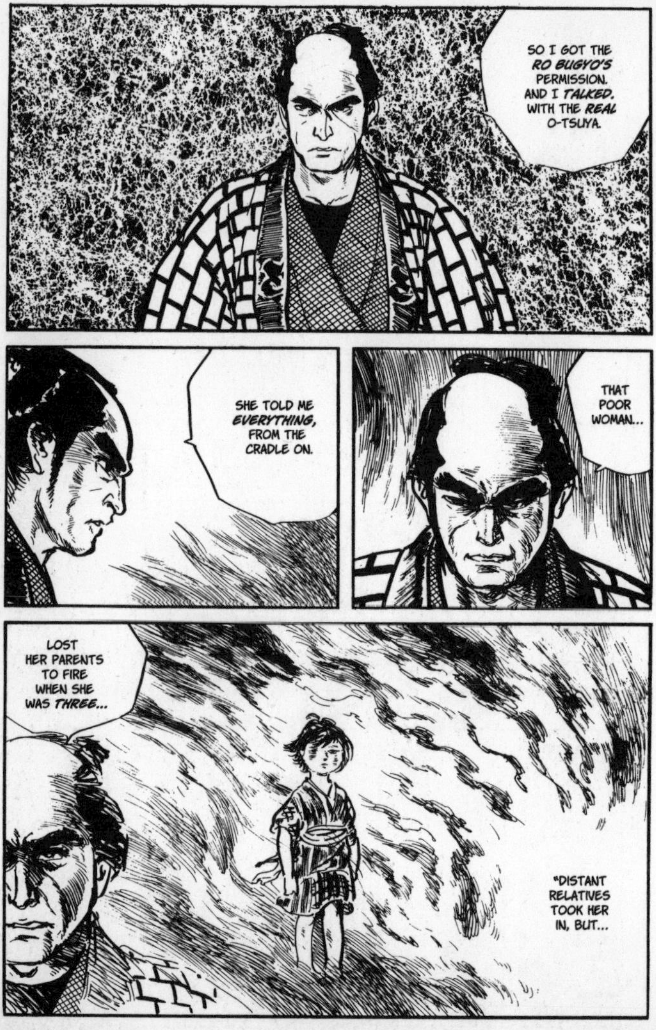
SO I GOT THE *RO BUGYO'S* PERMISSION. AND I *TALKED.* WITH THE *REAL* O-TSUYA.
SHE TOLD ME *EVERYTHING,* FROM THE CRADLE ON.
THAT POOR WOMAN...
LOST HER PARENTS TO FIRE WHEN SHE WAS *THREE...*
"DISTANT RELATIVES TOOK HER IN, BUT...

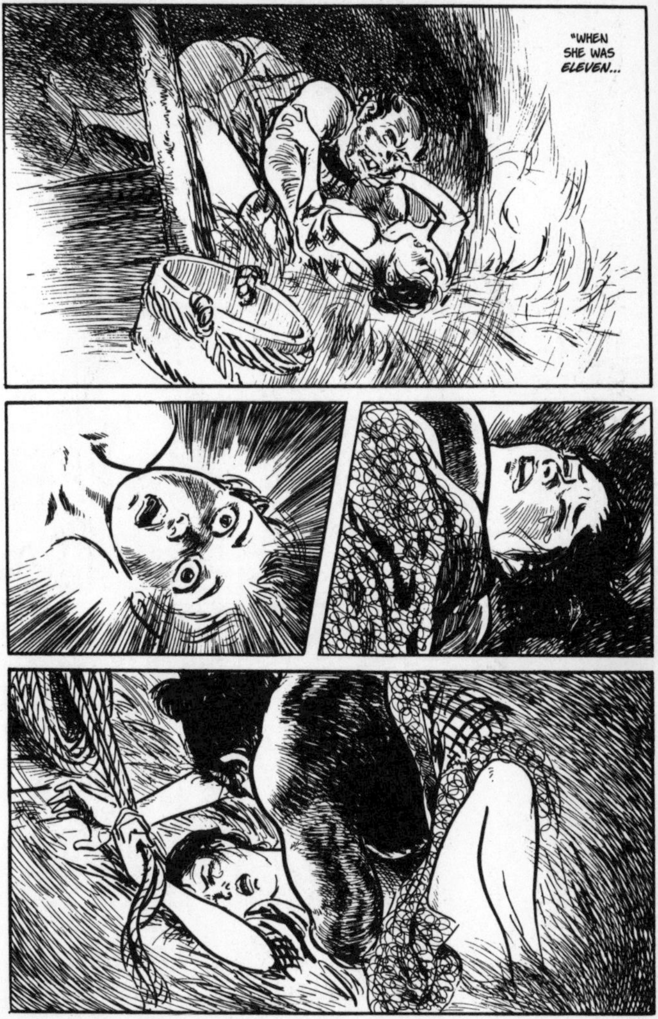
"WHEN SHE WAS ELEVEN...

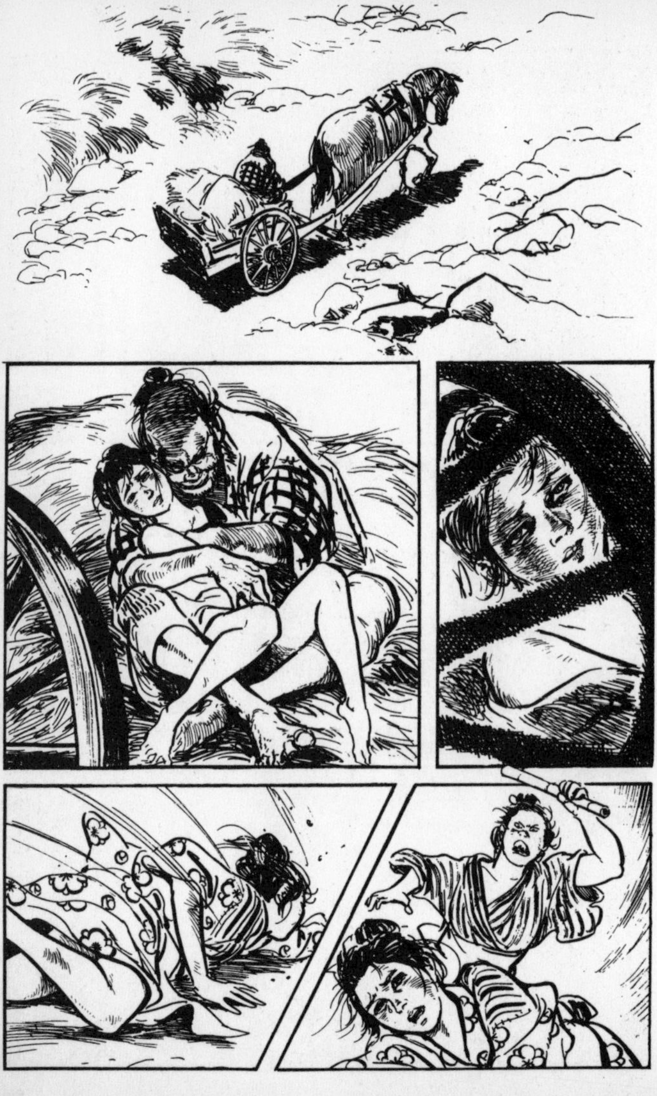

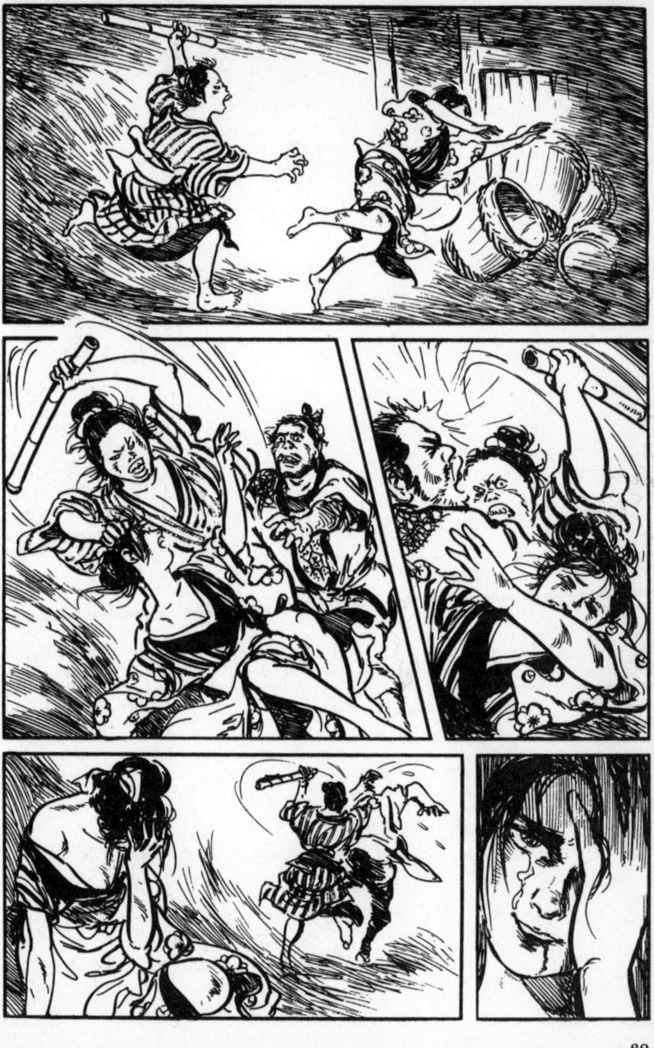

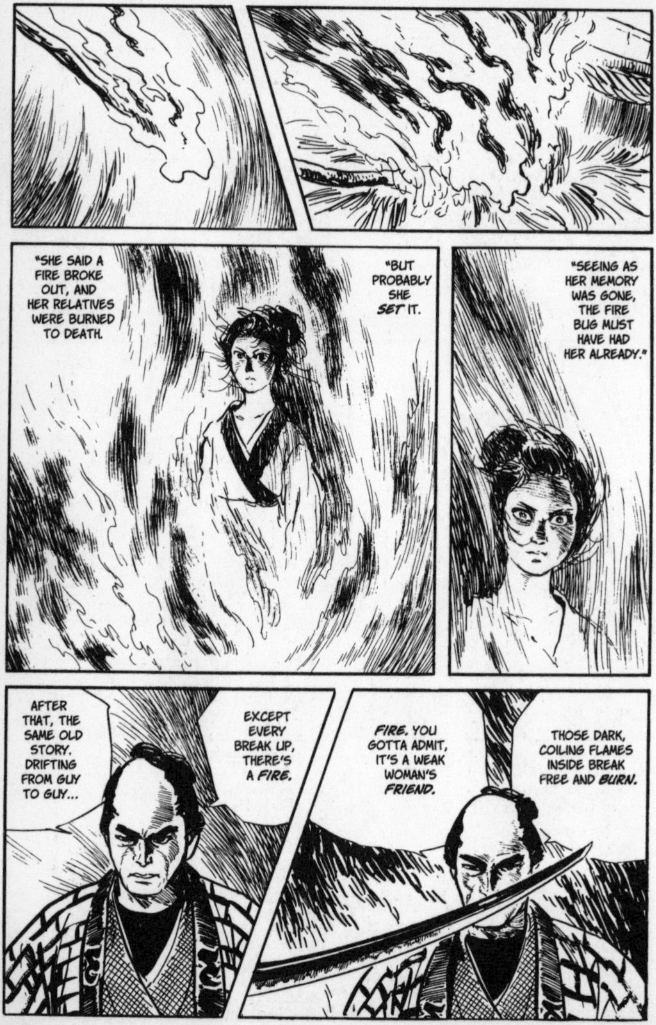
"SHE SAID A FIRE BROKE OUT, AND HER RELATIVES WERE BURNED TO DEATH.
"BUT PROBABLY SHE *SET* IT.
"SEEING AS HER MEMORY WAS GONE, THE FIRE BUG MUST HAVE HAD HER ALREADY."
AFTER THAT, THE SAME OLD STORY. DRIFTING FROM GUY TO GUY...
EXCEPT EVERY BREAK UP, THERE'S A *FIRE.*
FIRE. YOU GOTTA ADMIT, IT'S A WEAK WOMAN'S *FRIEND.*
THOSE DARK, COILING FLAMES INSIDE BREAK FREE AND *BURN.*

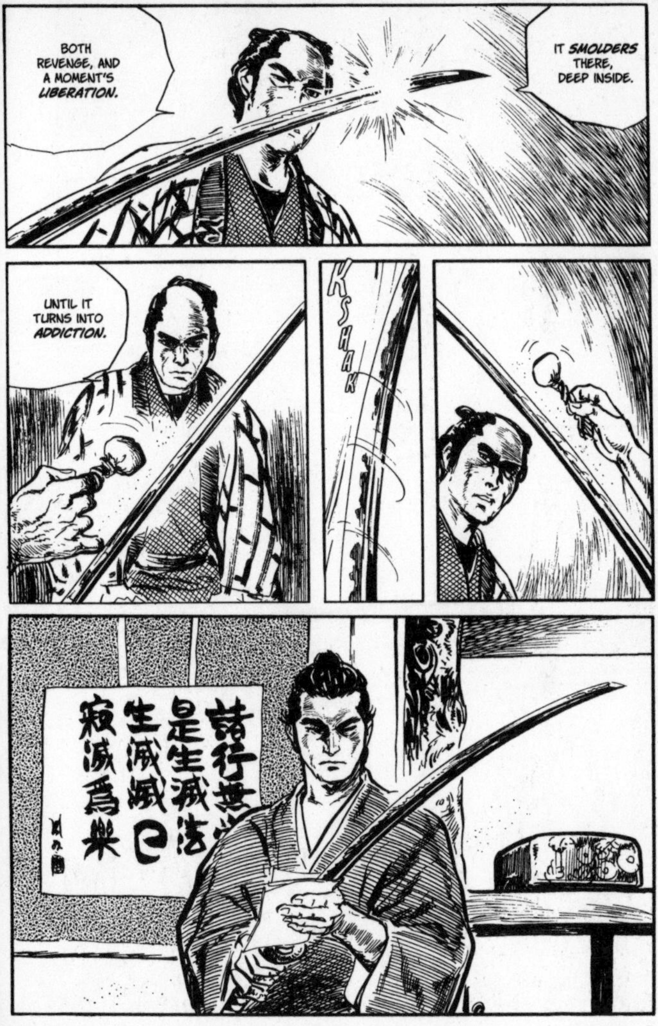
BOTH REVENGE, AND A MOMENT'S *LIBERATION.*
IT *SMOLDERS* THERE, DEEP INSIDE.
UNTIL IT TURNS INTO *ADDICTION.*
KSHAK
諸行無
是生滅法
生滅滅已
寂滅爲樂

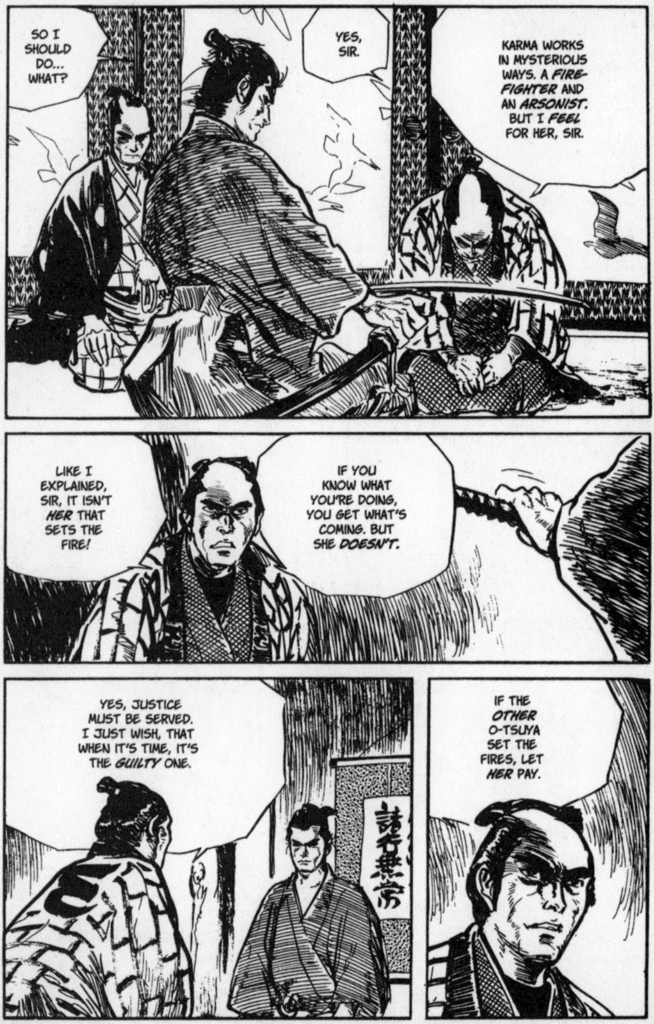
SO I SHOULD DO... WHAT?
YES, SIR.
KARMA WORKS IN MYSTERIOUS WAYS. A *FIRE-FIGHTER* AND AN *ARSONIST*. BUT I *FEEL* FOR HER, SIR.
LIKE I EXPLAINED, SIR, IT ISN'T *HER* THAT SETS THE FIRE!
IF YOU KNOW WHAT YOU'RE DOING, YOU GET WHAT'S COMING. BUT SHE *DOESN'T*.
YES, JUSTICE MUST BE SERVED. I JUST WISH, THAT WHEN IT'S TIME, IT'S THE *GUILTY* ONE.
諸行無常
IF THE *OTHER* O-TSUYA SET THE FIRES, LET *HER* PAY.

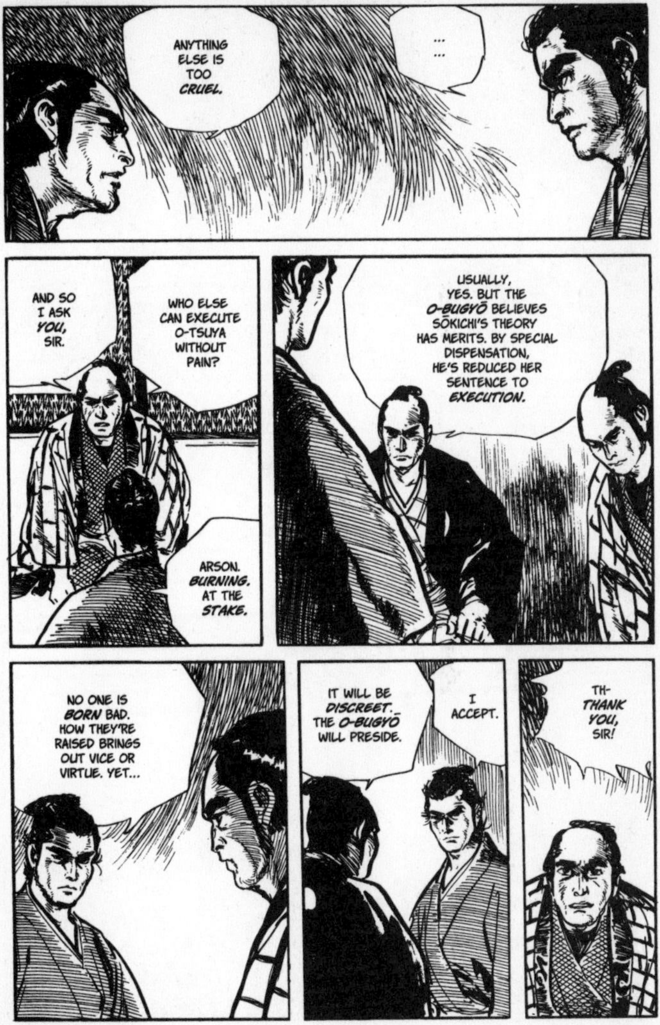
ANYTHING ELSE IS TOO CRUEL.
...
...
AND SO I ASK YOU, SIR.
WHO ELSE CAN EXECUTE O-TSUYA WITHOUT PAIN?
ARSON. BURNING. AT THE STAKE.
USUALLY, YES. BUT THE O-BUGYŌ BELIEVES SŌKICHI'S THEORY HAS MERITS. BY SPECIAL DISPENSATION, HE'S REDUCED HER SENTENCE TO EXECUTION.
NO ONE IS BORN BAD. HOW THEY'RE RAISED BRINGS OUT VICE OR VIRTUE. YET...
IT WILL BE DISCREET. THE O-BUGYŌ WILL PRESIDE.
I ACCEPT.
TH- THANK YOU, SIR!

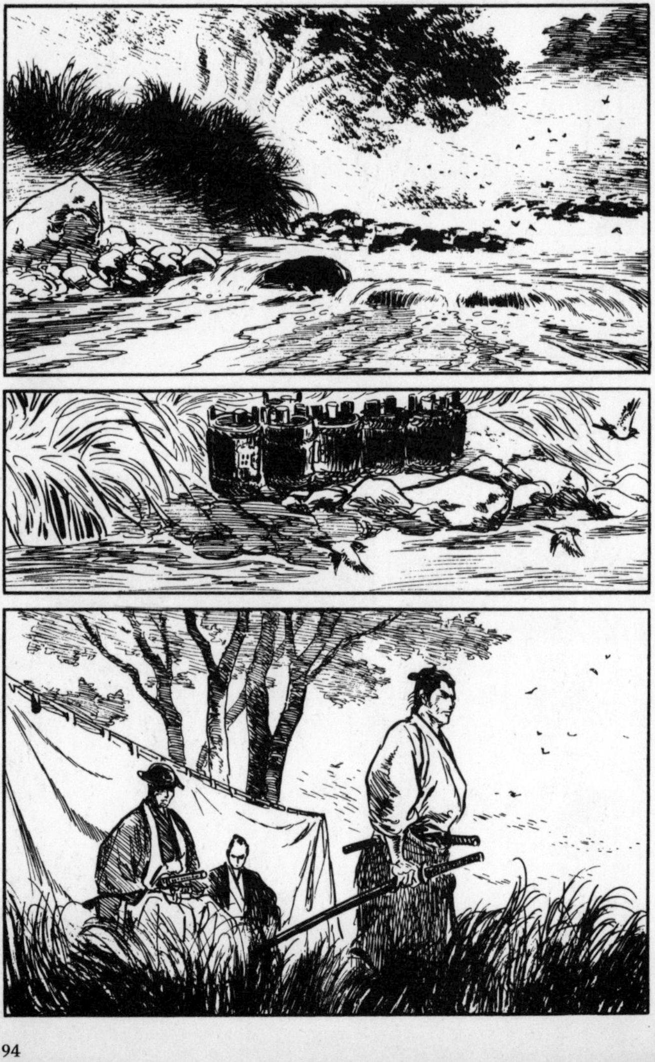

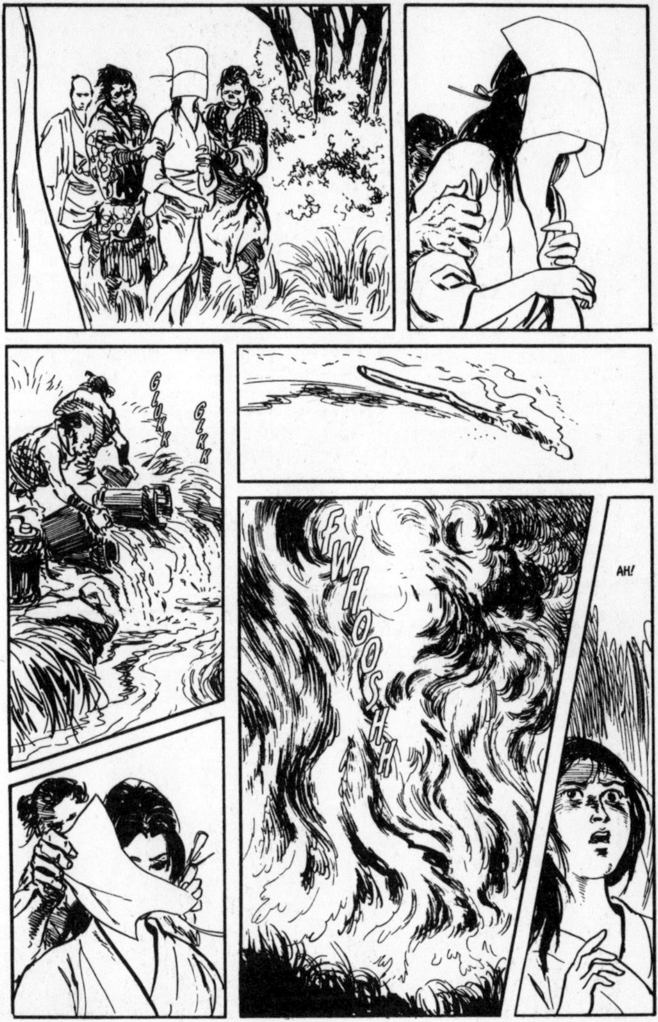
GLUKK
GLKK
FWHOOSHH
AH!

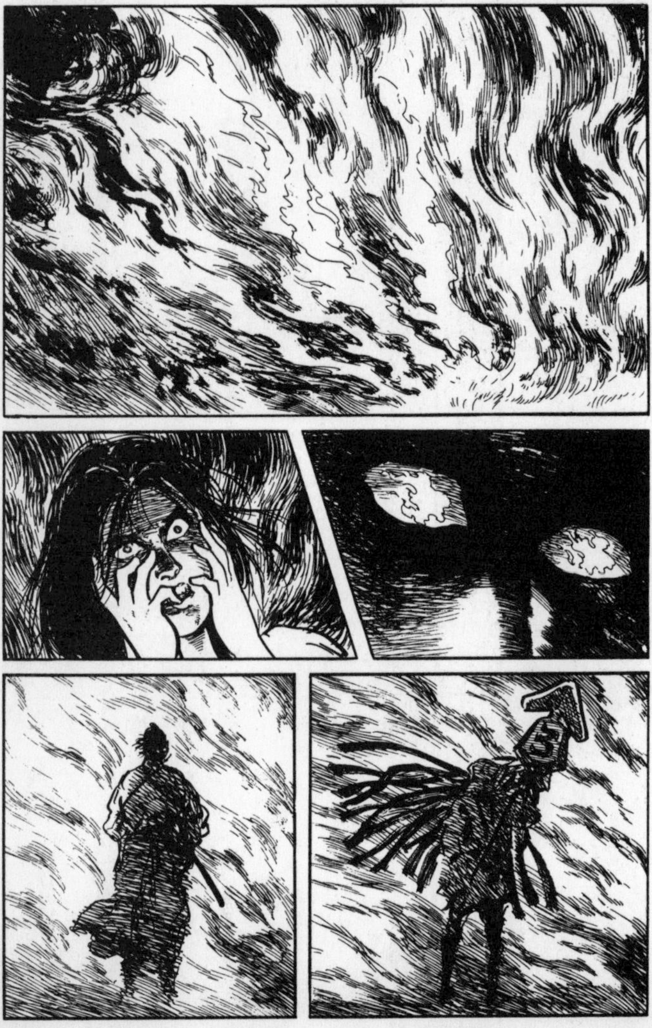

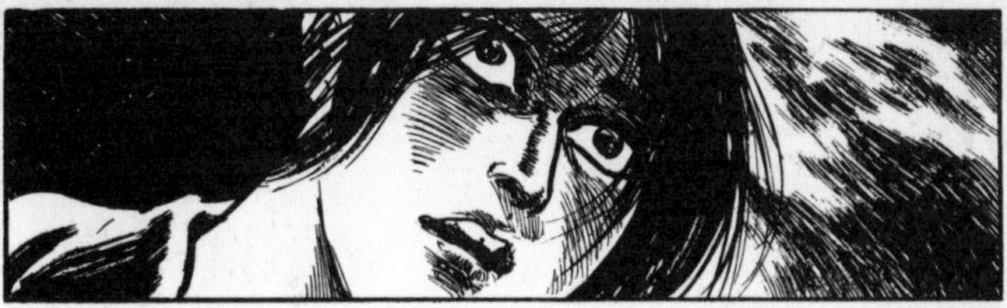

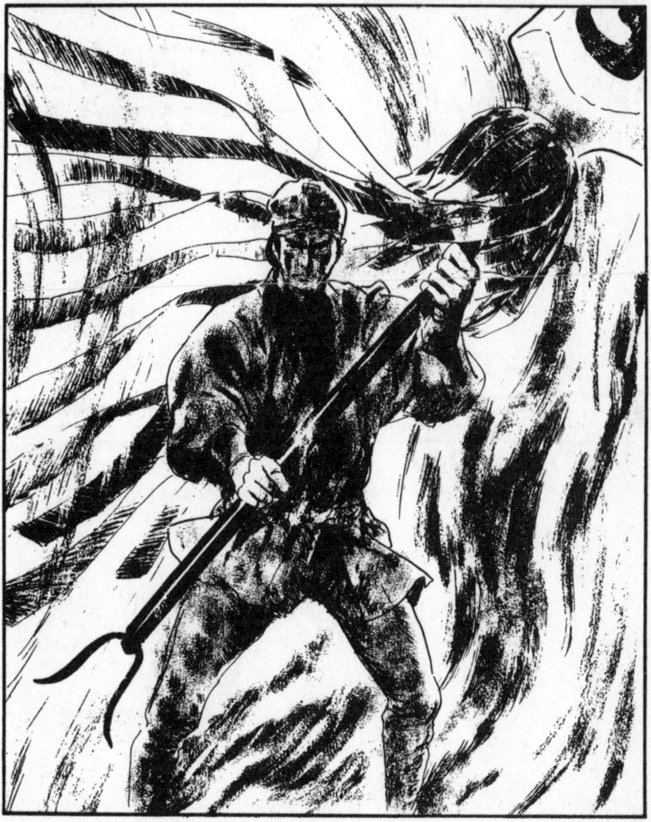

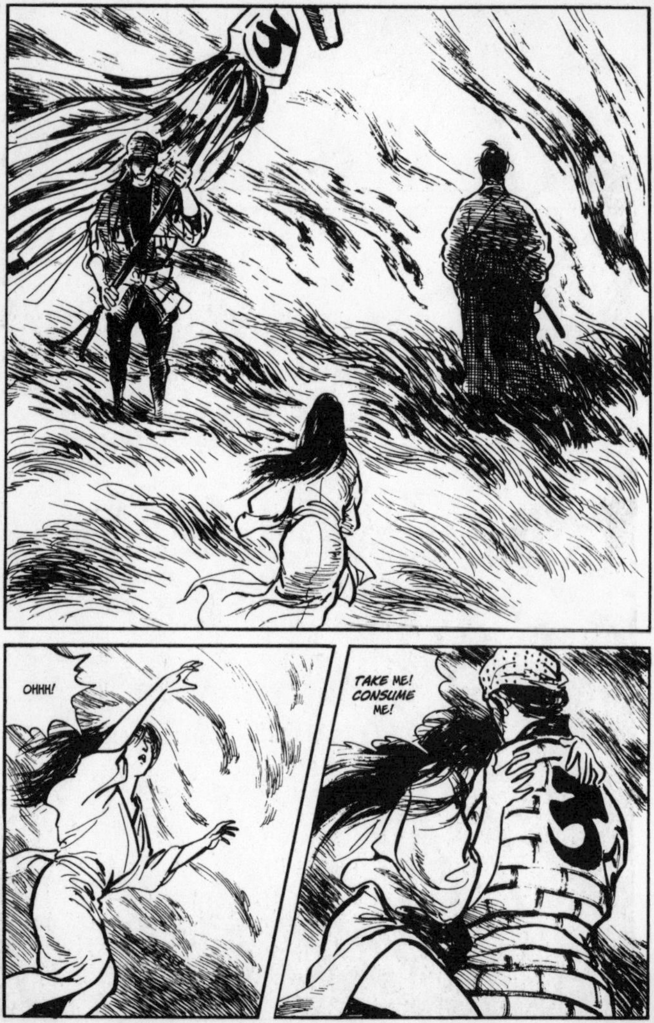
OHHH!
TAKE ME! CONSUME ME!

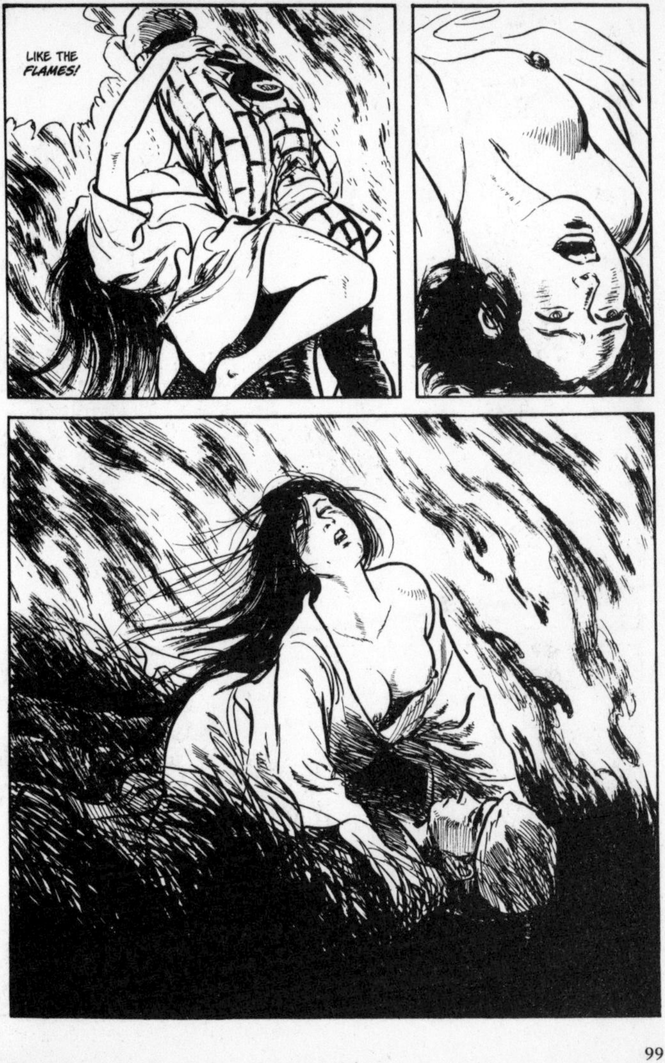
LIKE THE *FLAMES!*

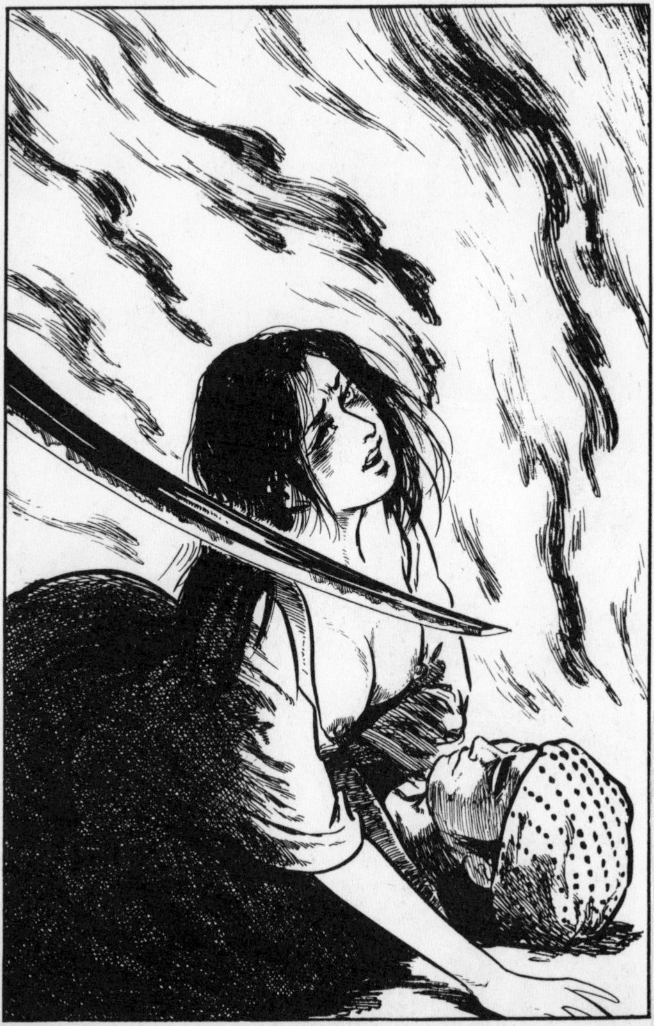

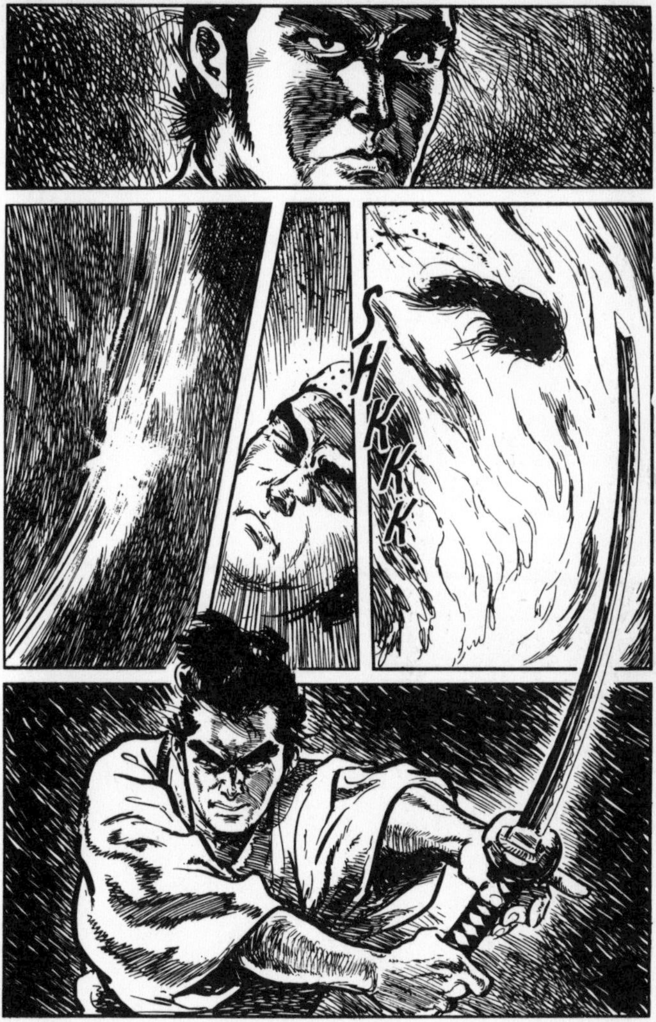
SHKKKK

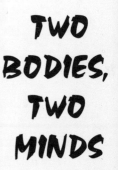

CUT SEVEN

TWO BODIES, TWO MINDS

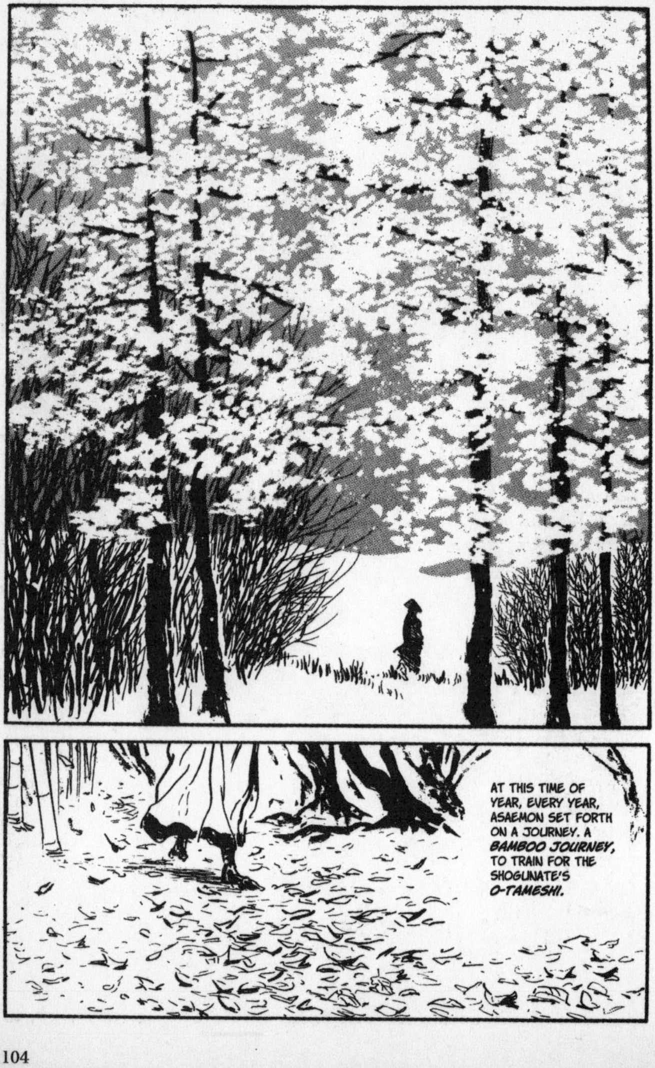
AT THIS TIME OF YEAR, EVERY YEAR, ASAEMON SET FORTH ON A JOURNEY. A *BAMBOO JOURNEY*, TO TRAIN FOR THE SHOGUNATE'S *O-TAMESHI.*

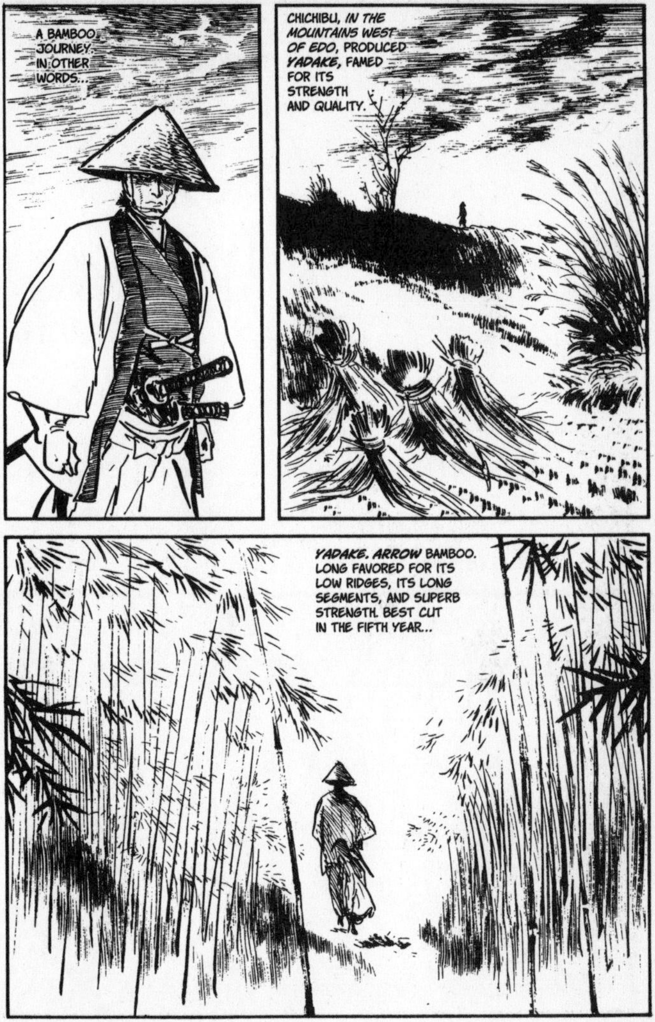
A BAMBOO JOURNEY. IN OTHER WORDS...
CHICHIBU, *IN THE MOUNTAINS WEST OF EDO*, PRODUCED *YADAKE*, FAMED FOR ITS STRENGTH AND QUALITY.
YADAKE. ARROW BAMBOO. LONG FAVORED FOR ITS LOW RIDGES, ITS LONG SEGMENTS, AND SUPERB STRENGTH. BEST CUT IN THE FIFTH YEAR...

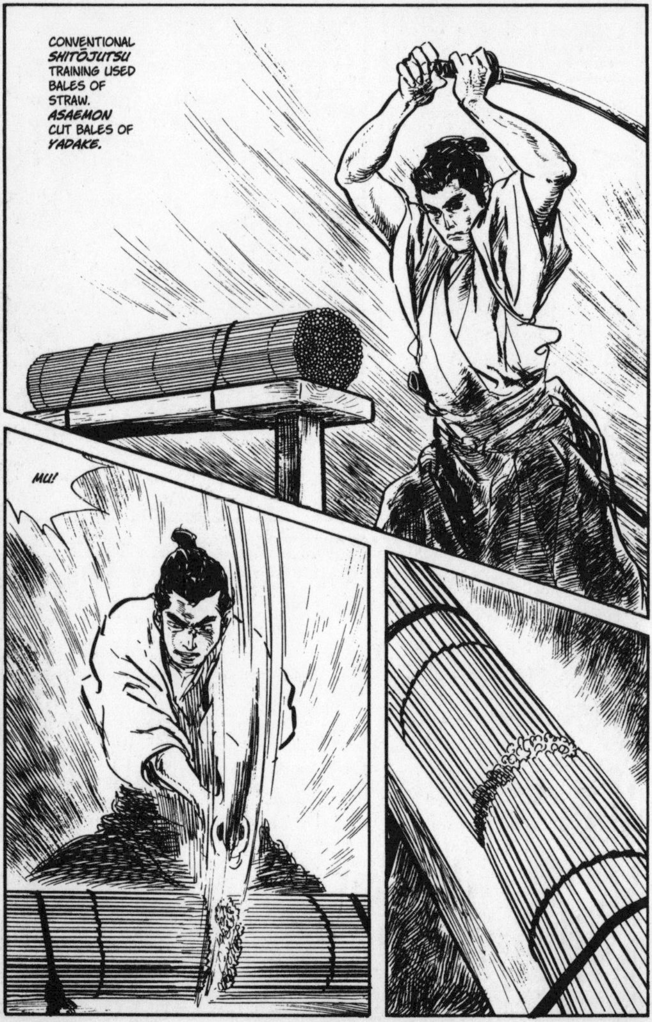

CONVENTIONAL *SHITŌJUTSU* TRAINING USED BALES OF STRAW. *ASAEMON* CUT BALES OF *YADAKE.*
MU!

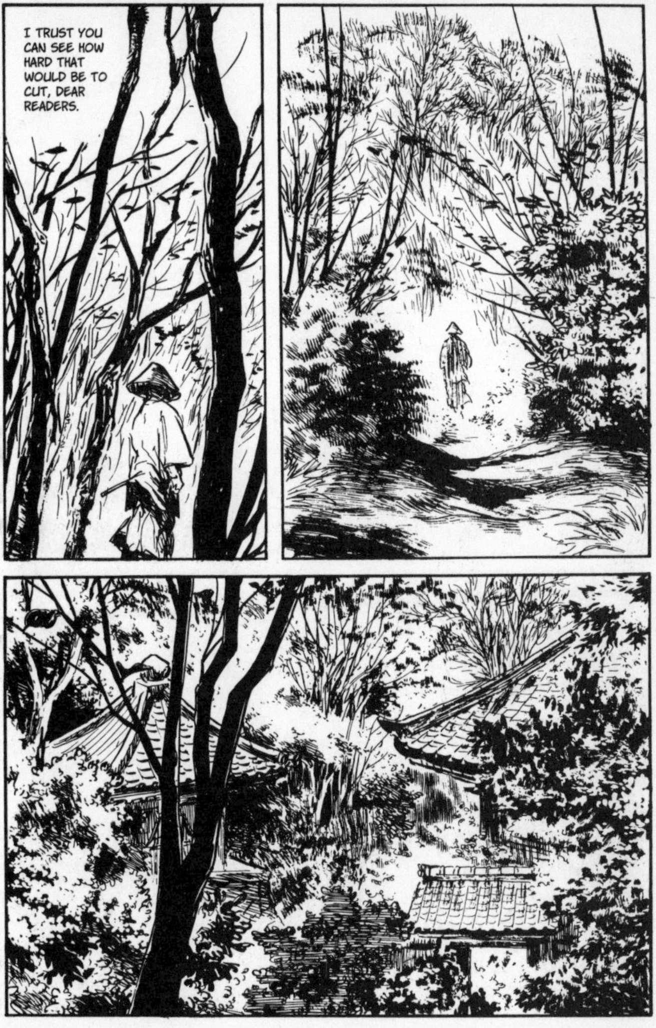
I TRUST YOU CAN SEE HOW HARD THAT WOULD BE TO CUT, DEAR READERS.

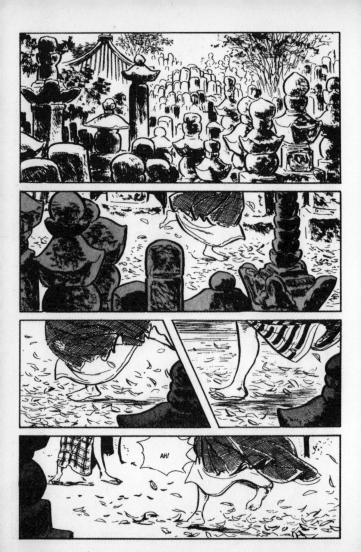

AH!

108

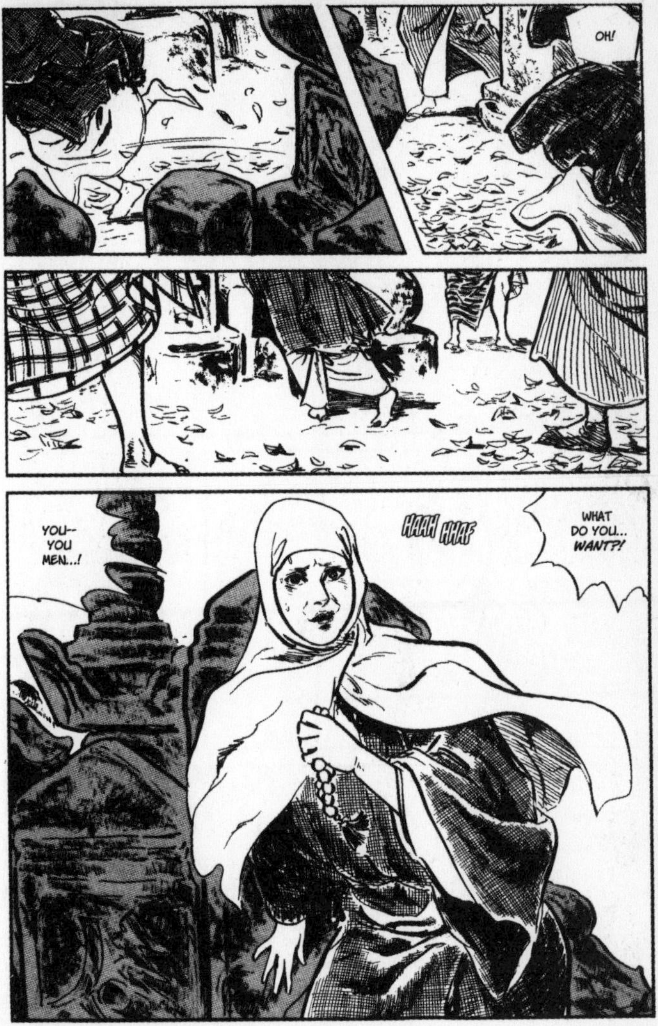
OH!
YOU--
YOU
MEN...!
HAAAH HHAF
WHAT
DO YOU...
WANT?!

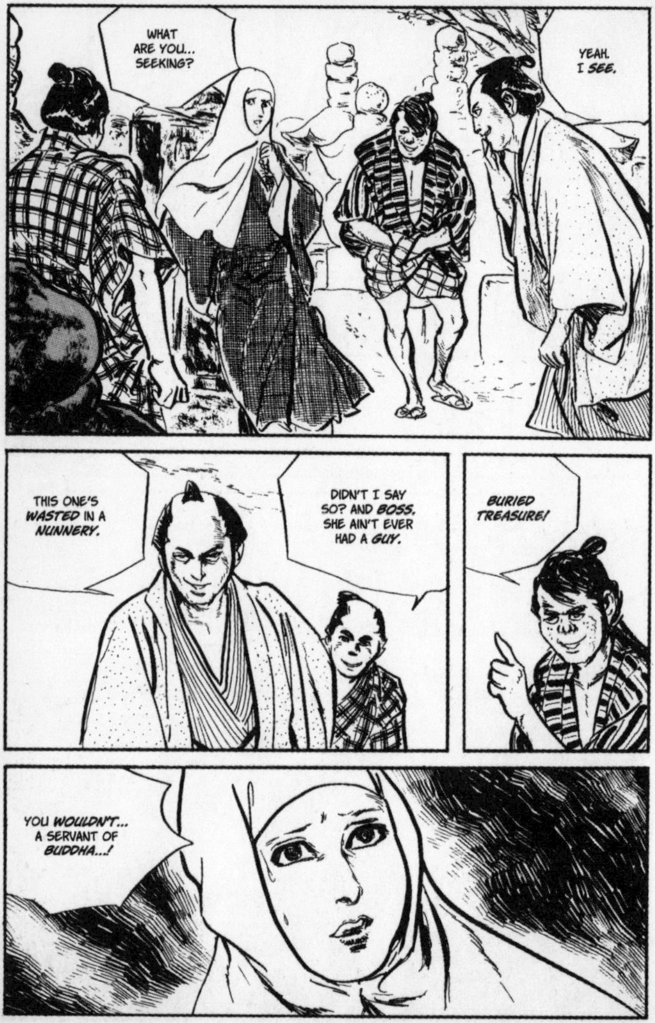
WHAT ARE YOU... SEEKING?
YEAH. I *SEE.*
THIS ONE'S *WASTED* IN A *NUNNERY.*
DIDN'T I SAY SO? AND *BOSS,* SHE AIN'T EVER HAD A *GUY.*
BURIED TREASURE!
YOU *WOULDN'T...* A SERVANT OF *BUDDHA...!*

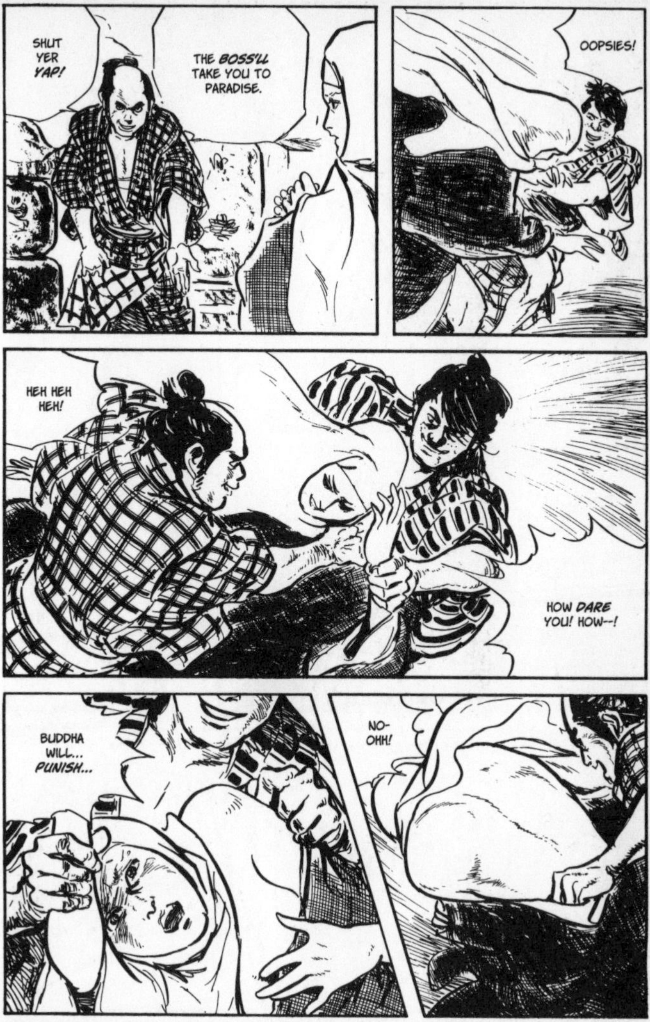
SHUT YER *YAP!*
THE *BOSS'LL* TAKE YOU TO PARADISE.
OOPSIES!
HEH HEH HEH!
HOW *DARE* YOU! HOW--!
BUDDHA WILL... *PUNISH...*
NO-OHH!

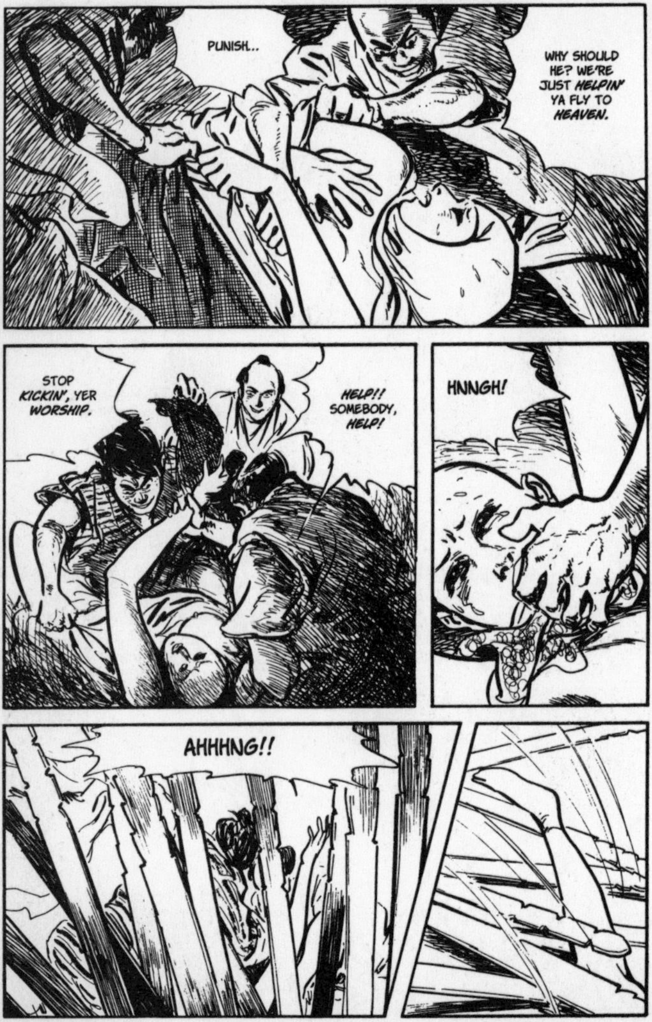
PUNISH...
WHY SHOULD HE? WE'RE JUST *HELPIN'* YA FLY TO *HEAVEN.*
STOP *KICKIN'*, YER *WORSHIP.*
HELP!! SOMEBODY, *HELP!*
HNNGH!
AHHHNG!!

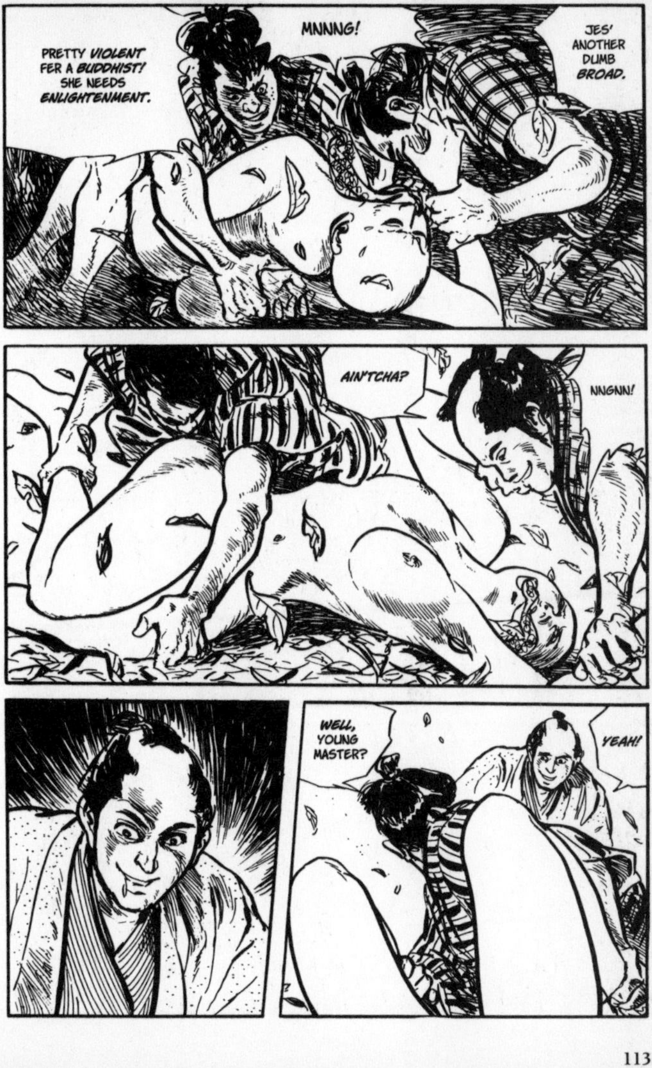
PRETTY VIOLENT FER A BUDDHIST! SHE NEEDS ENLIGHTENMENT.
MNNNG!
JES' ANOTHER DUMB BROAD.
AIN'TCHA?
NNGNN!
WELL, YOUNG MASTER?
YEAH!

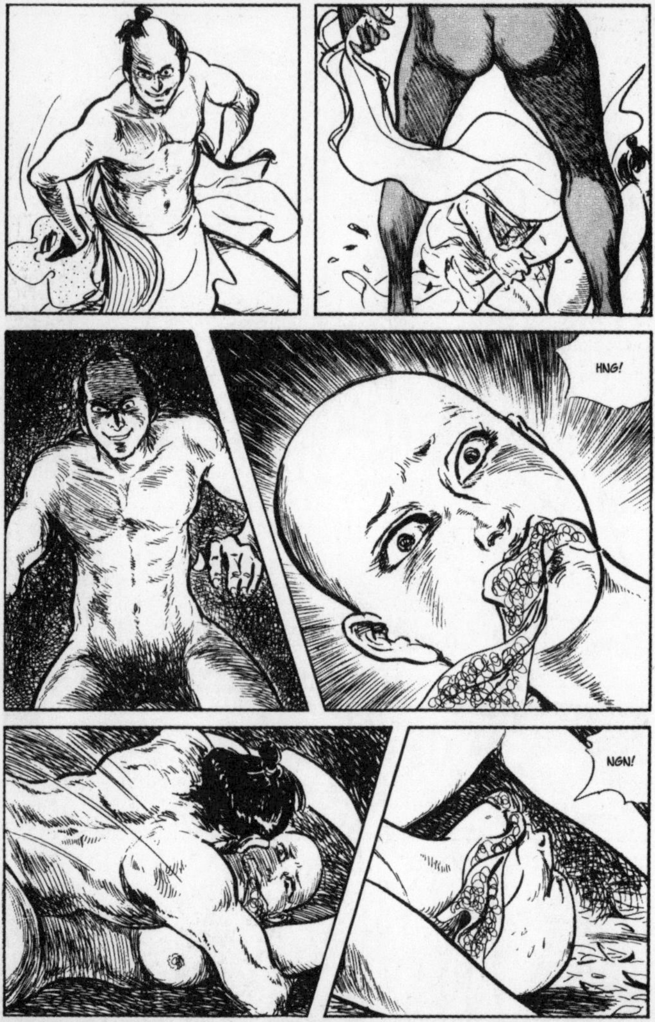
HNG!
NGN!

JUST AS I *THOUGHT.*

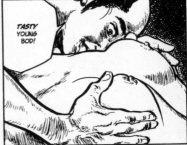

TASTY YOUNG BOD!

UHNNG!

YOU DON'T GOT A *HUBBY,* SO IT AIN'T EVEN A *SIN.*

PLAIN OLD *FORNICATION.* NO POINT *STRUGGLING!*

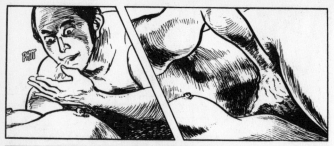

PHT!

NNGN!

ANNG!

KTAK KTAK KTAK

116

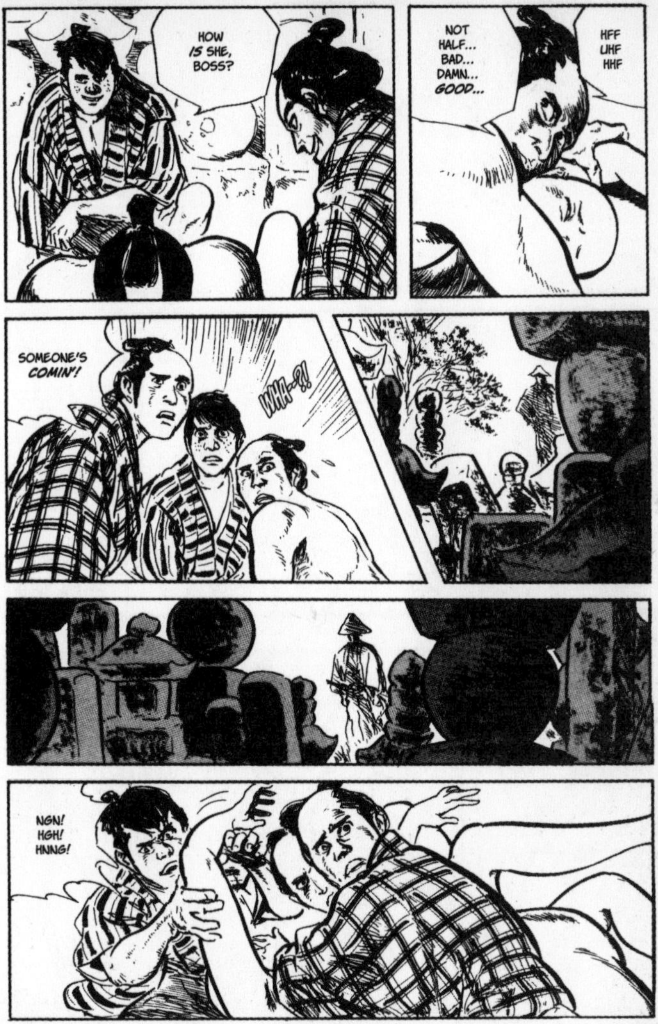
HOW
IS SHE,
BOSS?
NOT
HALF...
BAD...
DAMN...
GOOD...
HFF
UHF
HHF
SOMEONE'S
COMIN'!
WHA--?!
NGN!
HGH!
HNNG!

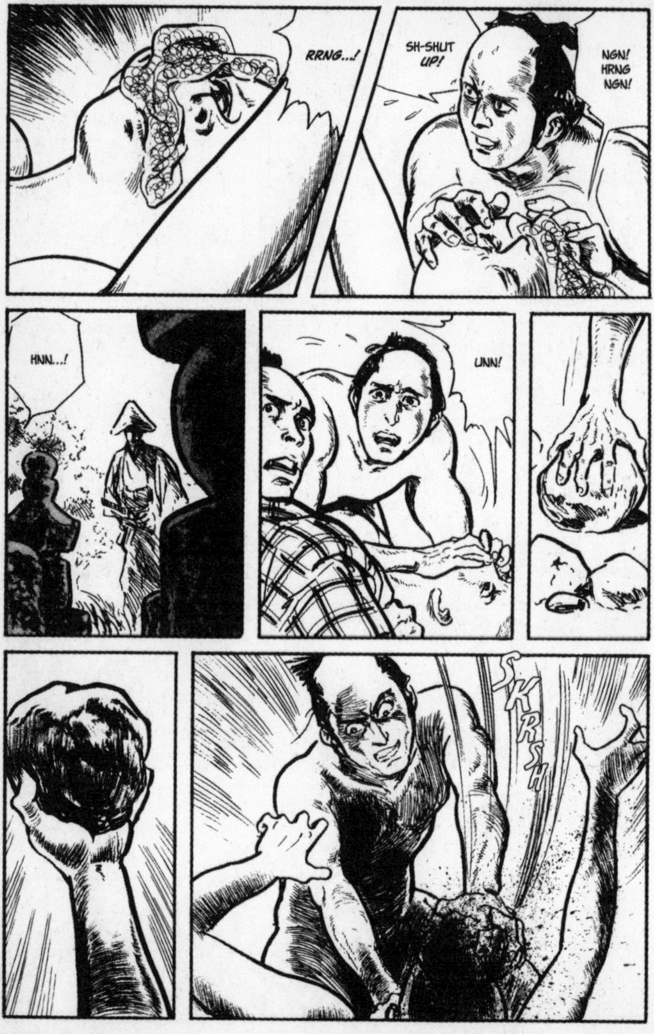
RRNG...!
SH-SHUT UP!
NGN! HRNG NGN!
HNN...!
UNN!
SKRSH

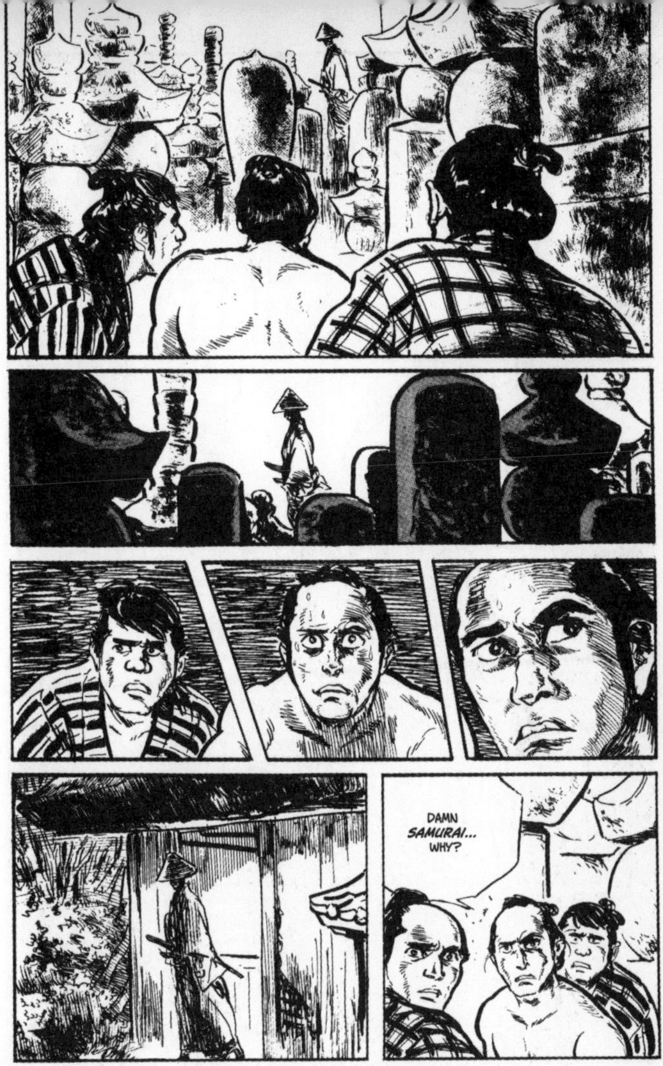
DAMN SAMURAI... WHY?

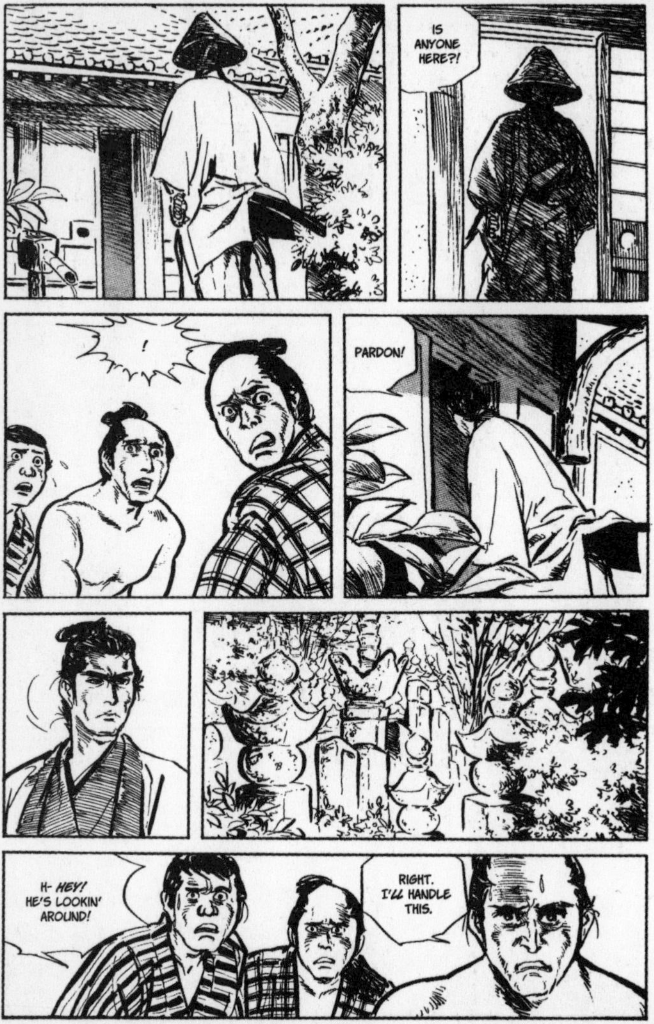
IS ANYONE HERE?!
!
PARDON!
H- HEY! HE'S LOOKIN' AROUND!
RIGHT. I'LL HANDLE THIS.

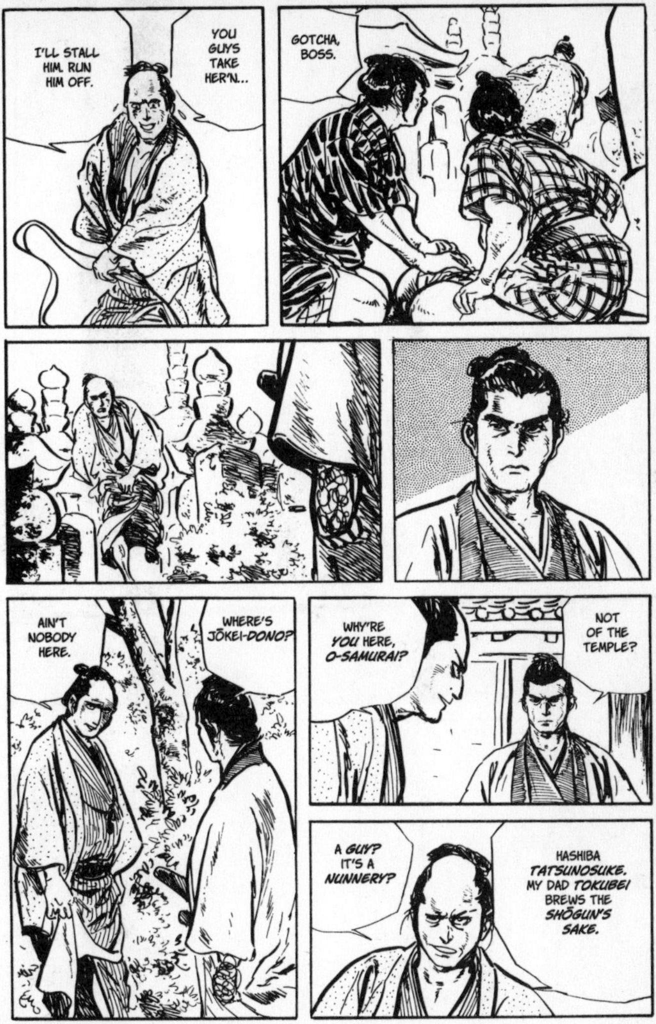
I'LL STALL HIM. RUN HIM OFF.
YOU GUYS TAKE HER'N...
GOTCHA, BOSS.
AIN'T NOBODY HERE.
WHERE'S JŌKEI-*DONO?*
WHY'RE *YOU* HERE, *O-SAMURAI?*
NOT OF THE TEMPLE?
A *GUY?* IT'S A *NUNNERY?*
HASHIBA *TATSUNOSUKE.* MY DAD *TOKUBEI* BREWS THE *SHŌGUN'S SAKE.*

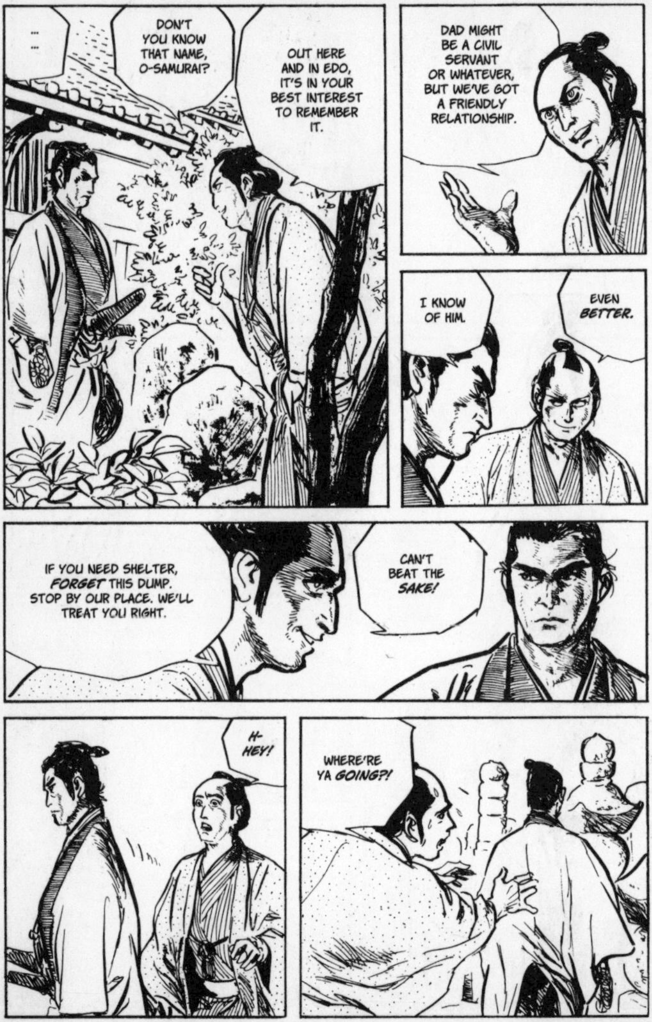
... ...
DON'T YOU KNOW THAT NAME, O-SAMURAI?
OUT HERE AND IN EDO, IT'S IN YOUR BEST INTEREST TO REMEMBER IT.
DAD MIGHT BE A CIVIL SERVANT OR WHATEVER, BUT WE'VE GOT A FRIENDLY RELATIONSHIP.
I KNOW OF HIM.
EVEN BETTER.
IF YOU NEED SHELTER, FORGET THIS DUMP. STOP BY OUR PLACE. WE'LL TREAT YOU RIGHT.
CAN'T BEAT THE SAKE!
H-HEY!
WHERE'RE YA GOING?!

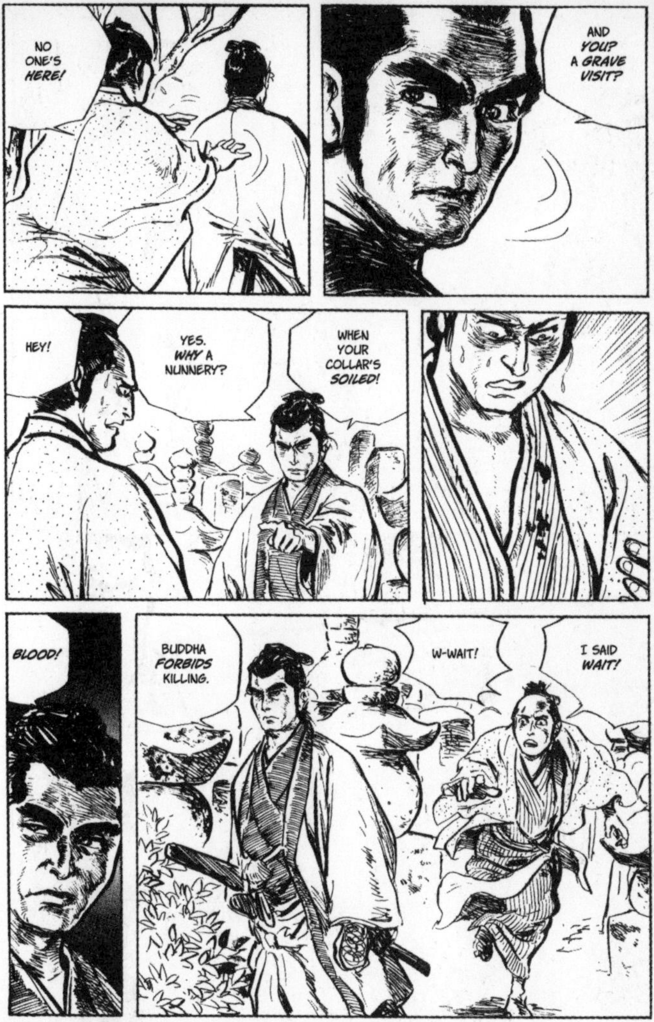
NO ONE'S HERE!
AND YOU? A GRAVE VISIT?
HEY!
YES. WHY A NUNNERY?
WHEN YOUR COLLAR'S SOILED!
BLOOD!
BUDDHA FORBIDS KILLING.
W-WAIT!
I SAID WAIT!

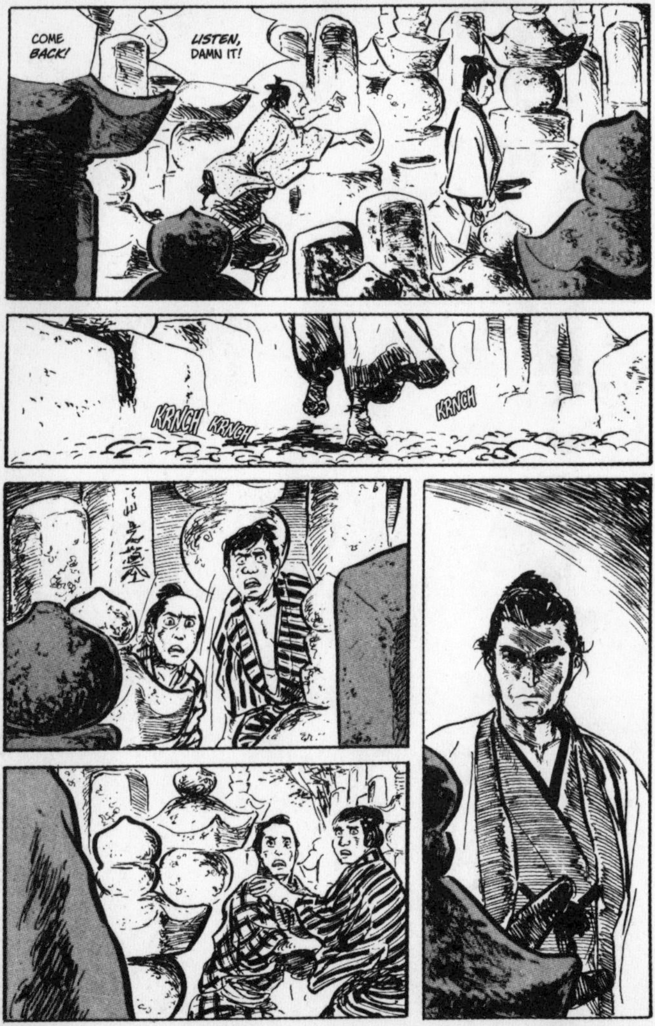
COME BACK!
LISTEN, DAMN IT!
KRNCH KRNCH
KRNCH

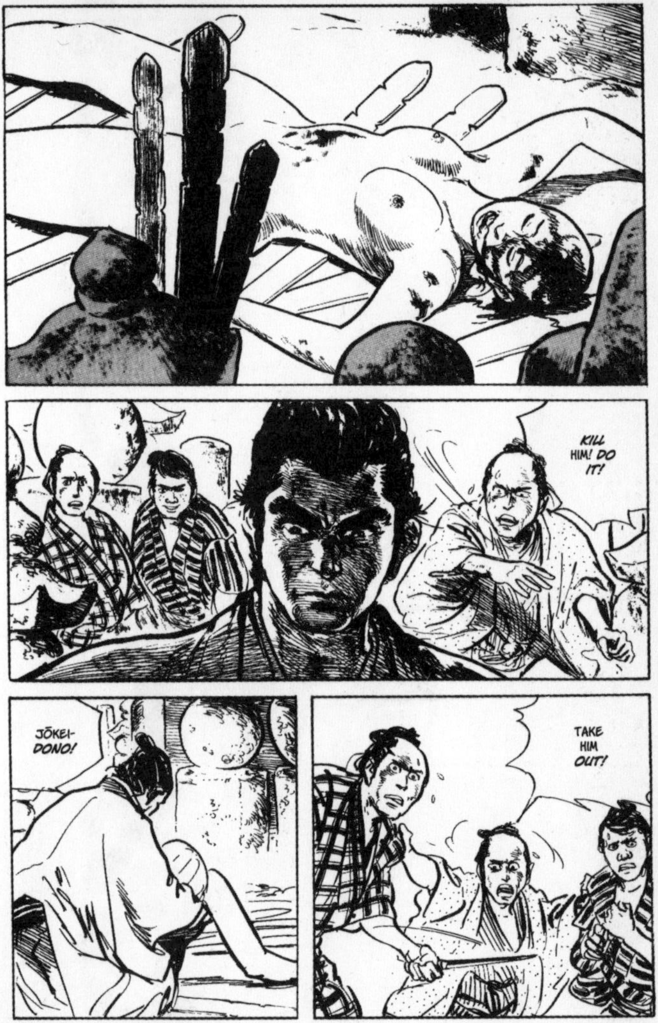
KILL HIM! DO IT!
JŌKEI-DONO!
TAKE HIM OUT!

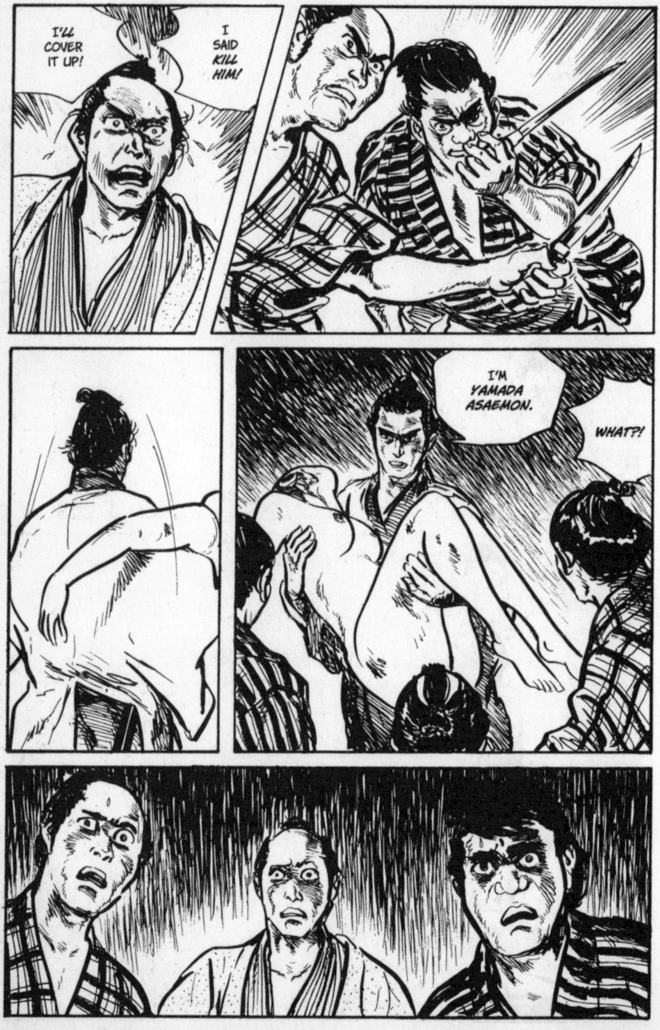
I'LL COVER IT UP!
I SAID KILL HIM!
I'M YAMADA ASAEMON.
WHAT?!

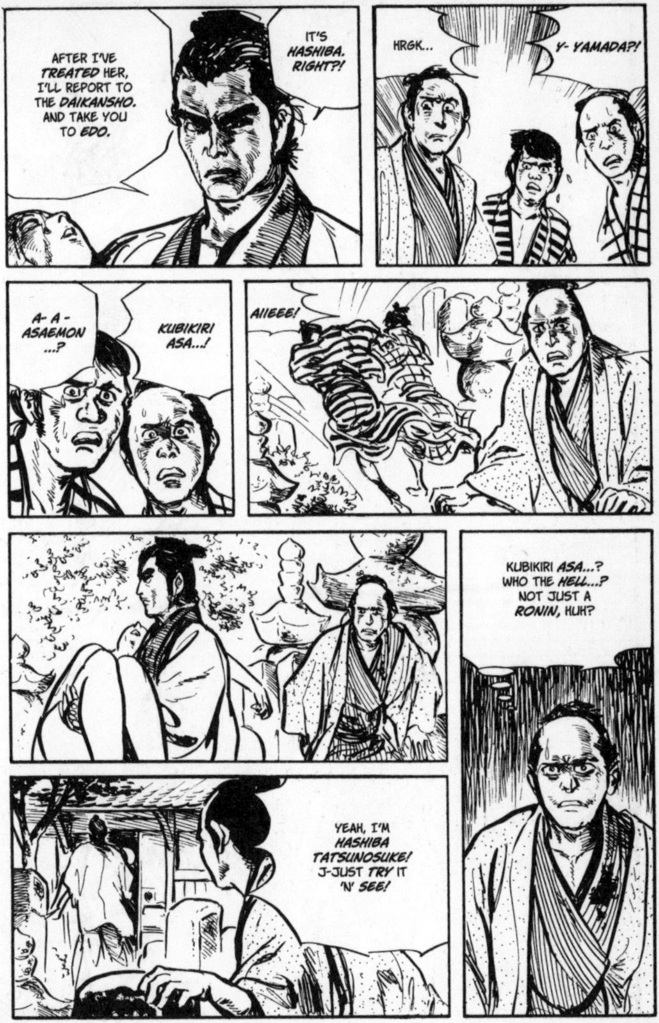
AFTER I'VE TREATED HER, I'LL REPORT TO THE DAIKANSHO. AND TAKE YOU TO EDO.
IT'S HASHIBA. RIGHT?!
HRGK...
Y- YAMADA?!
A- A- ASAEMON ...?
KUBIKIRI ASA...!
AIIEEE!
KUBIKIRI ASA...? WHO THE HELL...? NOT JUST A RONIN, HUH?
YEAH, I'M HASHIBA TATSUNOSUKE! J-JUST TRY IT 'N' SEE!

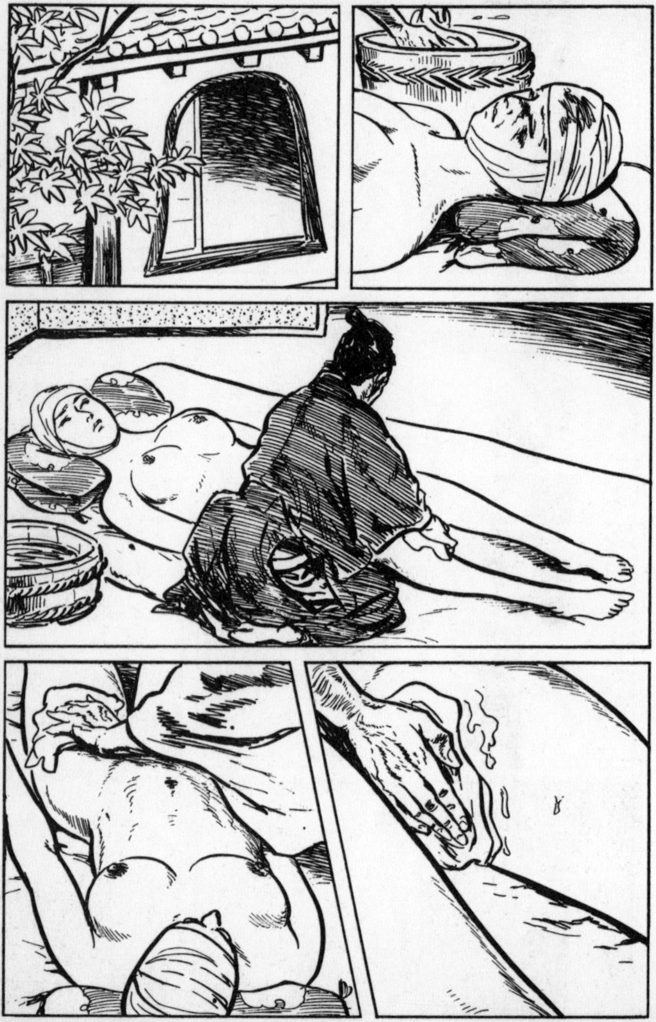

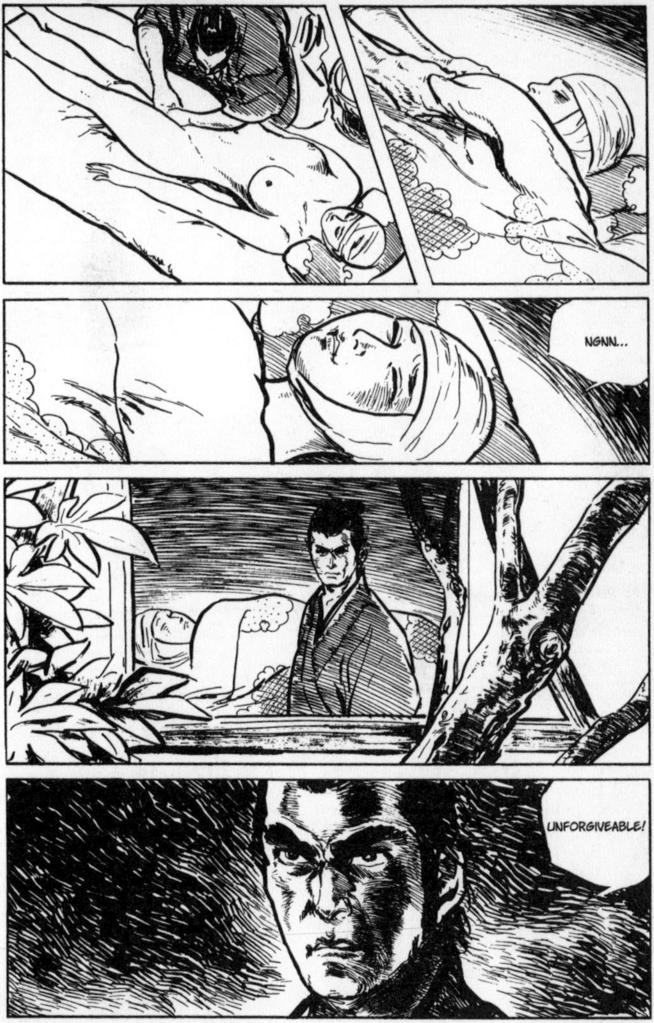
NGNN...
UNFORGIVEABLE!

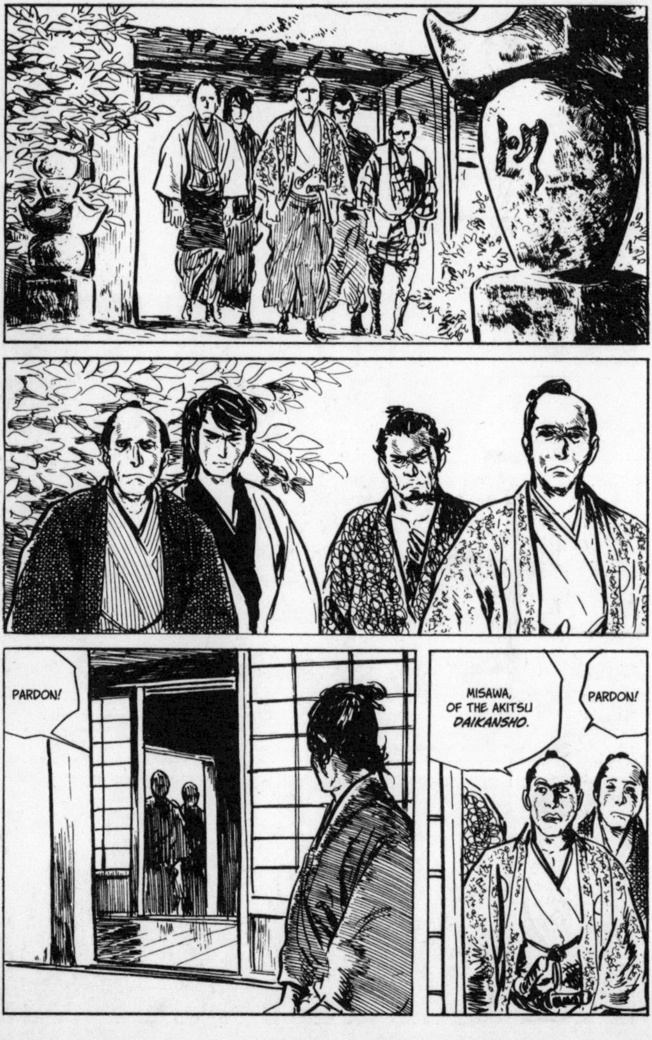
PARDON!
MISAWA, OF THE AKITSU *DAIKANSHO*.
PARDON!

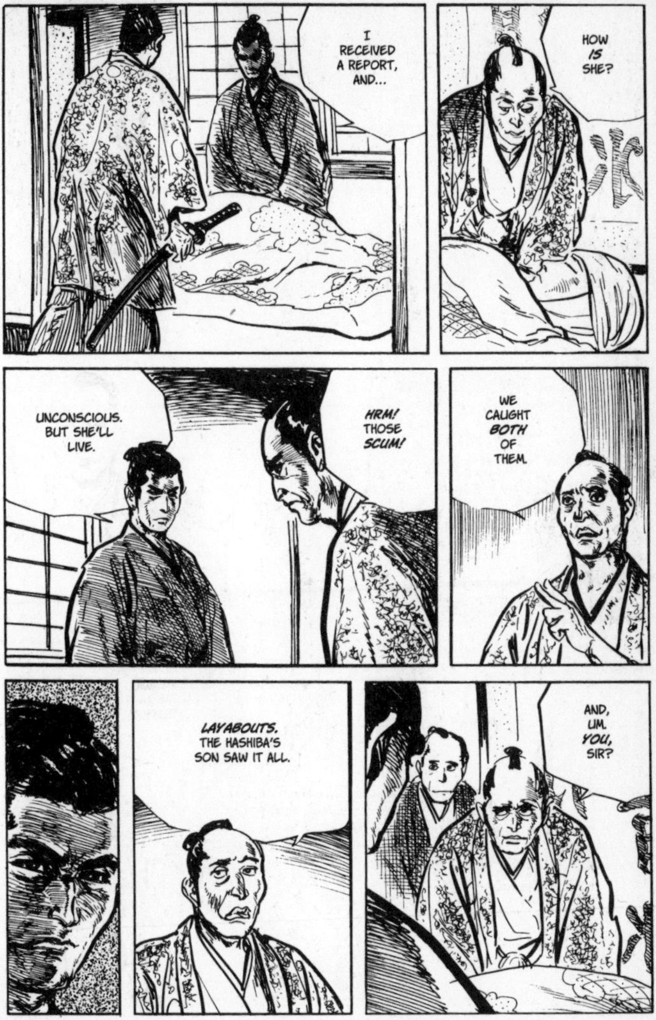
I RECEIVED A REPORT, AND...
HOW *IS* SHE?
UNCONSCIOUS. BUT SHE'LL LIVE.
HRM! THOSE *SCUM!*
WE CAUGHT *BOTH* OF THEM.
LAYABOUTS. THE HASHIBA'S SON SAW IT ALL.
AND, UM. *YOU,* SIR?

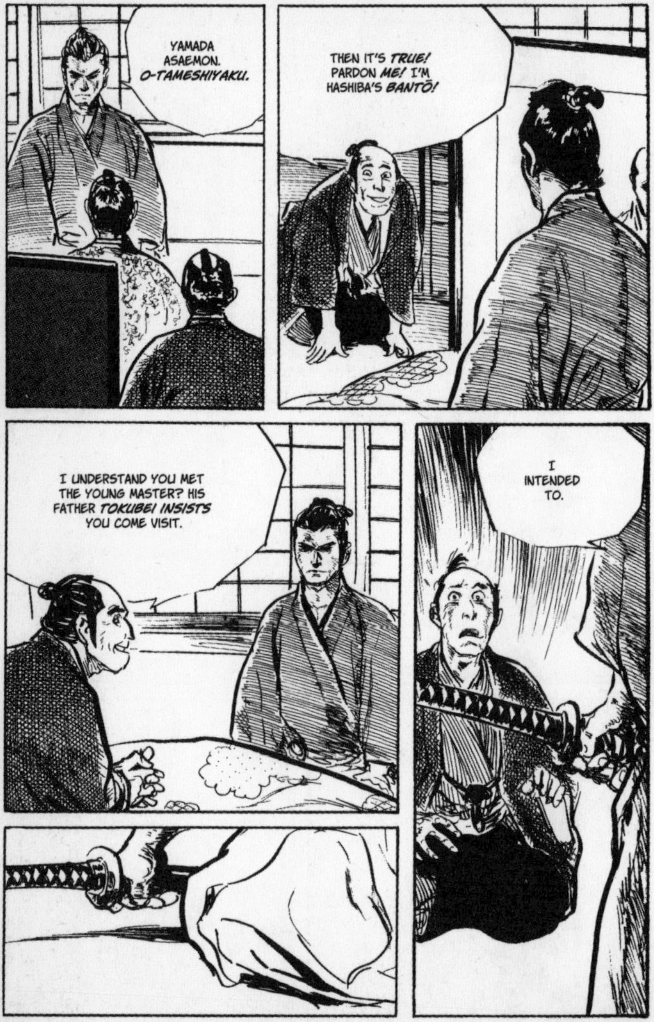
YAMADA ASAEMON. O-TAMESHIYAKU.
THEN IT'S TRUE! PARDON ME! I'M HASHIBA'S BANTŌ!
I UNDERSTAND YOU MET THE YOUNG MASTER? HIS FATHER TOKUBEI INSISTS YOU COME VISIT.
I INTENDED TO.

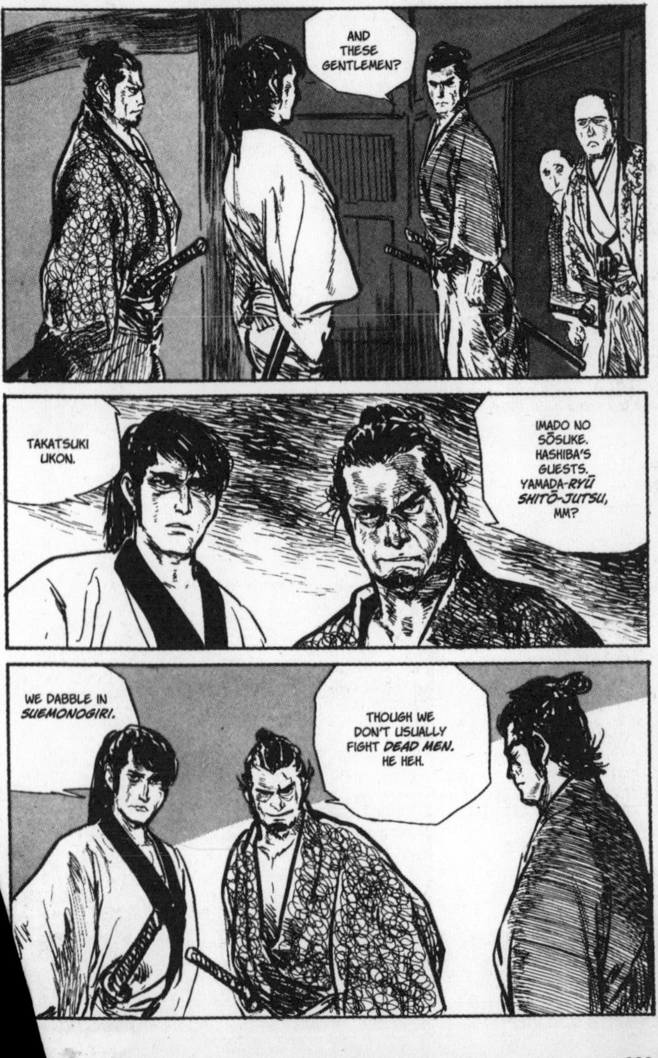
AND THESE GENTLEMEN?
TAKATSUKI UKON.
IMADO NO SŌSUKE. HASHIBA'S GUESTS. YAMADA-*RYŪ SHITŌ-JUTSU,* MM?
WE DABBLE IN *SUEMONOGIRI.*
THOUGH WE DON'T USUALLY FIGHT *DEAD MEN.* HE HEH.

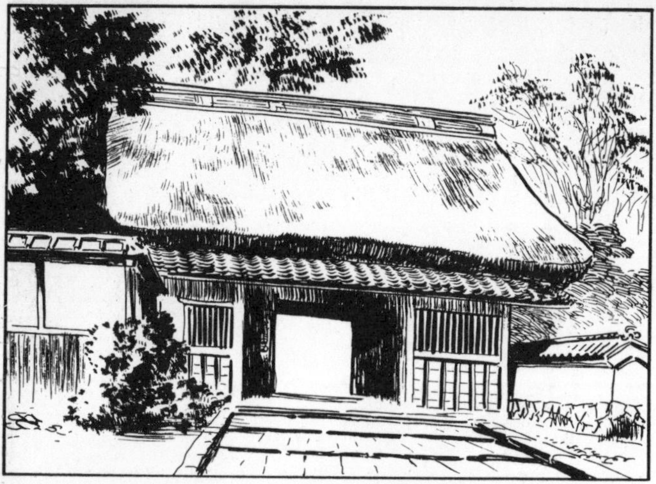

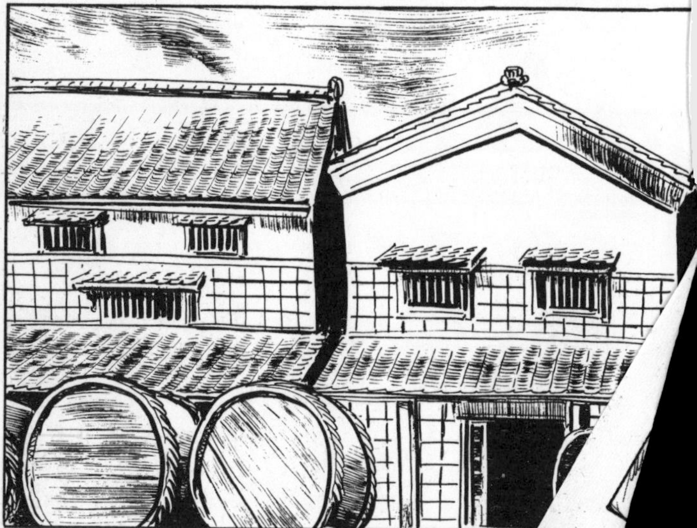

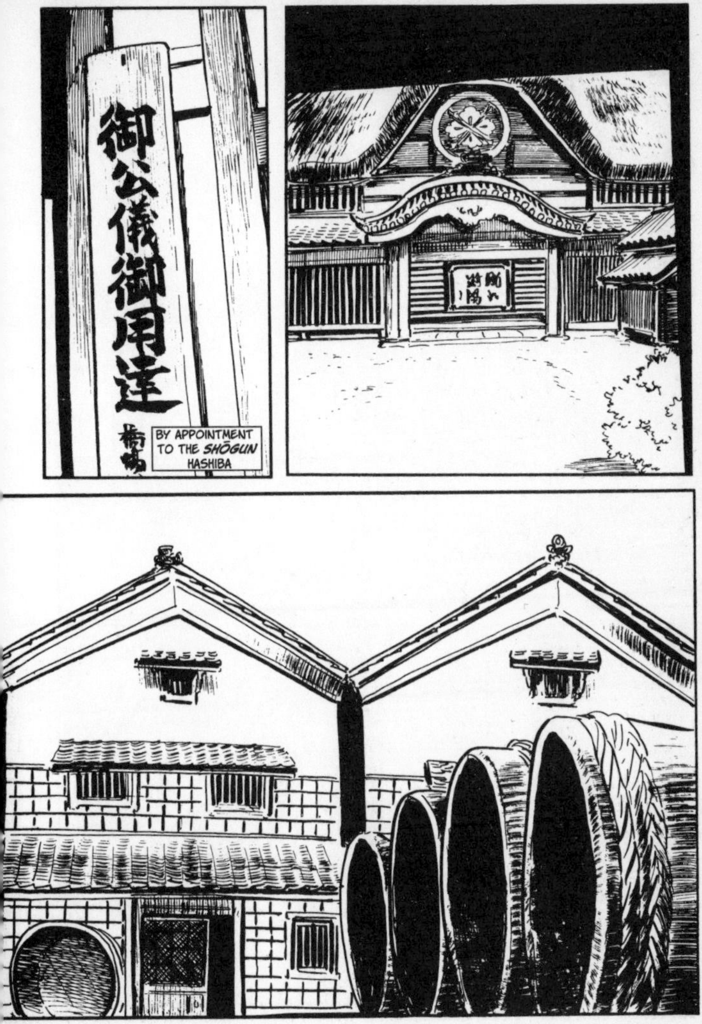
御公儀御用達
BY APPOINTMENT TO THE *SHŌGUN* HASHIBA

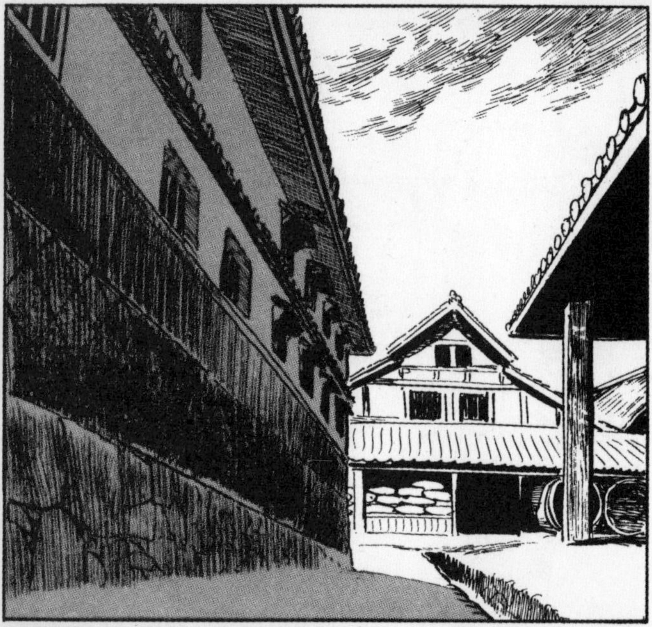

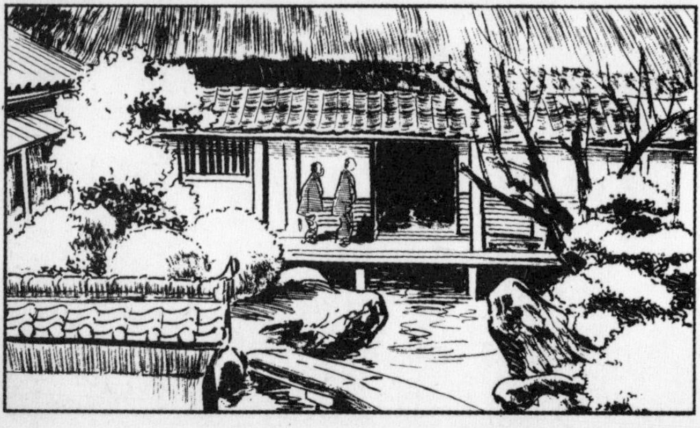

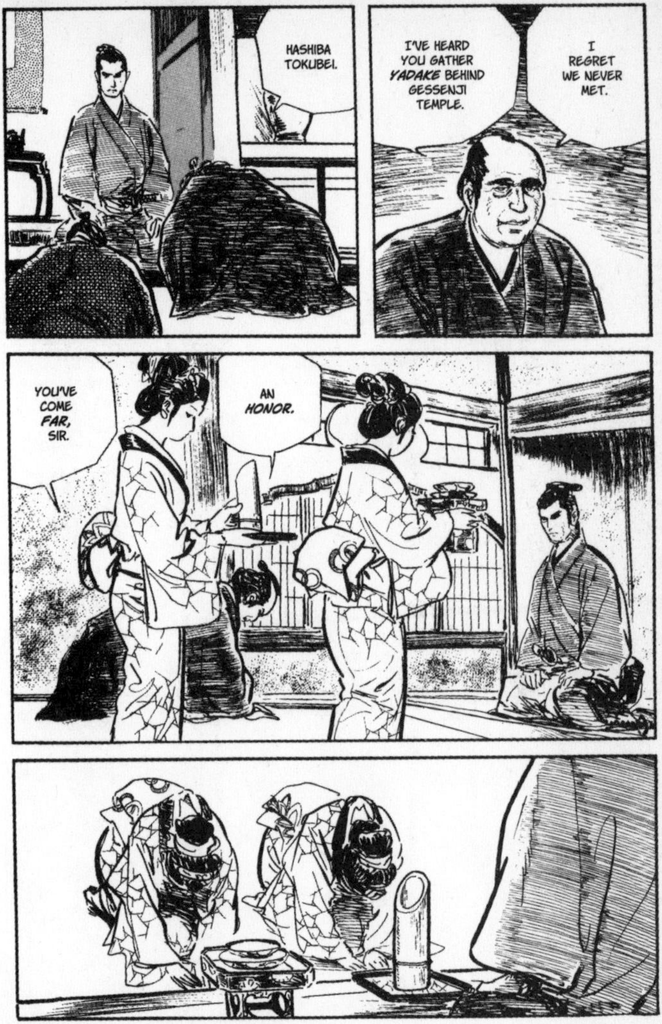
HASHIBA TOKUBEI.
I'VE HEARD YOU GATHER YADAKE BEHIND GESSENJI TEMPLE.
I REGRET WE NEVER MET.
YOU'VE COME FAR, SIR.
AN HONOR.

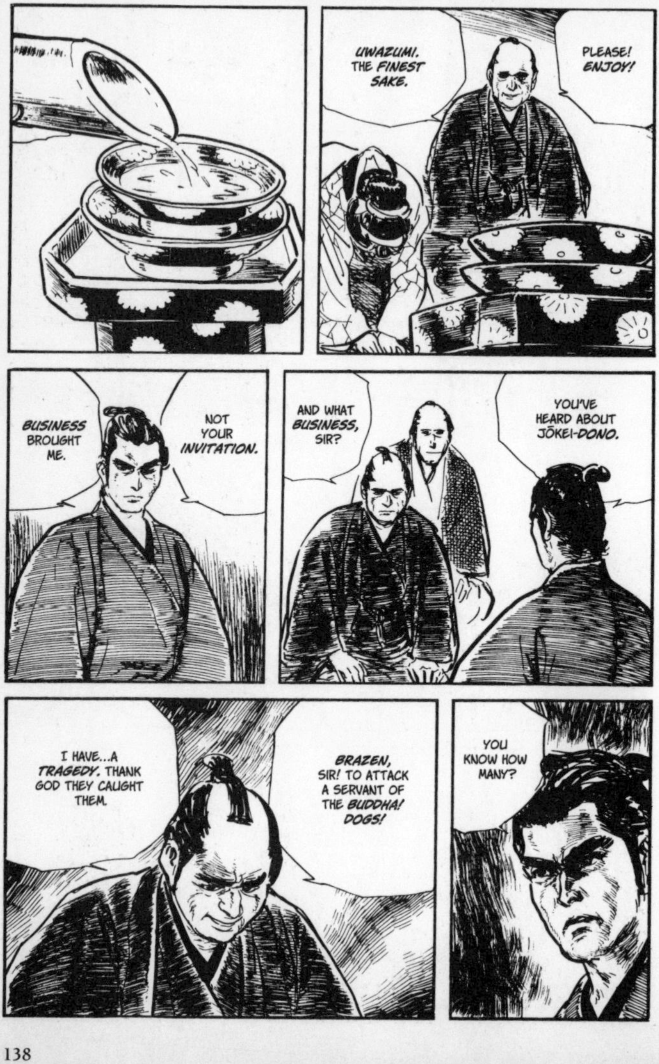
UWAZUMI. THE FINEST SAKE.
PLEASE! ENJOY!
BUSINESS BROUGHT ME.
NOT YOUR INVITATION.
AND WHAT BUSINESS, SIR?
YOU'VE HEARD ABOUT JŌKEI-DONO.
I HAVE...A TRAGEDY. THANK GOD THEY CAUGHT THEM.
BRAZEN, SIR! TO ATTACK A SERVANT OF THE BUDDHA! DOGS!
YOU KNOW HOW MANY?

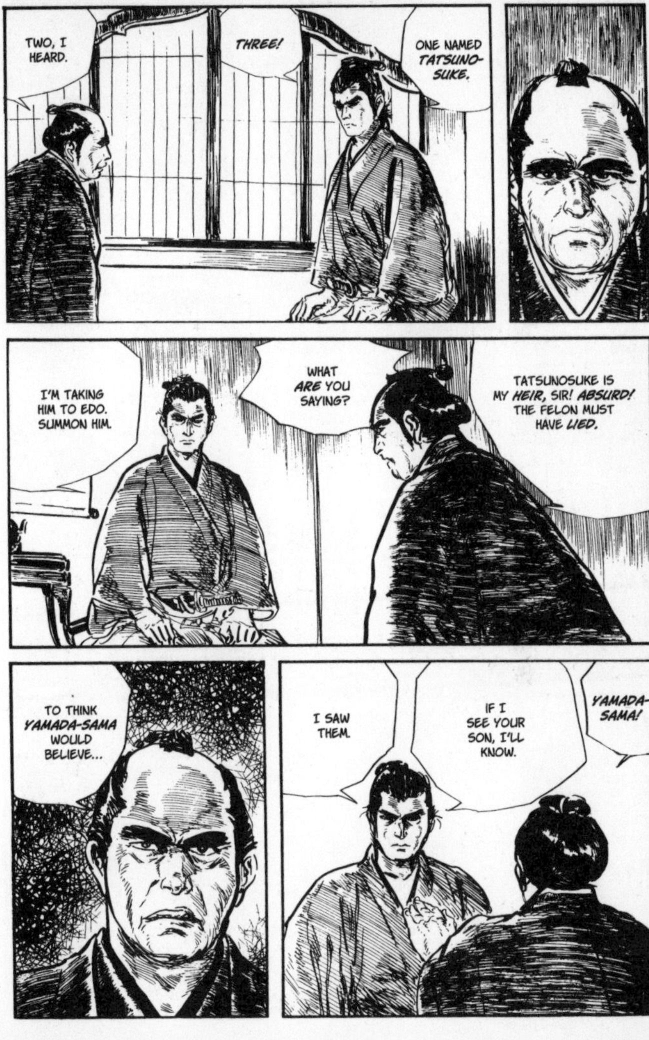

TWO, I HEARD.
THREE!
ONE NAMED TATSUNOSUKE.
I'M TAKING HIM TO EDO. SUMMON HIM.
WHAT ARE YOU SAYING?
TATSUNOSUKE IS MY HEIR, SIR! ABSURD! THE FELON MUST HAVE LIED.
TO THINK YAMADA-SAMA WOULD BELIEVE...
I SAW THEM.
IF I SEE YOUR SON, I'LL KNOW.
YAMADA-SAMA!

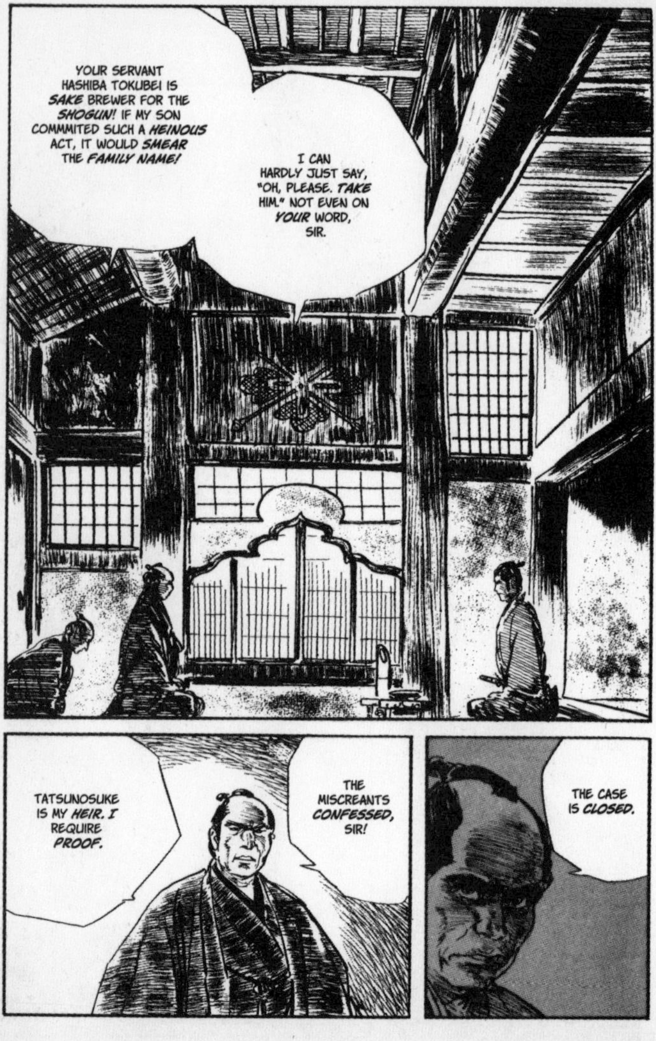
YOUR SERVANT HASHIBA TOKUBEI IS SAKE BREWER FOR THE SHOGUN! IF MY SON COMMMITED SUCH A HEINOUS ACT, IT WOULD SMEAR THE FAMILY NAME!
I CAN HARDLY JUST SAY, "OH, PLEASE. TAKE HIM." NOT EVEN ON YOUR WORD, SIR.
TATSUNOSUKE IS MY HEIR. I REQUIRE PROOF.
THE MISCREANTS CONFESSED, SIR!
THE CASE IS CLOSED.

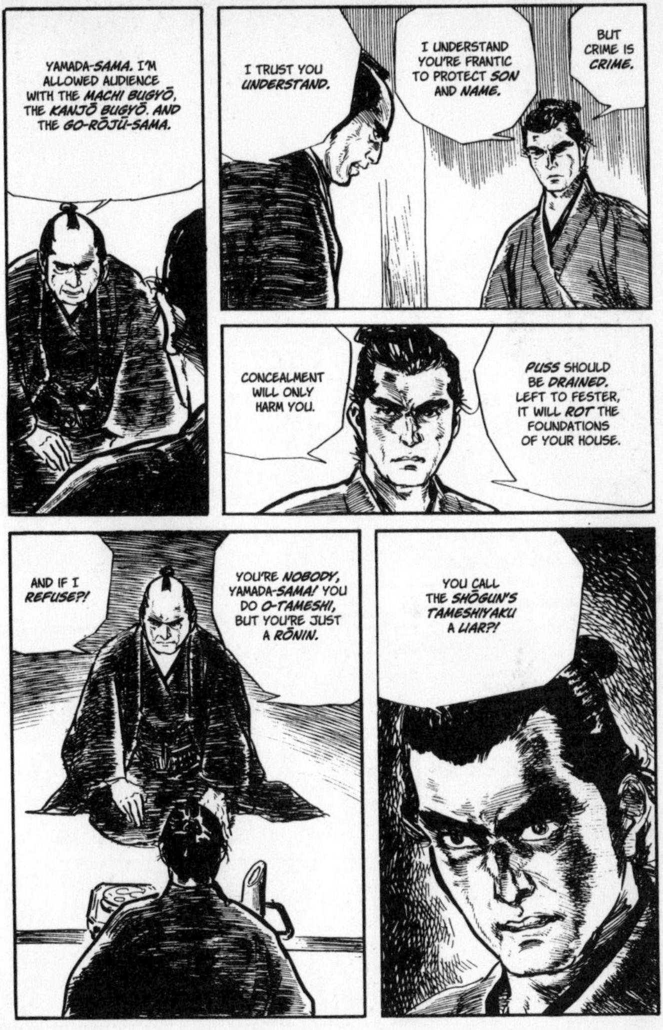
YAMADA-SAMA. I'M ALLOWED AUDIENCE WITH THE MACHI BUGYŌ, THE KANJŌ BUGYŌ. AND THE GO-RŌJŪ-SAMA.
I TRUST YOU UNDERSTAND.
I UNDERSTAND YOU'RE FRANTIC TO PROTECT SON AND NAME.
BUT CRIME IS CRIME.
CONCEALMENT WILL ONLY HARM YOU.
PUSS SHOULD BE DRAINED. LEFT TO FESTER, IT WILL ROT THE FOUNDATIONS OF YOUR HOUSE.
AND IF I REFUSE?!
YOU'RE NOBODY, YAMADA-SAMA! YOU DO O-TAMESHI, BUT YOU'RE JUST A RŌNIN.
YOU CALL THE SHŌGUN'S TAMESHIYAKU A LIAR?!

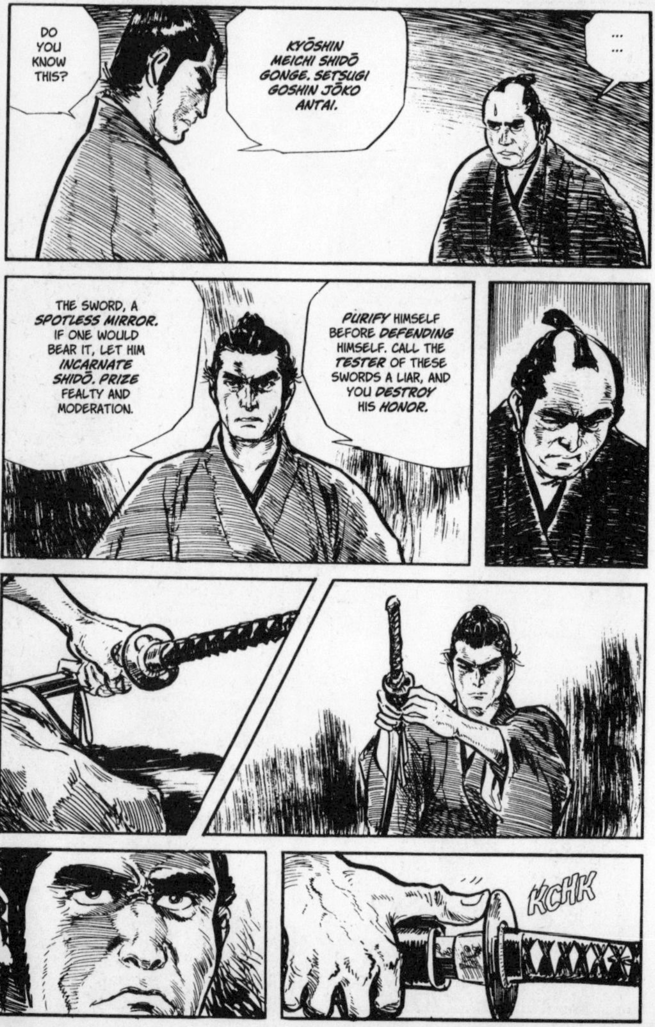
DO YOU KNOW THIS?
KYŌSHIN MEICHI SHIDŌ GONGE. SETSUGI GOSHIN JŌKO ANTAI.
... ...
THE SWORD, A SPOTLESS MIRROR. IF ONE WOULD BEAR IT, LET HIM INCARNATE SHIDŌ. PRIZE FEALTY AND MODERATION.
PURIFY HIMSELF BEFORE DEFENDING HIMSELF. CALL THE TESTER OF THESE SWORDS A LIAR, AND YOU DESTROY HIS HONOR.
KCHK

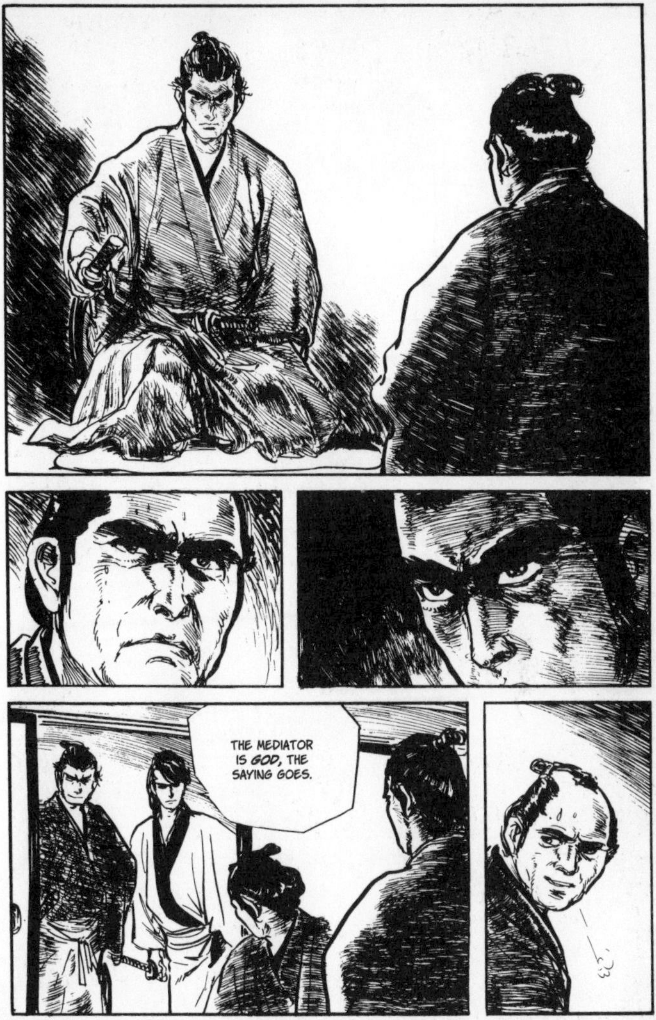
THE MEDIATOR IS *GOD*, THE SAYING GOES.

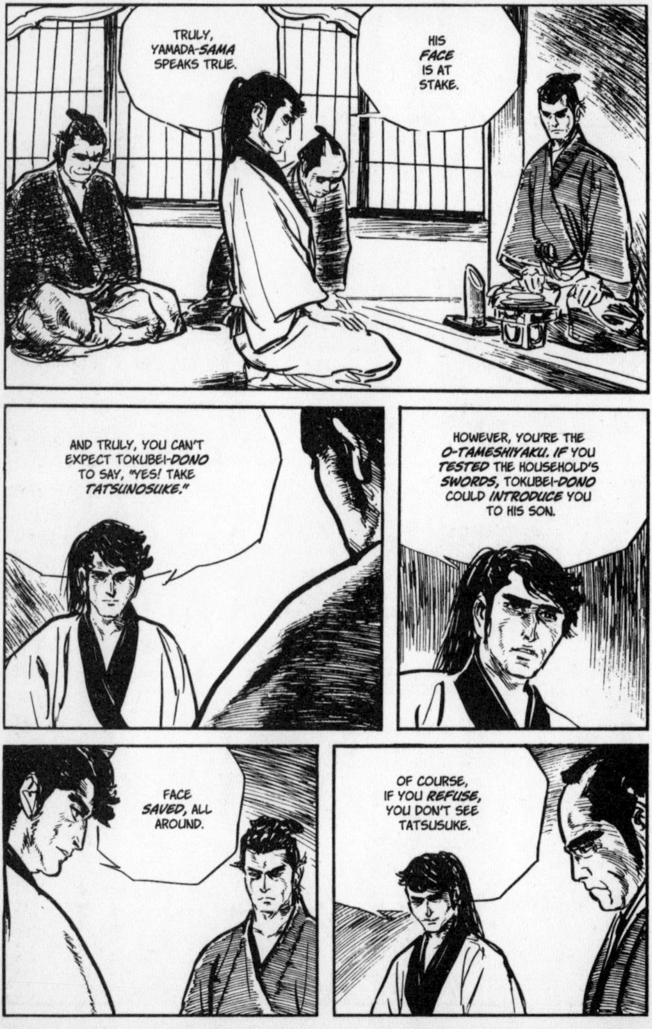
TRULY, YAMADA-*SAMA* SPEAKS TRUE.
HIS *FACE* IS AT STAKE.
AND TRULY, YOU CAN'T EXPECT TOKUBEI-*DONO* TO SAY, "YES! TAKE *TATSUNOSUKE.*"
HOWEVER, YOU'RE THE *O-TAMESHIYAKU. IF* YOU *TESTED* THE HOUSEHOLD'S *SWORDS,* TOKUBEI-*DONO* COULD *INTRODUCE* YOU TO HIS SON.
FACE *SAVED,* ALL AROUND.
OF COURSE, IF YOU *REFUSE,* YOU DON'T SEE TATSUSUKE.

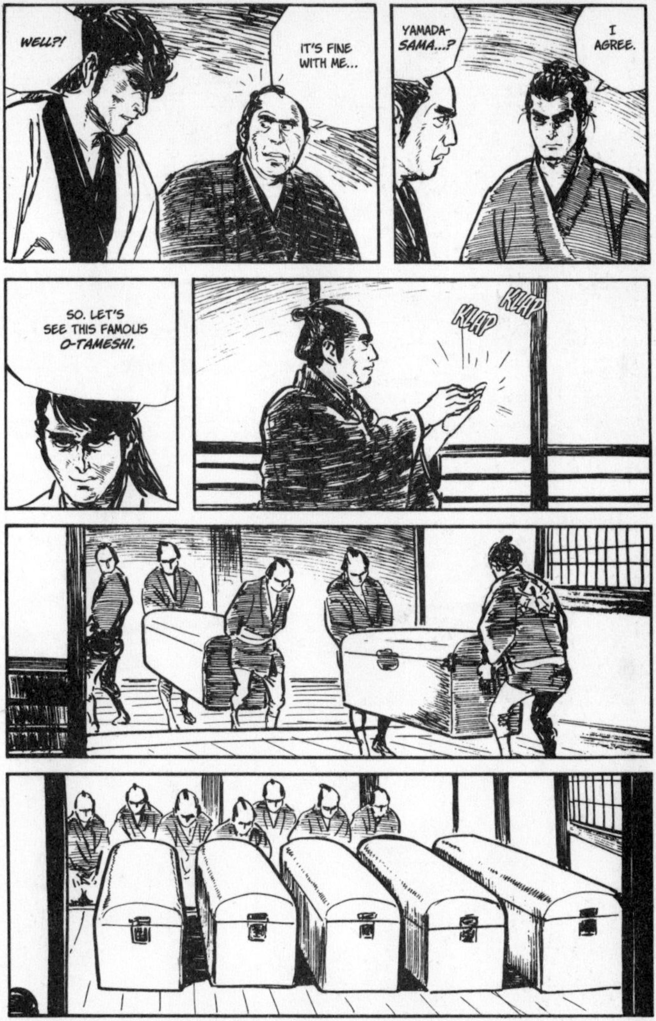
WELL?!
IT'S FINE WITH ME...
YAMADA-SAMA...?
I AGREE.
SO. LET'S SEE THIS FAMOUS O-TAMESHI.
KLAP
KLAP

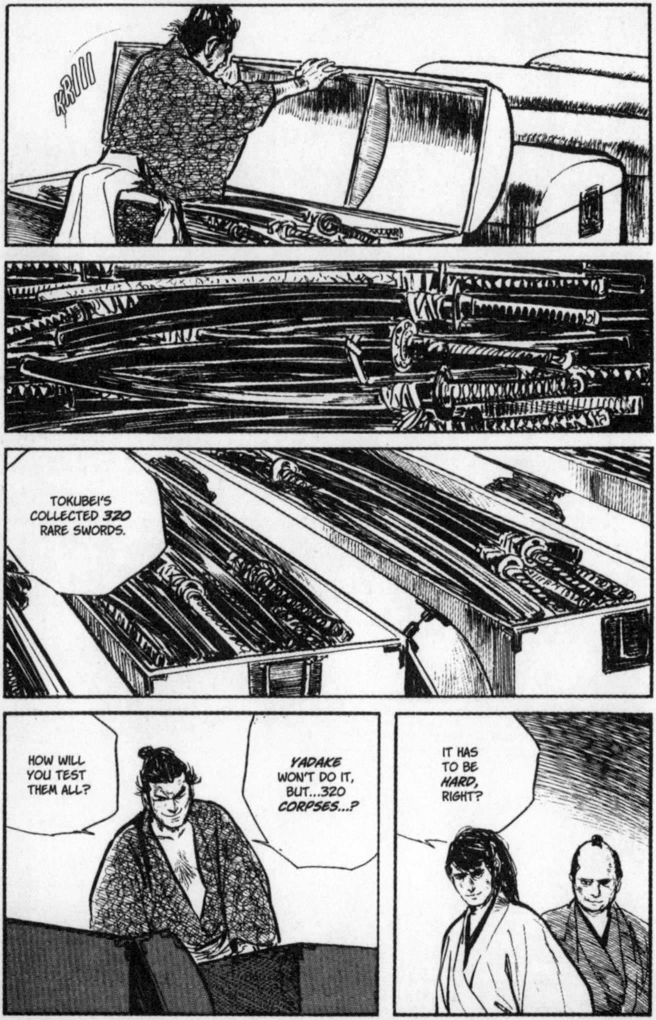
KRIII
TOKUBEI'S COLLECTED 320 RARE SWORDS.
HOW WILL YOU TEST THEM ALL?
YADAKE WON'T DO IT, BUT...320 CORPSES...?
IT HAS TO BE HARD, RIGHT?

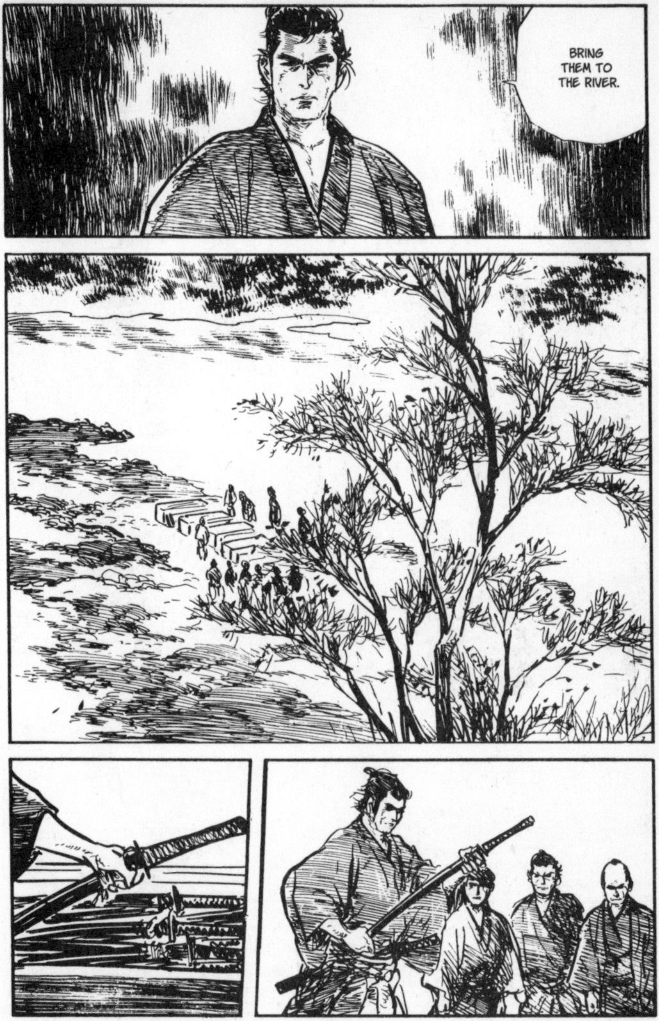
BRING THEM TO THE RIVER.

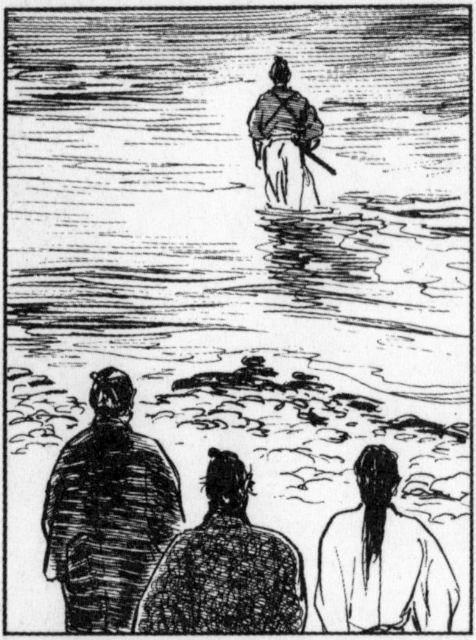
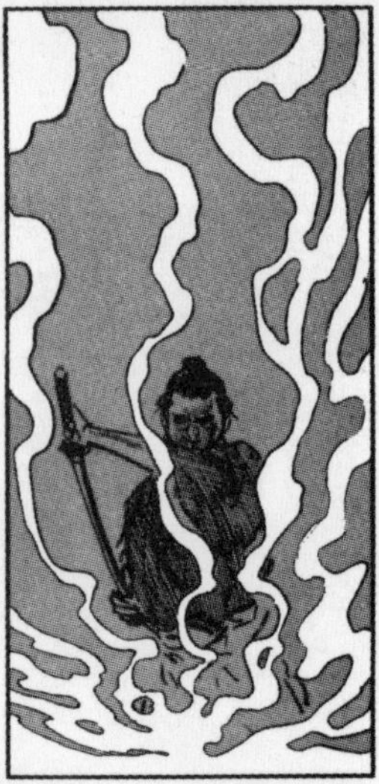
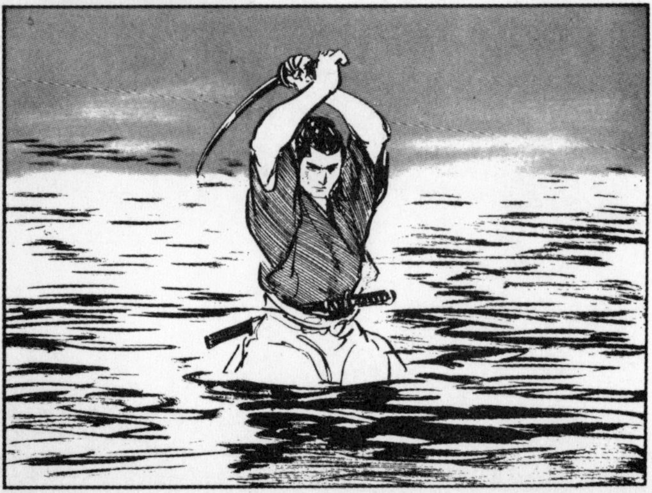

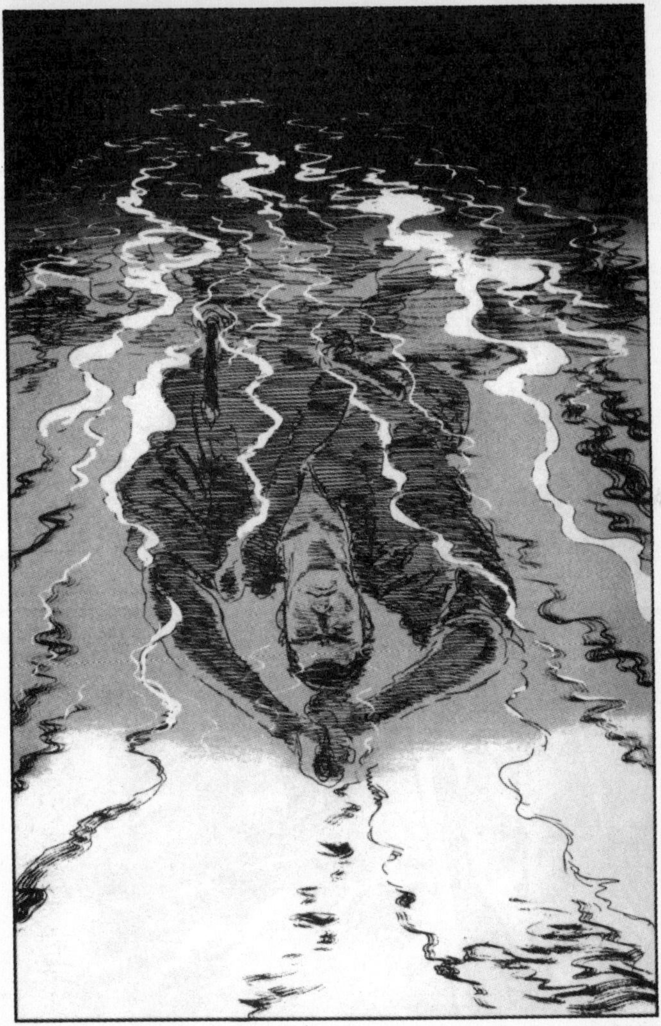

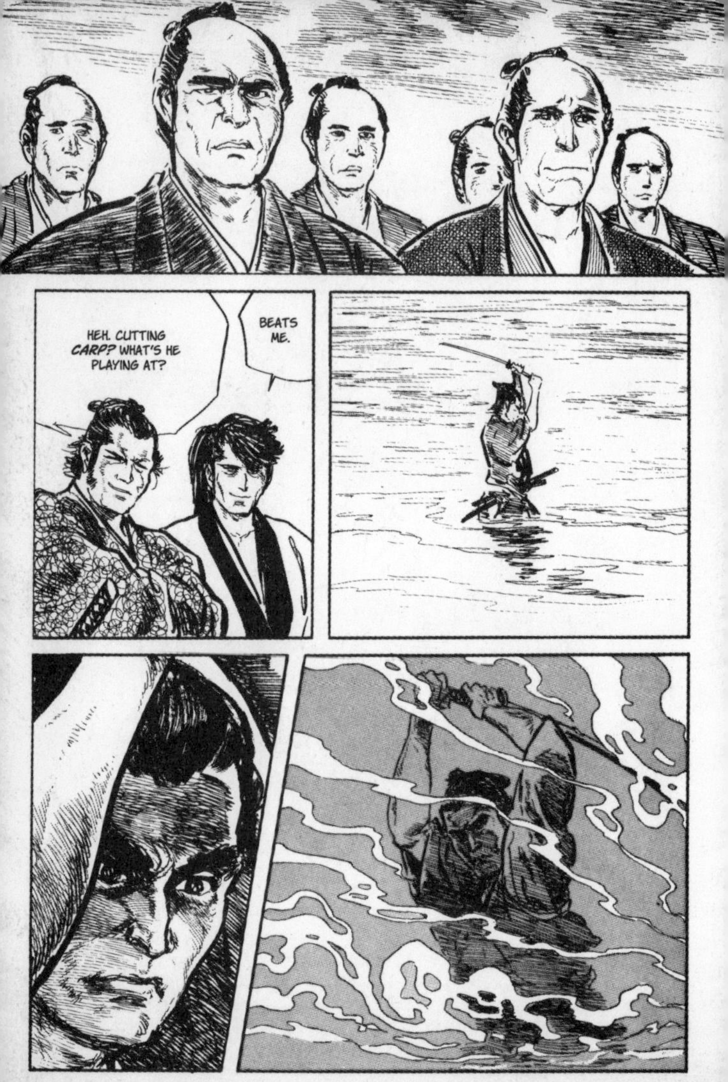
HEH. CUTTING *CARP?* WHAT'S HE PLAYING AT?
BEATS ME.

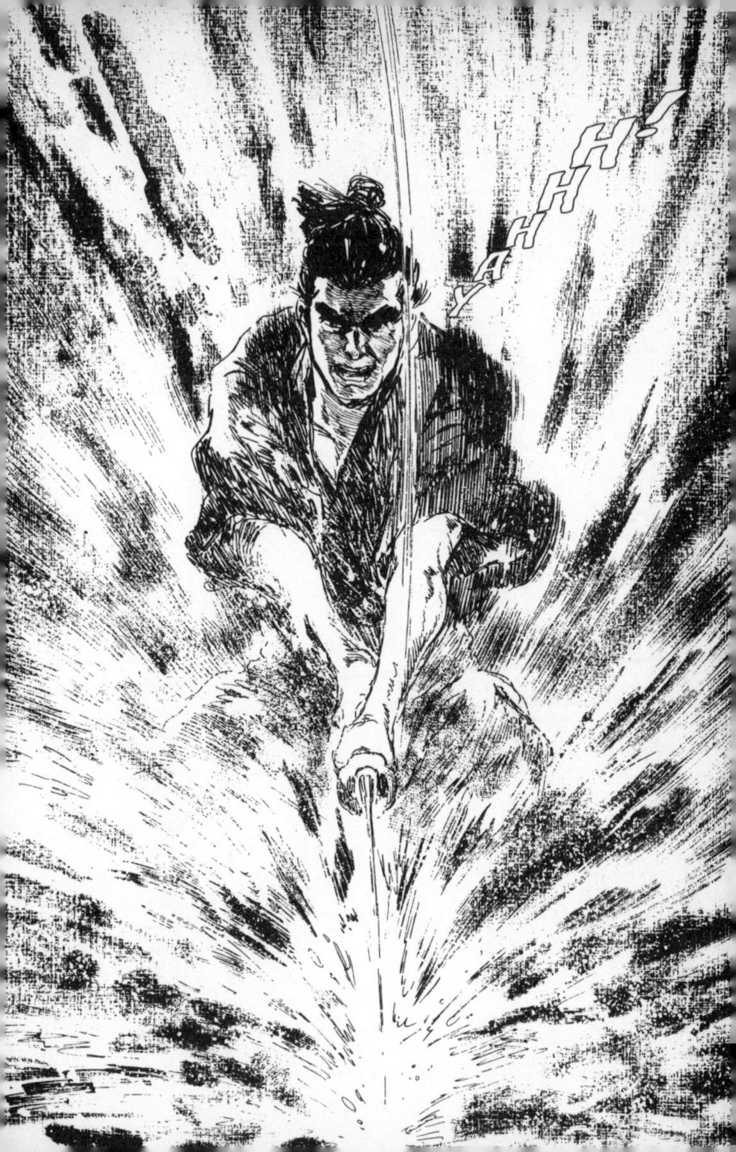
YAHHHH!

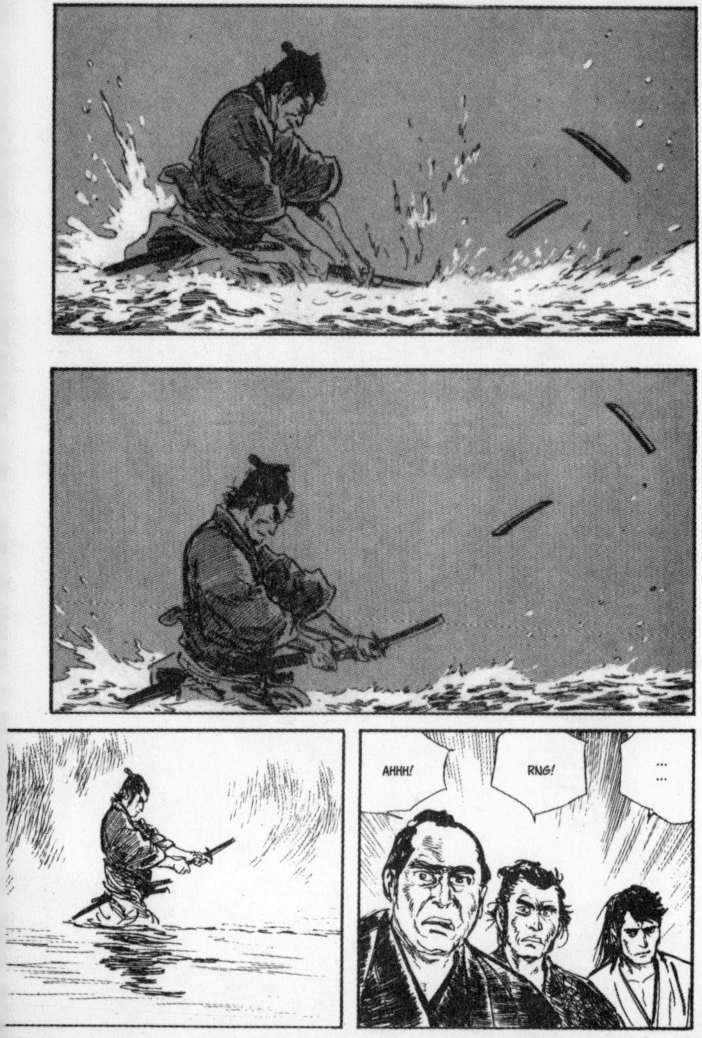
AHHH!
RNG!
...
...

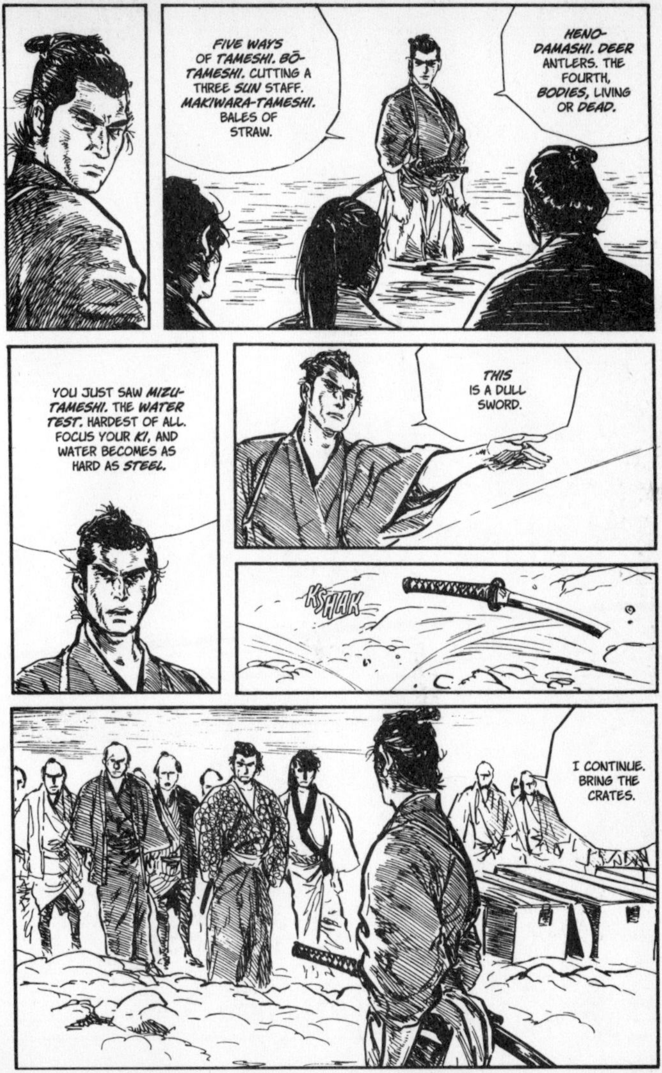
FIVE WAYS OF TAMESHI. BŌ-TAMESHI. CUTTING A THREE SUN STAFF. MAKIWARA-TAMESHI. BALES OF STRAW.
HENO-DAMASHI. DEER ANTLERS. THE FOURTH, BODIES, LIVING OR DEAD.
YOU JUST SAW MIZU-TAMESHI. THE WATER TEST. HARDEST OF ALL. FOCUS YOUR KI, AND WATER BECOMES AS HARD AS STEEL.
THIS IS A DULL SWORD.
KSHAK
I CONTINUE. BRING THE CRATES.

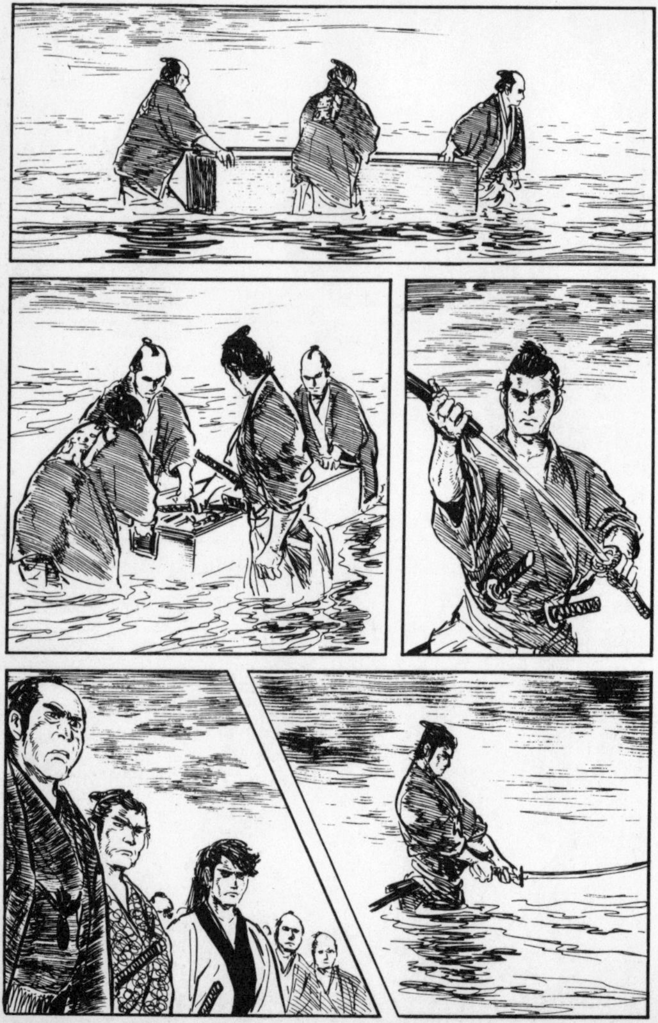

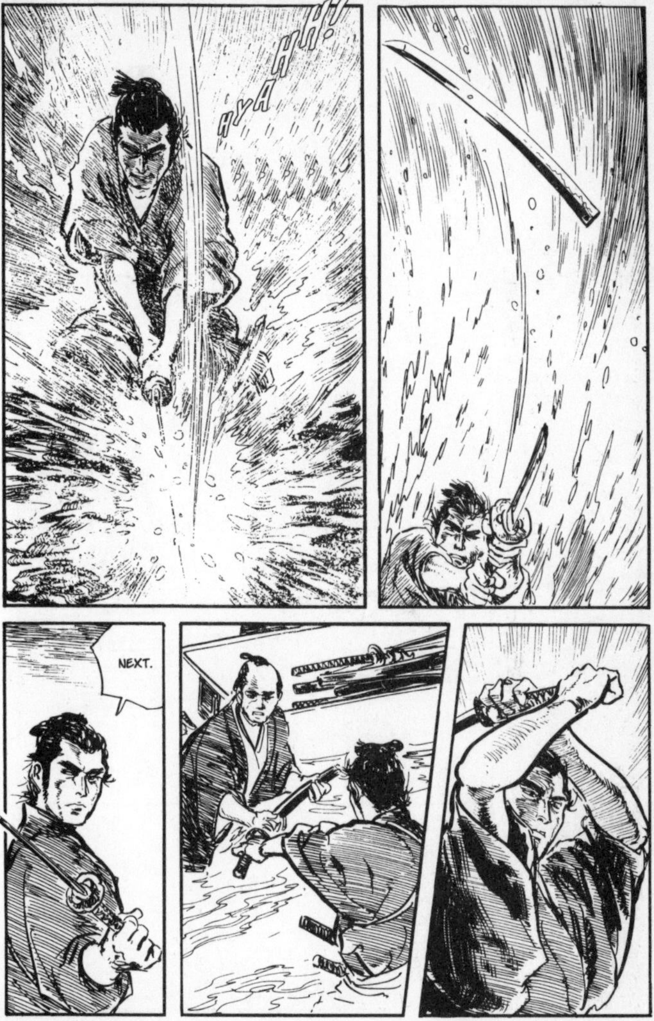
HYAAHH!!
NEXT.

SKNNG SWHRAK

TOHH!

KCHAK

HYAH!

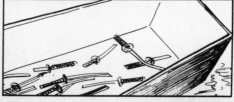

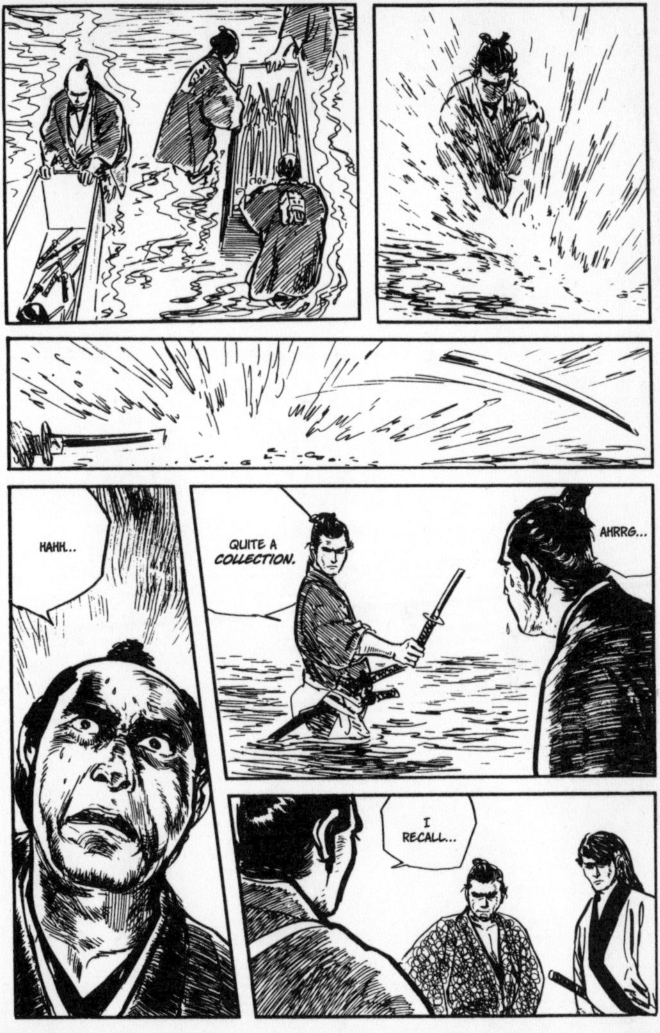
HAHH...
QUITE A COLLECTION.
AHRRG...
I RECALL...

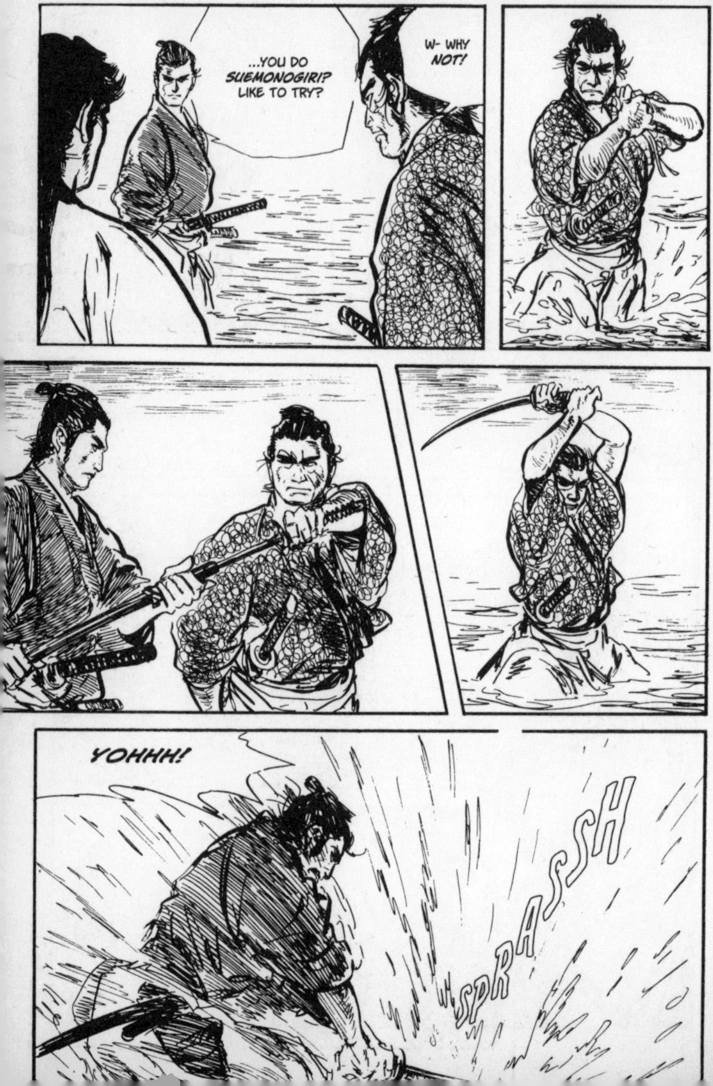
...YOU DO
SUEMONOGIRI!?
LIKE TO TRY?
W- WHY
NOT!
YOHHH!
SPRASSH

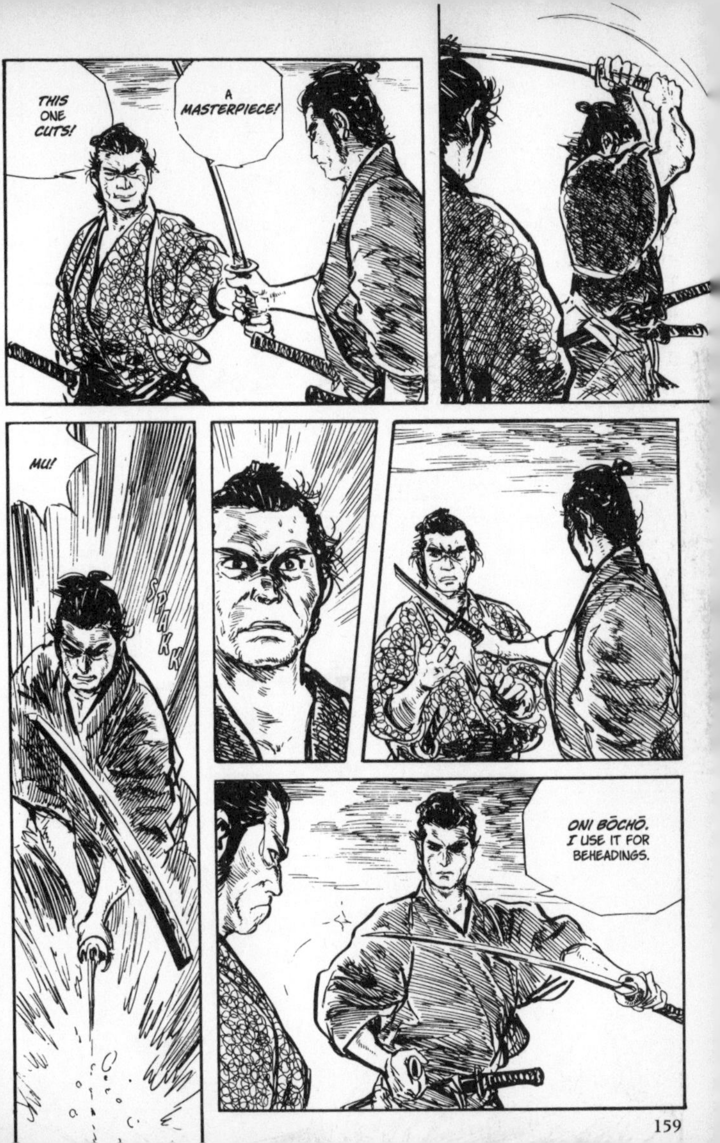
THIS ONE CUTS!
A MASTERPIECE!
MU!
SPAKK
ONI BŌCHŌ. I USE IT FOR BEHEADINGS.

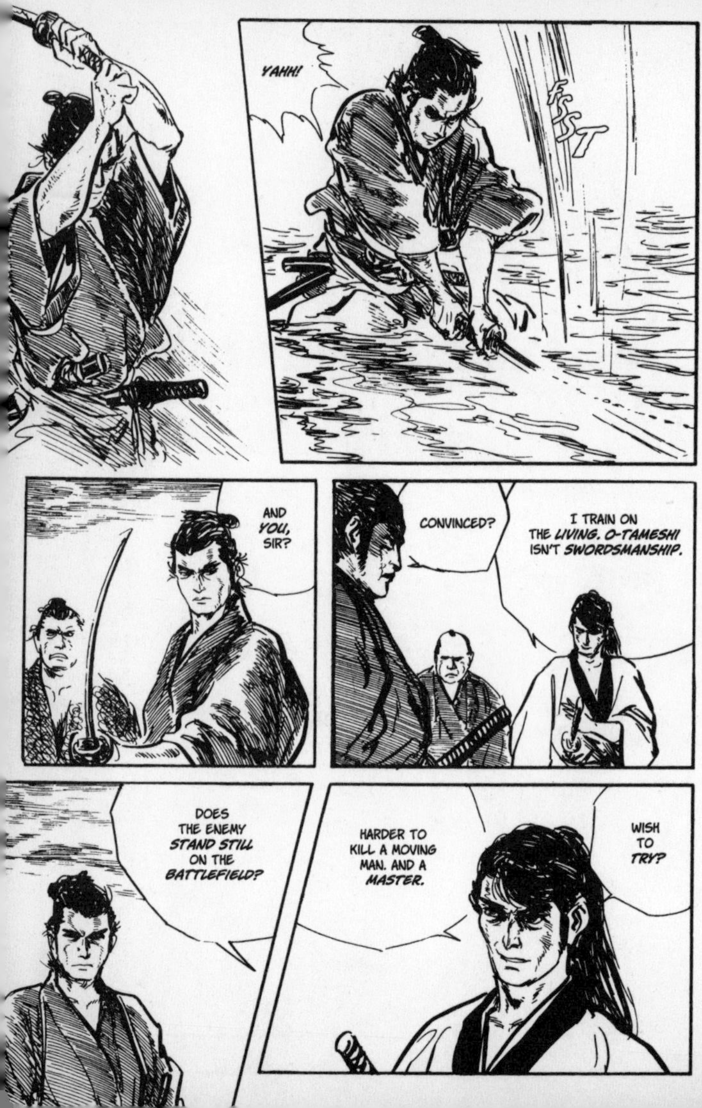
YAHH!
FSST
AND YOU, SIR?
CONVINCED?
I TRAIN ON THE LIVING. O-TAMESHI ISN'T SWORDSMANSHIP.
DOES THE ENEMY STAND STILL ON THE BATTLEFIELD?
HARDER TO KILL A MOVING MAN. AND A MASTER.
WISH TO TRY?

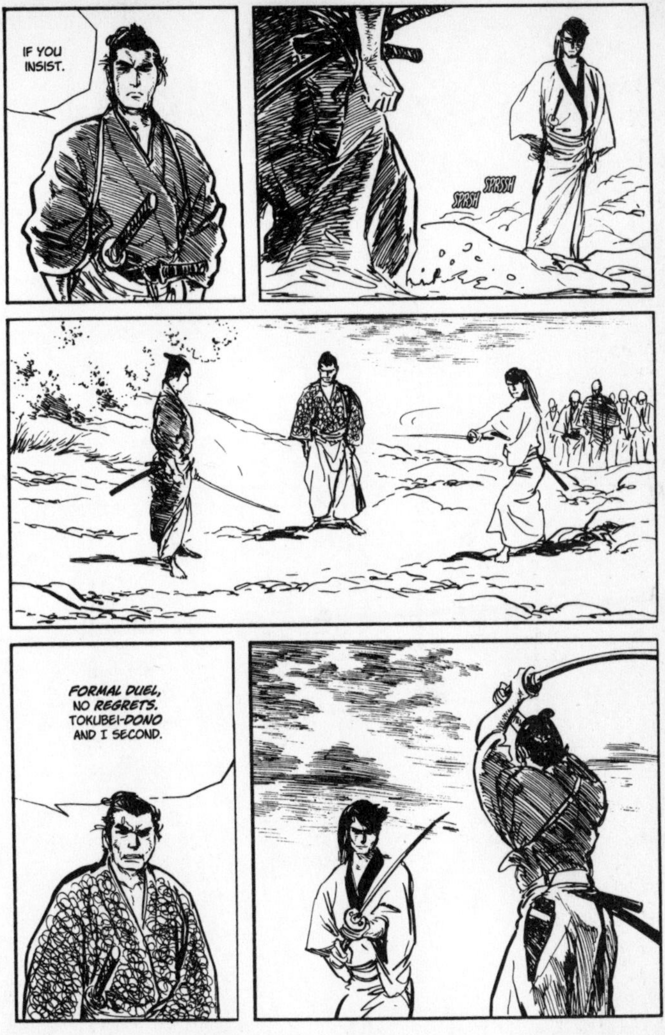
IF YOU INSIST.
SPRSH
SPRSSH
FORMAL DUEL, NO REGRETS. TOKUBEI-DONO AND I SECOND.

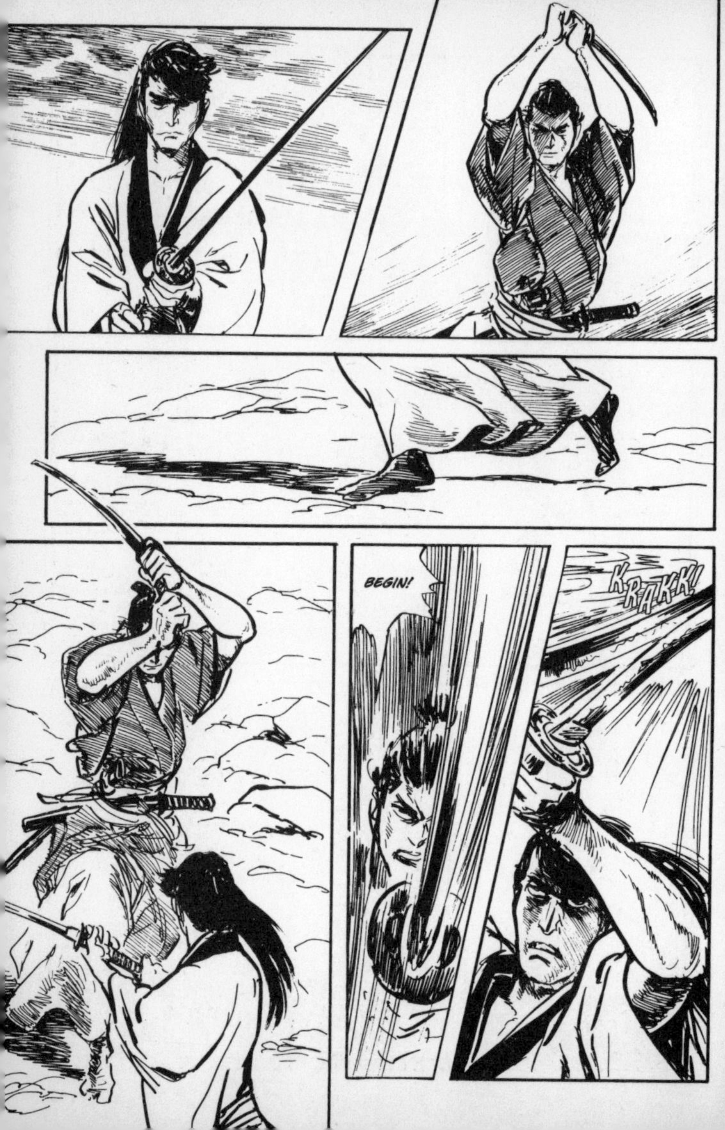
BEGIN!
KRAKK!

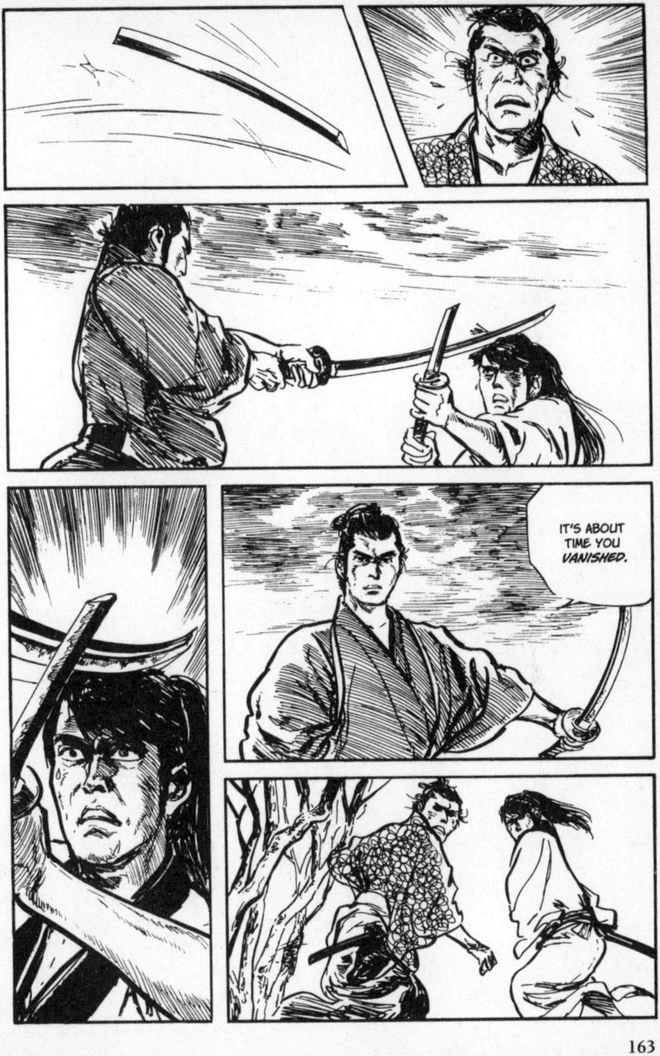
IT'S ABOUT
TIME YOU
VANISHED.

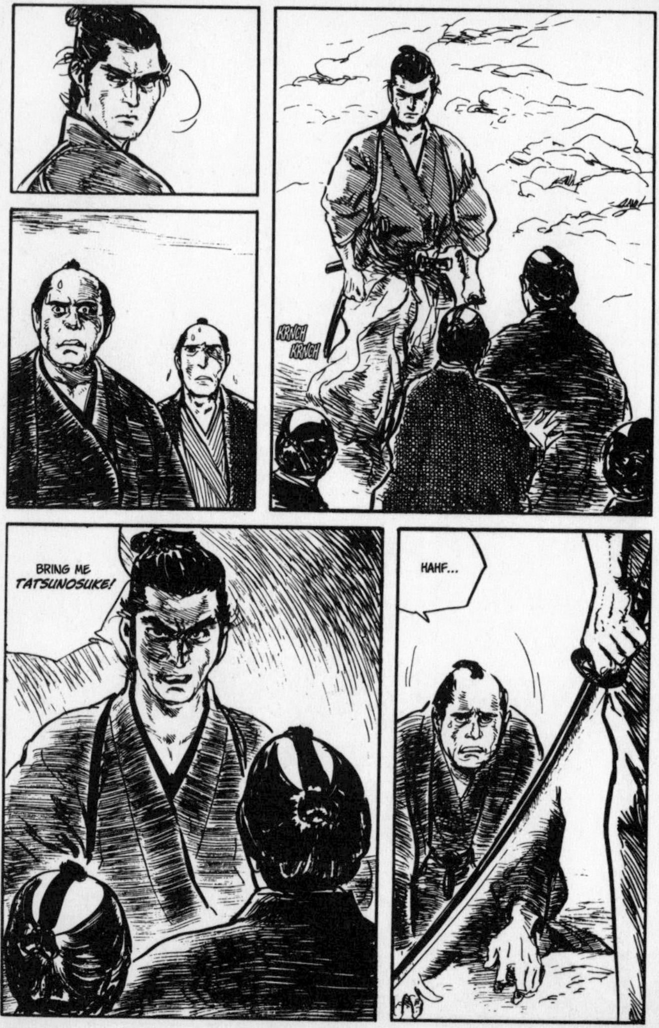
KRNCH
KRNCH
BRING ME TATSUNOSUKE!
HAHF...

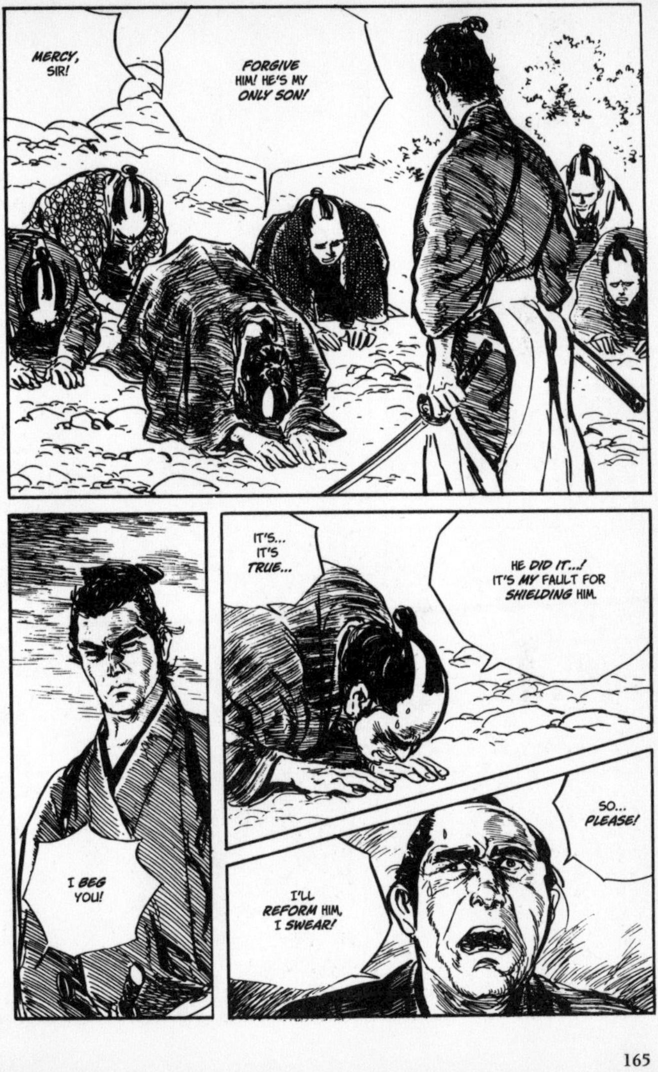
MERCY, SIR!
FORGIVE HIM! HE'S MY ONLY SON!
I BEG YOU!
IT'S... IT'S TRUE...
HE DID IT...! IT'S MY FAULT FOR SHIELDING HIM.
I'LL REFORM HIM, I SWEAR!
SO... PLEASE!

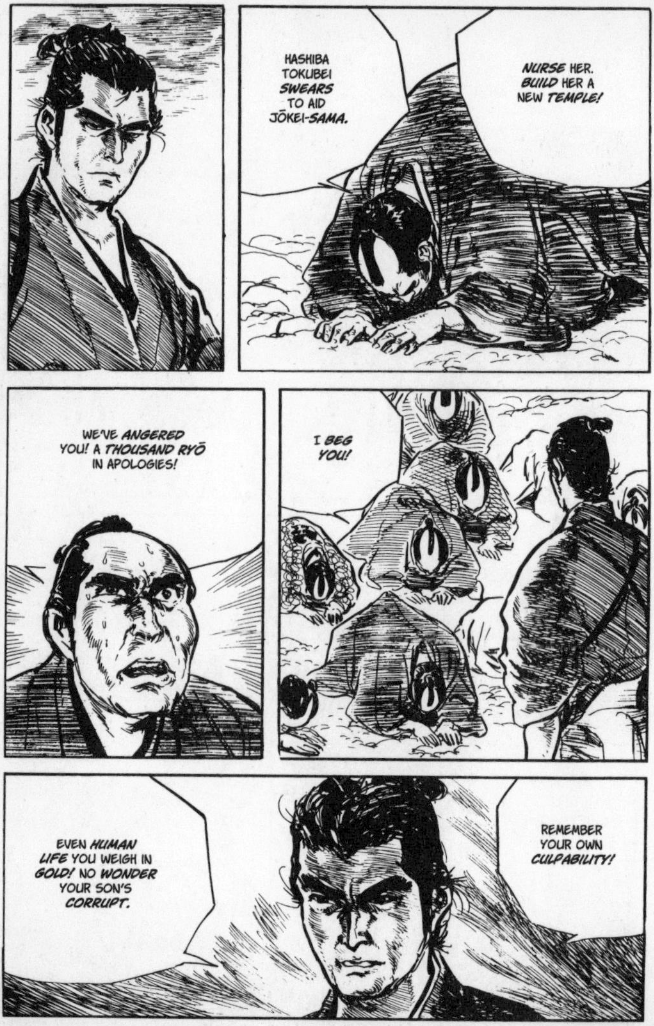
HASHIBA TOKUBEI SWEARS TO AID JŌKEI-SAMA.
NURSE HER. BUILD HER A NEW TEMPLE!
WE'VE ANGERED YOU! A THOUSAND RYŌ IN APOLOGIES!
I BEG YOU!
EVEN HUMAN LIFE YOU WEIGH IN GOLD! NO WONDER YOUR SON'S CORRUPT.
REMEMBER YOUR OWN CULPABILITY!

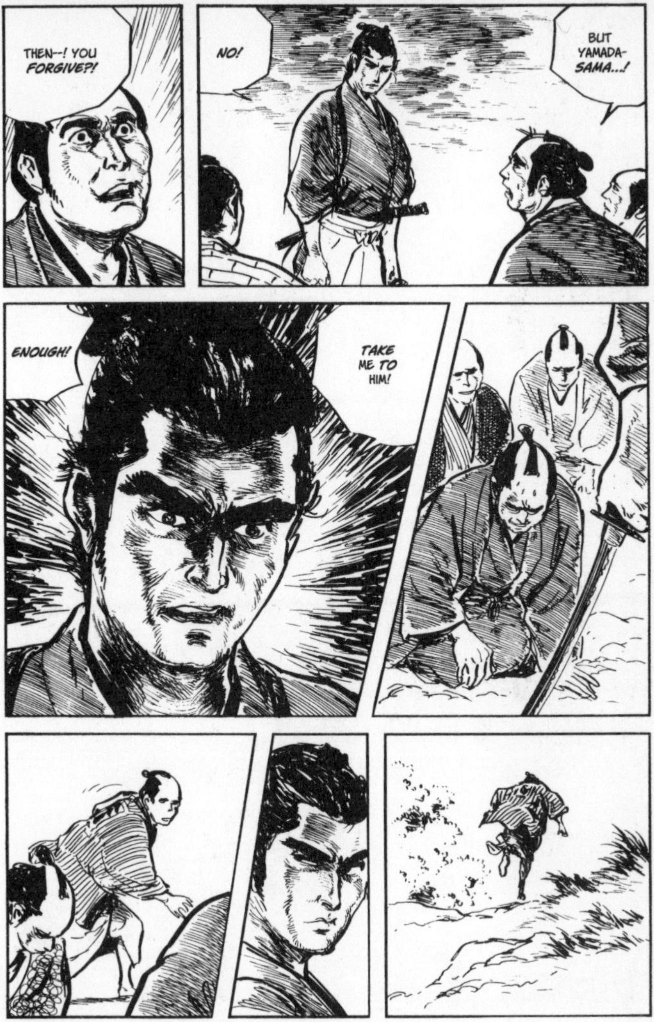
THEN--! YOU FORGIVE?!
NO!
BUT YAMADA-SAMA...!
ENOUGH!
TAKE ME TO HIM!

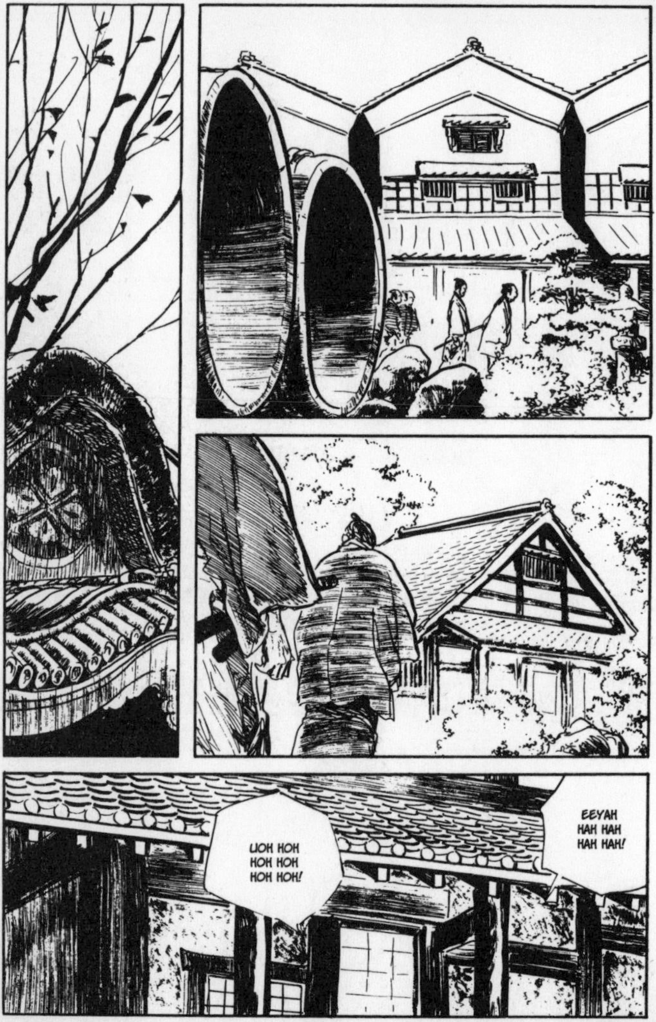
WOH HOH HOH HOH HOH HOH!
EEYAH HAH HAH HAH HAH!

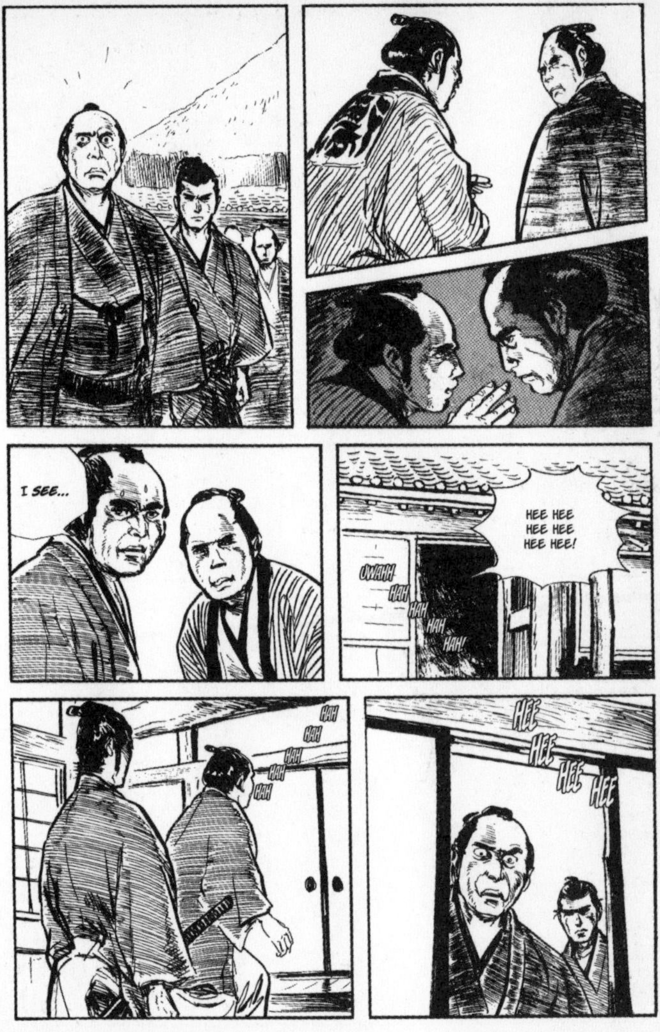
I SEE...
UWAHH
HAH
HAH
HAH
HAH!
HEE HEE HEE HEE HEE HEE!
HAH
HAH
HAH
HAH
HAH
HEE
HEE
HEE
HEE

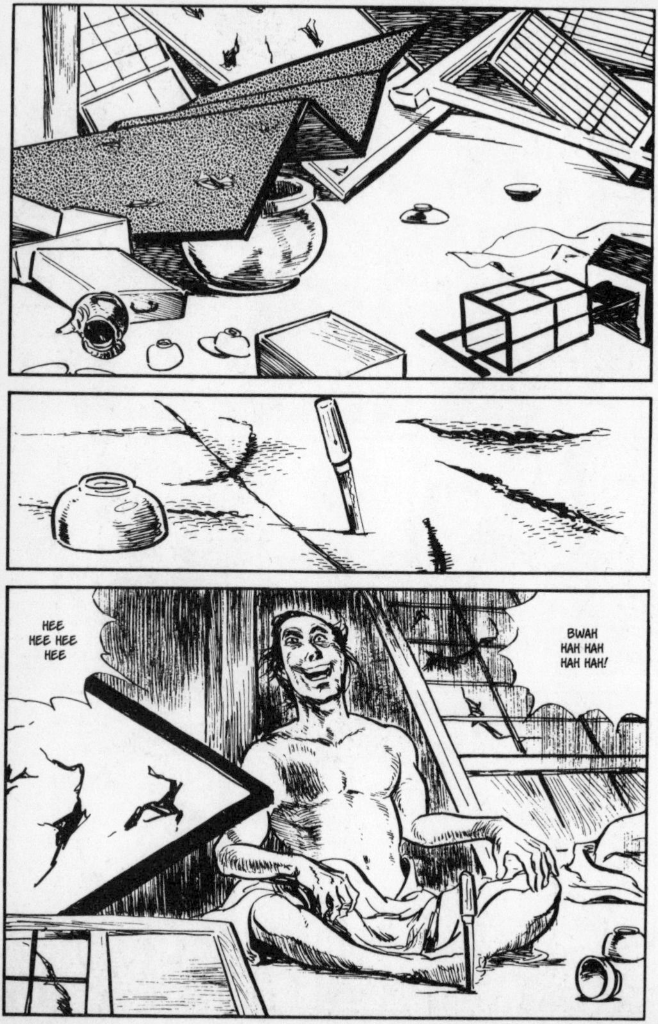
HEE
HEE HEE
HEE
BWAH
HAH HAH
HAH HAH!

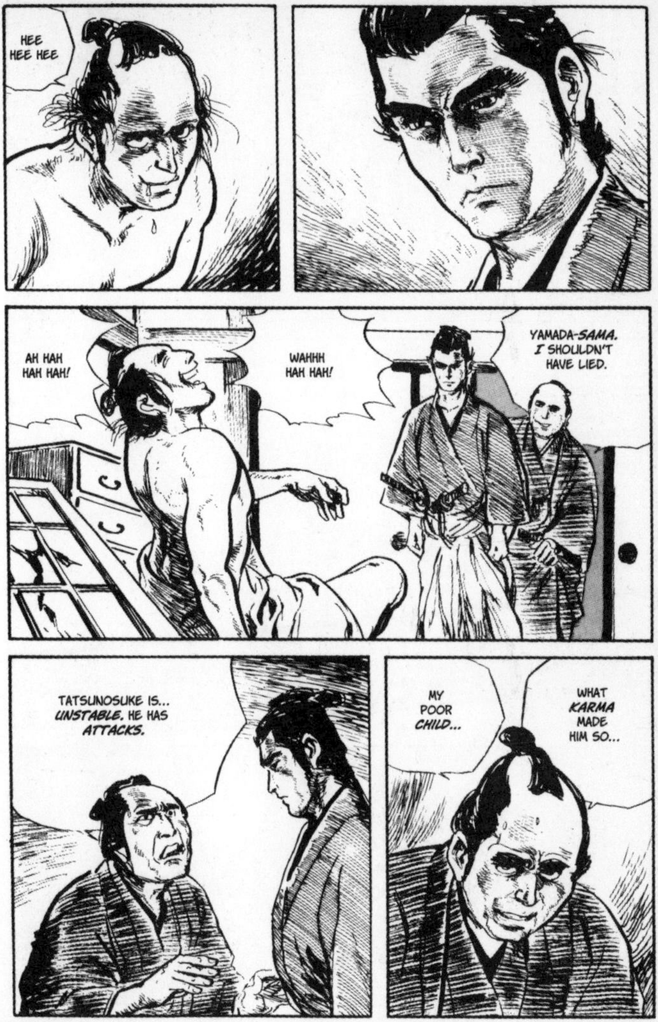
HEE HEE HEE
AH HAH HAH HAH!
WAHHH HAH HAH!
YAMADA-SAMA. I SHOULDN'T HAVE LIED.
TATSUNOSUKE IS... UNSTABLE. HE HAS ATTACKS.
MY POOR CHILD...
WHAT KARMA MADE HIM SO...

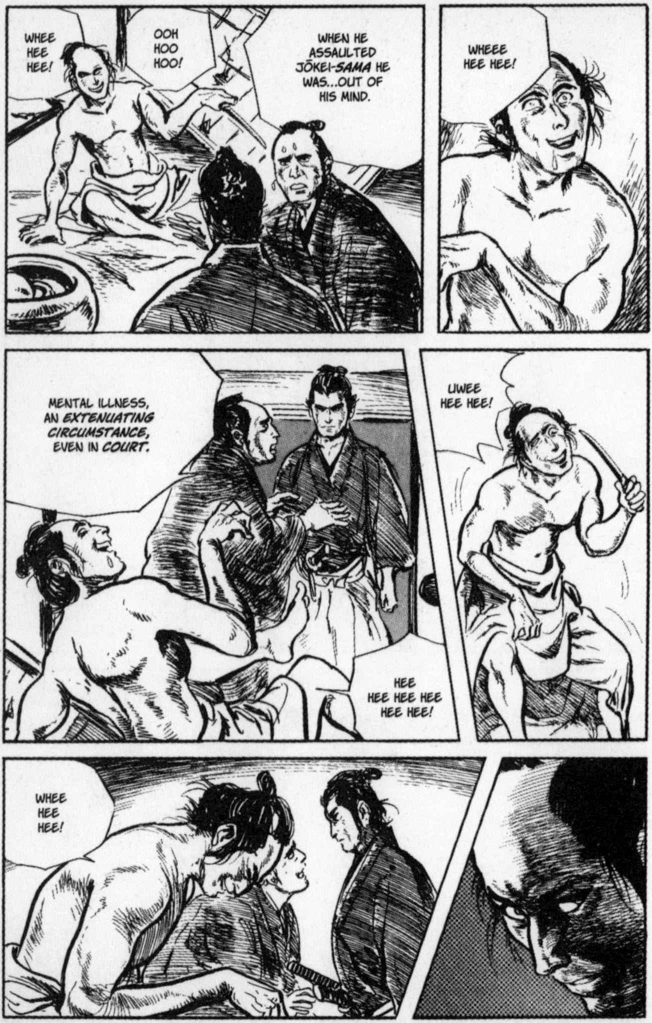
WHEE HEE HEE!
OOH HOO HOO!
WHEN HE ASSAULTED JŌKEI-*SAMA* HE WAS...OUT OF HIS MIND.
WHEEE HEE HEE!
MENTAL ILLNESS, AN *EXTENUATING CIRCUMSTANCE,* EVEN IN *COURT.*
HEE HEE HEE HEE HEE HEE!
UWEE HEE HEE!
WHEE HEE HEE!

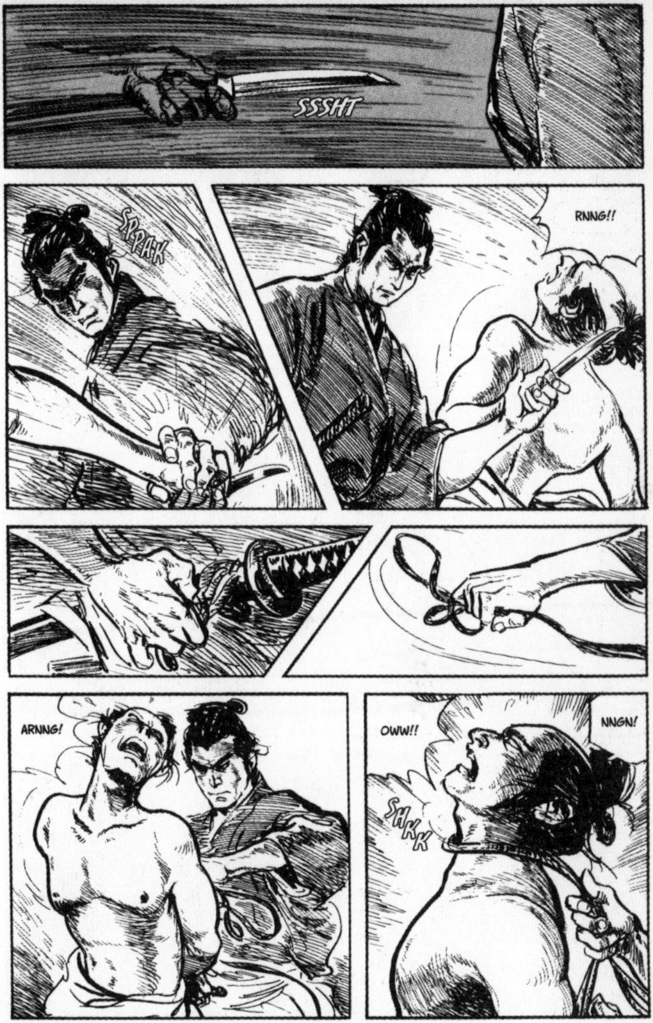
SSSHT
SPPAK
RNNG!!
ARNNG!
OWW!!
SHKK
NNGN!

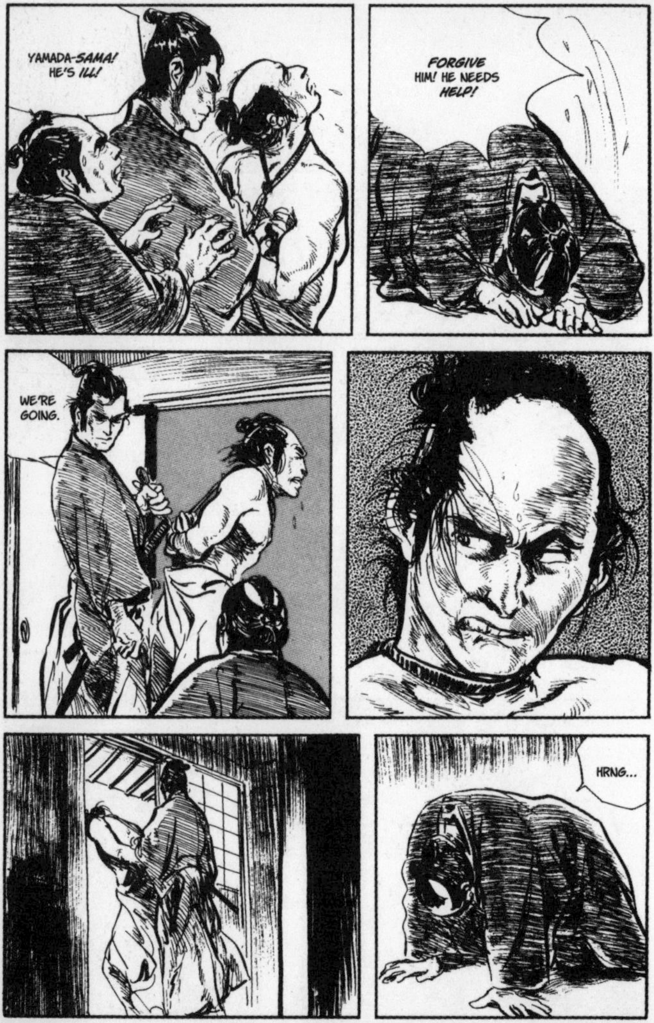
YAMADA-SAMA! HE'S ILL!
FORGIVE HIM! HE NEEDS HELP!
WE'RE GOING.
HRNG...

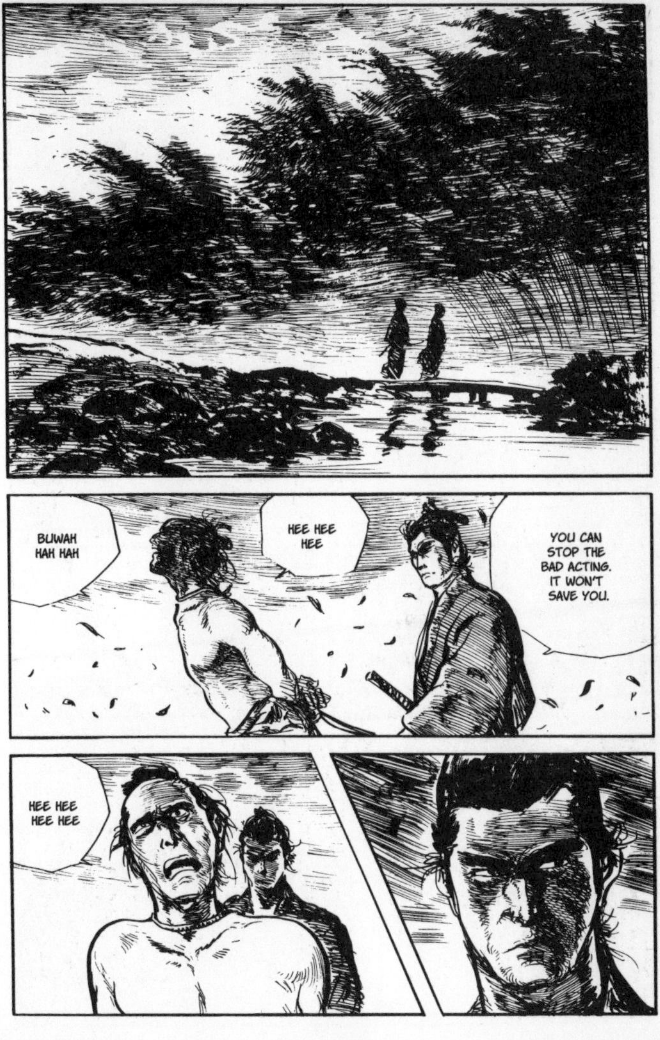
BUWAH HAH HAH
HEE HEE HEE
YOU CAN STOP THE BAD ACTING. IT WON'T SAVE YOU.
HEE HEE HEE HEE

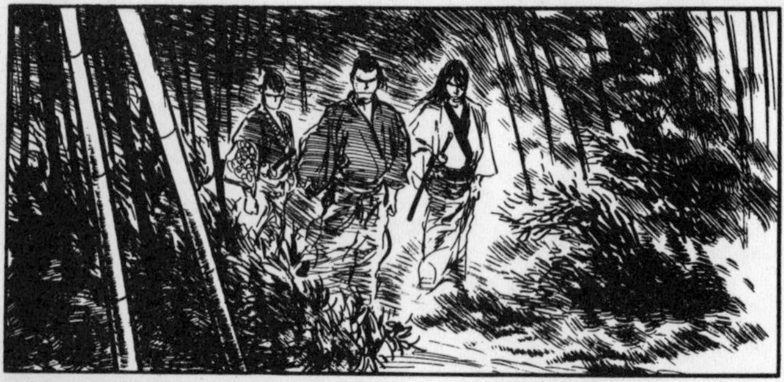

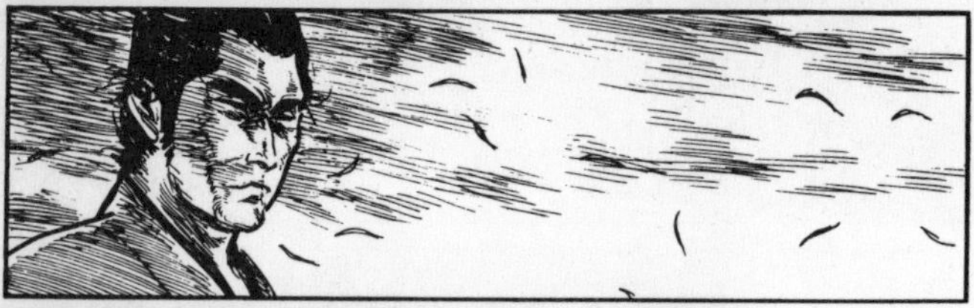

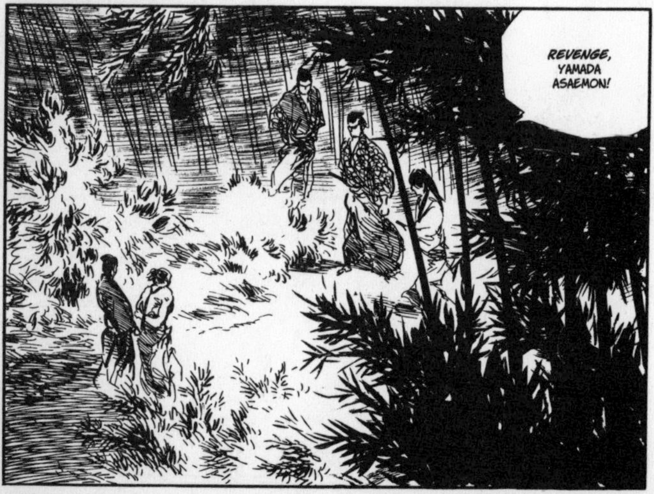
REVENGE, YAMADA ASAEMON!

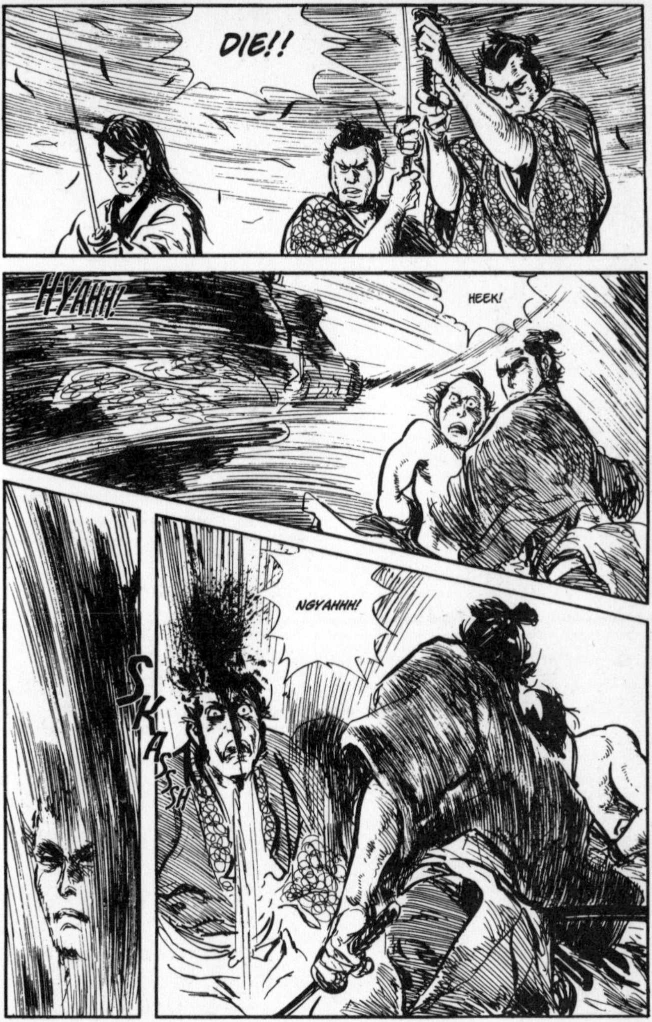
DIE!!
HYAHH!
HEEK!
NGYAHHH!
SKASSSH

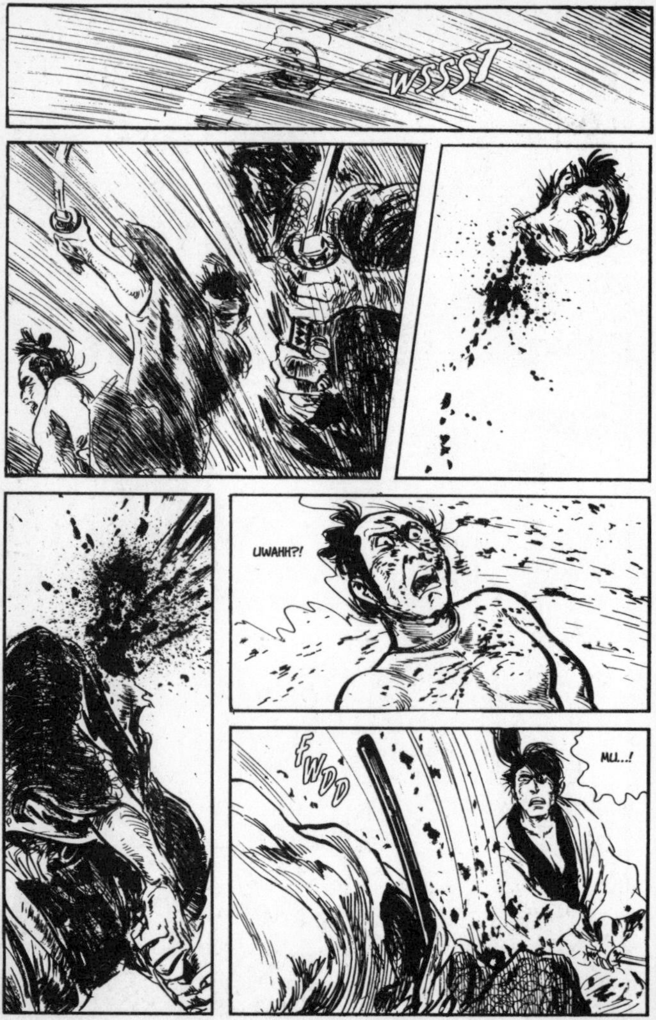
WSSST
UWAHH?!
FWDD
MU...!

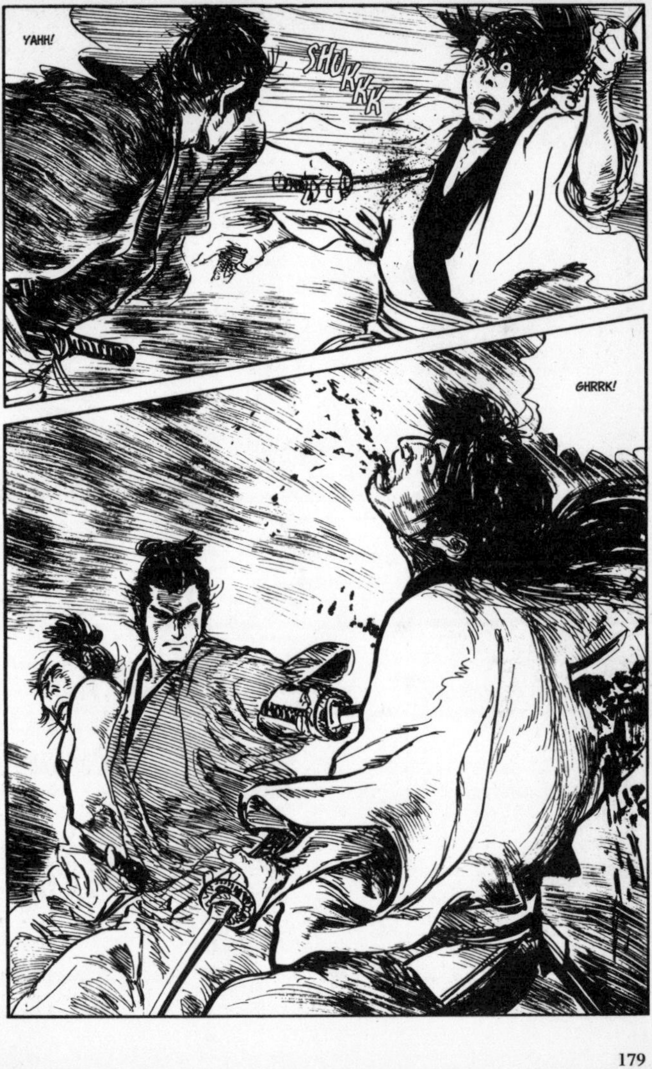
YAHH!
SHUKKK
GHRRK!

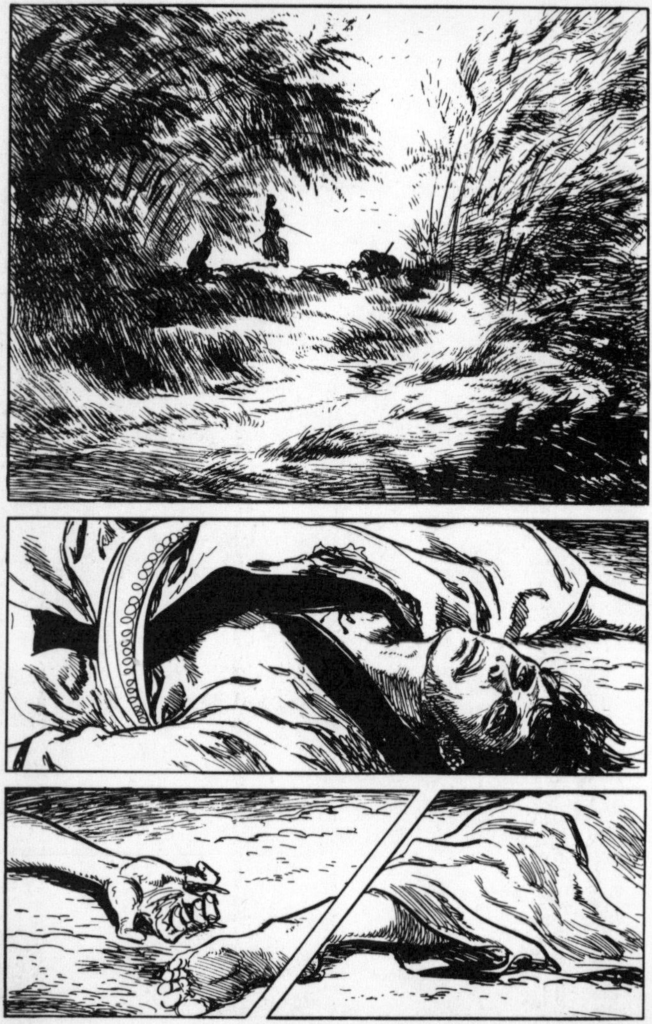

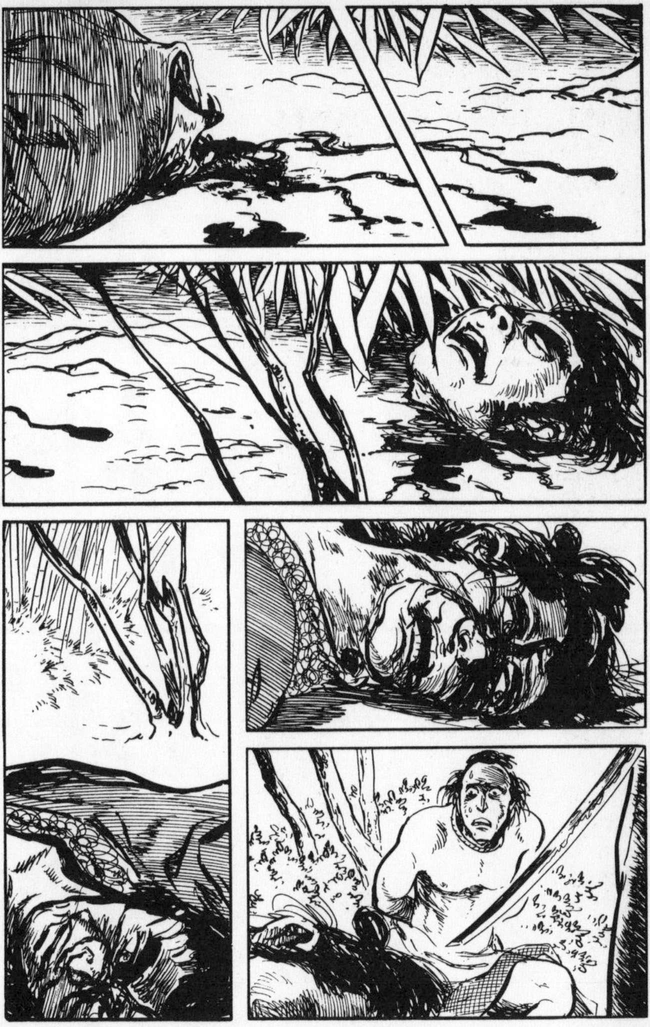

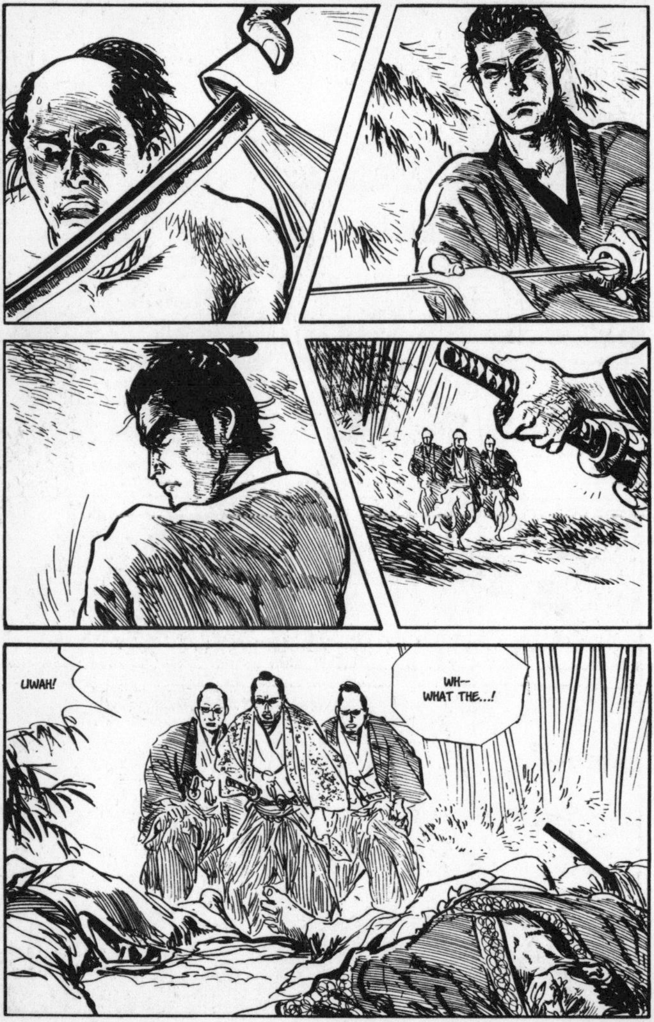
UWAH!
WH--
WHAT THE...!

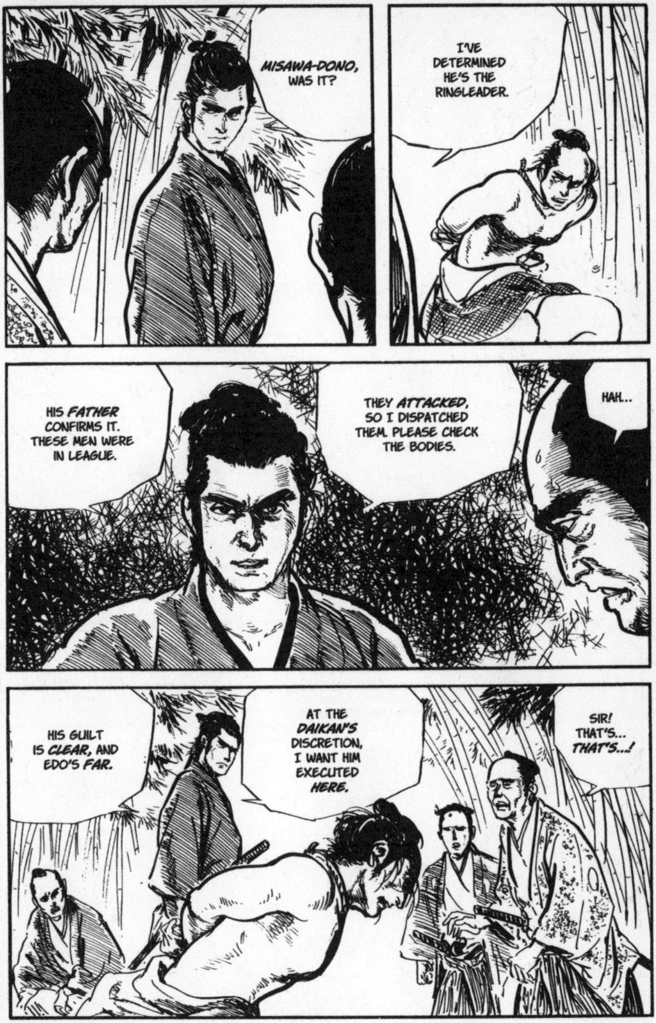
MISAWA-DONO, WAS IT?
I'VE DETERMINED HE'S THE RINGLEADER.
HIS FATHER CONFIRMS IT. THESE MEN WERE IN LEAGUE.
THEY ATTACKED, SO I DISPATCHED THEM. PLEASE CHECK THE BODIES.
HAH...
HIS GUILT IS CLEAR, AND EDO'S FAR.
AT THE DAIKAN'S DISCRETION, I WANT HIM EXECUTED HERE.
SIR! THAT'S... THAT'S...!

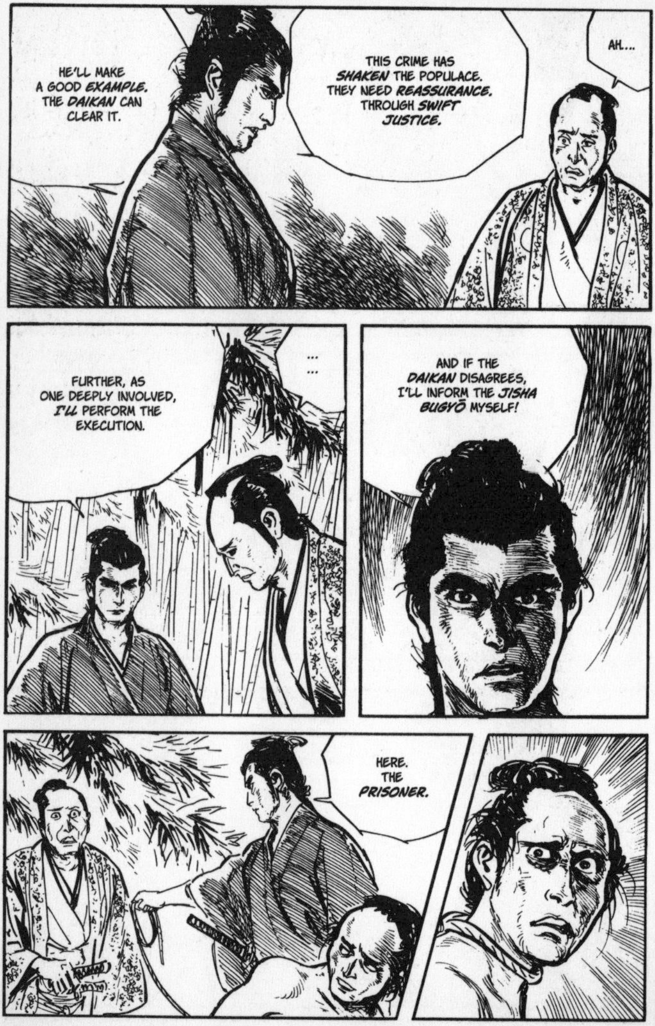
HE'LL MAKE A GOOD *EXAMPLE.* THE *DAIKAN* CAN CLEAR IT.
THIS CRIME HAS *SHAKEN* THE POPULACE. THEY NEED *REASSURANCE.* THROUGH *SWIFT JUSTICE.*
AH...
FURTHER, AS ONE DEEPLY INVOLVED, *I'LL* PERFORM THE EXECUTION.
...
...
AND IF THE *DAIKAN* DISAGREES, I'LL INFORM THE *JISHA BUGYŌ* MYSELF!
HERE. THE *PRISONER.*

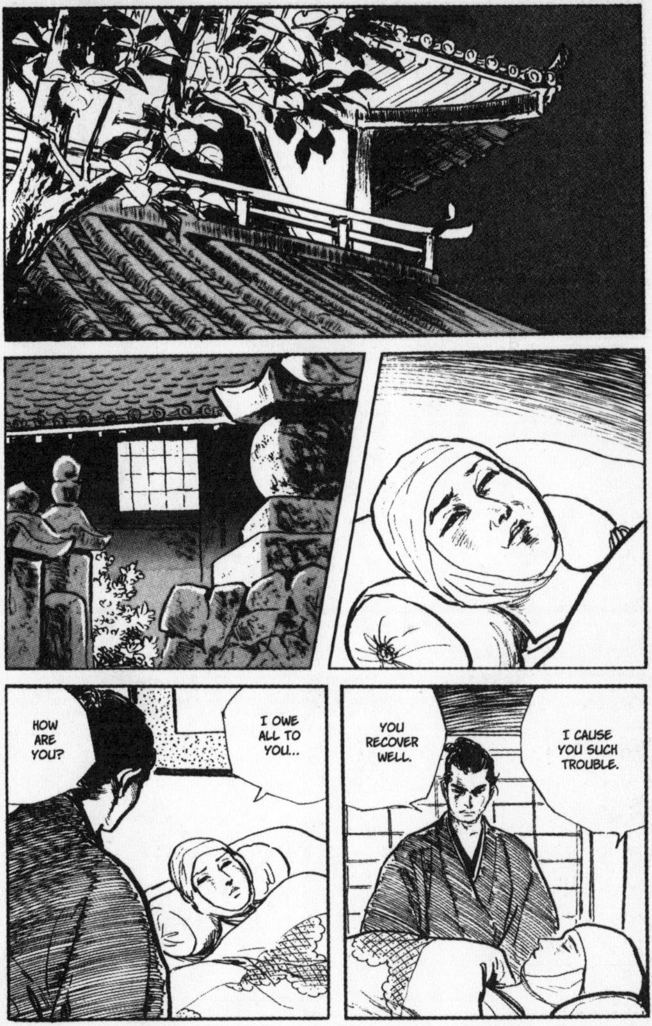
HOW ARE YOU?
I OWE ALL TO YOU...
YOU RECOVER WELL.
I CAUSE YOU SUCH TROUBLE.

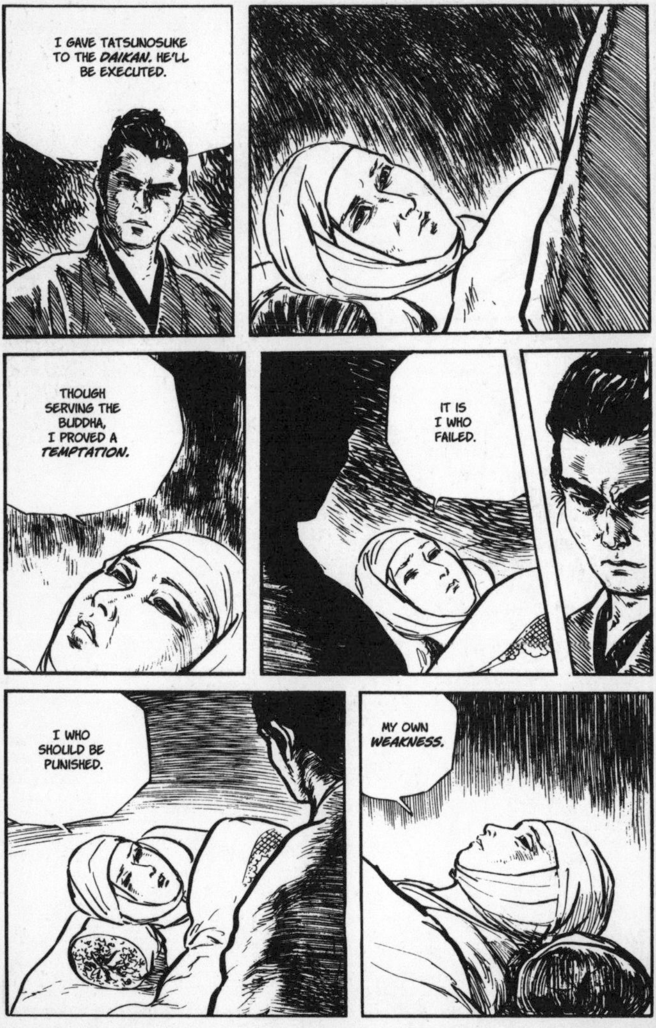
I GAVE TATSUNOSUKE TO THE *DAIKAN*. HE'LL BE EXECUTED.
THOUGH SERVING THE BUDDHA, I PROVED A *TEMPTATION.*
IT IS I WHO FAILED.
I WHO SHOULD BE PUNISHED.
MY OWN *WEAKNESS.*

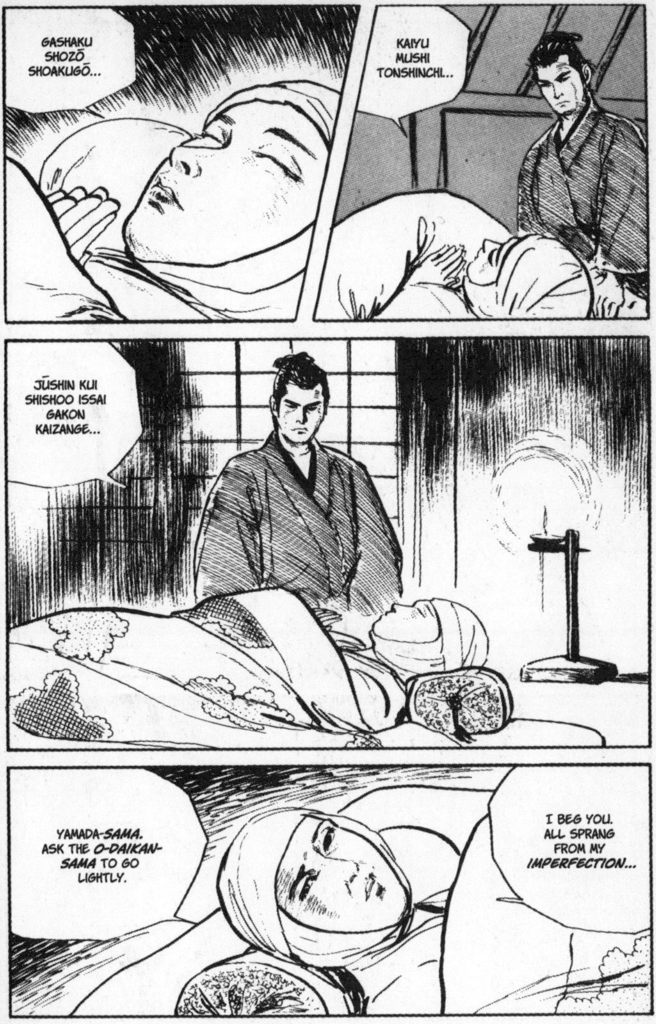
GASHAKU SHOZŌ SHOAKUGŌ...
KAIYU MUSHI TONSHINCHI...
JŪSHIN KUI SHISHOO ISSAI GAKON KAIZANGE...
YAMADA-*SAMA*. ASK THE *O-DAIKAN-SAMA* TO GO LIGHTLY.
I BEG YOU. ALL SPRANG FROM MY *IMPERFECTION*...

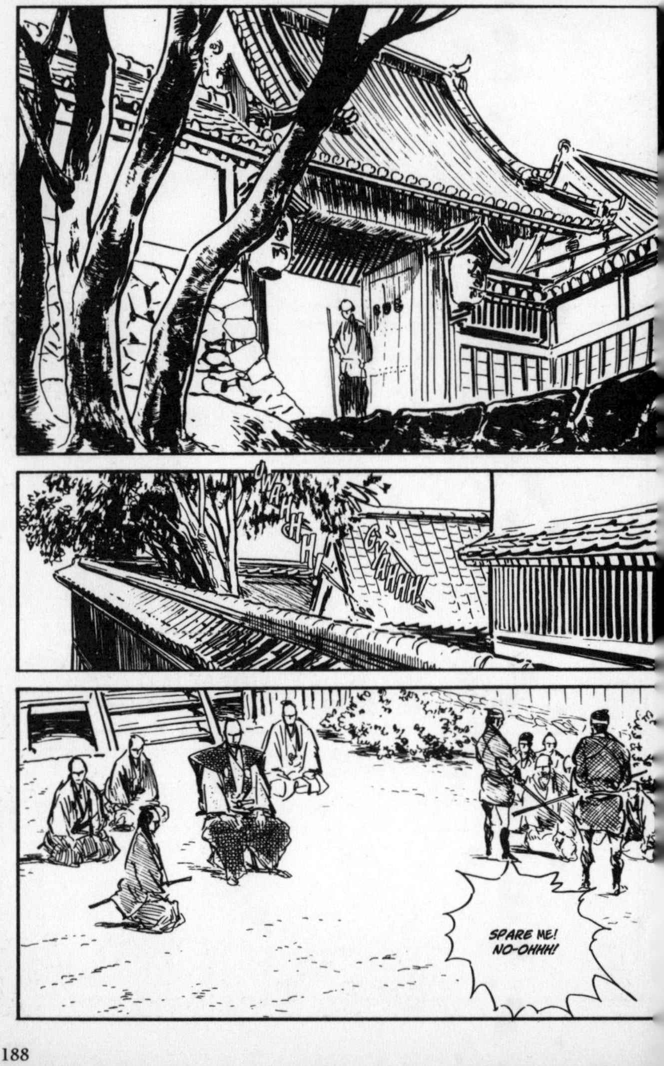
UWAHHH!
GYAHHH!
SPARE ME! NO-OHHH!

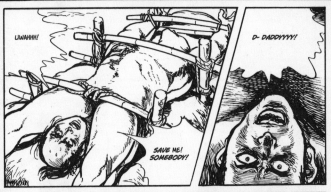

UWAHHH!

D- DADDYYYY!

SAVE ME! SOMEBODY!

T- TATSUNO-SUKE!!

AHHH! NOHHH!!

189

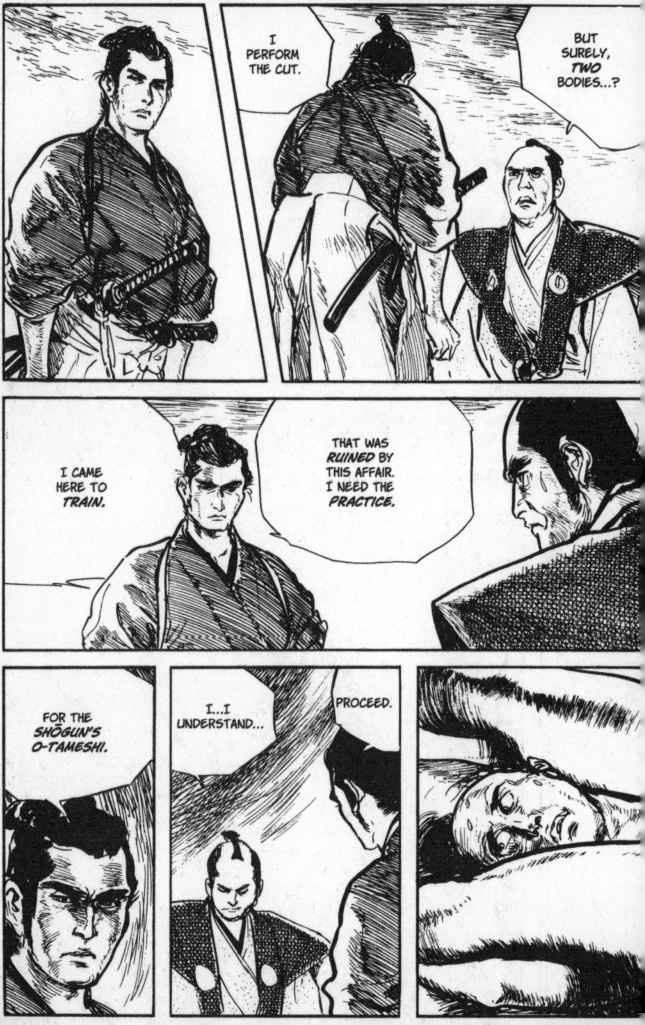
I PERFORM THE CUT.
BUT SURELY, TWO BODIES...?
I CAME HERE TO TRAIN.
THAT WAS RUINED BY THIS AFFAIR. I NEED THE PRACTICE.
FOR THE SHŌGUN'S O-TAMESHI.
I...I UNDERSTAND...
PROCEED.

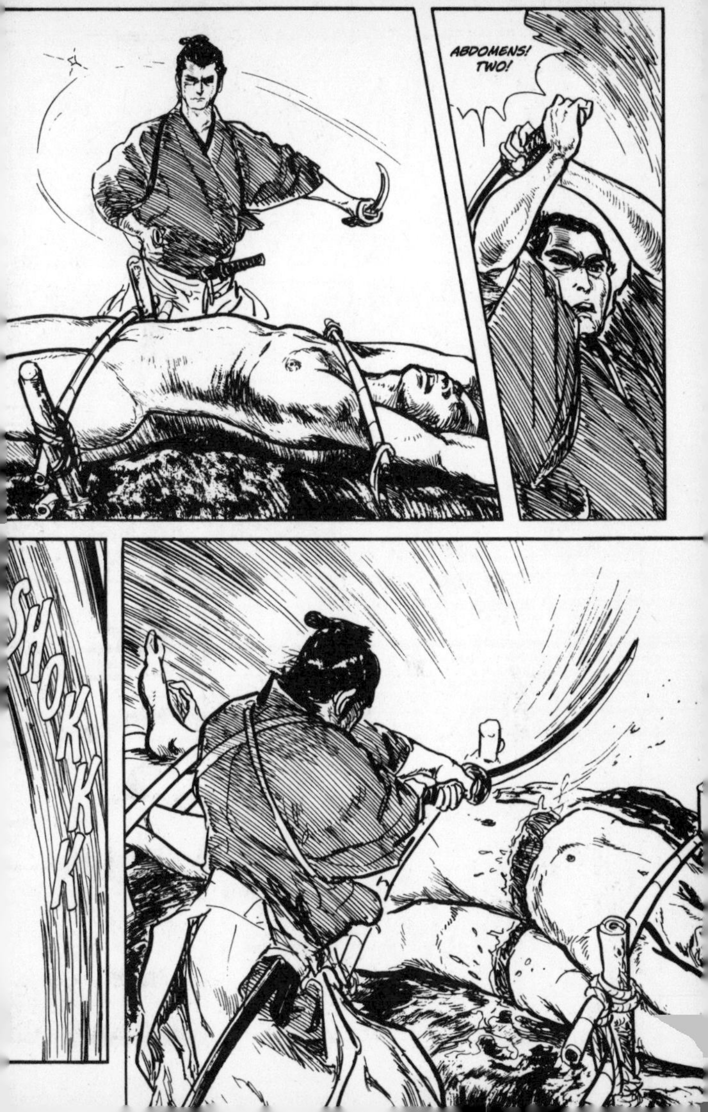
ABDOMENS! TWO!
SHOKKK

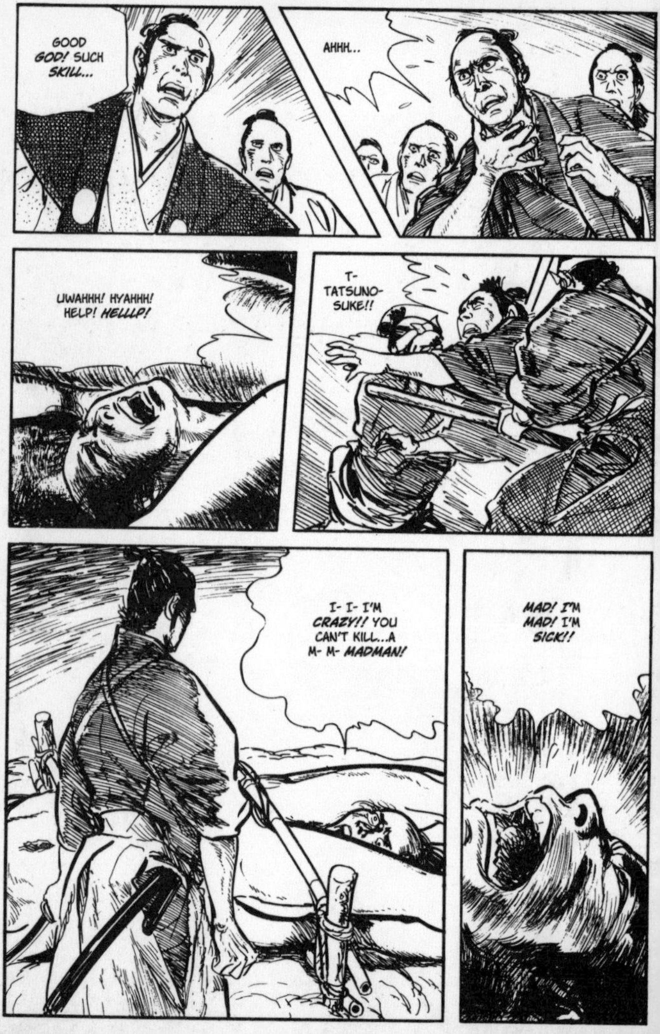
GOOD GOD! SUCH SKILL...
AHHH...
UWAHHH! HYAHHH! HELP! HELLLP!
T- TATSUNOSUKE!!
I- I- I'M CRAZY!! YOU CAN'T KILL...A M- M- MADMAN!
MAD! I'M MAD! I'M SICK!!

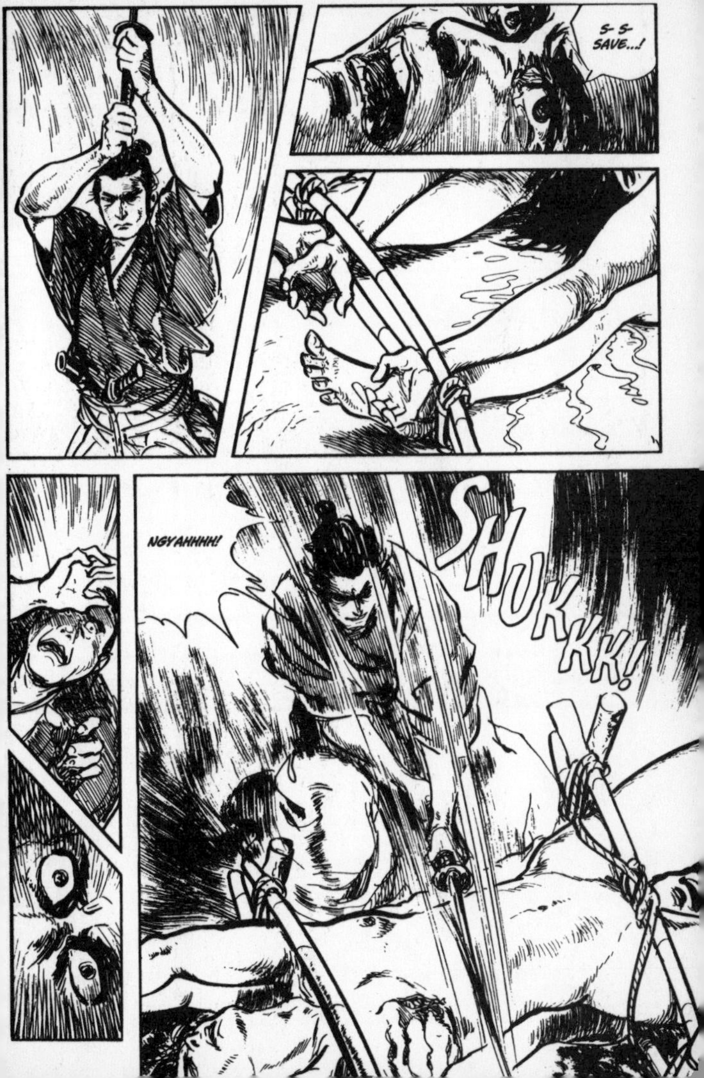
S-S-
SAVE...!
NGYAHHHH!
SHUKKKK!

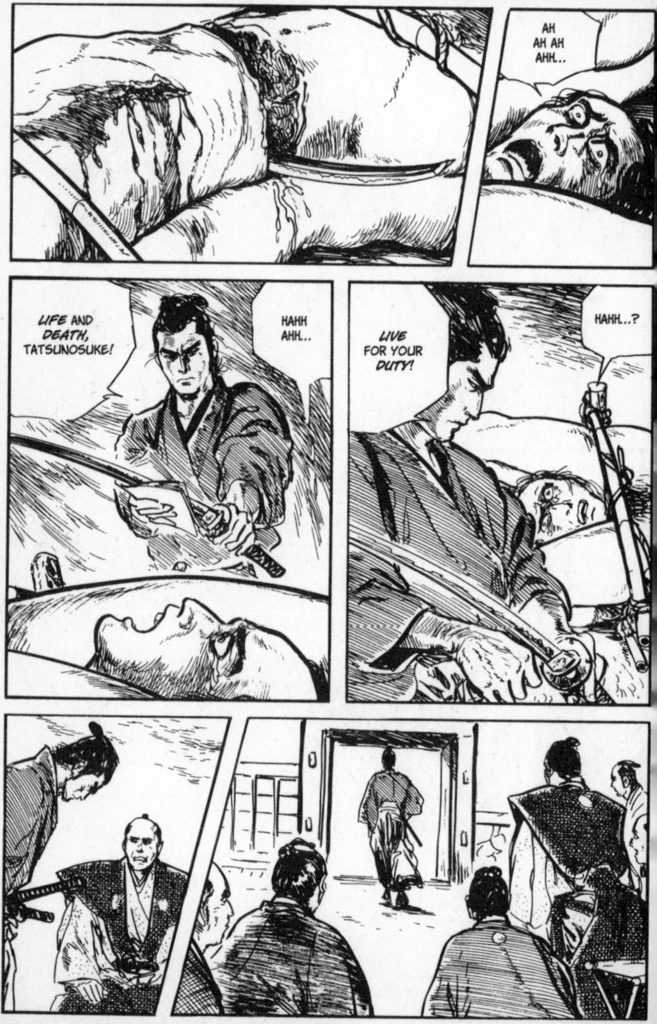
AH
AH AH AHH...
LIFE AND DEATH, TATSUNOSUKE!
HAHH AHH...
LIVE FOR YOUR DUTY!
HAHH...?

the eighth

A Taka-daimono for an Irezomotsu

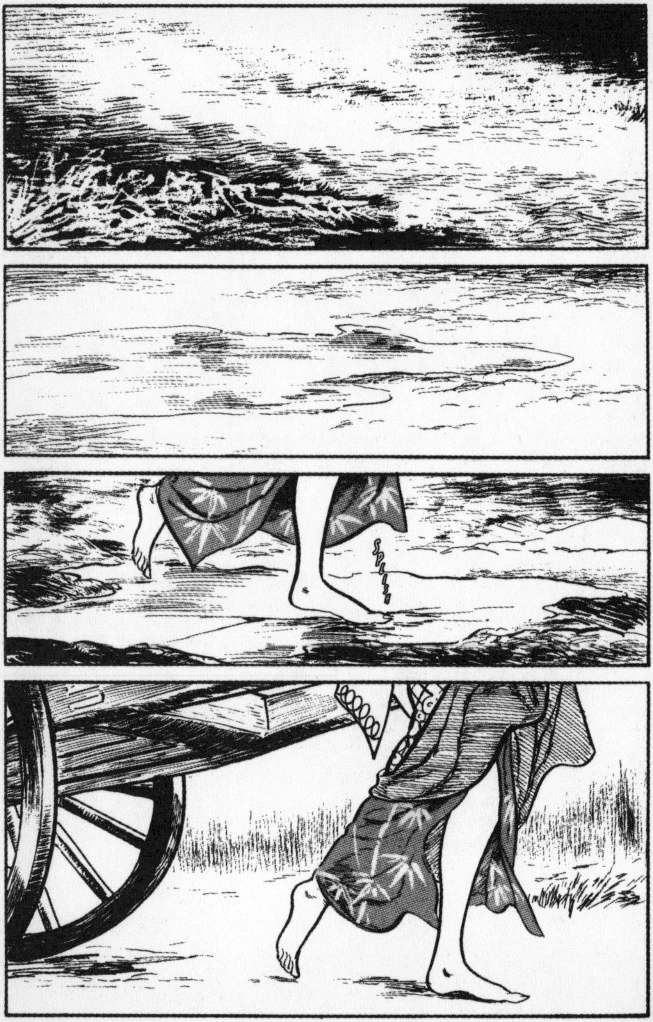
SPLISH

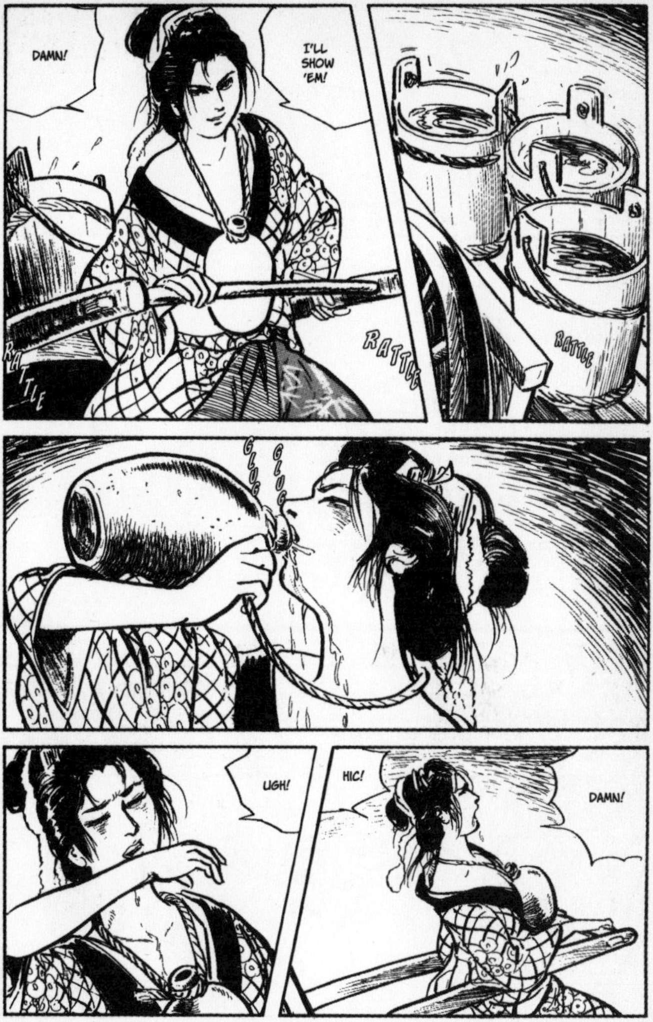
DAMN!
I'LL SHOW 'EM!
RATTLE
RATTLE
RATTLE
GLUG GLUG
UGH!
HIC!
DAMN!

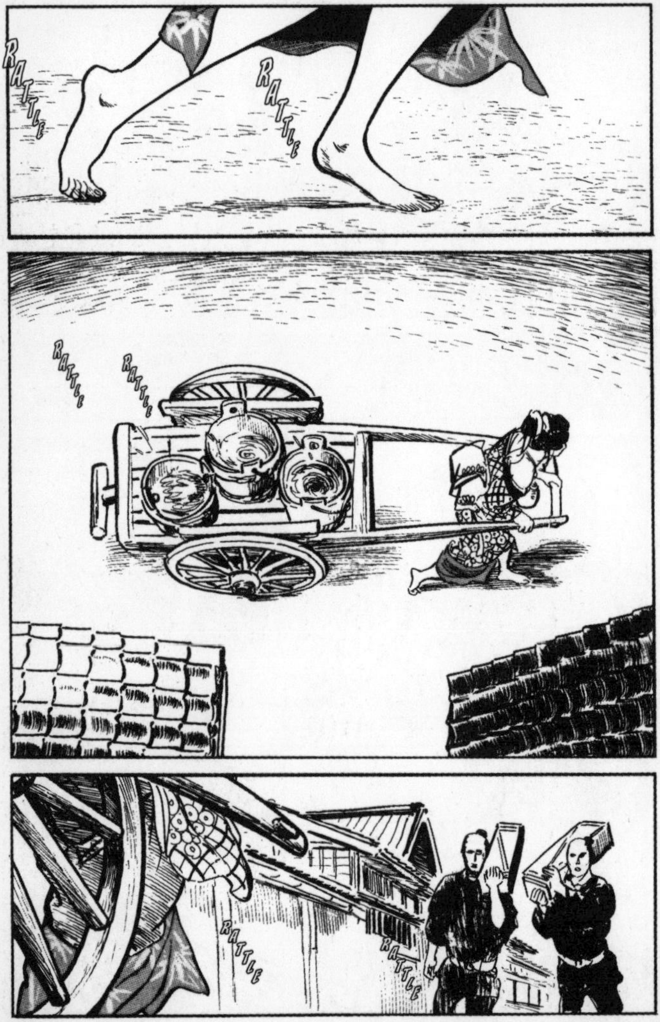
RATTLE
RATTLE
RATTLE
RATTLE
RATTLE
RATTLE

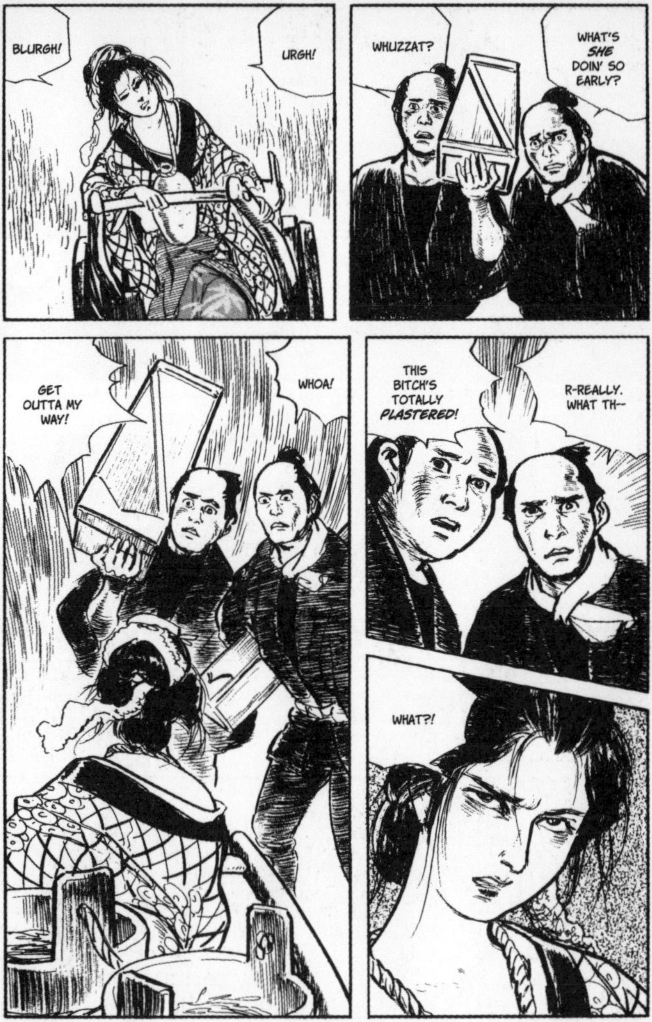
BLURGH!
URGH!
WHUZZAT?
WHAT'S *SHE* DOIN' SO EARLY?
GET OUTTA MY WAY!
WHOA!
THIS BITCH'S TOTALLY *PLASTERED!*
R-REALLY. WHAT TH--
WHAT?!

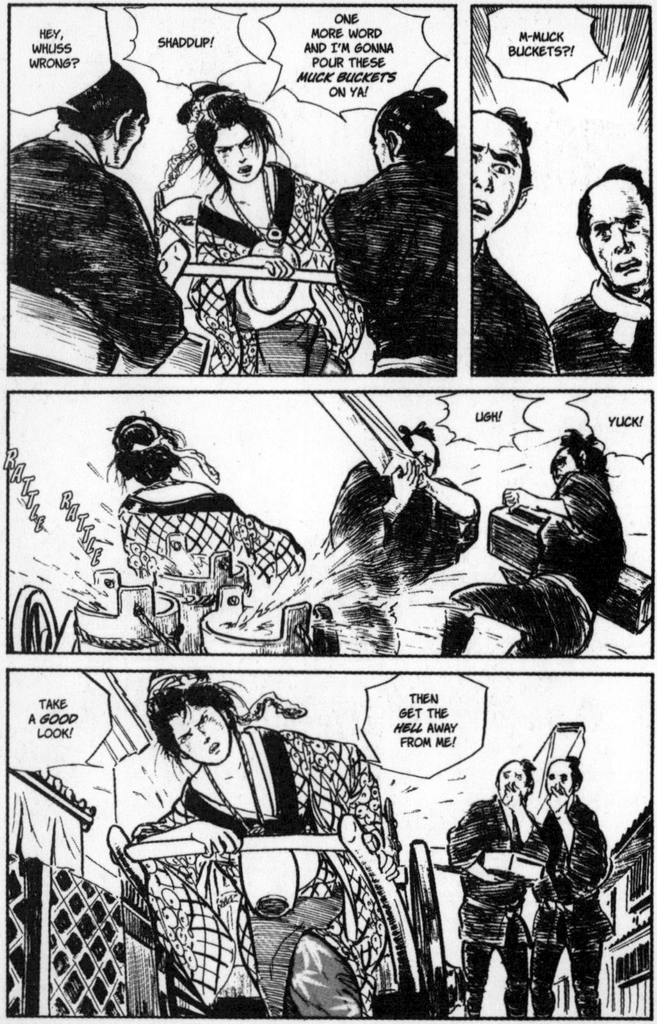
HEY, WHUSS WRONG?
SHADDUP!
ONE MORE WORD AND I'M GONNA POUR THESE *MUCK BUCKETS* ON YA!
M-MUCK BUCKETS?!
RATTLE
RATTLE
UGH!
YUCK!
TAKE A *GOOD* LOOK!
THEN GET THE *HELL* AWAY FROM ME!

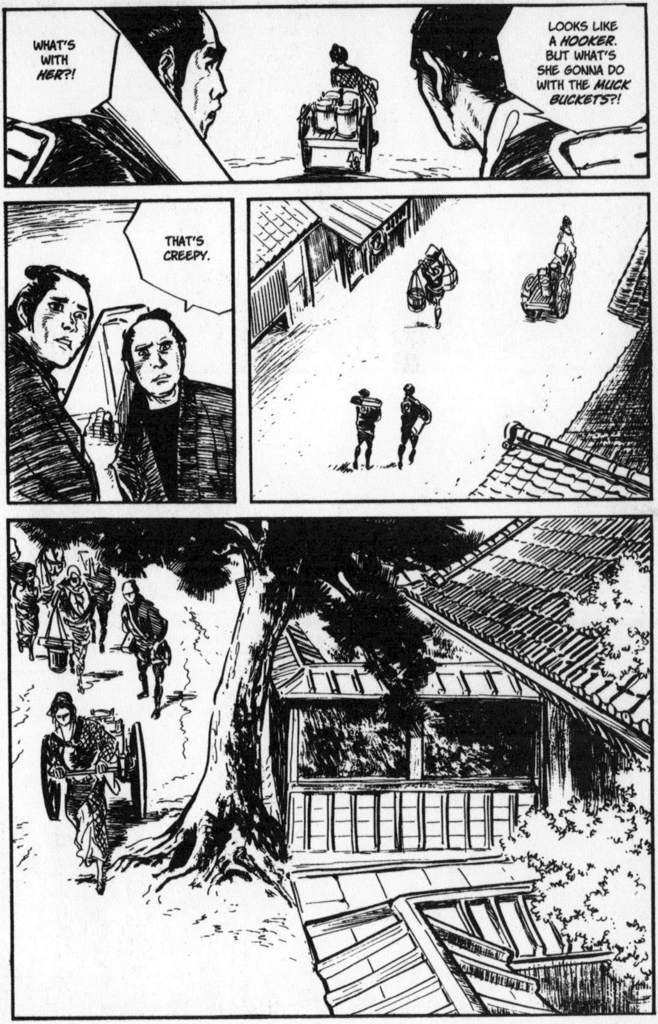
WHAT'S WITH HER?!
LOOKS LIKE A HOOKER. BUT WHAT'S SHE GONNA DO WITH THE MUCK BUCKETS?!
THAT'S CREEPY.

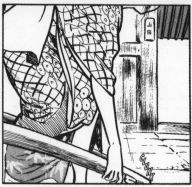

WHAT'S WRONG WITH HER?

HUH?

SHE'S WEIRD.

SHE'S GOING TO THE *EXECUTIONER'S* PLACE!

DAMN!

YOU DAMN EXECUTIONER...

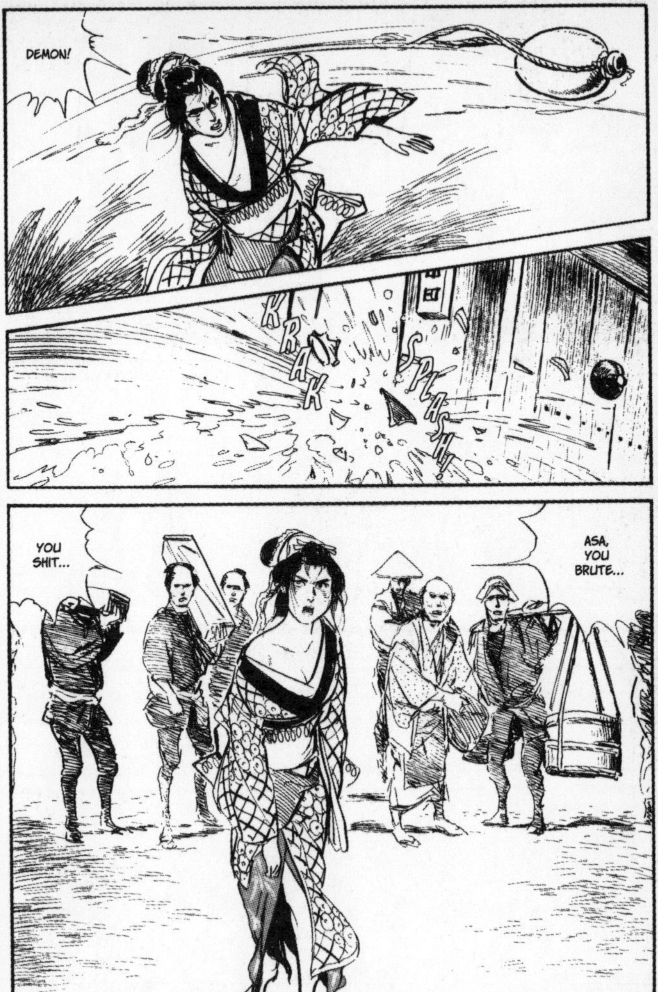
DEMON!
KRAK
SPLASH!
YOU SHIT...
ASA, YOU BRUTE...

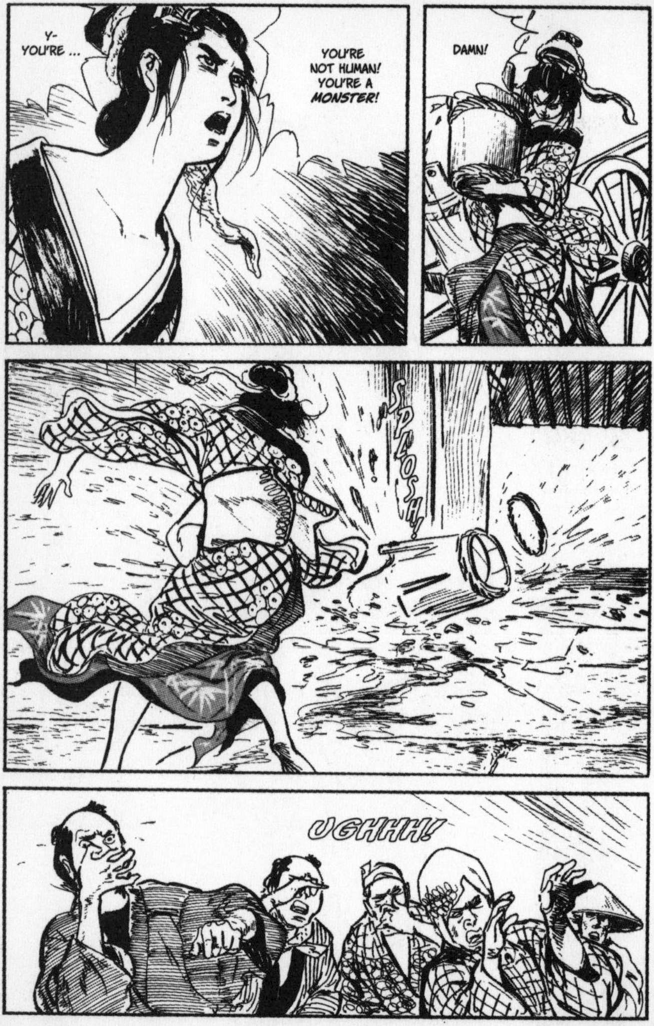
Y-
YOU'RE ...
YOU'RE NOT HUMAN! YOU'RE A *MONSTER!*
DAMN!
SPLOOSH!
UGHHH!

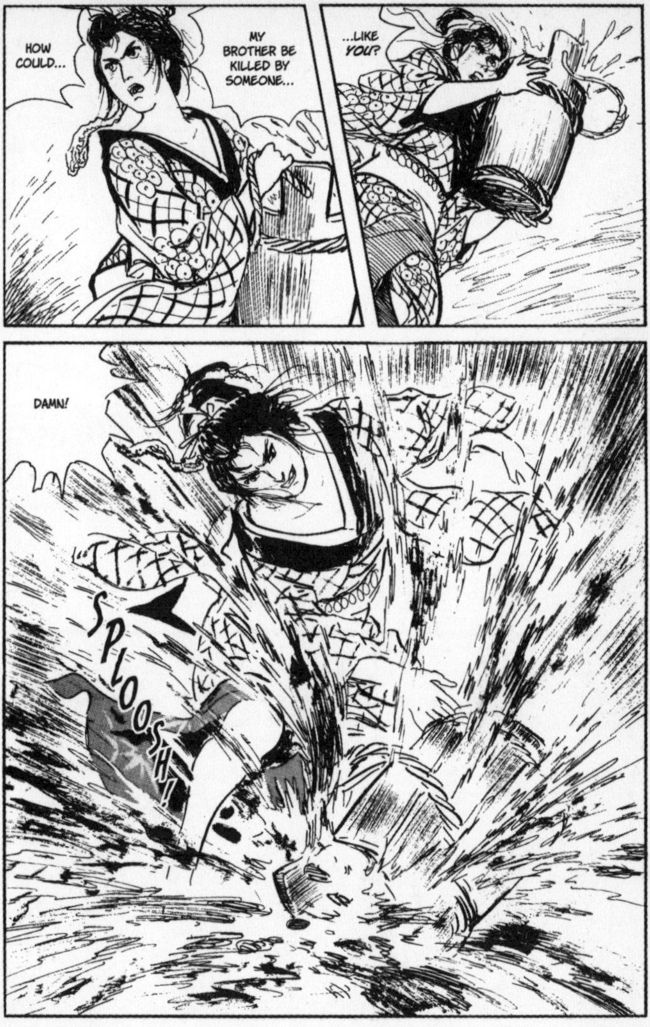
HOW COULD...
MY BROTHER BE KILLED BY SOMEONE...
...LIKE *YOU*?
DAMN!
SPLOOSH!

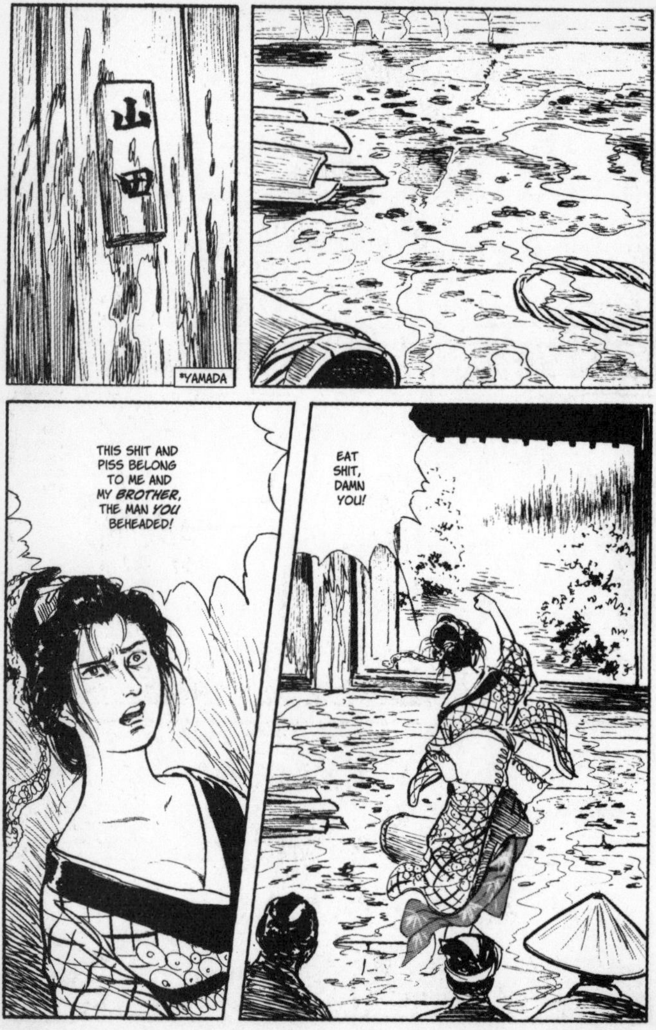
山田
*YAMADA
THIS SHIT AND PISS BELONG TO ME AND MY *BROTHER*, THE MAN *YOU* BEHEADED!
EAT SHIT, DAMN YOU!

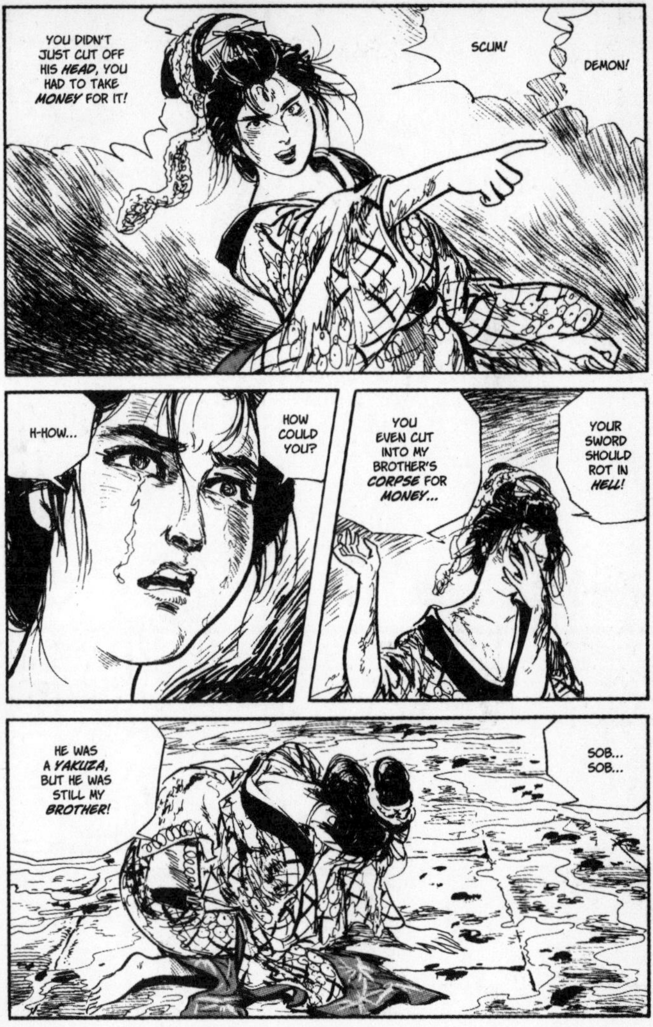

YOU DIDN'T JUST CUT OFF HIS *HEAD*, YOU HAD TO TAKE *MONEY* FOR IT!
SCUM!
DEMON!
H-HOW...
HOW COULD YOU?
YOU EVEN CUT INTO MY BROTHER'S *CORPSE* FOR *MONEY*...
YOUR SWORD SHOULD ROT IN *HELL*!
HE WAS A *YAKUZA*, BUT HE WAS STILL MY *BROTHER*!
SOB... SOB...

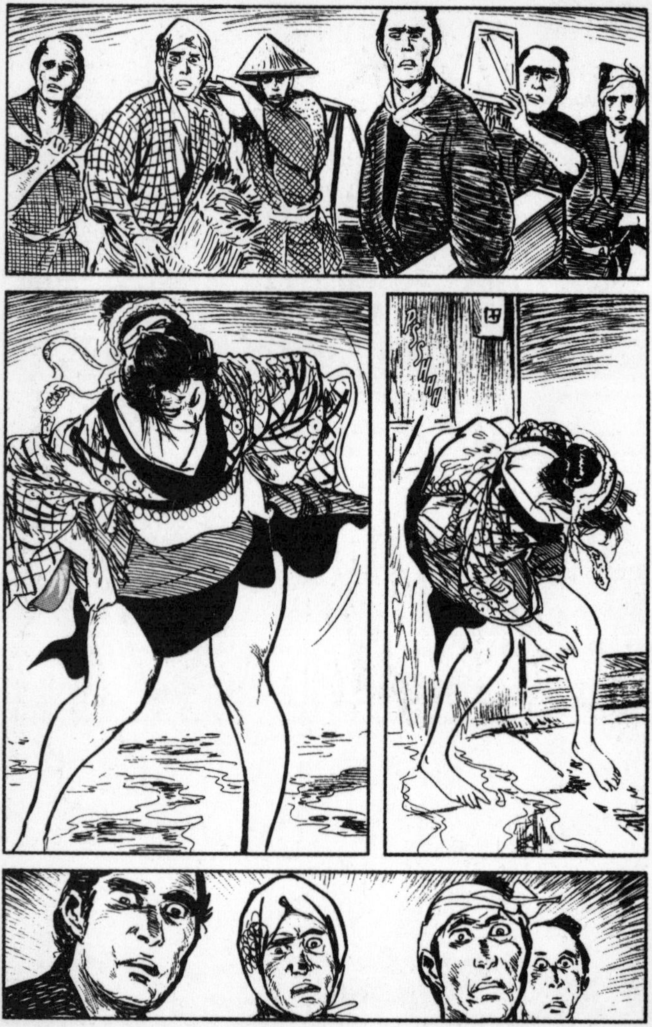
PSSHHH

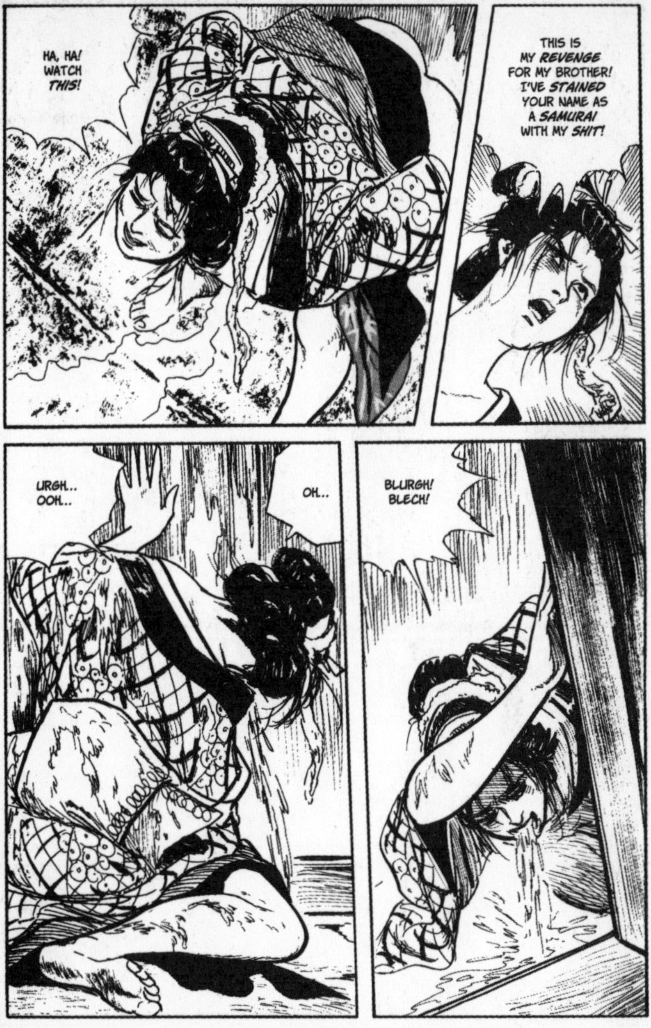
HA, HA! WATCH THIS!
THIS IS MY REVENGE FOR MY BROTHER! I'VE STAINED YOUR NAME AS A SAMURAI WITH MY SHIT!
URGH... OOH...
OH...
BLURGH! BLECH!

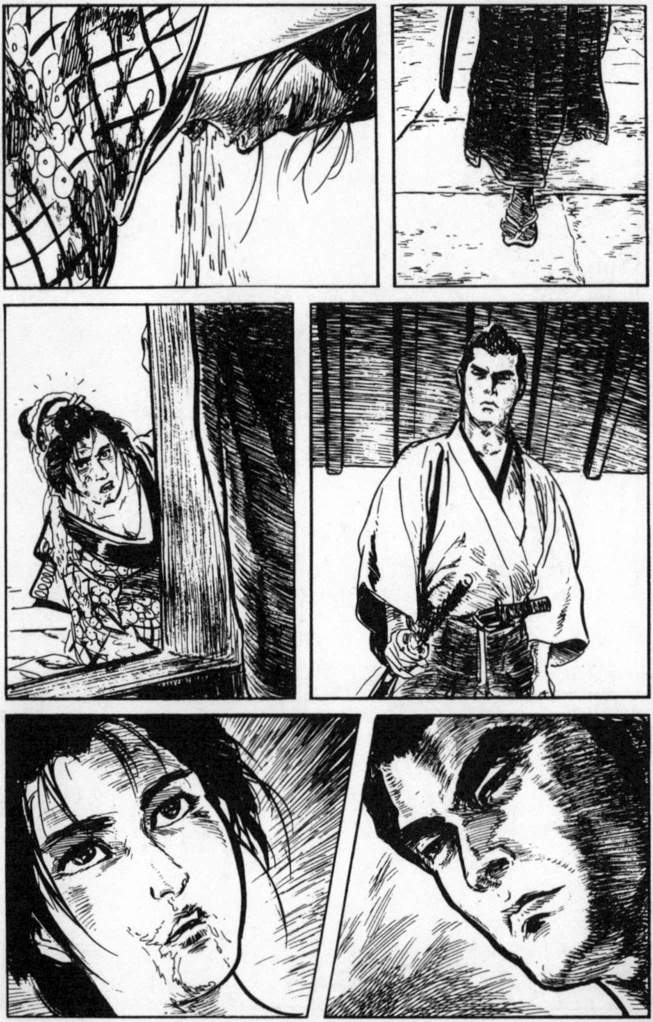

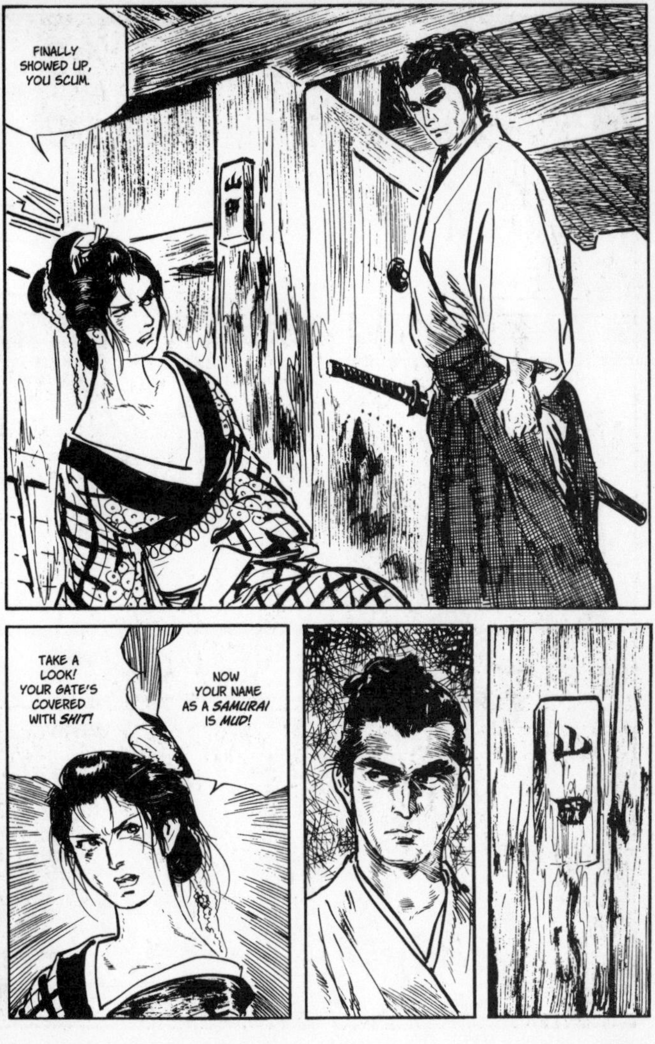
FINALLY SHOWED UP, YOU SCUM.
TAKE A LOOK! YOUR GATE'S COVERED WITH *SHIT*!
NOW YOUR NAME AS A *SAMURAI* IS *MUD*!

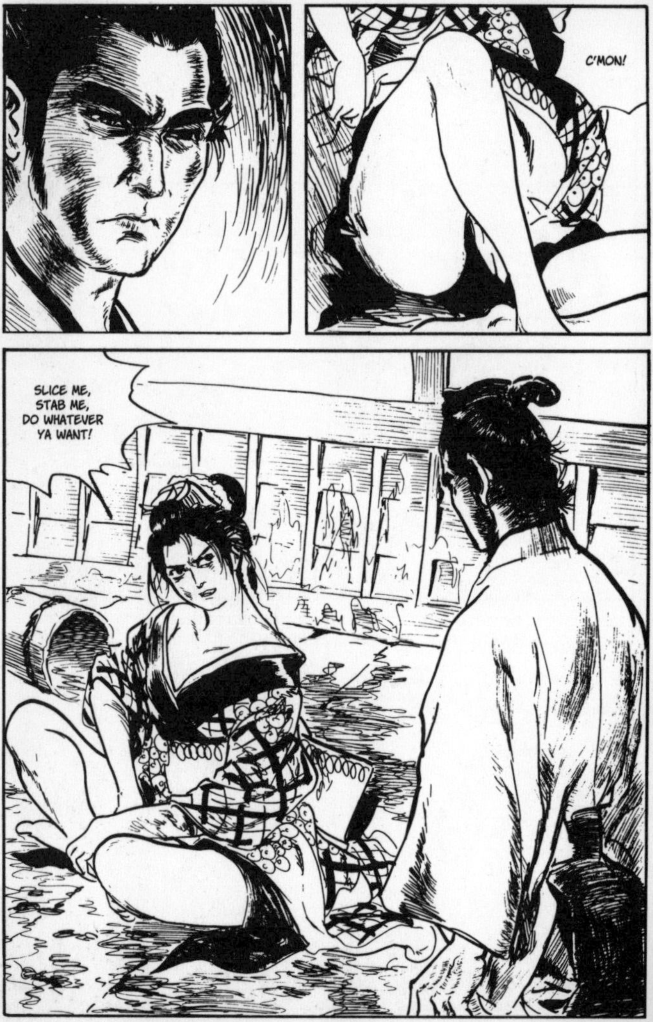
C'MON!
SLICE ME, STAB ME, DO WHATEVER YA WANT!

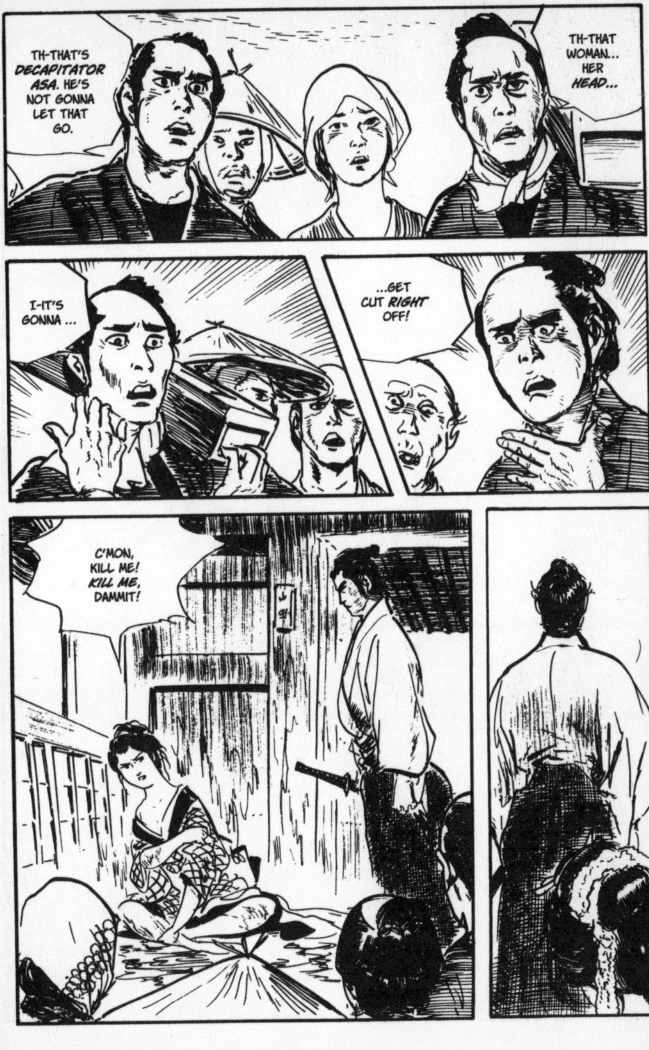
TH-THAT'S *DECAPITATOR ASA*. HE'S NOT GONNA LET THAT GO.
TH-THAT WOMAN... HER *HEAD*...
I-IT'S GONNA ...
...GET CUT *RIGHT* OFF!
C'MON, KILL ME! *KILL ME*, DAMMIT!

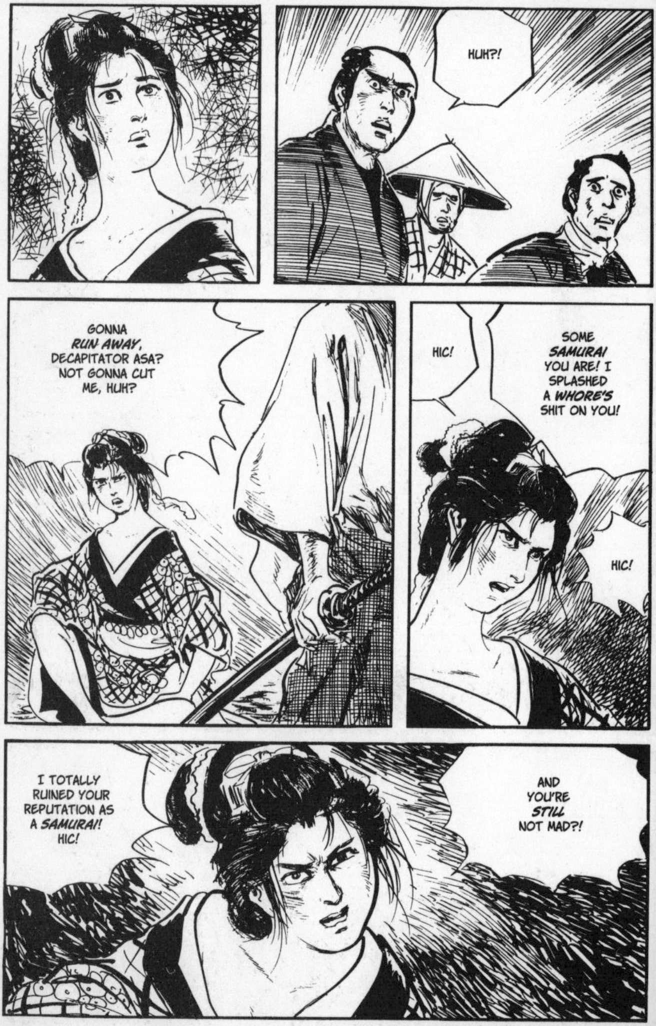
HUH?!
GONNA RUN AWAY, DECAPITATOR ASA? NOT GONNA CUT ME, HUH?
HIC!
SOME SAMURAI YOU ARE! I SPLASHED A WHORE'S SHIT ON YOU!
HIC!
I TOTALLY RUINED YOUR REPUTATION AS A SAMURAI! HIC!
AND YOU'RE STILL NOT MAD?!

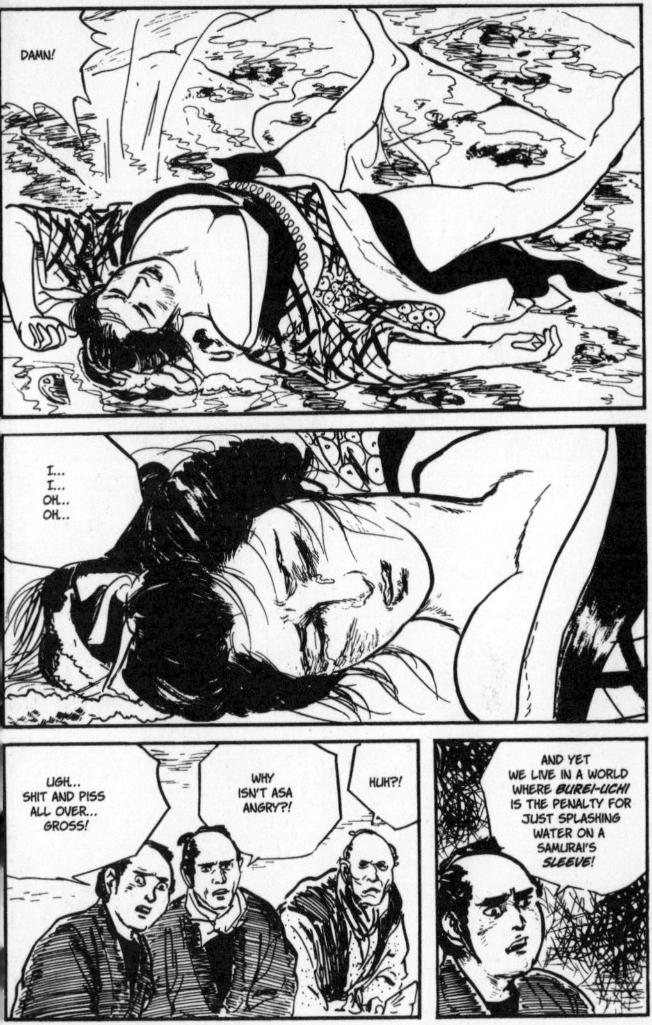
DAMN!
I... I... OH.. OH..
UGH... SHIT AND PISS ALL OVER... GROSS!
WHY ISN'T ASA ANGRY?!
HUH?!
AND YET WE LIVE IN A WORLD WHERE *BUREI-UCHI* IS THE PENALTY FOR JUST SPLASHING WATER ON A SAMURAI'S *SLEEVE*!

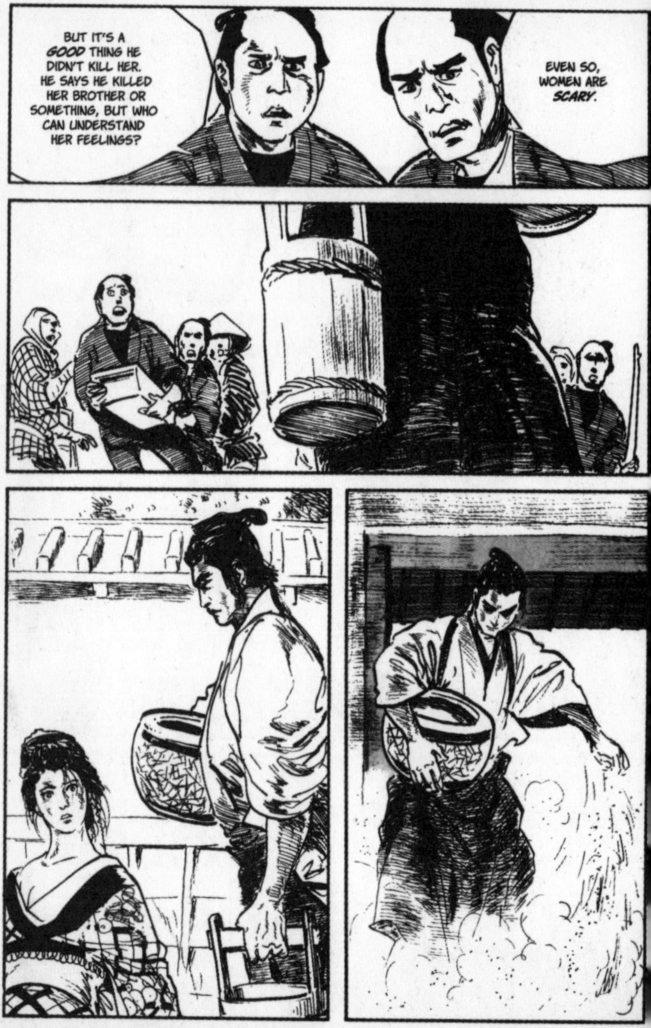
BUT IT'S A *GOOD* THING HE DIDN'T KILL HER. HE SAYS HE KILLED HER BROTHER OR SOMETHING, BUT WHO CAN UNDERSTAND HER FEELINGS?
EVEN SO, WOMEN ARE *SCARY*.

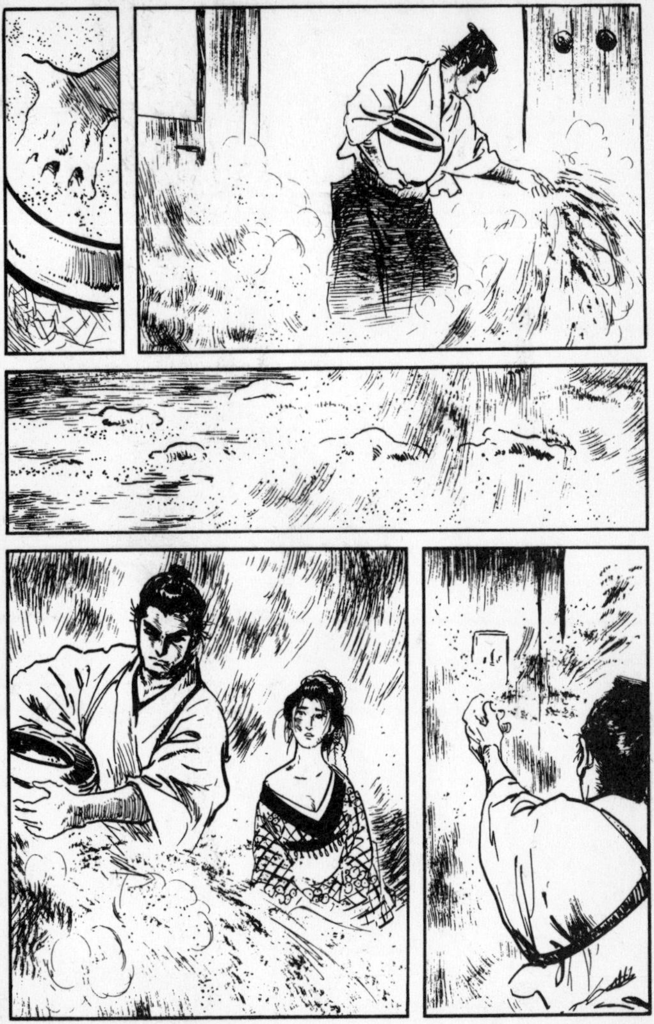

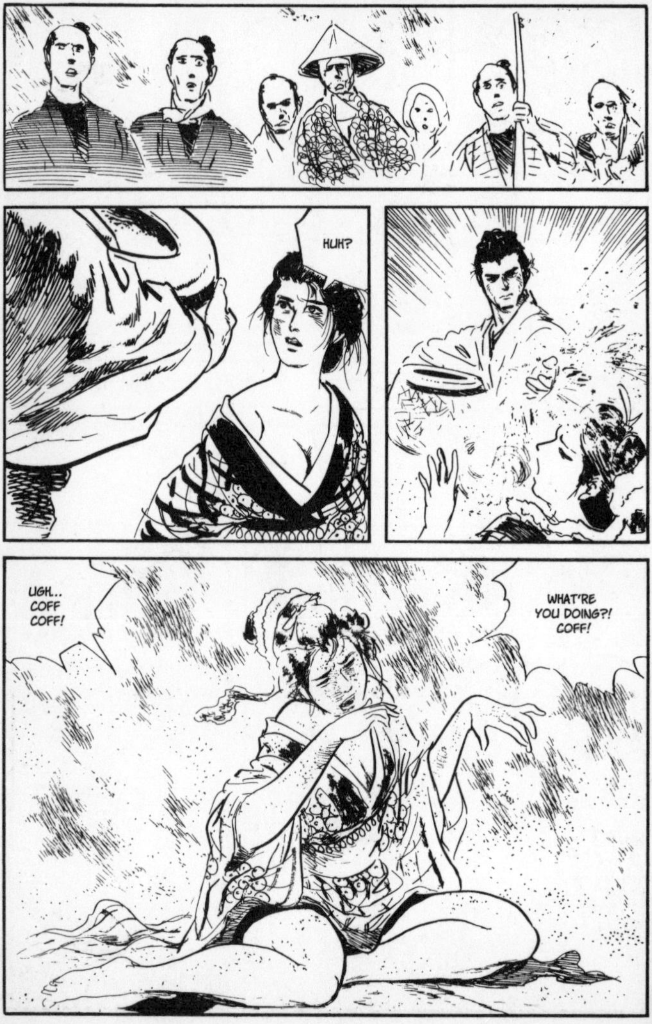
HUH?
UGH... COFF COFF!
WHAT'RE YOU DOING?! COFF!

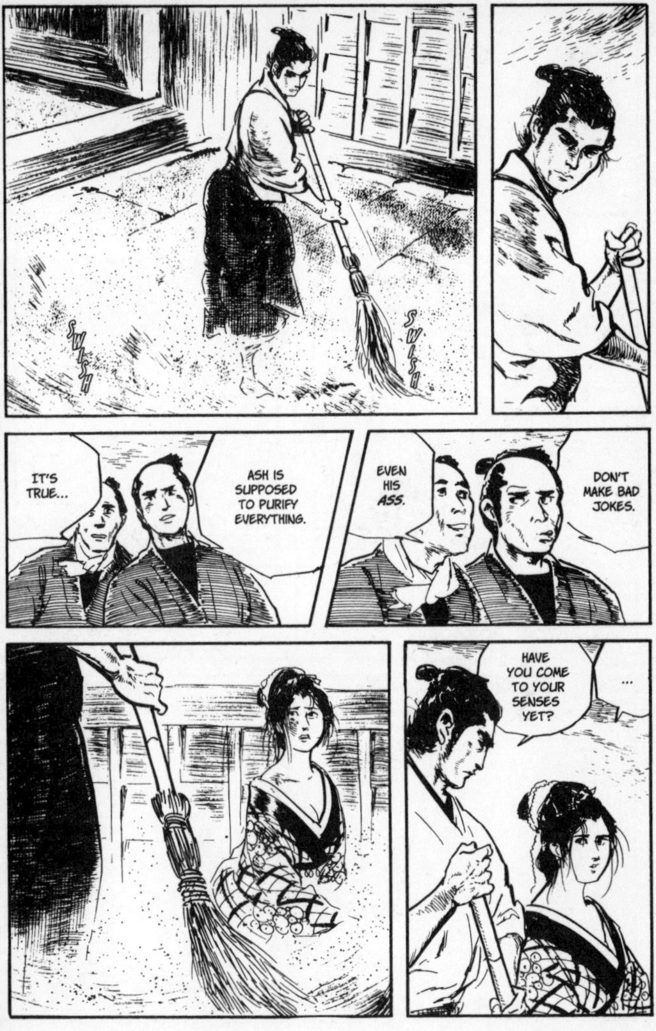
SWISH
SWISH
IT'S TRUE...
ASH IS SUPPOSED TO PURIFY EVERYTHING.
EVEN HIS ASS.
DON'T MAKE BAD JOKES.
HAVE YOU COME TO YOUR SENSES YET?
...

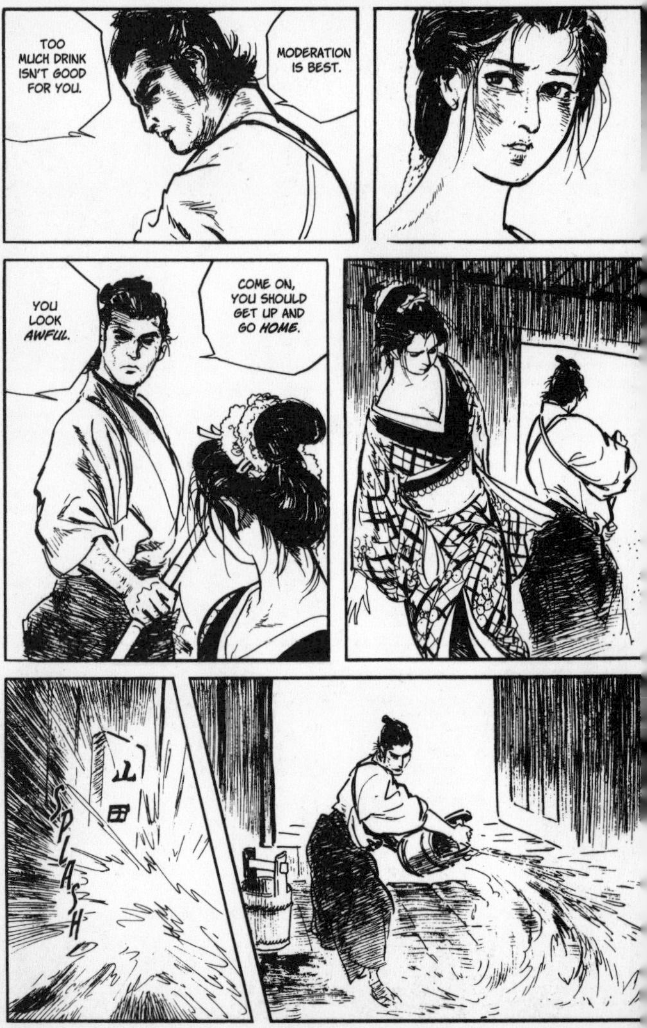
TOO MUCH DRINK ISN'T GOOD FOR YOU.
MODERATION IS BEST.
YOU LOOK *AWFUL.*
COME ON, YOU SHOULD GET UP AND GO *HOME*.
SPLASH

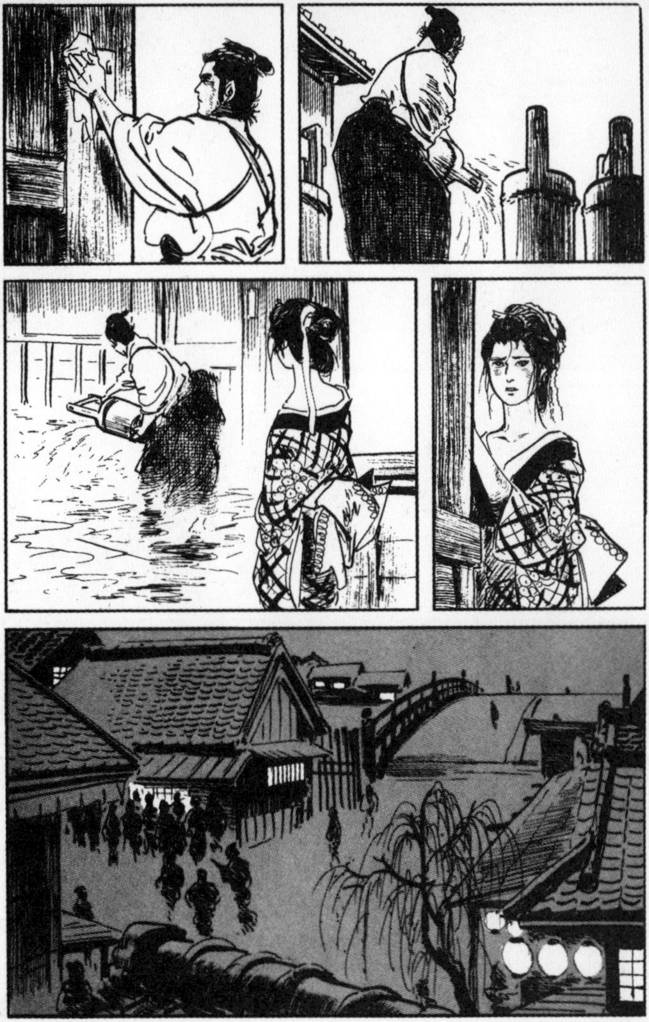

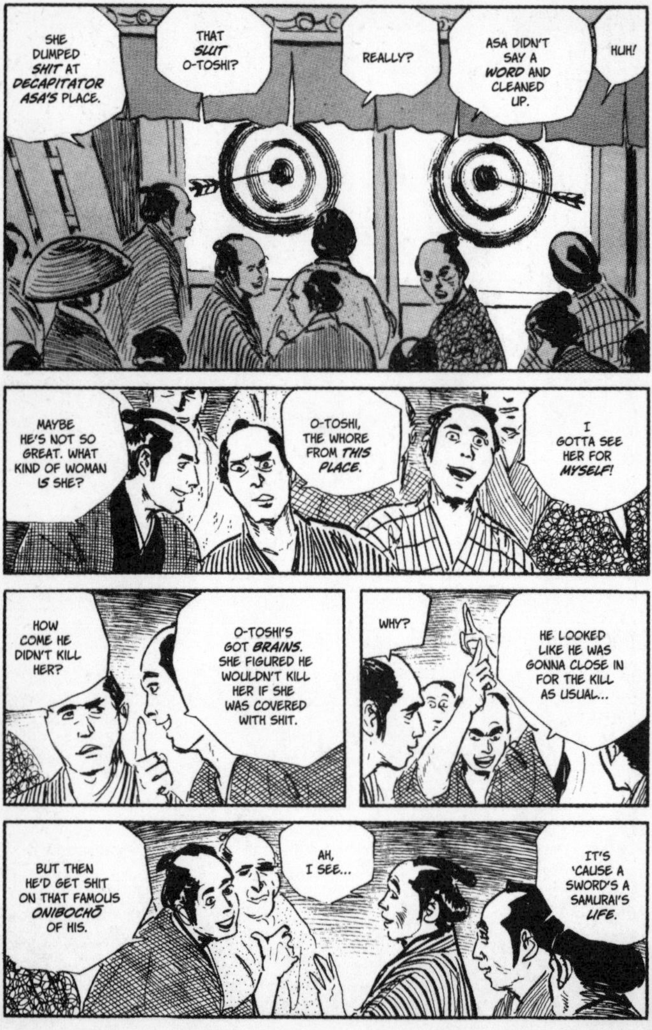
SHE DUMPED SHIT AT DECAPITATOR ASA'S PLACE.
THAT SLUT O-TOSHI?
REALLY?
ASA DIDN'T SAY A WORD AND CLEANED UP.
HUH!
MAYBE HE'S NOT SO GREAT. WHAT KIND OF WOMAN IS SHE?
O-TOSHI, THE WHORE FROM THIS PLACE.
I GOTTA SEE HER FOR MYSELF!
HOW COME HE DIDN'T KILL HER?
O-TOSHI'S GOT BRAINS. SHE FIGURED HE WOULDN'T KILL HER IF SHE WAS COVERED WITH SHIT.
WHY?
HE LOOKED LIKE HE WAS GONNA CLOSE IN FOR THE KILL AS USUAL...
BUT THEN HE'D GET SHIT ON THAT FAMOUS ONIBOCHŌ OF HIS.
AH, I SEE...
IT'S 'CAUSE A SWORD'S A SAMURAI'S LIFE.

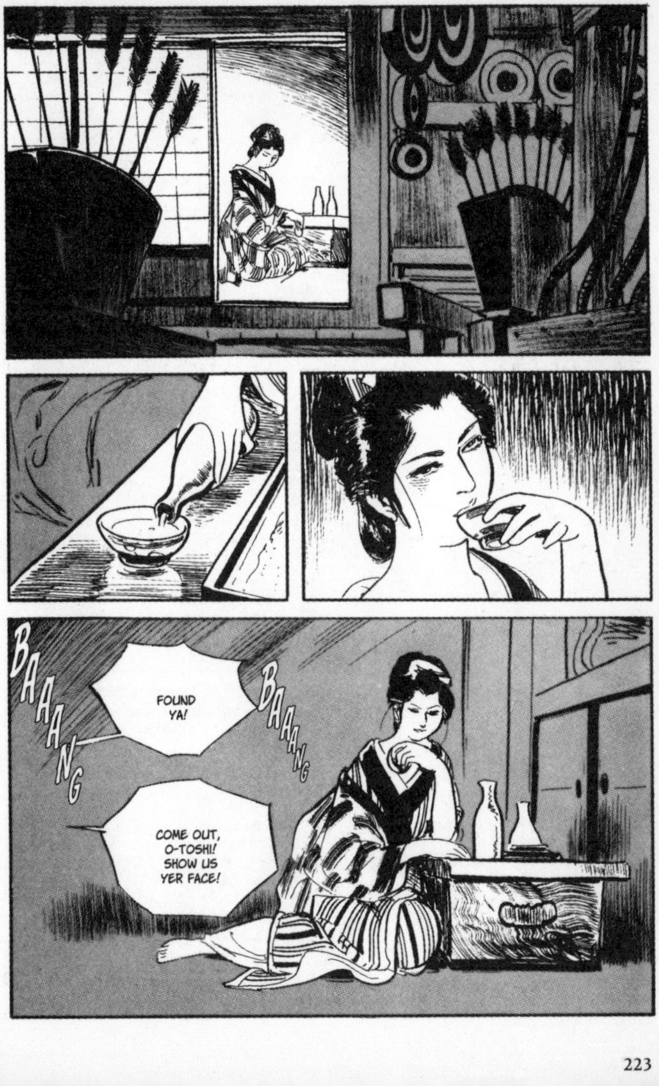
BAAANG
FOUND YA!
BAAANG
COME OUT, O-TOSHI! SHOW US YER FACE!

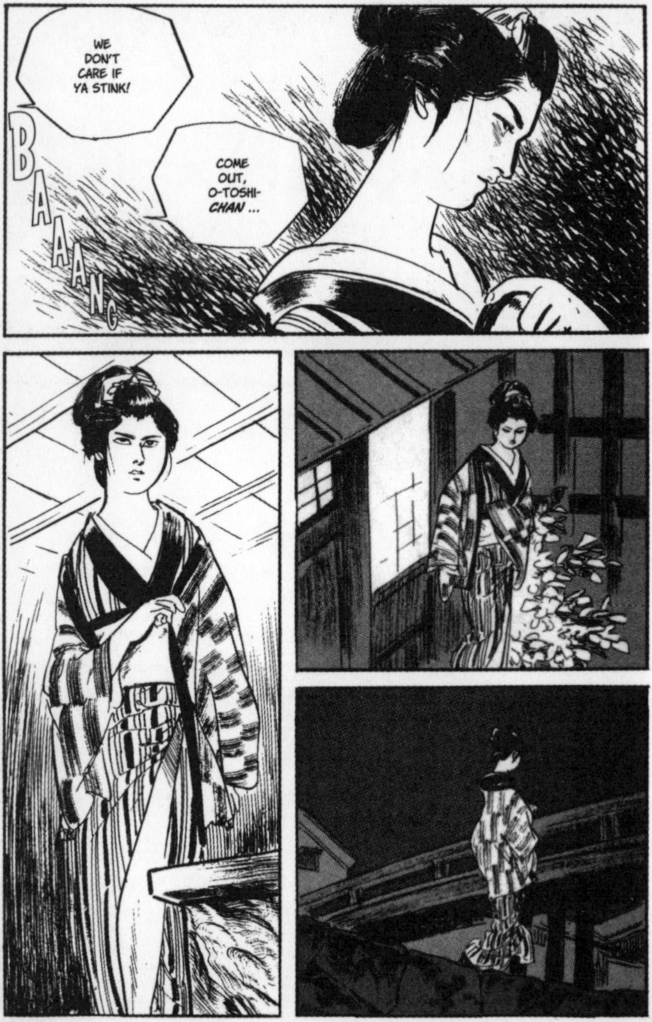

WE DON'T CARE IF YA STINK!
BAAAANG
COME OUT, O-TOSHI-*CHAN* ...

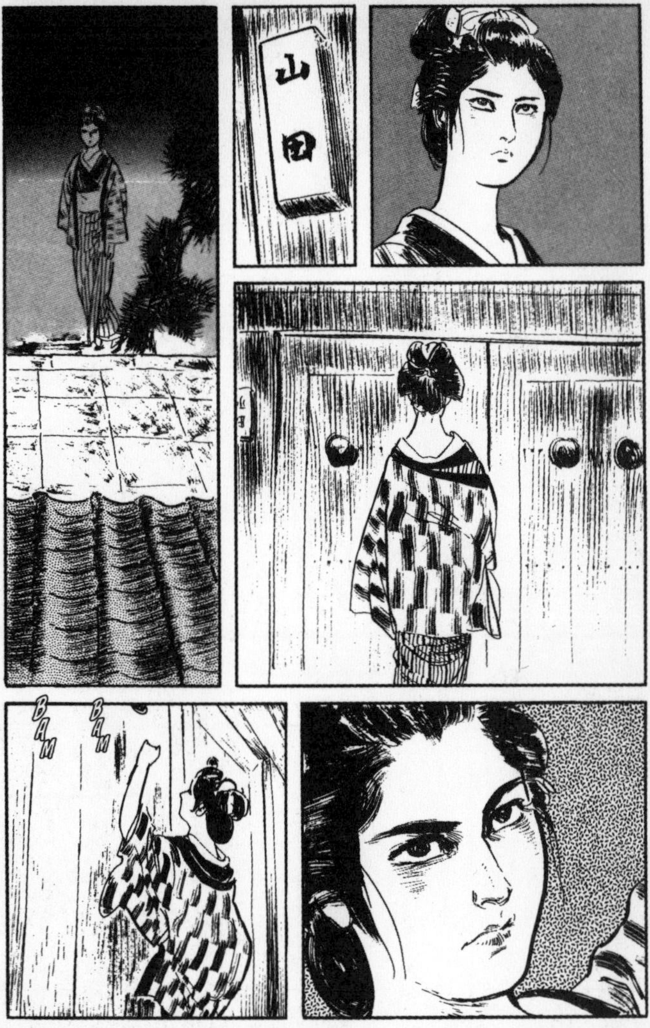
山田
BAM
BAM

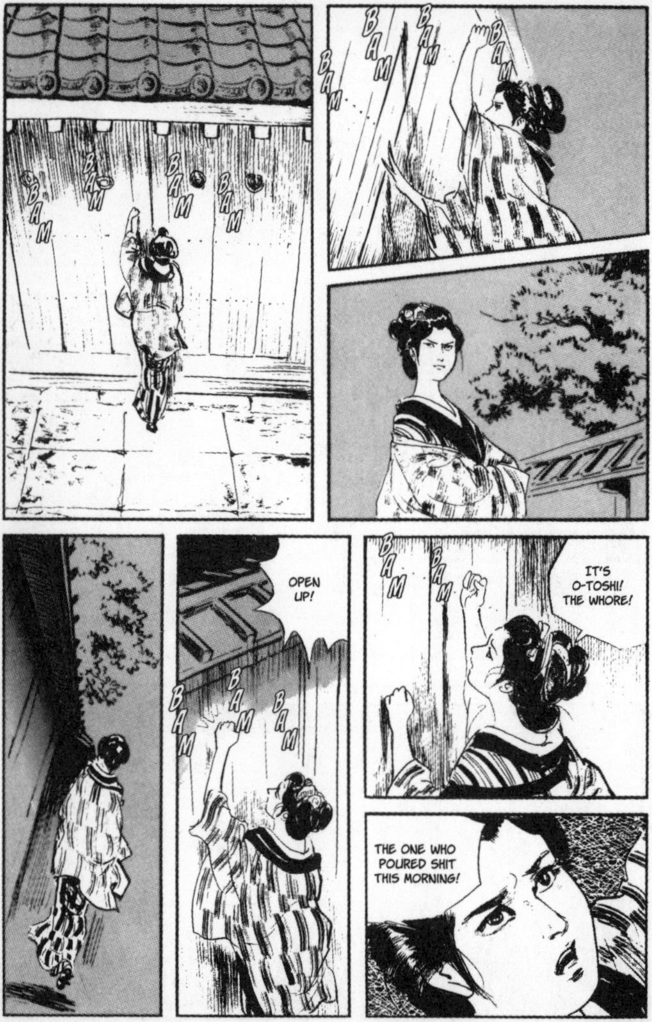
BAM
BAM
BAM
BAM
BAM
BAM
BAM
BAM
BAM
BAM
OPEN UP!
BAM
BAM
IT'S O-TOSHI! THE WHORE!
THE ONE WHO POURED SHIT THIS MORNING!

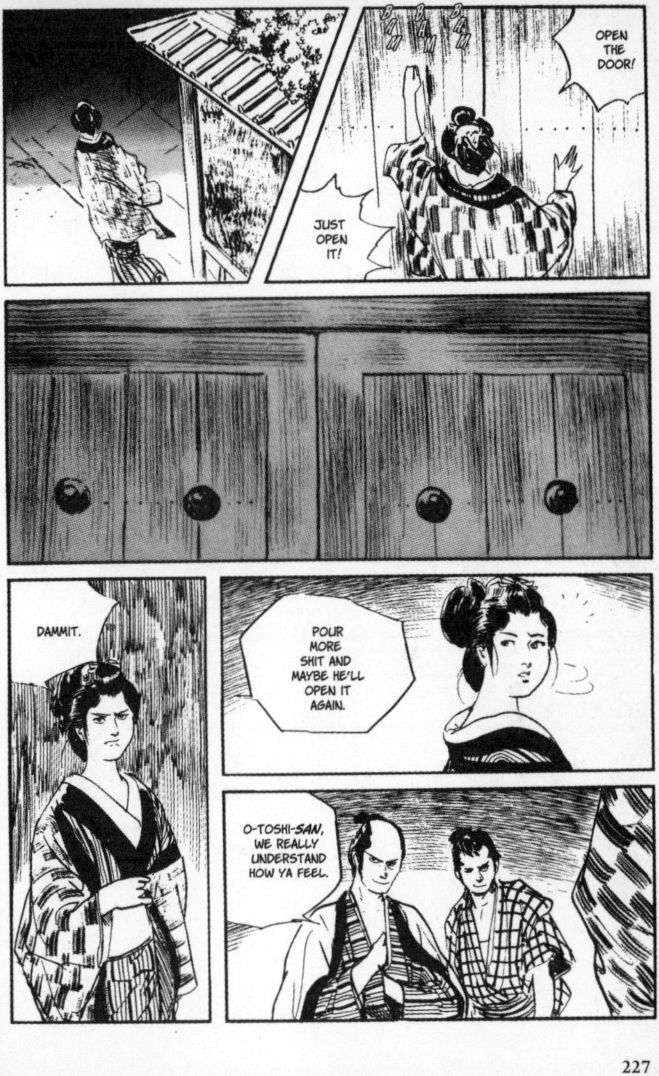
BAM BAM BAM
OPEN THE DOOR!
JUST OPEN IT!
DAMMIT.
POUR MORE SHIT AND MAYBE HE'LL OPEN IT AGAIN.
O-TOSHI-*SAN*, WE REALLY UNDERSTAND HOW YA FEEL.

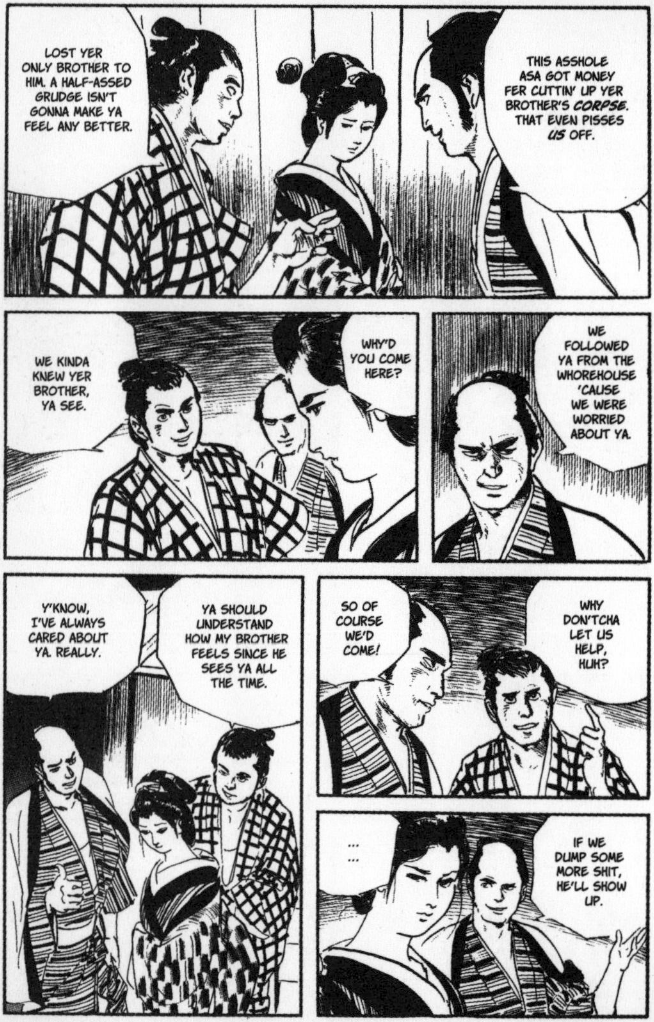

LOST YER ONLY BROTHER TO HIM. A HALF-ASSED GRUDGE ISN'T GONNA MAKE YA FEEL ANY BETTER.
THIS ASSHOLE ASA GOT MONEY FER CUTTIN' UP YER BROTHER'S *CORPSE*. THAT EVEN PISSES *US* OFF.
WE KINDA KNEW YER BROTHER, YA SEE.
WHY'D YOU COME HERE?
WE FOLLOWED YA FROM THE WHOREHOUSE 'CAUSE WE WERE WORRIED ABOUT YA.
Y'KNOW, I'VE ALWAYS CARED ABOUT YA. REALLY.
YA SHOULD UNDERSTAND HOW MY BROTHER FEELS SINCE HE SEES YA ALL THE TIME.
SO OF COURSE WE'D COME!
WHY DON'TCHA LET US HELP, HUH?
...
...
IF WE DUMP SOME MORE SHIT, HE'LL SHOW UP.

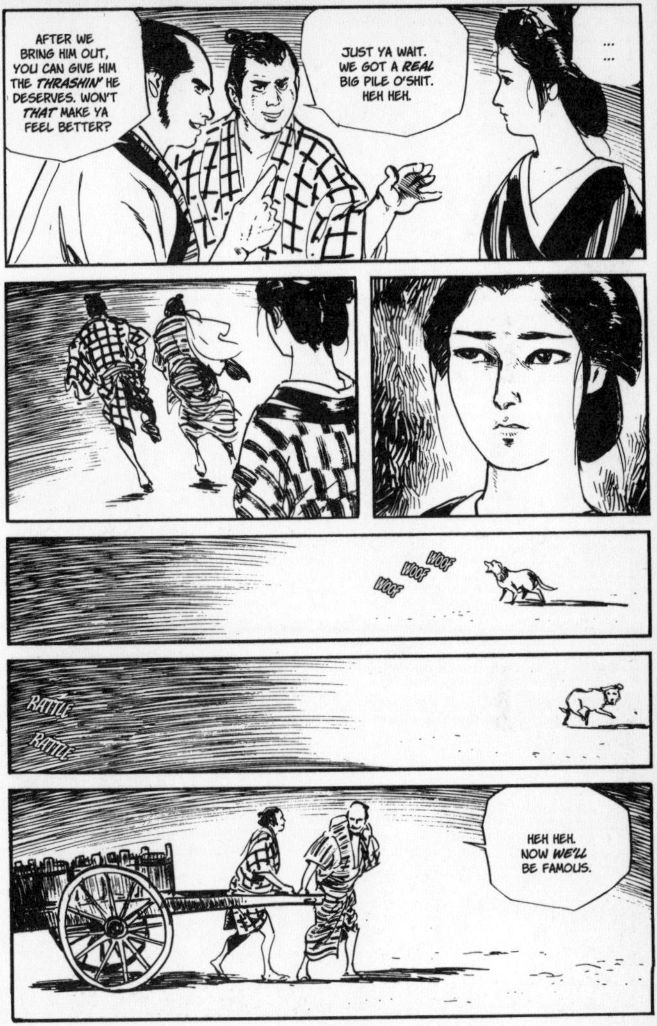
AFTER WE BRING HIM OUT, YOU CAN GIVE HIM THE *THRASHIN'* HE DESERVES. WON'T *THAT* MAKE YA FEEL BETTER?
JUST YA WAIT. WE GOT A *REAL* BIG PILE O'SHIT. HEH HEH.
...
...
WOOF
WOOF
WOOF
RATTLE
RATTLE
HEH HEH. NOW *WE'LL* BE FAMOUS.

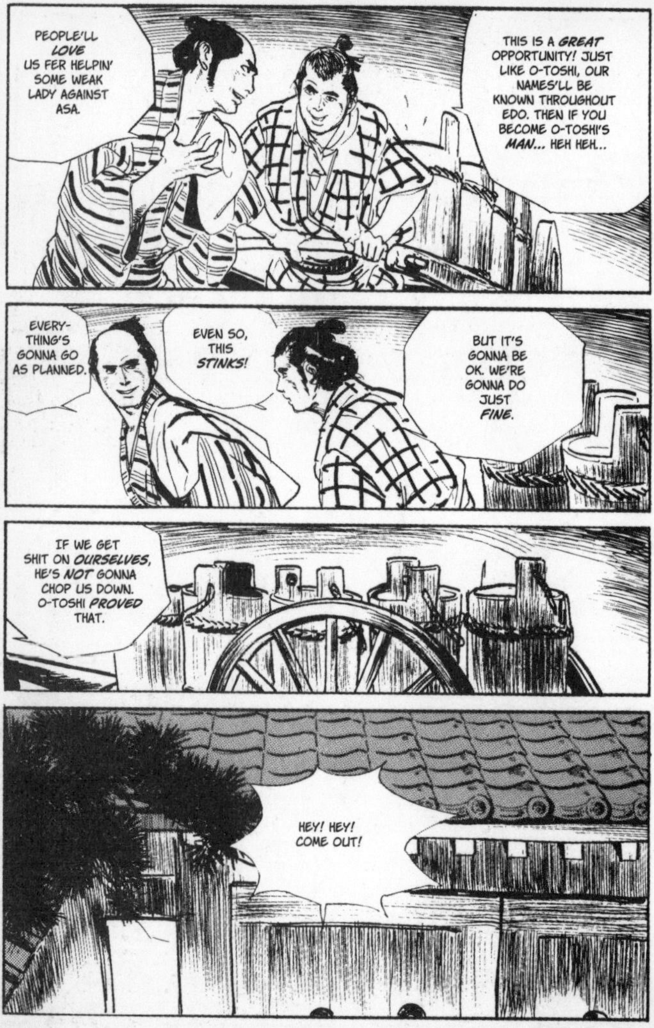
PEOPLE'LL LOVE US FER HELPIN' SOME WEAK LADY AGAINST ASA.
THIS IS A GREAT OPPORTUNITY! JUST LIKE O-TOSHI, OUR NAMES'LL BE KNOWN THROUGHOUT EDO. THEN IF YOU BECOME O-TOSHI'S MAN... HEH HEH...
EVERY-THING'S GONNA GO AS PLANNED.
EVEN SO, THIS STINKS!
BUT IT'S GONNA BE OK. WE'RE GONNA DO JUST FINE.
IF WE GET SHIT ON OURSELVES, HE'S NOT GONNA CHOP US DOWN. O-TOSHI PROVED THAT.
HEY! HEY! COME OUT!

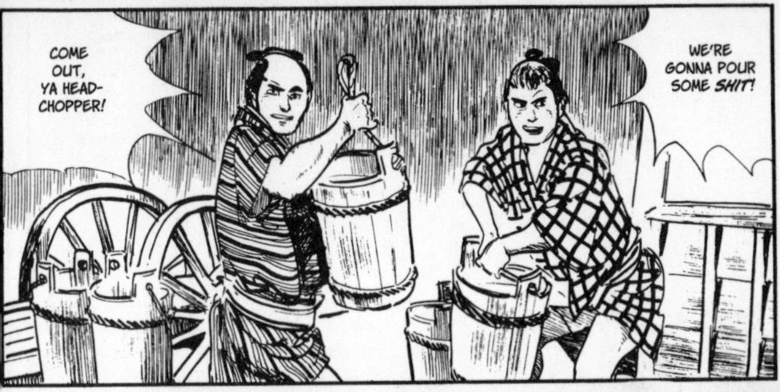
COME OUT, YA HEAD-CHOPPER!
WE'RE GONNA POUR SOME *SHIT*!
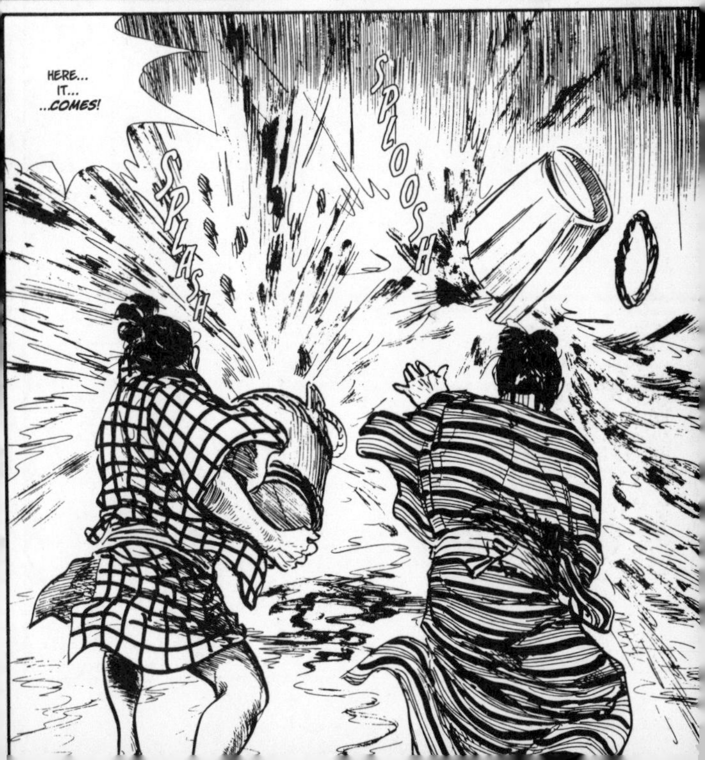
HERE... IT... ...*COMES*!
SPLASH
SPLOOSH

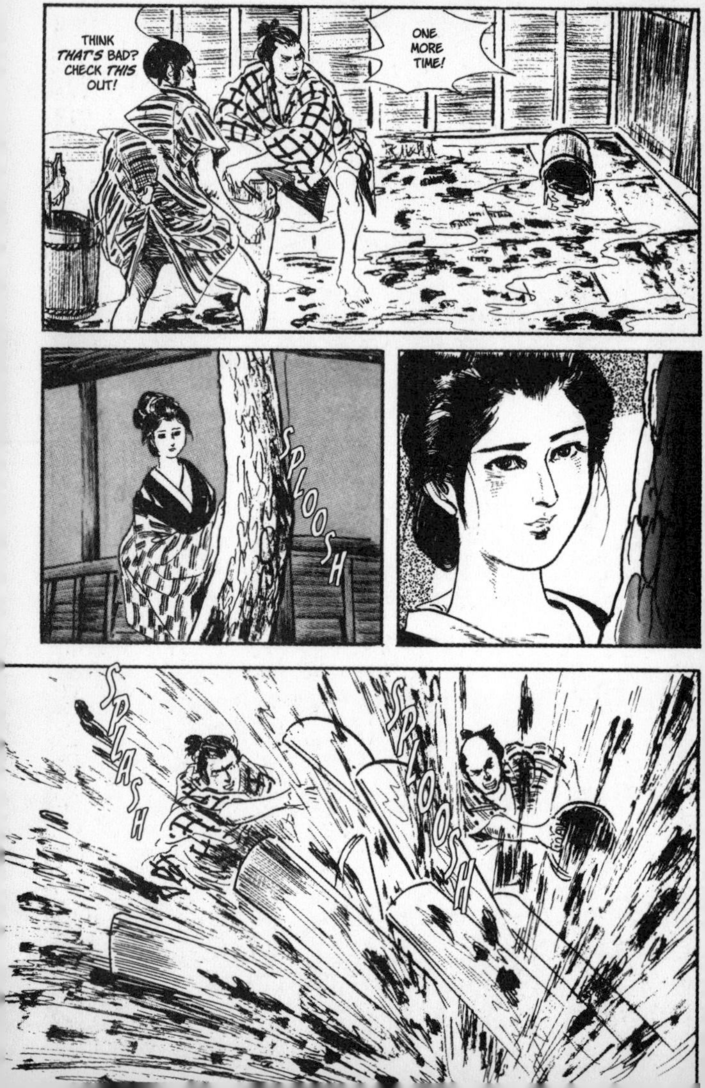
THINK THAT'S BAD? CHECK THIS OUT!
ONE MORE TIME!
SPLOOSH
SPLASH
SPLOOSH

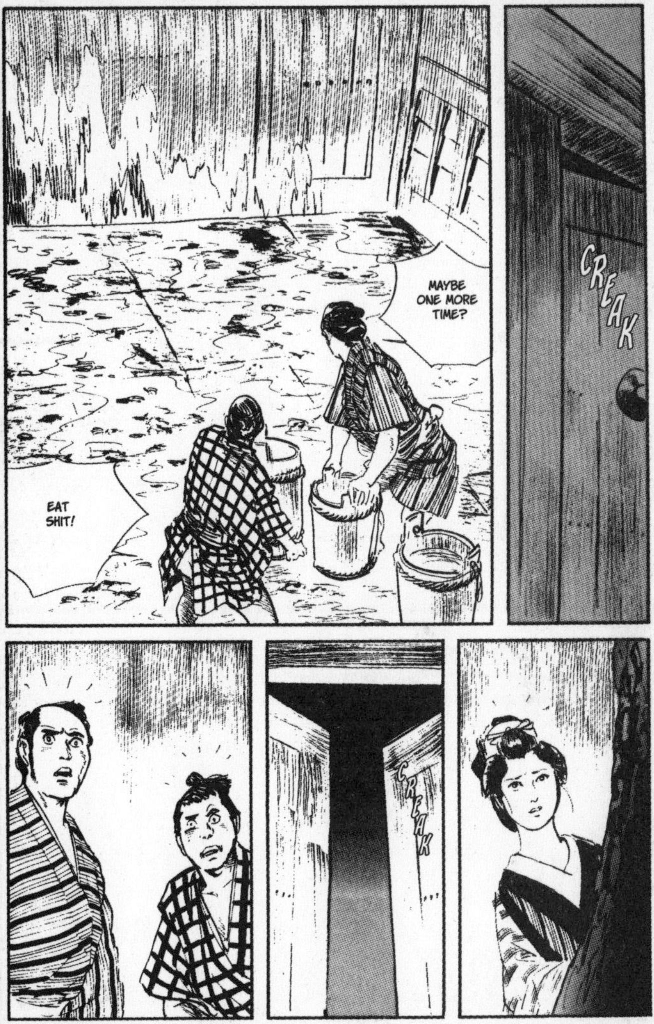
MAYBE ONE MORE TIME?
EAT SHIT!
CREAK
CREAK

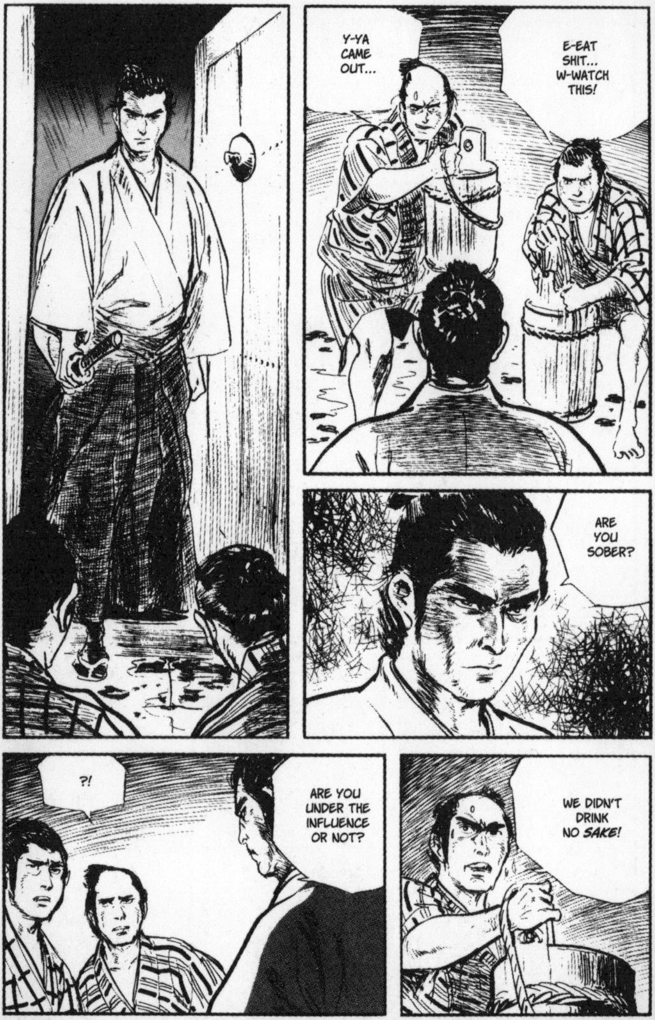
Y-YA CAME OUT...
E-EAT SHIT... W-WATCH THIS!
ARE YOU SOBER?
?!
ARE YOU UNDER THE INFLUENCE OR NOT?
WE DIDN'T DRINK NO *SAKE*!

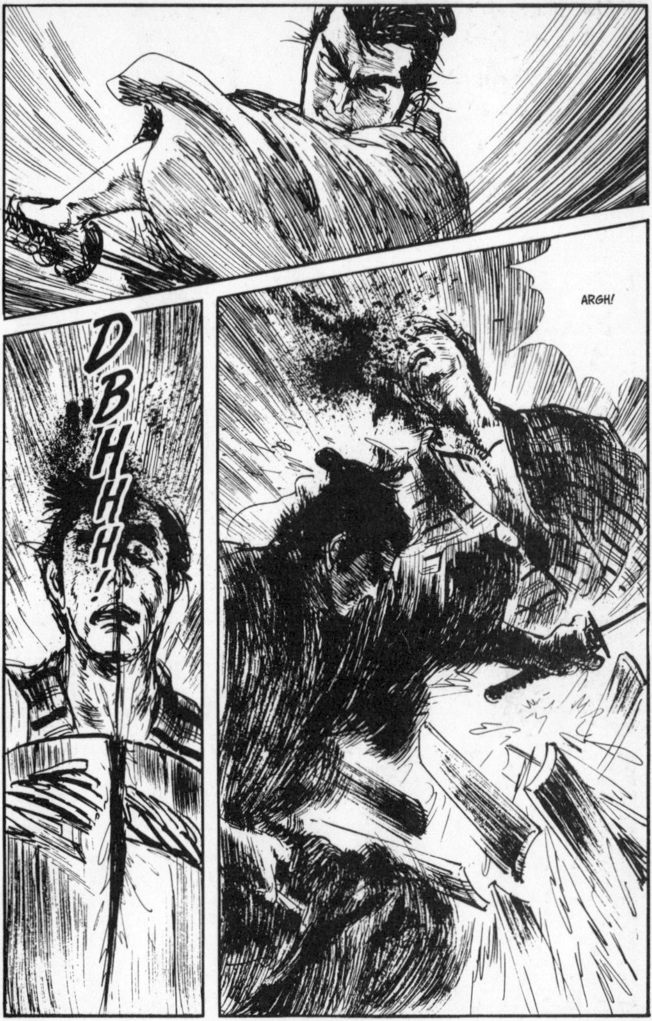
DBHHHH!
ARGH!

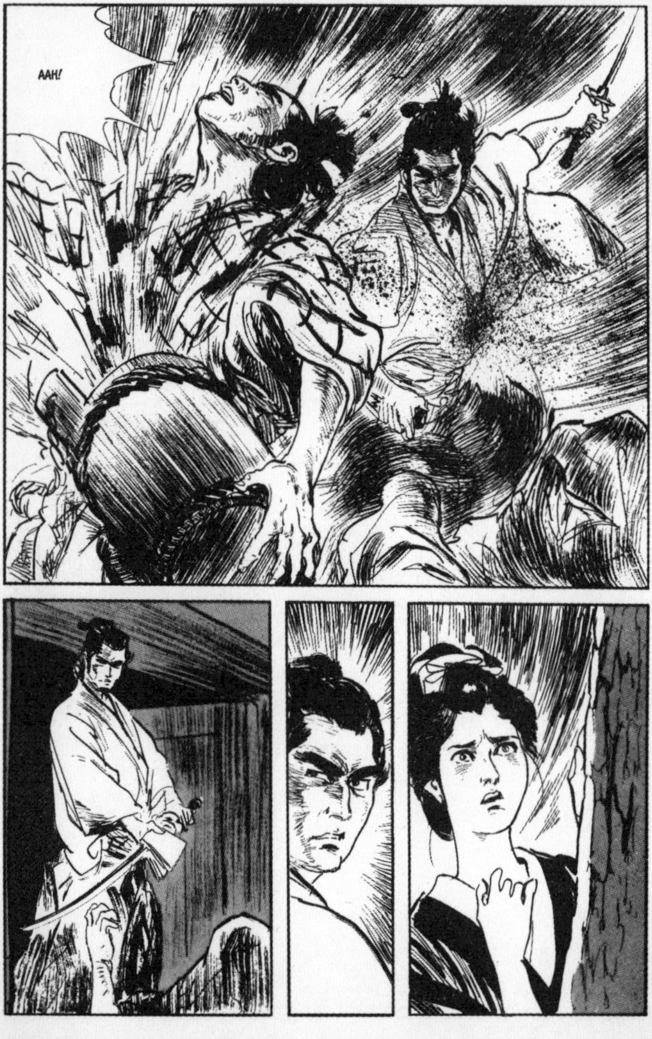
AAH!

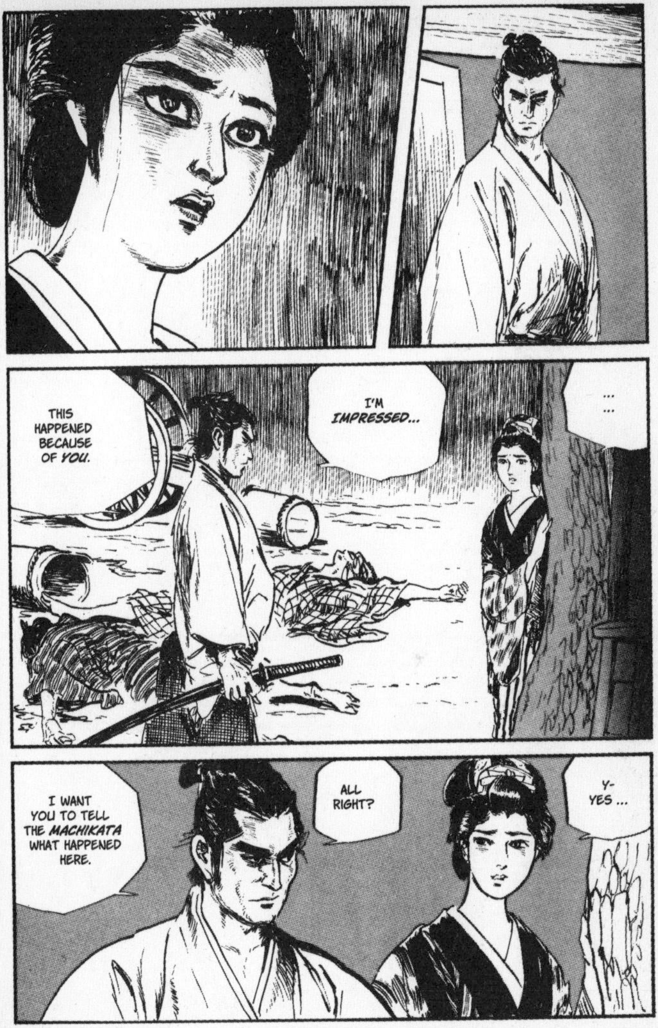
THIS HAPPENED BECAUSE OF *YOU*.
I'M *IMPRESSED*...
...
...
I WANT YOU TO TELL THE *MACHIKATA* WHAT HAPPENED HERE.
ALL RIGHT?
Y- YES ...

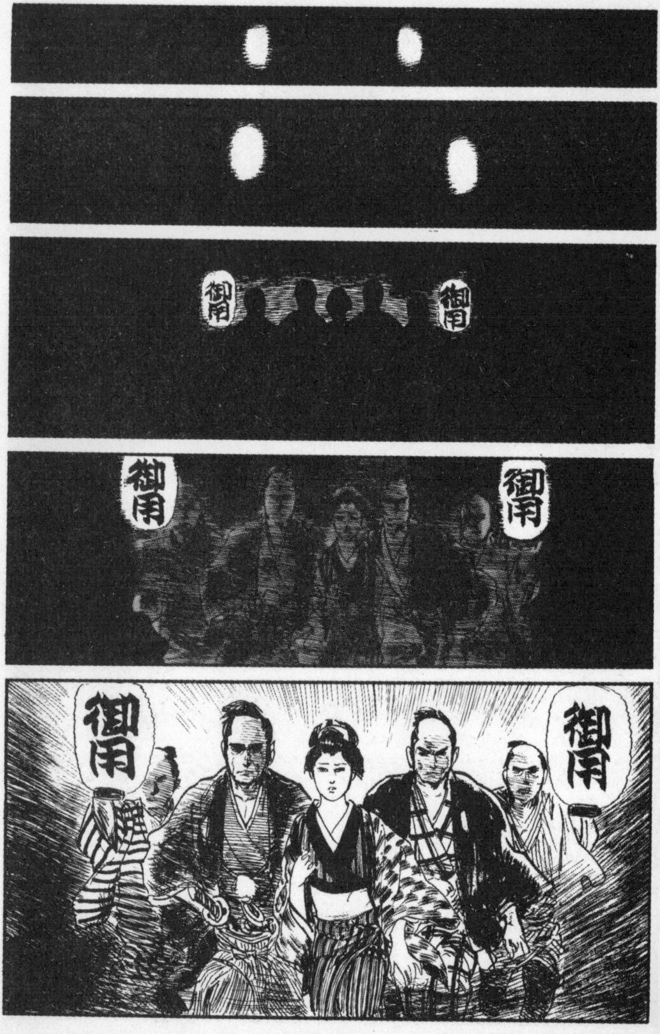
御用
御用
御用
御用
御用
御用

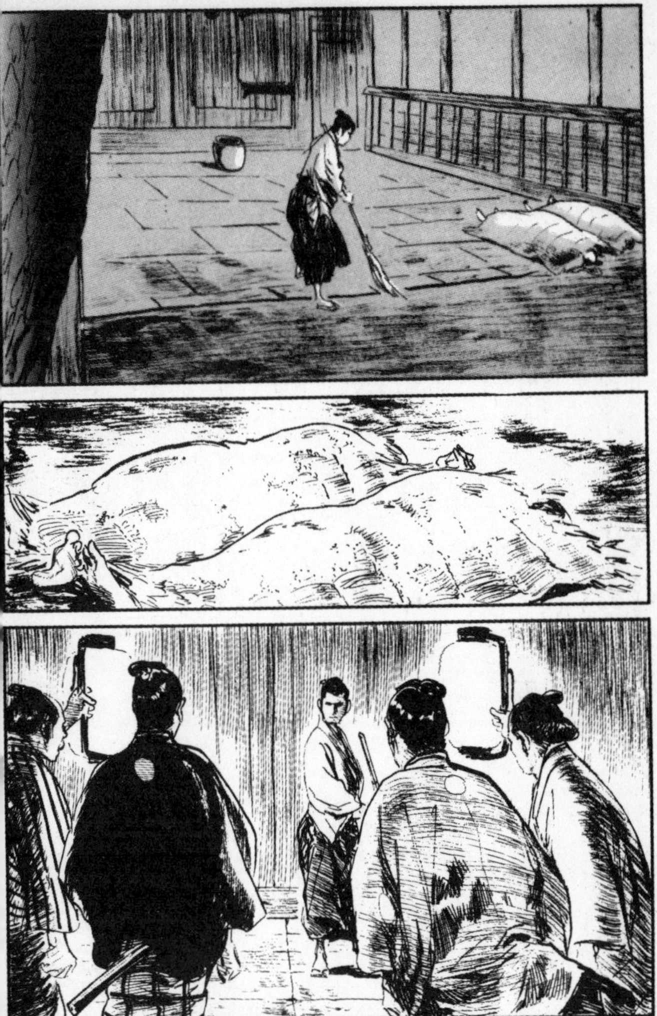

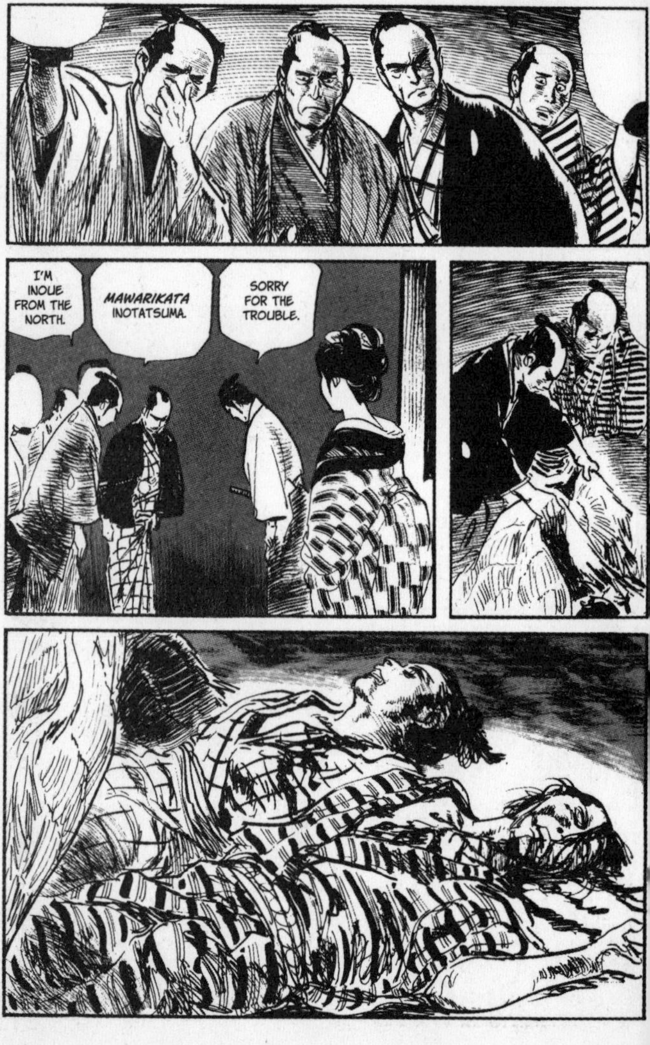
I'M INOUE FROM THE NORTH.
MAWARIKATA INOTATSUMA.
SORRY FOR THE TROUBLE.

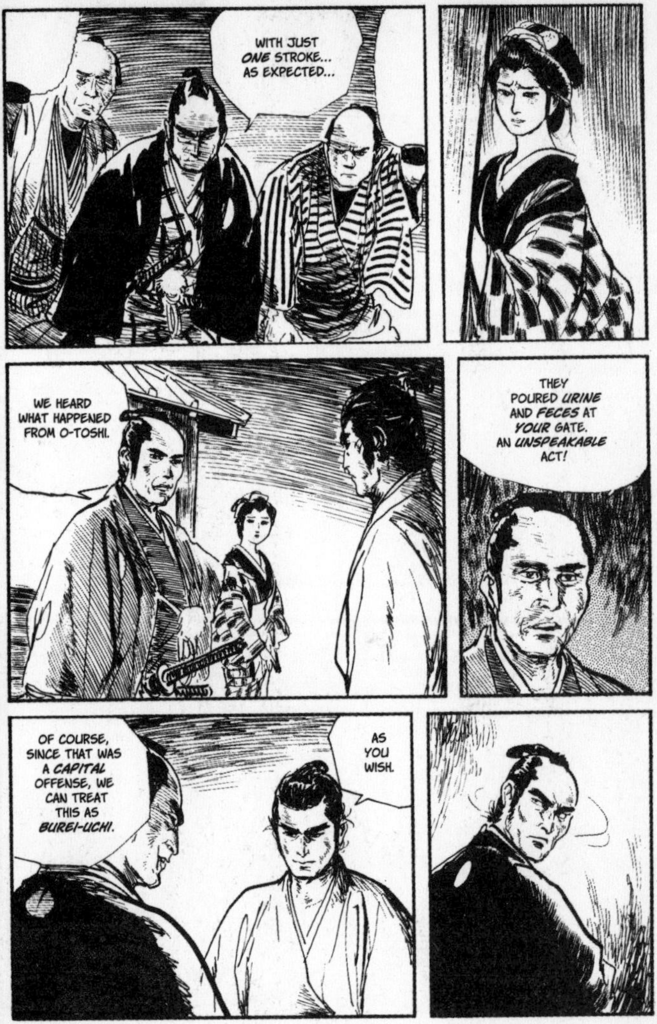
WITH JUST ONE STROKE... AS EXPECTED...
WE HEARD WHAT HAPPENED FROM O-TOSHI.
THEY POURED URINE AND FECES AT YOUR GATE. AN UNSPEAKABLE ACT!
OF COURSE, SINCE THAT WAS A CAPITAL OFFENSE, WE CAN TREAT THIS AS BUREI-UCHI.
AS YOU WISH.

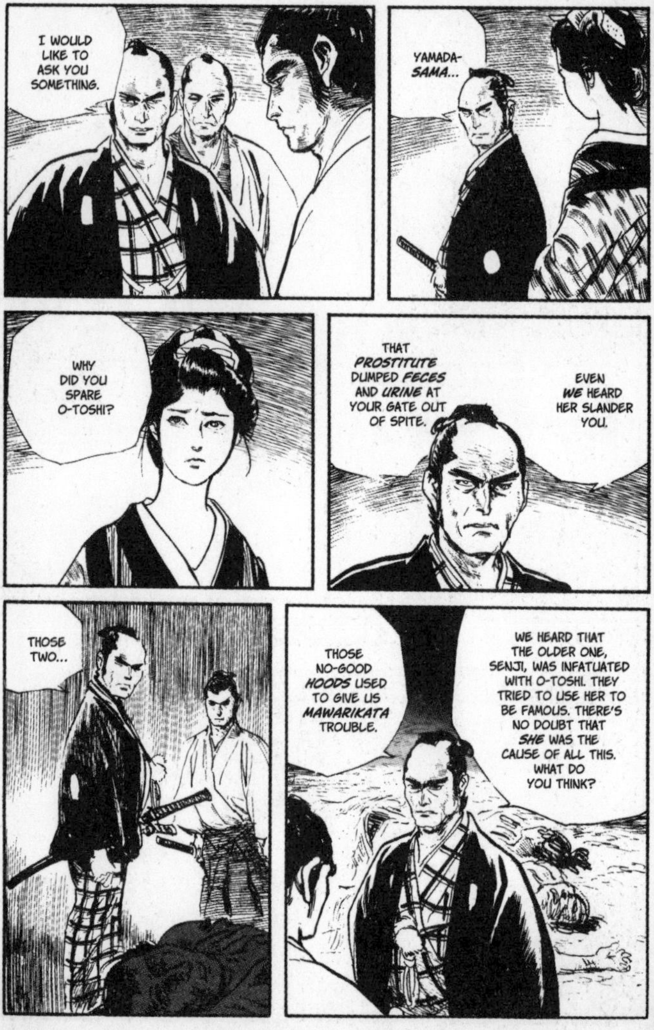
I WOULD LIKE TO ASK YOU SOMETHING.
YAMADA-SAMA...
WHY DID YOU SPARE O-TOSHI?
THAT PROSTITUTE DUMPED FECES AND URINE AT YOUR GATE OUT OF SPITE.
EVEN WE HEARD HER SLANDER YOU.
THOSE TWO...
THOSE NO-GOOD HOODS USED TO GIVE US MAWARIKATA TROUBLE.
WE HEARD THAT THE OLDER ONE, SENJI, WAS INFATUATED WITH O-TOSHI. THEY TRIED TO USE HER TO BE FAMOUS. THERE'S NO DOUBT THAT SHE WAS THE CAUSE OF ALL THIS. WHAT DO YOU THINK?

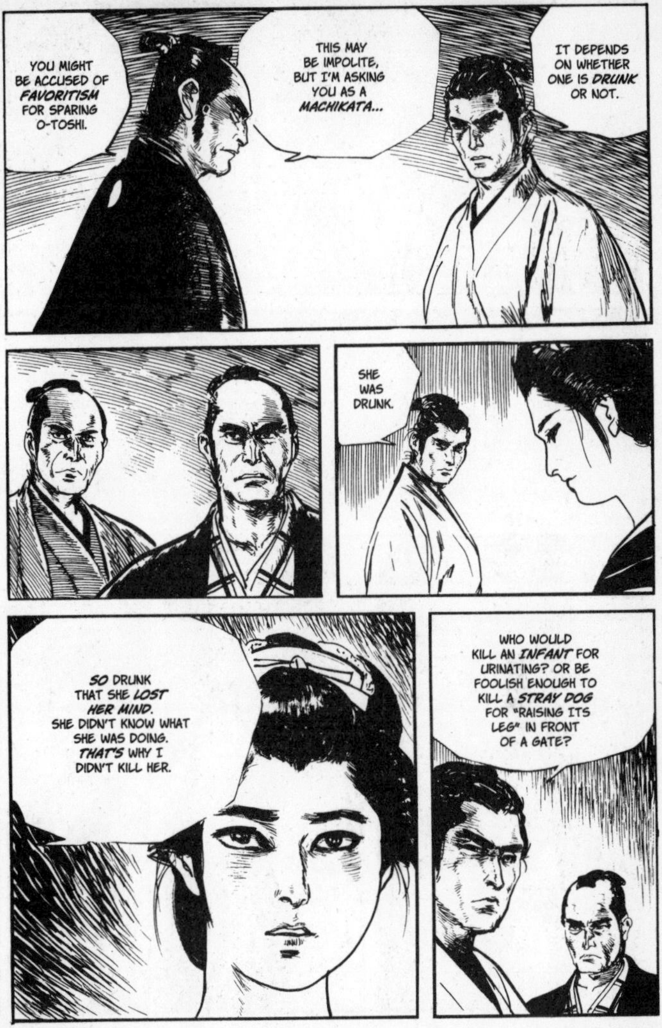
YOU MIGHT BE ACCUSED OF FAVORITISM FOR SPARING O-TOSHI.
THIS MAY BE IMPOLITE, BUT I'M ASKING YOU AS A MACHIKATA...
IT DEPENDS ON WHETHER ONE IS DRUNK OR NOT.
SHE WAS DRUNK.
SO DRUNK THAT SHE LOST HER MIND. SHE DIDN'T KNOW WHAT SHE WAS DOING. THAT'S WHY I DIDN'T KILL HER.
WHO WOULD KILL AN INFANT FOR URINATING? OR BE FOOLISH ENOUGH TO KILL A STRAY DOG FOR "RAISING ITS LEG" IN FRONT OF A GATE?

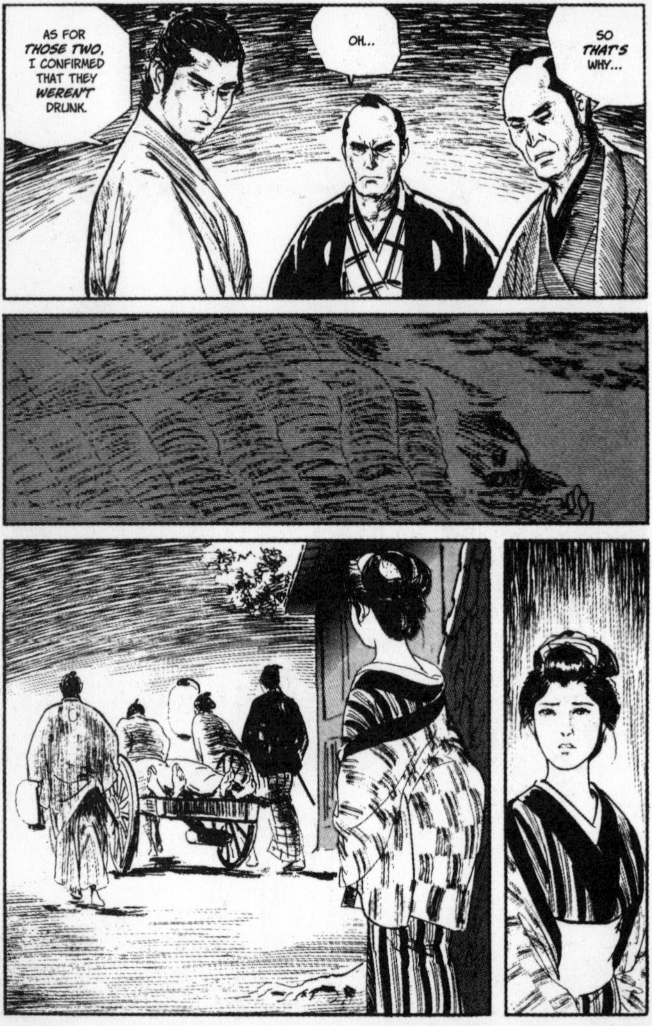
AS FOR *THOSE TWO*, I CONFIRMED THAT THEY *WEREN'T* DRUNK.
OH...
SO *THAT'S* WHY...

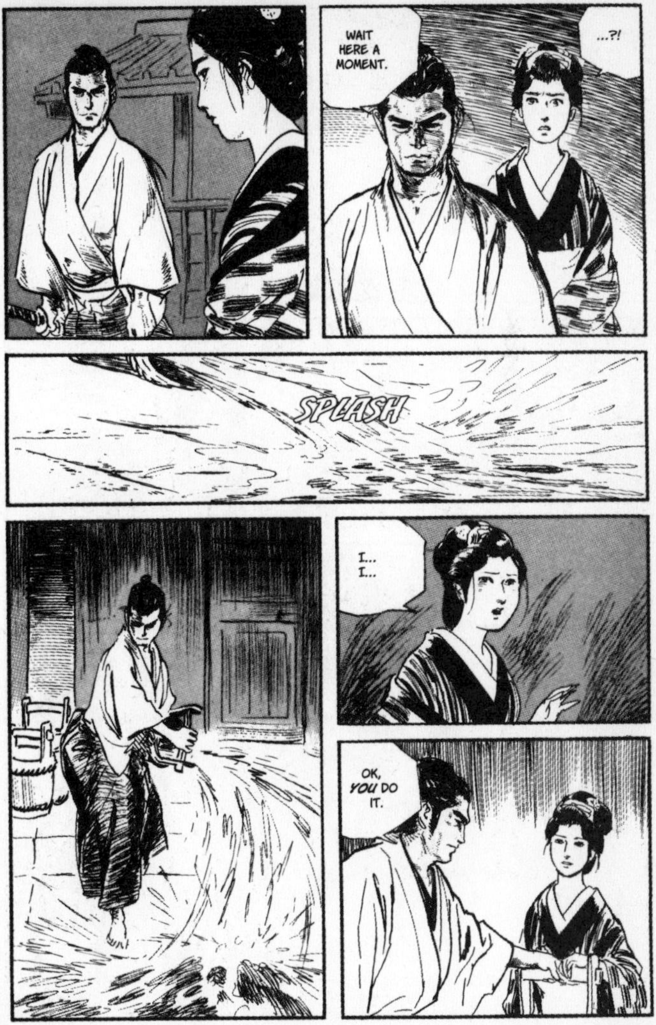
WAIT HERE A MOMENT.
...?!
SPLASH
I... I...
OK, YOU DO IT.

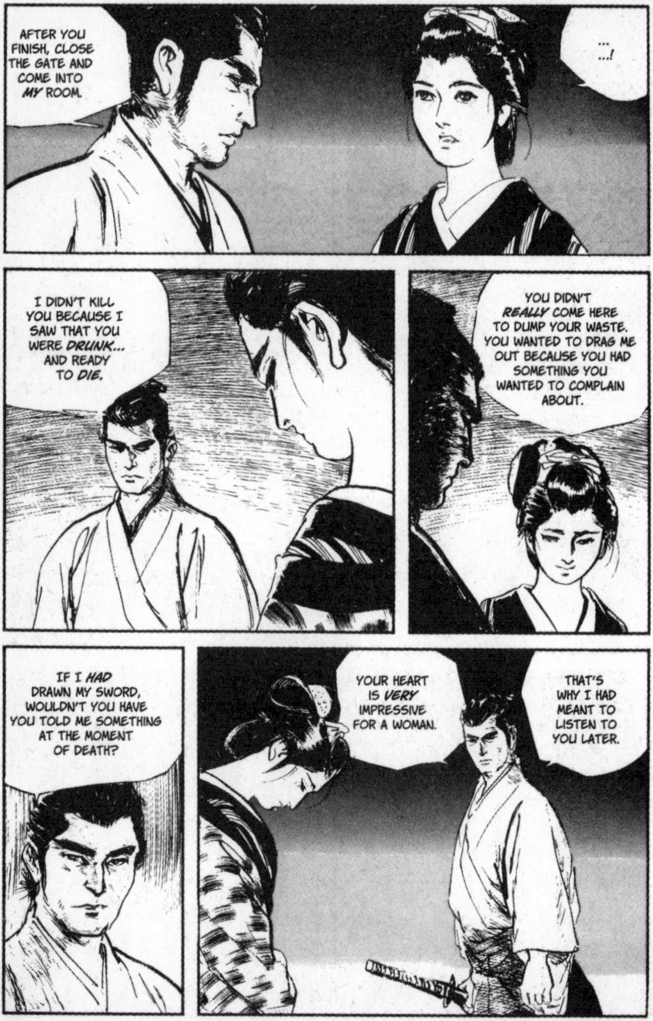
AFTER YOU FINISH, CLOSE THE GATE AND COME INTO *MY* ROOM.
... ...!
I DIDN'T KILL YOU BECAUSE I SAW THAT YOU WERE *DRUNK*... AND READY TO *DIE*.
YOU DIDN'T *REALLY* COME HERE TO DUMP YOUR WASTE. YOU WANTED TO DRAG ME OUT BECAUSE YOU HAD SOMETHING YOU WANTED TO COMPLAIN ABOUT.
IF I *HAD* DRAWN MY SWORD, WOULDN'T YOU HAVE YOU TOLD ME SOMETHING AT THE MOMENT OF DEATH?
YOUR HEART IS *VERY* IMPRESSIVE FOR A WOMAN.
THAT'S WHY I HAD MEANT TO LISTEN TO YOU LATER.

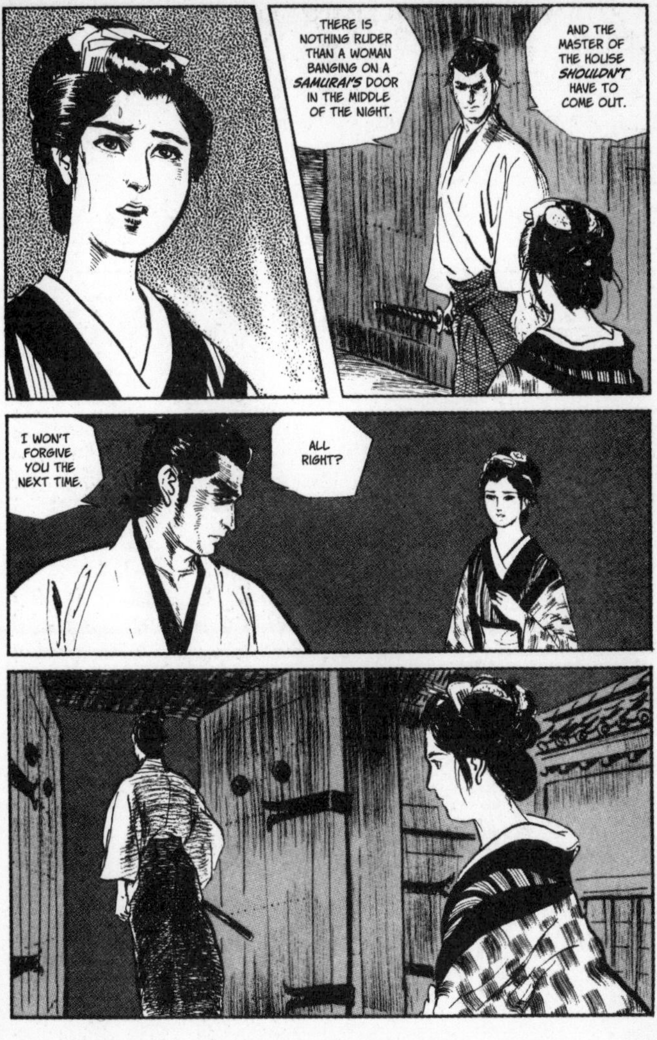
THERE IS NOTHING RUDER THAN A WOMAN BANGING ON A *SAMURAI'S* DOOR IN THE MIDDLE OF THE NIGHT.
AND THE MASTER OF THE HOUSE *SHOULDN'T* HAVE TO COME OUT.
I WON'T FORGIVE YOU THE NEXT TIME.
ALL RIGHT?

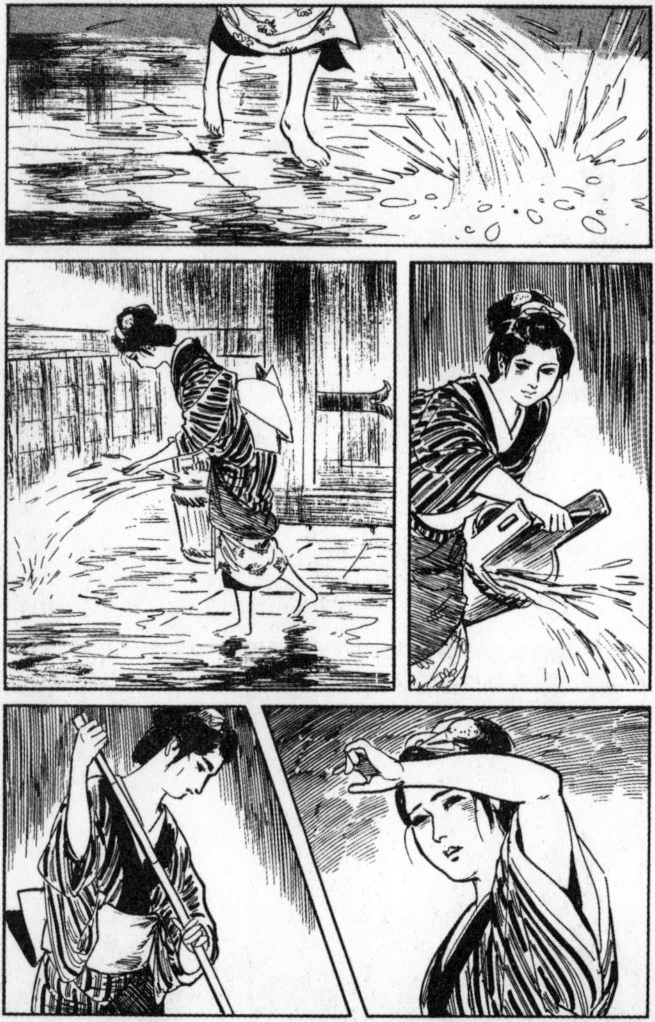

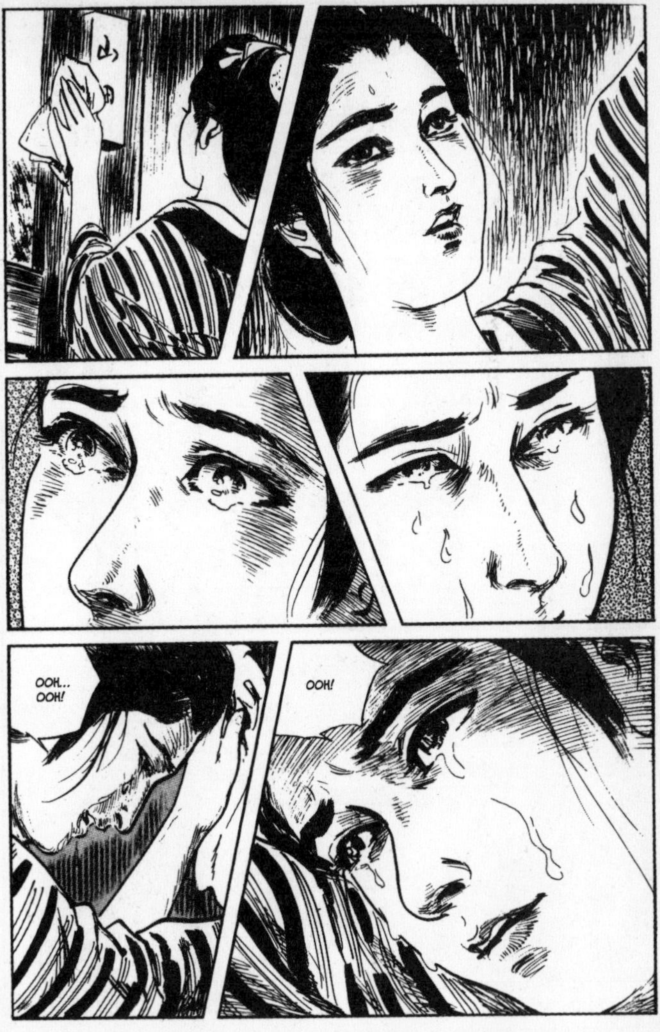
OOH... OOH!
OOH!

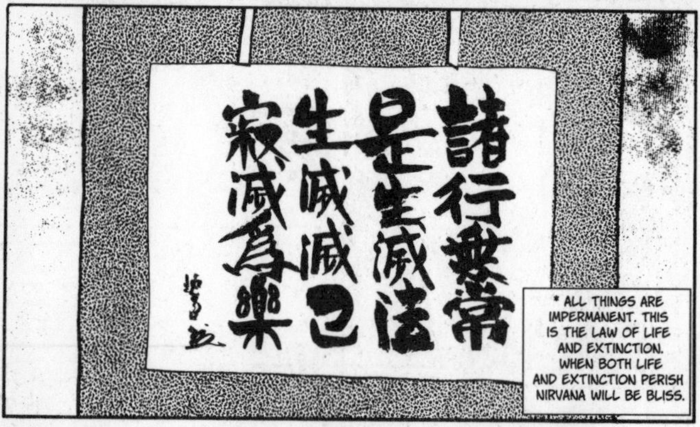
諸行無常
是生滅法
生滅滅已
寂滅為樂
* ALL THINGS ARE IMPERMANENT. THIS IS THE LAW OF LIFE AND EXTINCTION. WHEN BOTH LIFE AND EXTINCTION PERISH NIRVANA WILL BE BLISS.

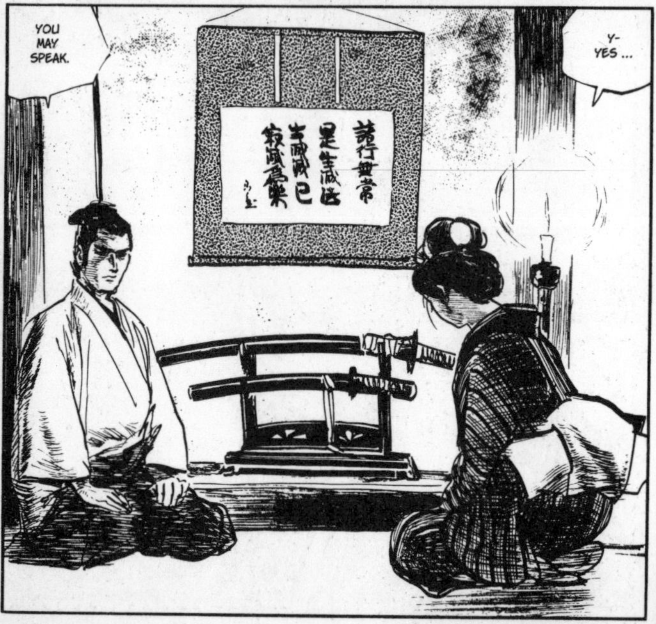
YOU MAY SPEAK.
Y- YES ...

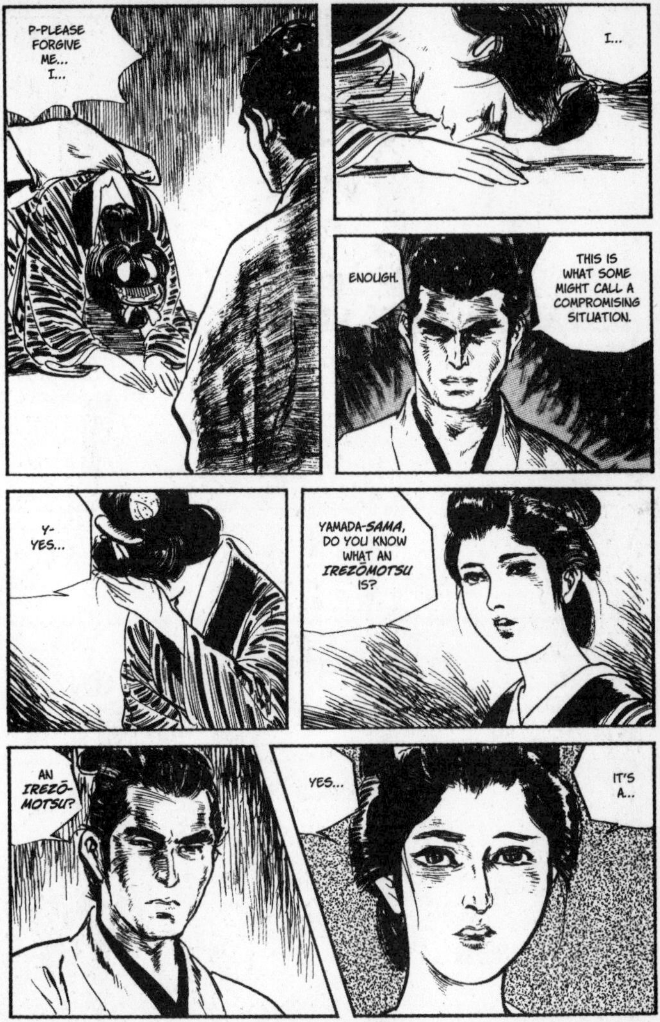
P-PLEASE FORGIVE ME... I...
I...
ENOUGH.
THIS IS WHAT SOME MIGHT CALL A COMPROMISING SITUATION.
Y-YES...
YAMADA-*SAMA*, DO YOU KNOW WHAT AN *IREZŌMOTSU* IS?
AN *IREZŌ-MOTSU*?
YES...
IT'S A...

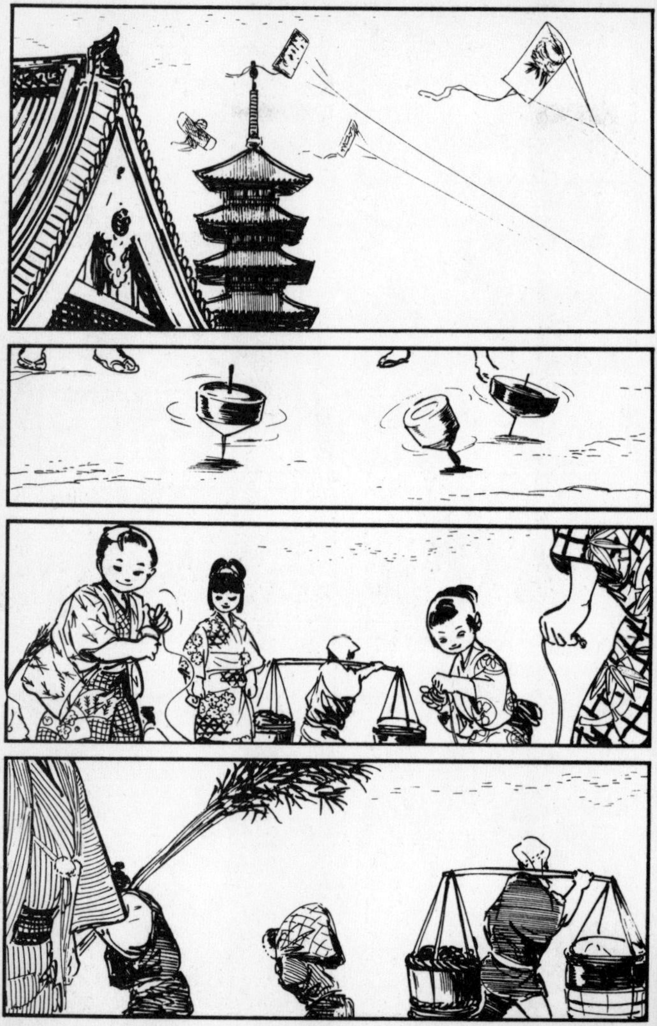

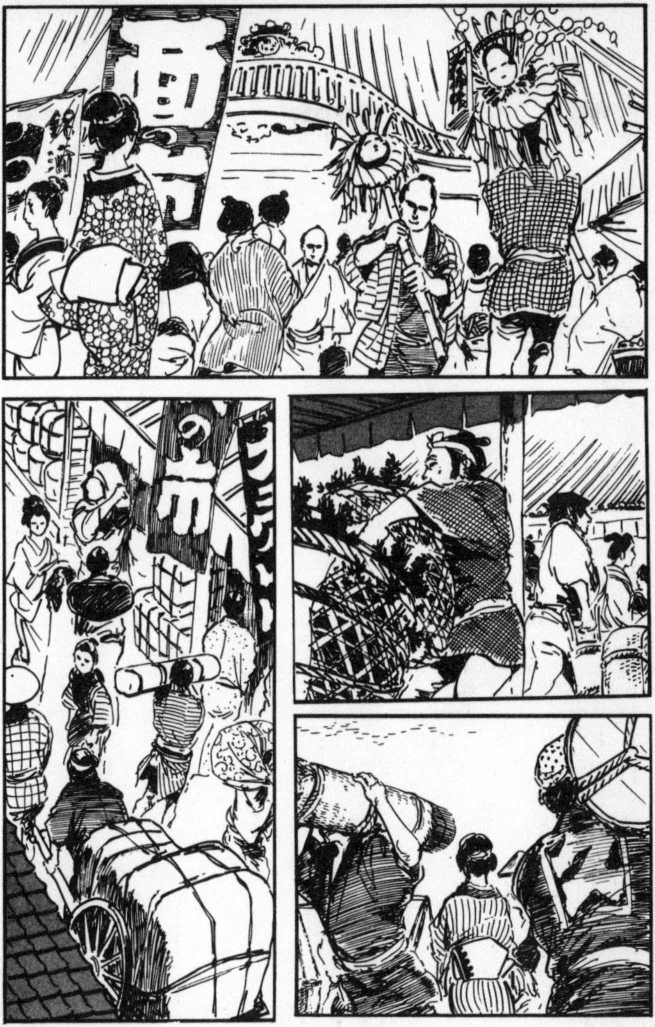

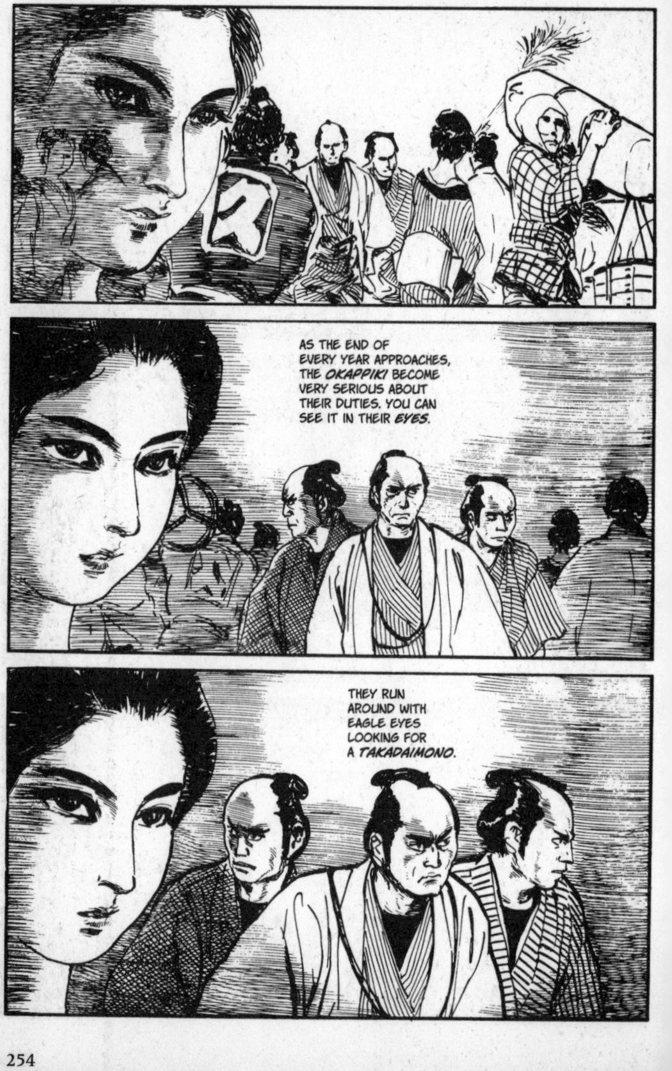
AS THE END OF EVERY YEAR APPROACHES, THE *OKAPPIKI* BECOME VERY SERIOUS ABOUT THEIR DUTIES. YOU CAN SEE IT IN THEIR *EYES*.
THEY RUN AROUND WITH EAGLE EYES LOOKING FOR A *TAKADAIMONO*.

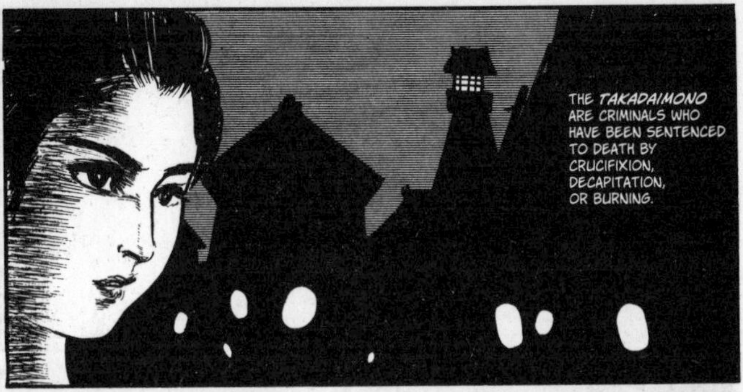
THE *TAKADAIMONO* ARE CRIMINALS WHO HAVE BEEN SENTENCED TO DEATH BY CRUCIFIXION, DECAPITATION, OR BURNING.

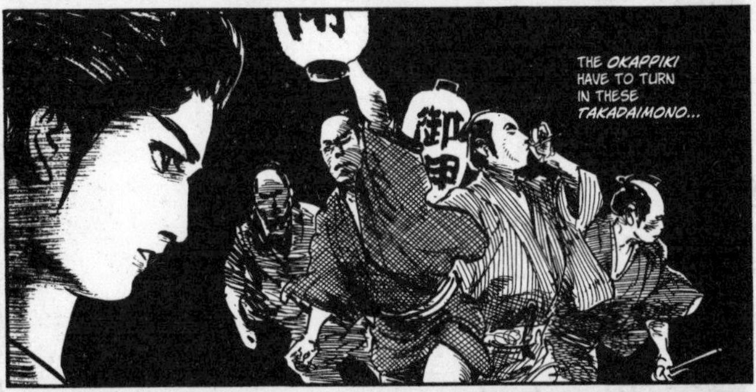
THE *OKAPPIKI* HAVE TO TURN IN THESE *TAKADAIMONO*...

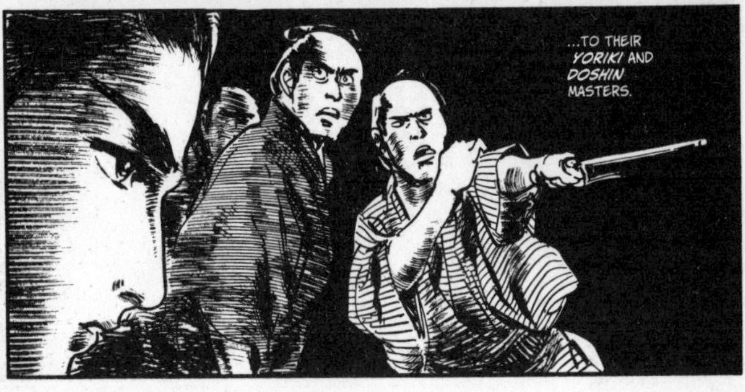
...TO THEIR *YORIKI* AND *DOSHIN* MASTERS.

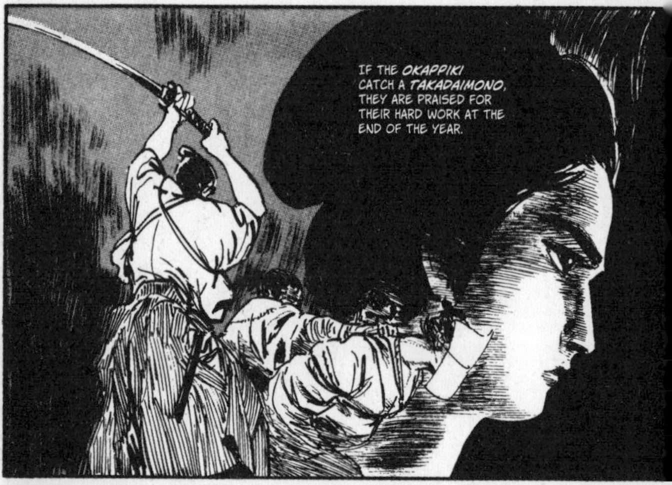
IF THE *OKAPPIKI* CATCH A *TAKADAIMONO*, THEY ARE PRAISED FOR THEIR HARD WORK AT THE END OF THE YEAR.
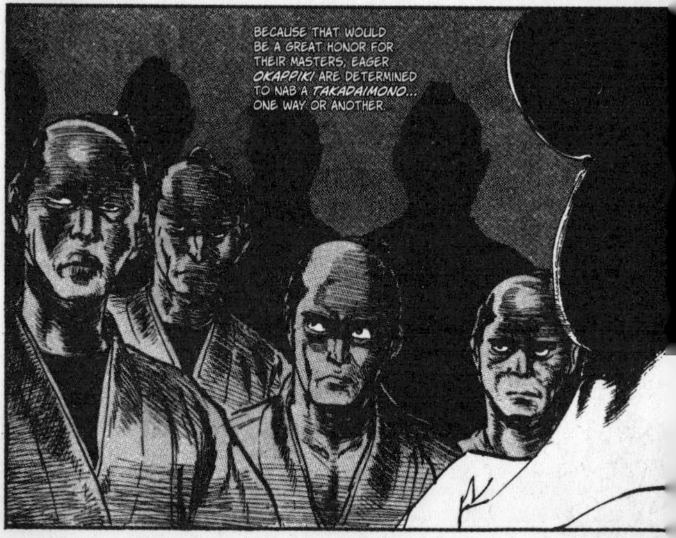
BECAUSE THAT WOULD BE A GREAT HONOR FOR THEIR MASTERS, EAGER *OKAPPIKI* ARE DETERMINED TO NAB A *TAKADAIMONO*... ONE WAY OR ANOTHER.

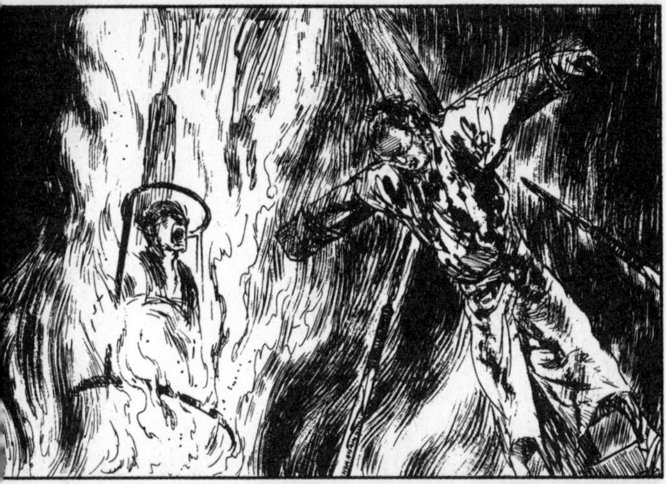

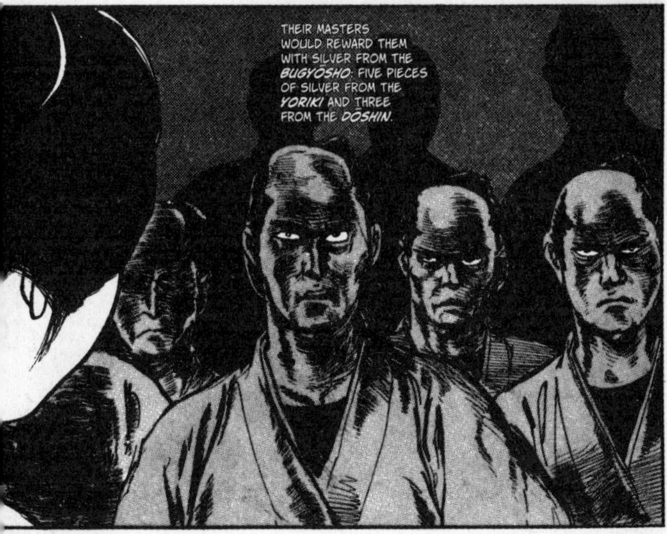
THEIR MASTERS WOULD REWARD THEM WITH SILVER FROM THE *BUGYŌSHO*: FIVE PIECES OF SILVER FROM THE *YORIKI* AND THREE FROM THE *DŌSHIN*.

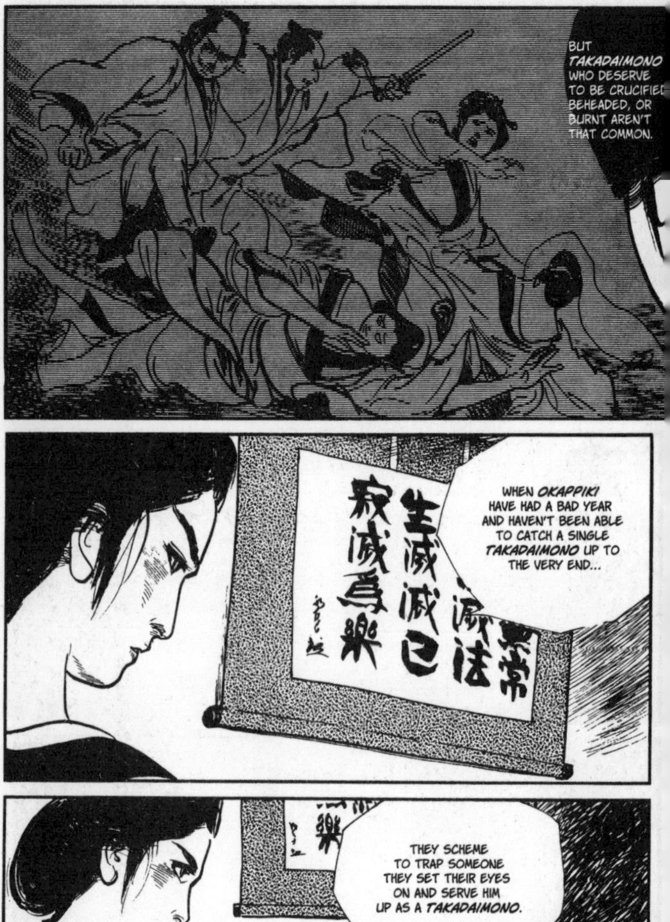
BUT *TAKADAIMONO* WHO DESERVE TO BE CRUCIFIED BEHEADED, OR BURNT AREN'T THAT COMMON.
WHEN *OKAPPIKI* HAVE HAD A BAD YEAR AND HAVEN'T BEEN ABLE TO CATCH A SINGLE *TAKADAIMONO* UP TO THE VERY END...
THEY SCHEME TO TRAP SOMEONE THEY SET THEIR EYES ON AND SERVE HIM UP AS A *TAKADAIMONO*.

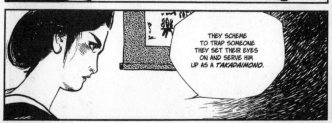

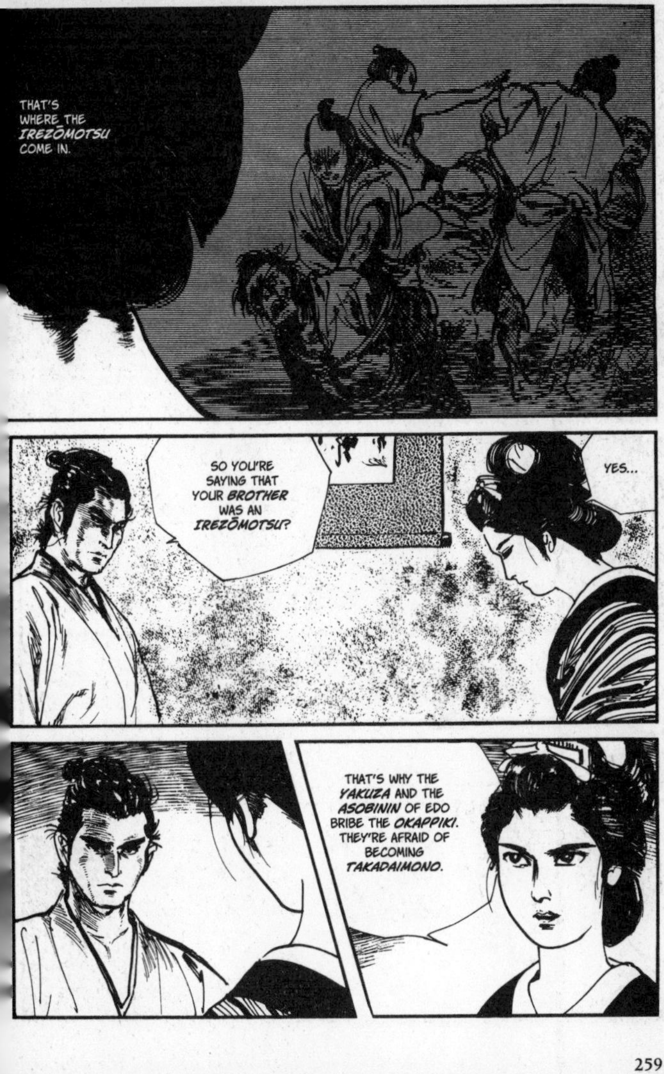
THAT'S WHERE THE IREZŌMOTSU COME IN.
SO YOU'RE SAYING THAT YOUR BROTHER WAS AN IREZŌMOTSU?
YES...
THAT'S WHY THE YAKUZA AND THE ASOBININ OF EDO BRIBE THE OKAPPIKI. THEY'RE AFRAID OF BECOMING TAKADAIMONO.

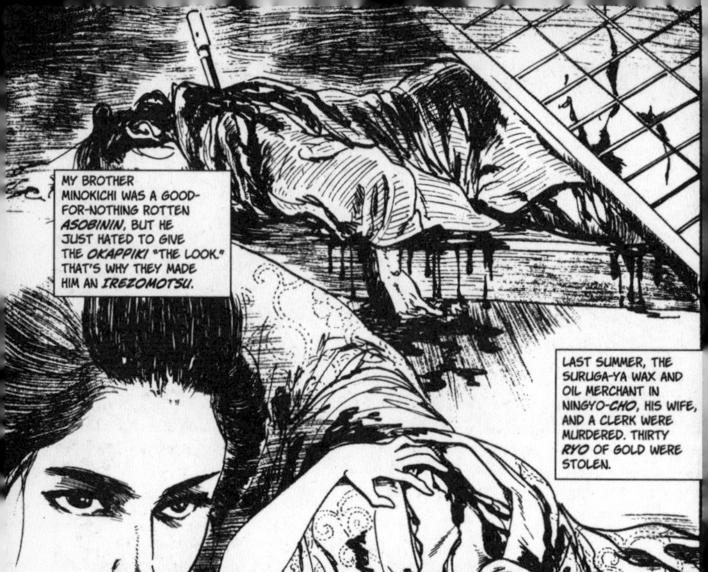
MY BROTHER MINOKICHI WAS A GOOD-FOR-NOTHING ROTTEN *ASOBININ*, BUT HE JUST HATED TO GIVE THE *OKAPPIKI* "THE LOOK." THAT'S WHY THEY MADE HIM AN *IREZOMOTSU*.
LAST SUMMER, THE SURUGA-YA WAX AND OIL MERCHANT IN NINGYO-*CHO*, HIS WIFE, AND A CLERK WERE MURDERED. THIRTY *RYO* OF GOLD WERE STOLEN.

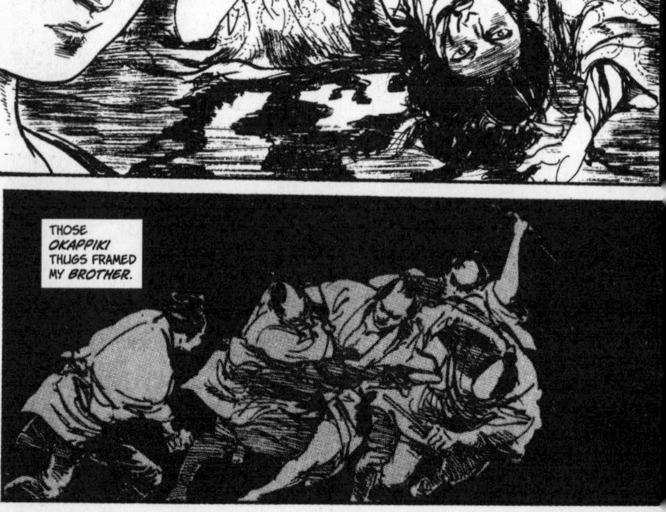
THOSE *OKAPPIKI* THUGS FRAMED MY *BROTHER*.

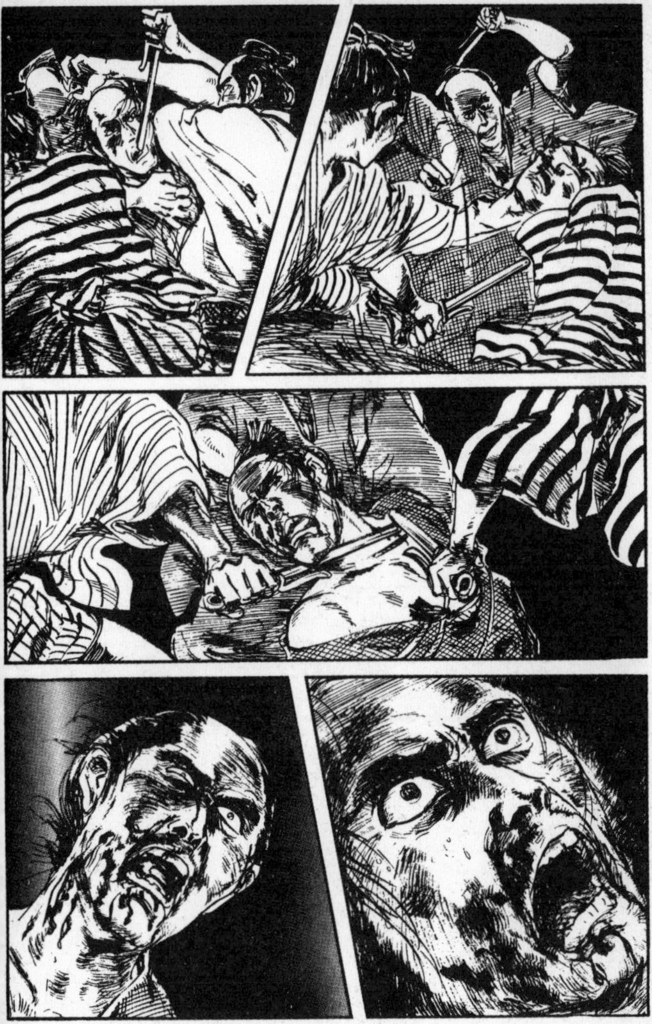

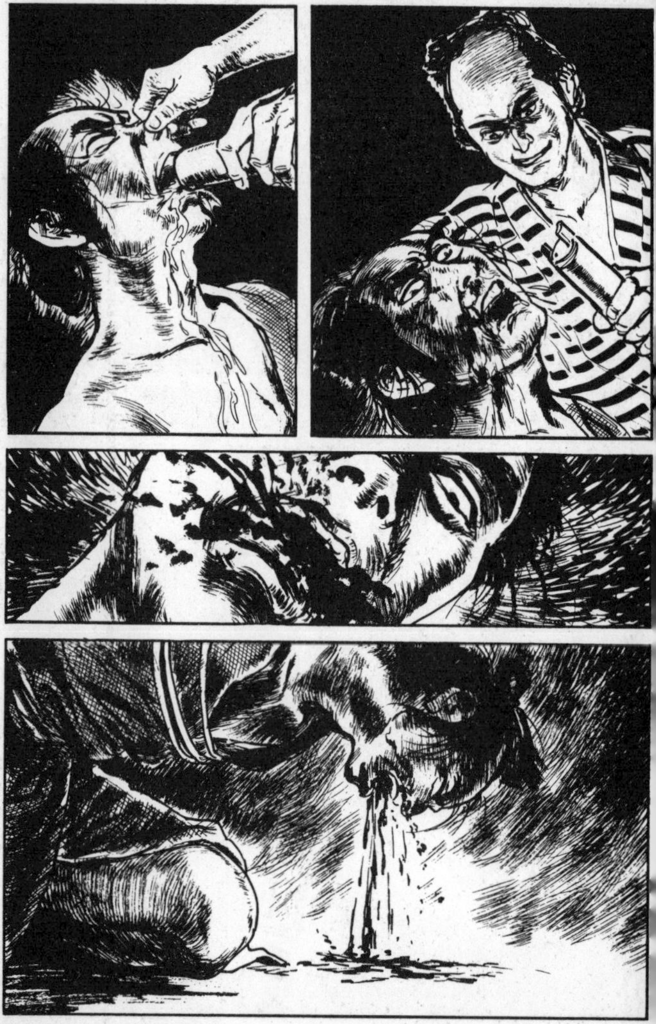

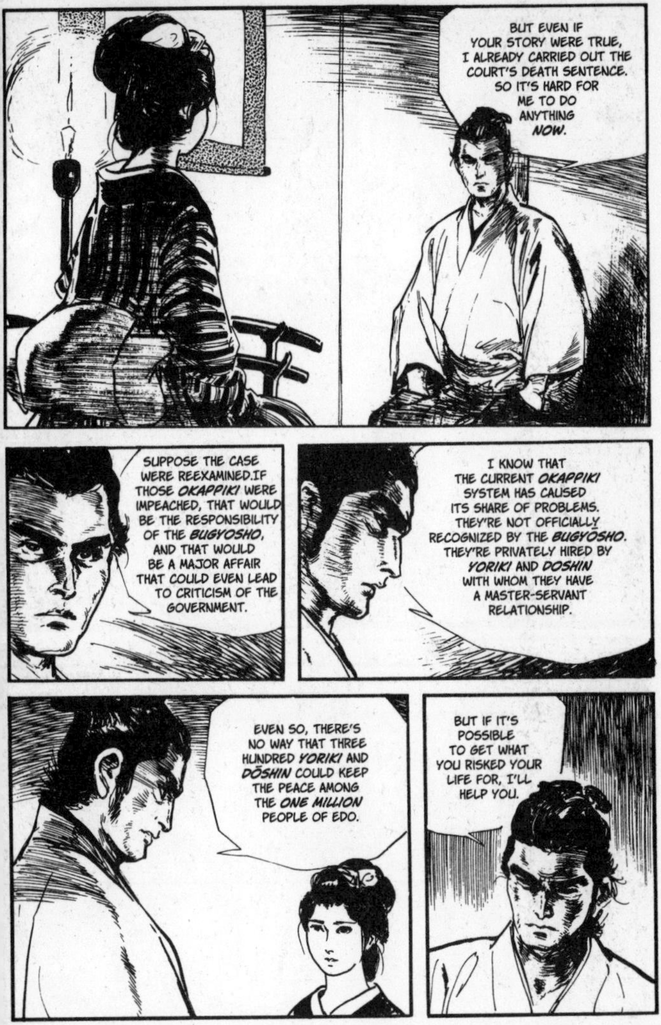
BUT EVEN IF YOUR STORY WERE TRUE, I ALREADY CARRIED OUT THE COURT'S DEATH SENTENCE. SO IT'S HARD FOR ME TO DO ANYTHING *NOW*.
SUPPOSE THE CASE WERE REEXAMINED.IF THOSE *OKAPPIKI* WERE IMPEACHED, THAT WOULD BE THE RESPONSIBILITY OF THE *BUGYOSHO*, AND THAT WOULD BE A MAJOR AFFAIR THAT COULD EVEN LEAD TO CRITICISM OF THE GOVERNMENT.
I KNOW THAT THE CURRENT *OKAPPIKI* SYSTEM HAS CAUSED ITS SHARE OF PROBLEMS. THEY'RE NOT OFFICIALLY RECOGNIZED BY THE *BUGYŌSHO*. THEY'RE PRIVATELY HIRED BY *YORIKI* AND *DOSHIN* WITH WHOM THEY HAVE A MASTER-SERVANT RELATIONSHIP.
EVEN SO, THERE'S NO WAY THAT THREE HUNDRED *YORIKI* AND *DŌSHIN* COULD KEEP THE PEACE AMONG THE *ONE MILLION* PEOPLE OF EDO.
BUT IF IT'S POSSIBLE TO GET WHAT YOU RISKED YOUR LIFE FOR, I'LL HELP YOU.

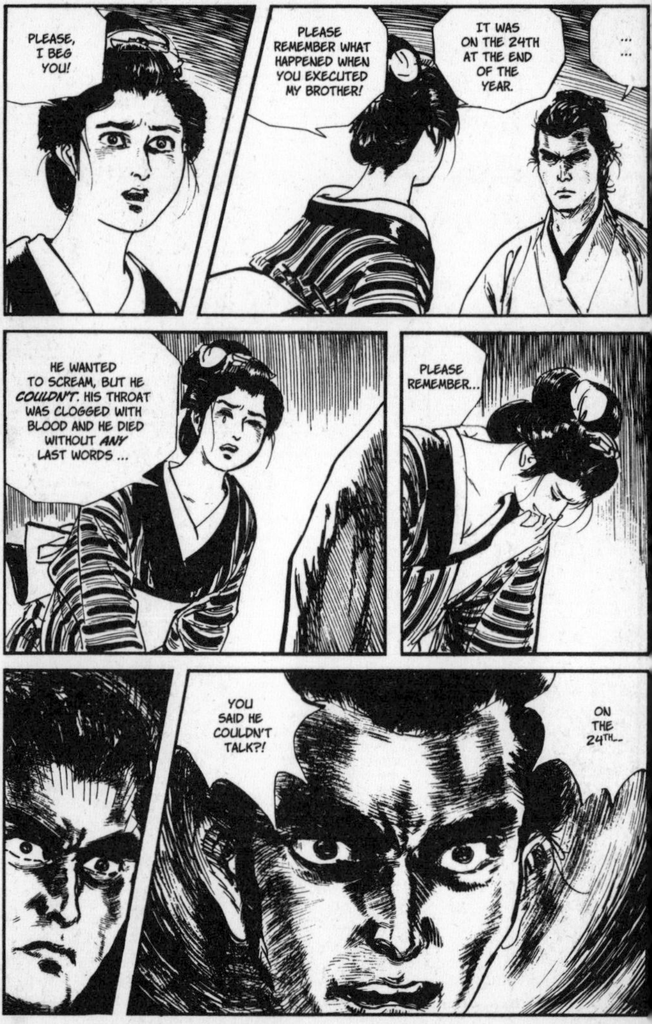
PLEASE, I BEG YOU!
PLEASE REMEMBER WHAT HAPPENED WHEN YOU EXECUTED MY BROTHER!
IT WAS ON THE 24TH AT THE END OF THE YEAR.
... ...
HE WANTED TO SCREAM, BUT HE *COULDN'T*. HIS THROAT WAS CLOGGED WITH BLOOD AND HE DIED WITHOUT *ANY* LAST WORDS ...
PLEASE REMEMBER...
YOU SAID HE COULDN'T TALK?!
ON THE 24TH...

AHHH...
OOH...
ARGH...

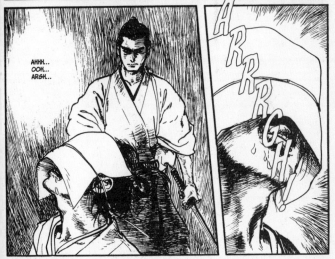

ARRRGH!

265

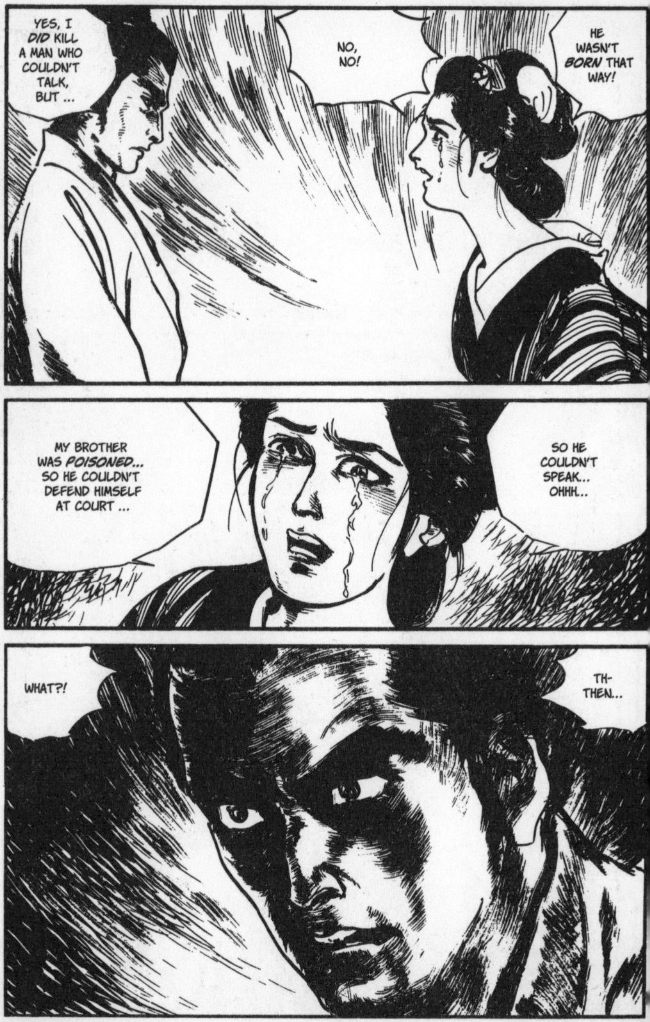
YES, I *DID* KILL A MAN WHO COULDN'T TALK, BUT ...
NO, NO!
HE WASN'T *BORN* THAT WAY!
MY BROTHER WAS *POISONED*... SO HE COULDN'T DEFEND HIMSELF AT COURT ...
SO HE COULDN'T SPEAK... OHHH...
WHAT?!
TH- THEN...

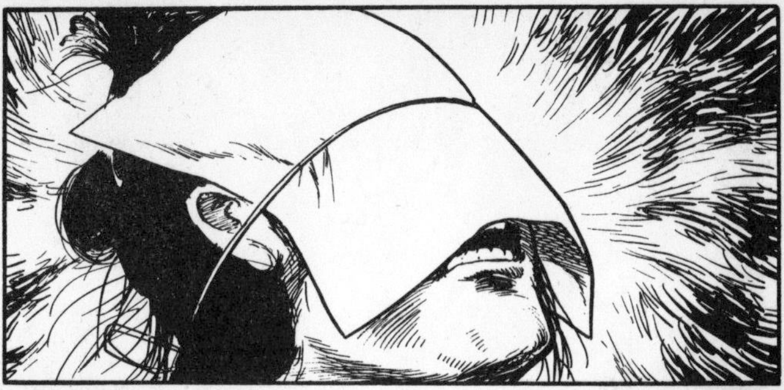
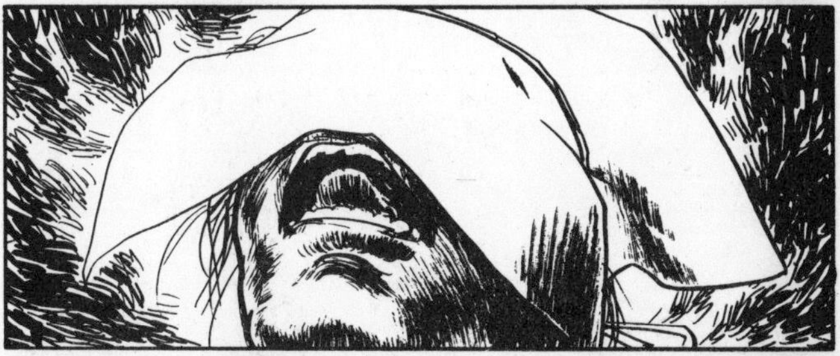
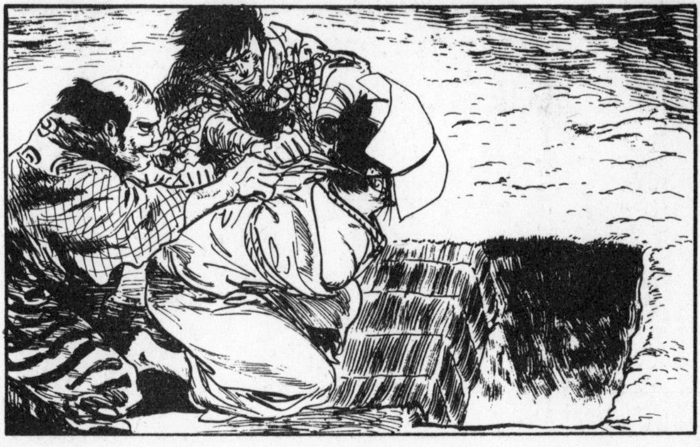

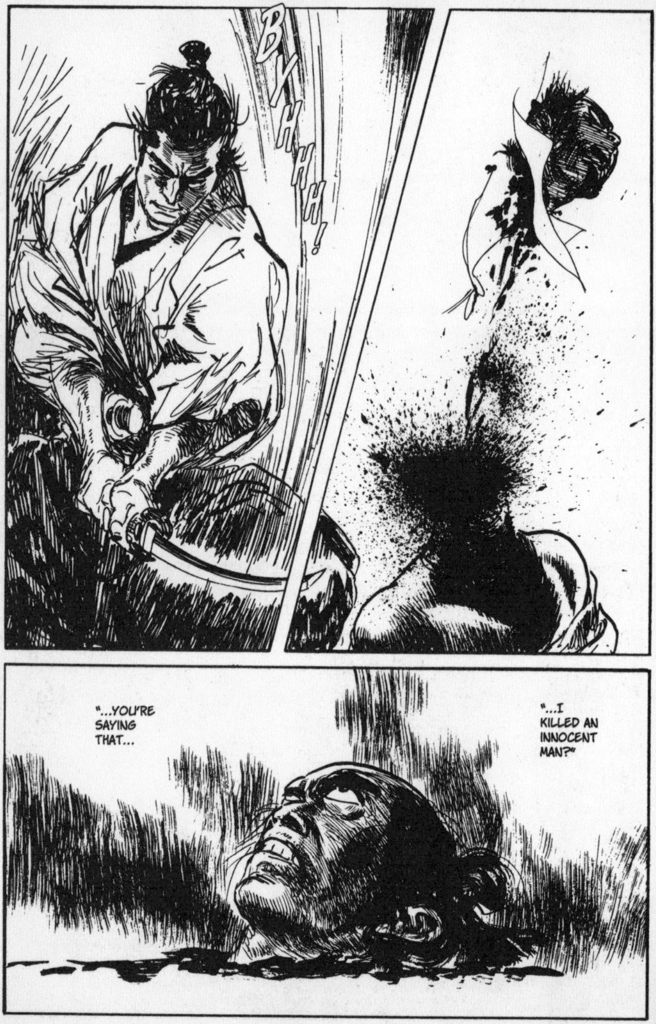
BYHHHH!
"...YOU'RE SAYING THAT...
"...I KILLED AN INNOCENT MAN?"

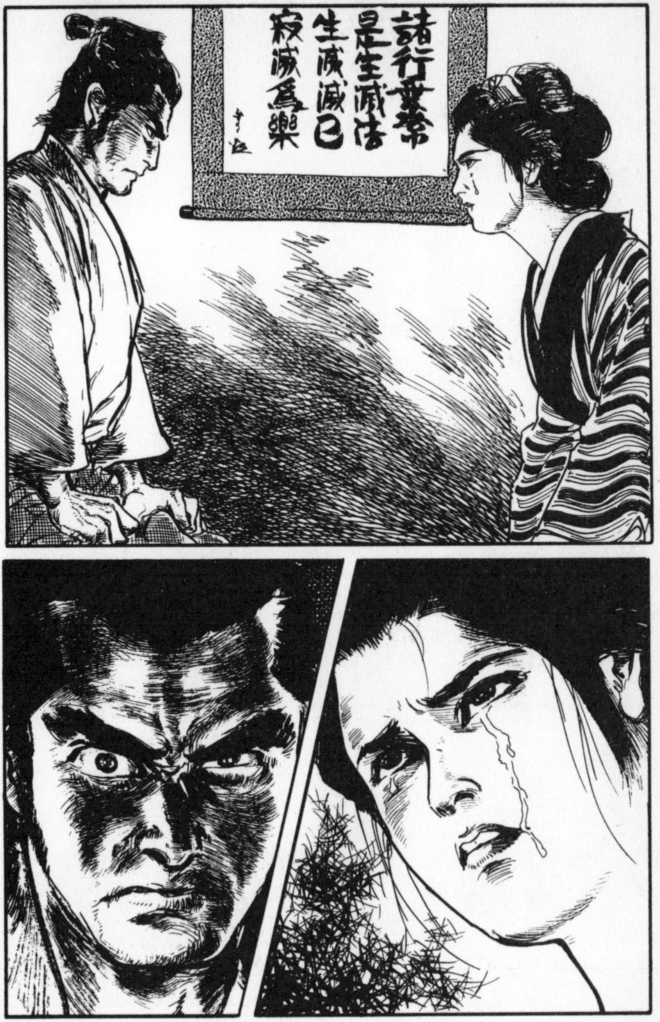
諸行無常
是生滅法
生滅滅已
寂滅爲樂

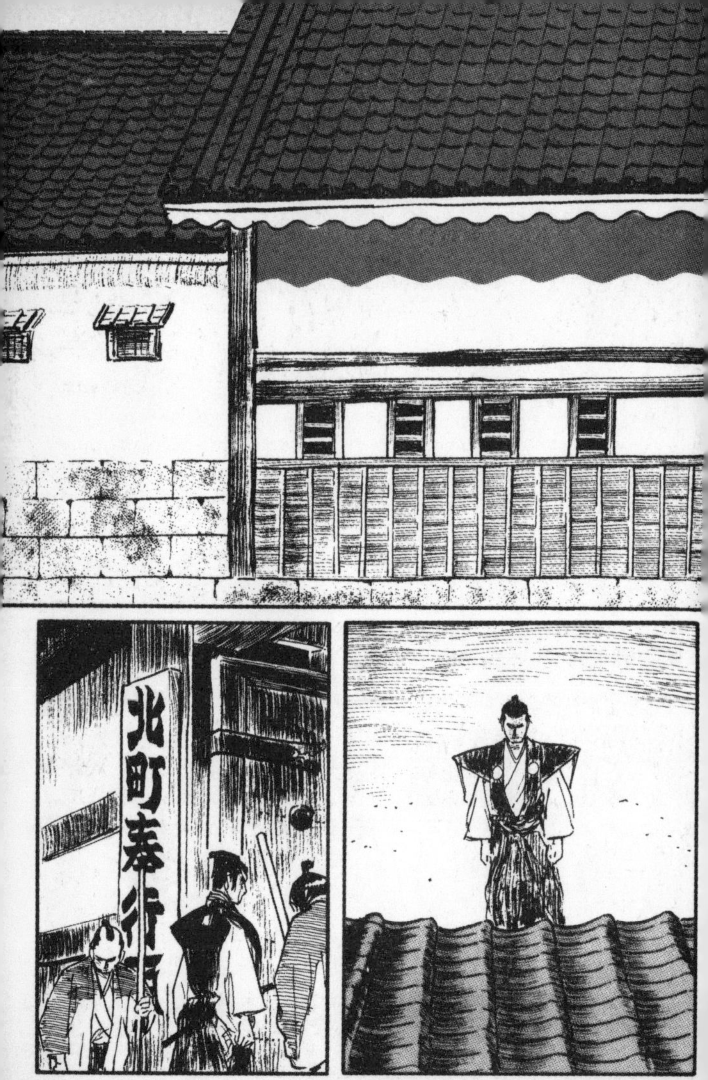
北町奉行

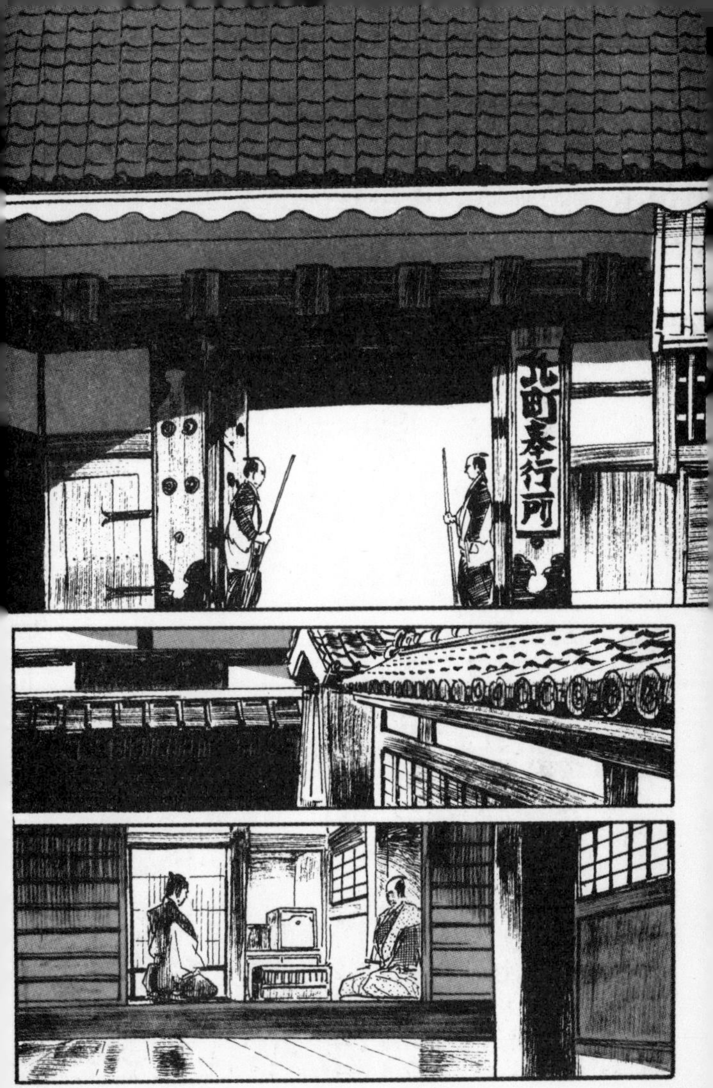
北町奉行所

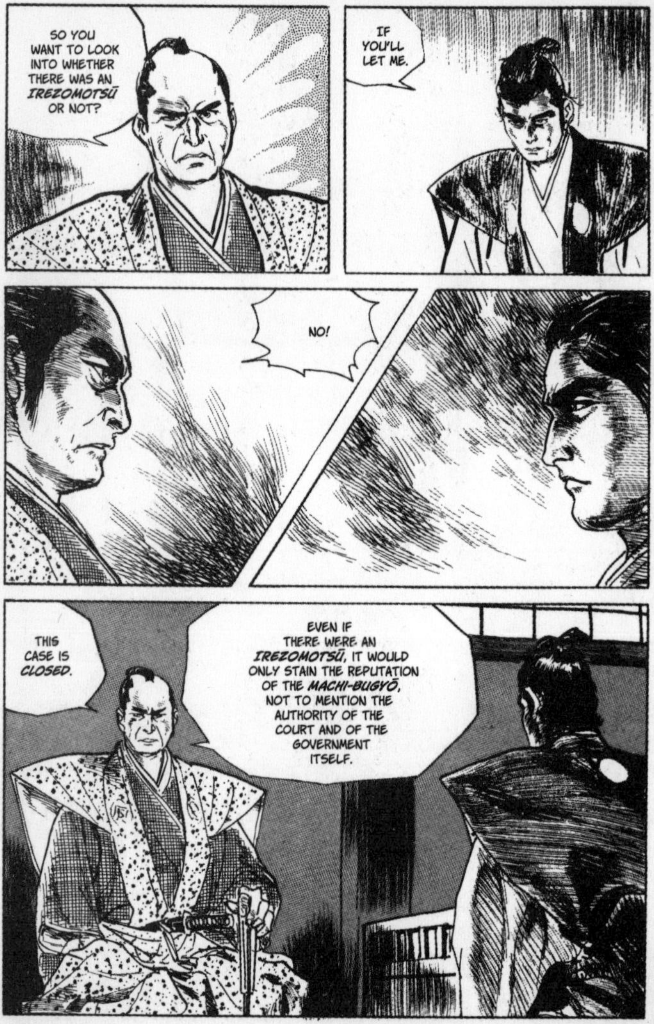
SO YOU WANT TO LOOK INTO WHETHER THERE WAS AN *IREZOMOTSŪ* OR NOT?
IF YOU'LL LET ME.
NO!
THIS CASE IS *CLOSED*.
EVEN IF THERE WERE AN *IREZOMOTSŪ*, IT WOULD ONLY STAIN THE REPUTATION OF THE *MACHI-BUGYŌ*, NOT TO MENTION THE AUTHORITY OF THE COURT AND OF THE GOVERNMENT ITSELF.

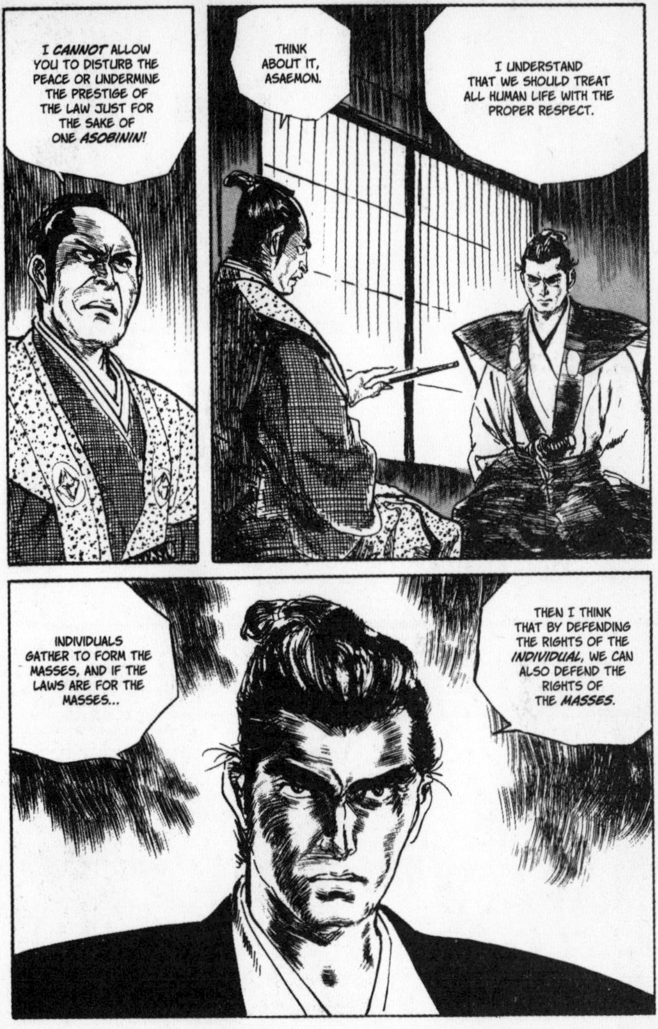

I *CANNOT* ALLOW YOU TO DISTURB THE PEACE OR UNDERMINE THE PRESTIGE OF THE LAW JUST FOR THE SAKE OF ONE *ASOBININ*!
THINK ABOUT IT, ASAEMON.
I UNDERSTAND THAT WE SHOULD TREAT ALL HUMAN LIFE WITH THE PROPER RESPECT.
INDIVIDUALS GATHER TO FORM THE MASSES, AND IF THE LAWS ARE FOR THE MASSES...
THEN I THINK THAT BY DEFENDING THE RIGHTS OF THE *INDIVIDUAL*, WE CAN ALSO DEFEND THE RIGHTS OF THE *MASSES*.

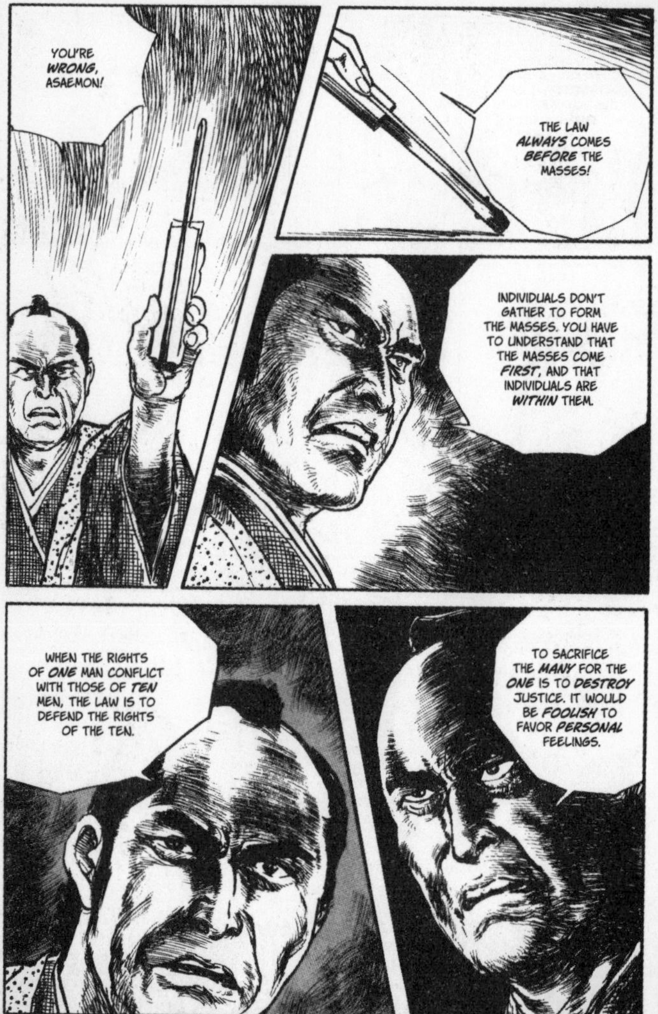
YOU'RE *WRONG*, ASAEMON!
THE LAW *ALWAYS* COMES *BEFORE* THE MASSES!
INDIVIDUALS DON'T GATHER TO FORM THE MASSES. YOU HAVE TO UNDERSTAND THAT THE MASSES COME *FIRST*, AND THAT INDIVIDUALS ARE *WITHIN* THEM.
WHEN THE RIGHTS OF *ONE* MAN CONFLICT WITH THOSE OF *TEN* MEN, THE LAW IS TO DEFEND THE RIGHTS OF THE TEN.
TO SACRIFICE THE *MANY* FOR THE *ONE* IS TO *DESTROY* JUSTICE. IT WOULD BE *FOOLISH* TO FAVOR *PERSONAL* FEELINGS.

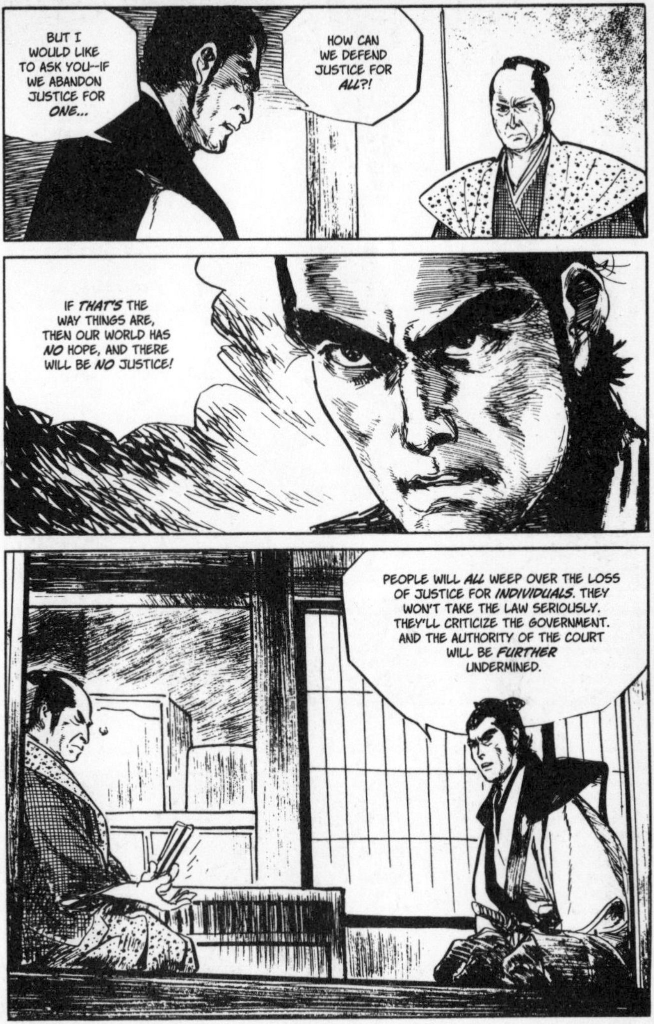
BUT I WOULD LIKE TO ASK YOU--IF WE ABANDON JUSTICE FOR *ONE...*
HOW CAN WE DEFEND JUSTICE FOR *ALL?!*
IF *THAT'S* THE WAY THINGS ARE, THEN OUR WORLD HAS *NO* HOPE, AND THERE WILL BE *NO* JUSTICE!
PEOPLE WILL *ALL* WEEP OVER THE LOSS OF JUSTICE FOR *INDIVIDUALS*. THEY WON'T TAKE THE LAW SERIOUSLY. THEY'LL CRITICIZE THE GOVERNMENT. AND THE AUTHORITY OF THE COURT WILL BE *FURTHER* UNDERMINED.

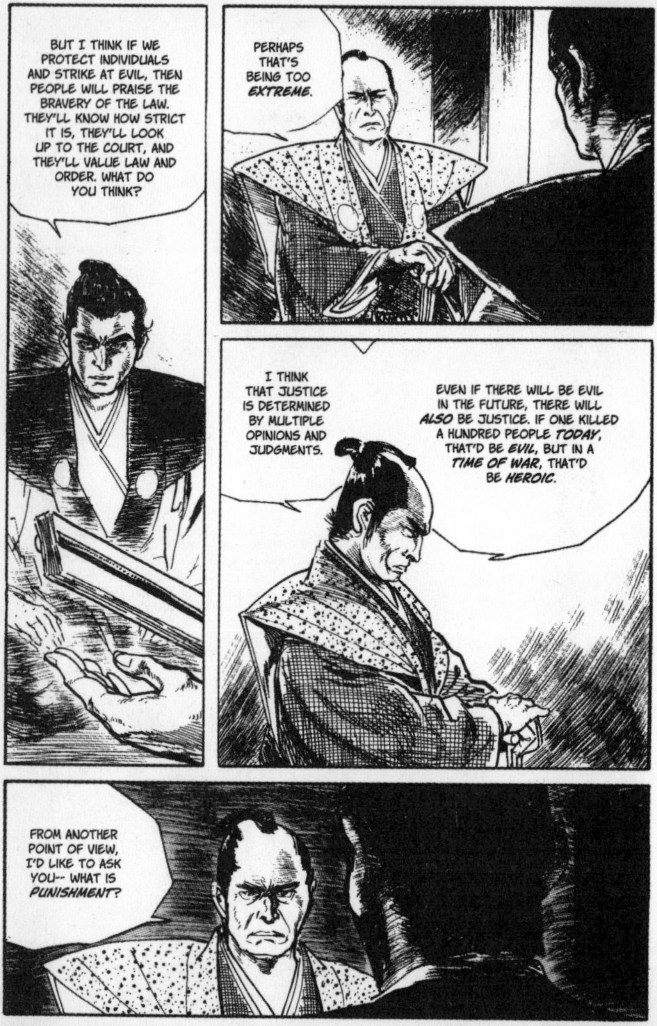
BUT I THINK IF WE PROTECT INDIVIDUALS AND STRIKE AT EVIL, THEN PEOPLE WILL PRAISE THE BRAVERY OF THE LAW. THEY'LL KNOW HOW STRICT IT IS, THEY'LL LOOK UP TO THE COURT, AND THEY'LL VALUE LAW AND ORDER. WHAT DO YOU THINK?
PERHAPS THAT'S BEING TOO *EXTREME*.
I THINK THAT JUSTICE IS DETERMINED BY MULTIPLE OPINIONS AND JUDGMENTS.
EVEN IF THERE WILL BE EVIL IN THE FUTURE, THERE WILL *ALSO* BE JUSTICE. IF ONE KILLED A HUNDRED PEOPLE *TODAY*, THAT'D BE *EVIL*, BUT IN A *TIME OF WAR*, THAT'D BE *HEROIC*.
FROM ANOTHER POINT OF VIEW, I'D LIKE TO ASK YOU-- WHAT IS *PUNISHMENT*?

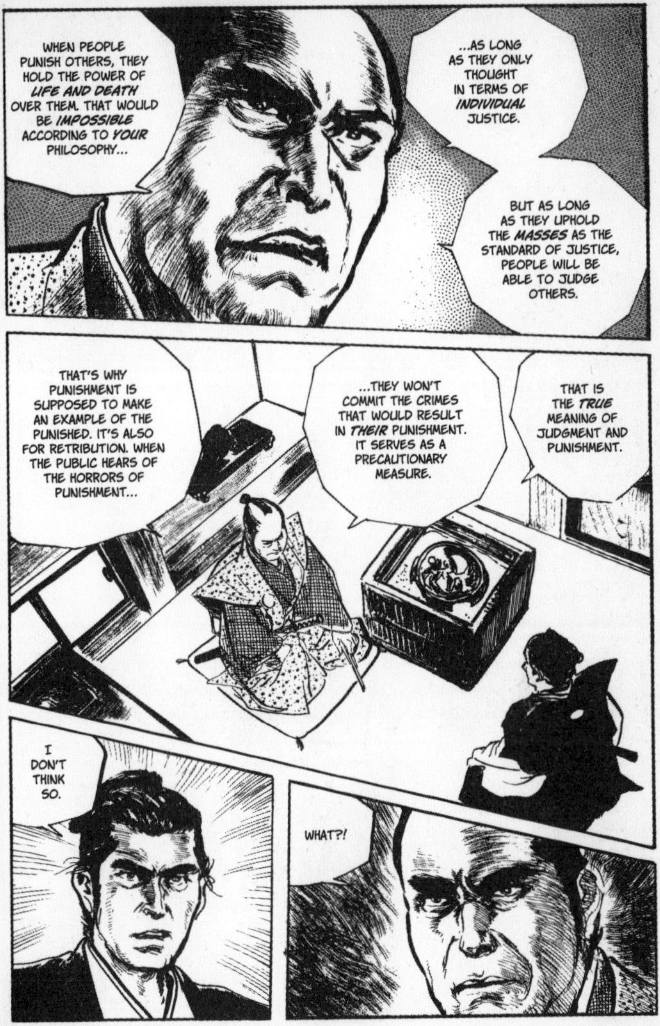
WHEN PEOPLE PUNISH OTHERS, THEY HOLD THE POWER OF *LIFE AND DEATH* OVER THEM. THAT WOULD BE *IMPOSSIBLE* ACCORDING TO *YOUR* PHILOSOPHY...
...AS LONG AS THEY ONLY THOUGHT IN TERMS OF *INDIVIDUAL* JUSTICE.
BUT AS LONG AS THEY UPHOLD THE *MASSES* AS THE STANDARD OF JUSTICE, PEOPLE WILL BE ABLE TO JUDGE OTHERS.
THAT'S WHY PUNISHMENT IS SUPPOSED TO MAKE AN EXAMPLE OF THE PUNISHED. IT'S ALSO FOR RETRIBUTION. WHEN THE PUBLIC HEARS OF THE HORRORS OF PUNISHMENT...
...THEY WON'T COMMIT THE CRIMES THAT WOULD RESULT IN *THEIR* PUNISHMENT. IT SERVES AS A PRECAUTIONARY MEASURE.
THAT IS THE *TRUE* MEANING OF JUDGMENT AND PUNISHMENT.
I DON'T THINK SO.
WHAT?!

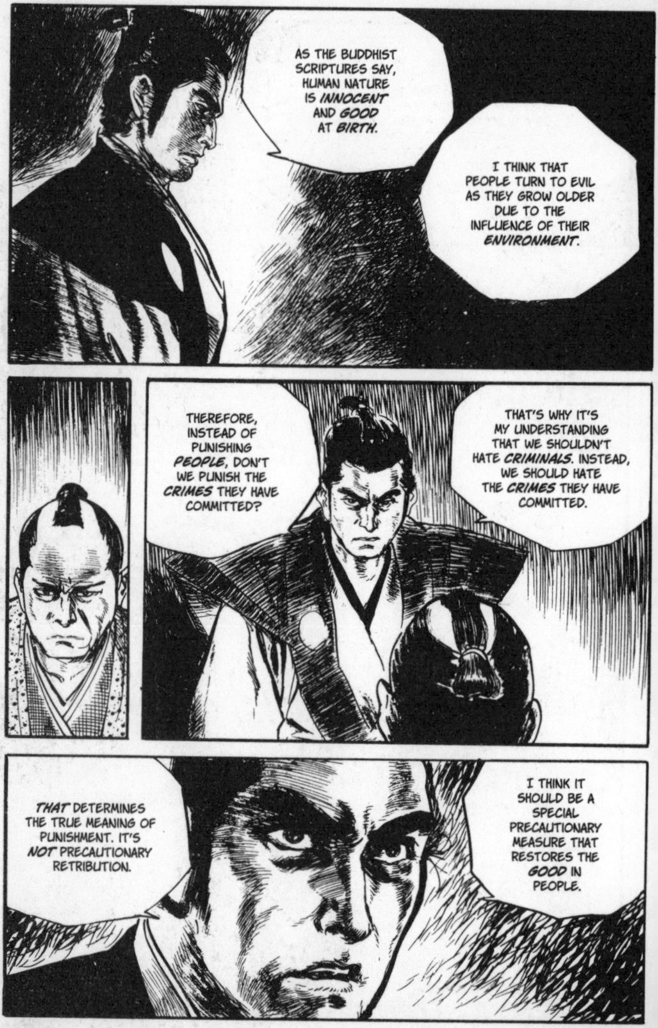
AS THE BUDDHIST SCRIPTURES SAY, HUMAN NATURE IS INNOCENT AND GOOD AT BIRTH.
I THINK THAT PEOPLE TURN TO EVIL AS THEY GROW OLDER DUE TO THE INFLUENCE OF THEIR ENVIRONMENT.
THEREFORE, INSTEAD OF PUNISHING PEOPLE, DON'T WE PUNISH THE CRIMES THEY HAVE COMMITTED?
THAT'S WHY IT'S MY UNDERSTANDING THAT WE SHOULDN'T HATE CRIMINALS. INSTEAD, WE SHOULD HATE THE CRIMES THEY HAVE COMMITTED.
THAT DETERMINES THE TRUE MEANING OF PUNISHMENT. IT'S NOT PRECAUTIONARY RETRIBUTION.
I THINK IT SHOULD BE A SPECIAL PRECAUTIONARY MEASURE THAT RESTORES THE GOOD IN PEOPLE.

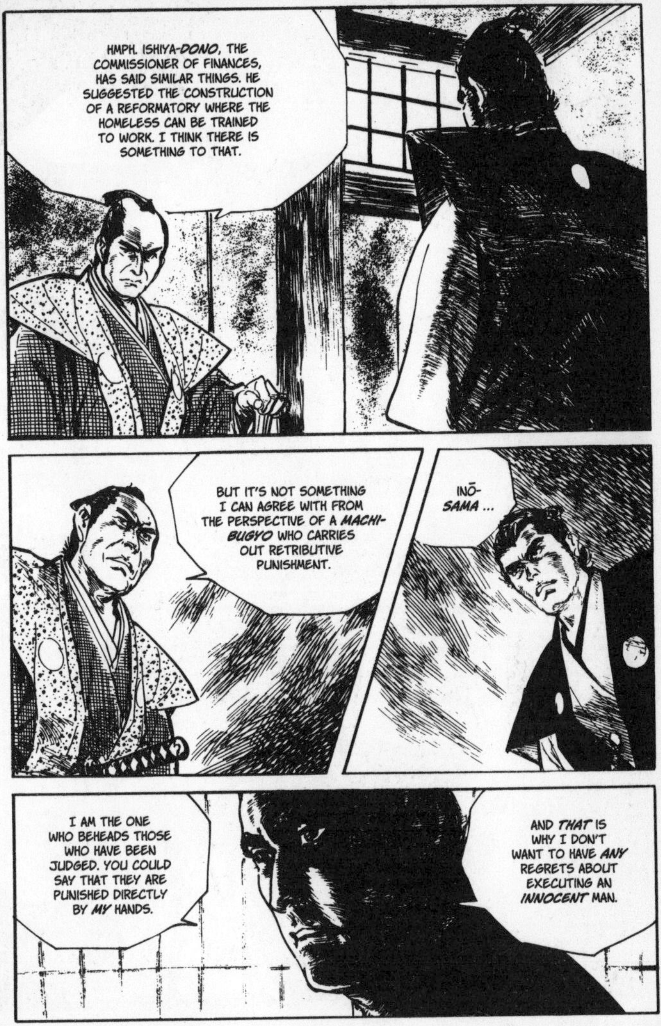
HMPH. ISHIYA-*DONO*, THE COMMISSIONER OF FINANCES, HAS SAID SIMILAR THINGS. HE SUGGESTED THE CONSTRUCTION OF A REFORMATORY WHERE THE HOMELESS CAN BE TRAINED TO WORK. I THINK THERE IS SOMETHING TO THAT.
BUT IT'S NOT SOMETHING I CAN AGREE WITH FROM THE PERSPECTIVE OF A *MACHI-BUGYO* WHO CARRIES OUT RETRIBUTIVE PUNISHMENT.
INŌ-*SAMA* ...
I AM THE ONE WHO BEHEADS THOSE WHO HAVE BEEN JUDGED. YOU COULD SAY THAT THEY ARE PUNISHED DIRECTLY BY *MY* HANDS.
AND *THAT* IS WHY I DON'T WANT TO HAVE *ANY* REGRETS ABOUT EXECUTING AN *INNOCENT* MAN.

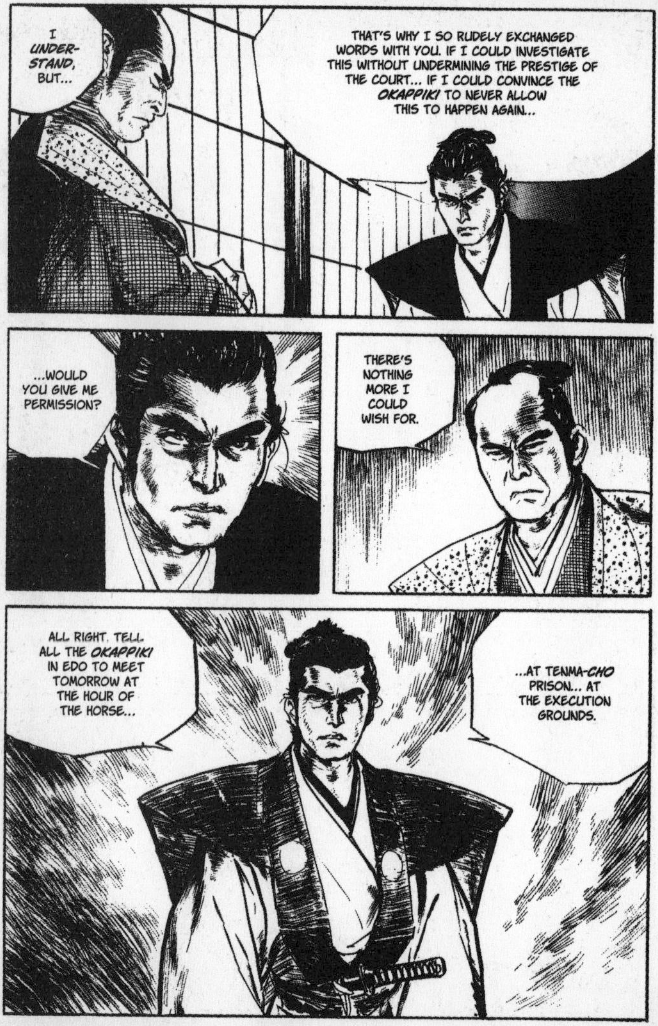
I UNDER-STAND, BUT...
THAT'S WHY I SO RUDELY EXCHANGED WORDS WITH YOU. IF I COULD INVESTIGATE THIS WITHOUT UNDERMINING THE PRESTIGE OF THE COURT... IF I COULD CONVINCE THE *OKAPPIKI* TO NEVER ALLOW THIS TO HAPPEN AGAIN...
...WOULD YOU GIVE ME PERMISSION?
THERE'S NOTHING MORE I COULD WISH FOR.
ALL RIGHT. TELL ALL THE *OKAPPIKI* IN EDO TO MEET TOMORROW AT THE HOUR OF THE HORSE...
...AT TENMA-*CHO* PRISON... AT THE EXECUTION GROUNDS.

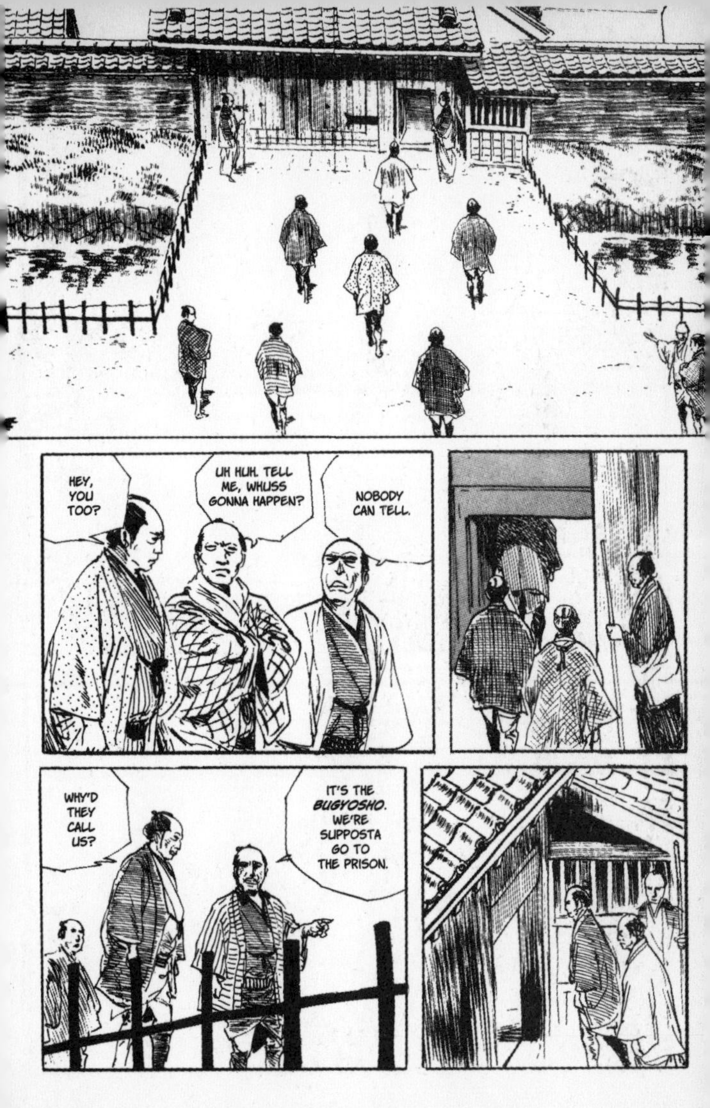
HEY, YOU TOO?
UH HUH. TELL ME, WHUSS GONNA HAPPEN?
NOBODY CAN TELL.
WHY'D THEY CALL US?
IT'S THE *BUGYOSHO*. WE'RE SUPPOSTA GO TO THE PRISON.

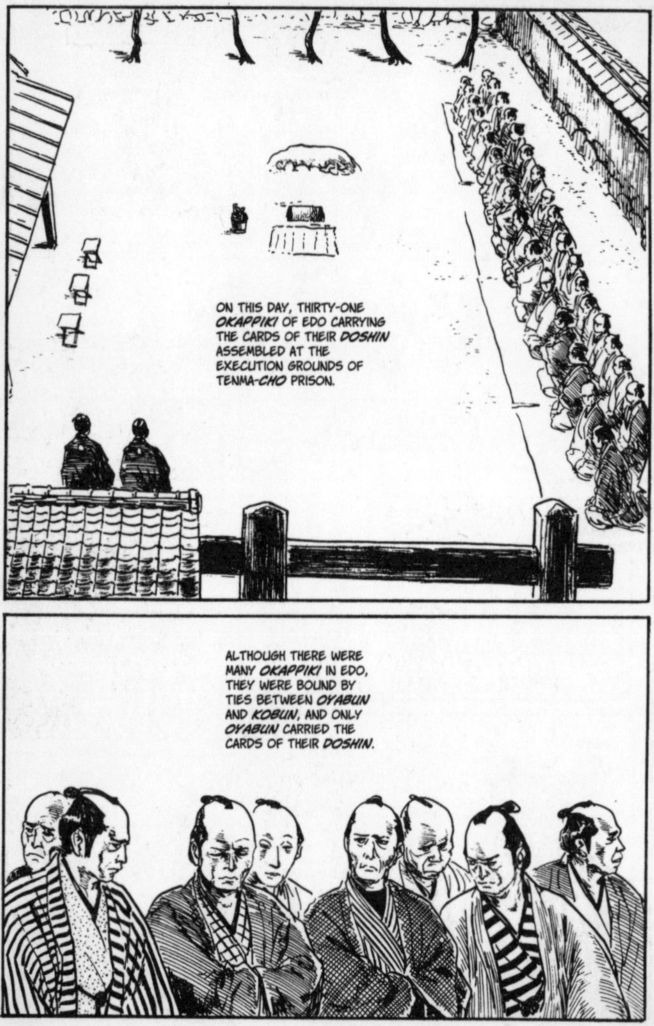
ON THIS DAY, THIRTY-ONE *OKAPPIKI* OF EDO CARRYING THE CARDS OF THEIR *DOSHIN* ASSEMBLED AT THE EXECUTION GROUNDS OF TENMA-*CHO* PRISON.
ALTHOUGH THERE WERE MANY *OKAPPIKI* IN EDO, THEY WERE BOUND BY TIES BETWEEN *OYABUN* AND *KOBUN*, AND ONLY *OYABUN* CARRIED THE CARDS OF THEIR *DOSHIN*.

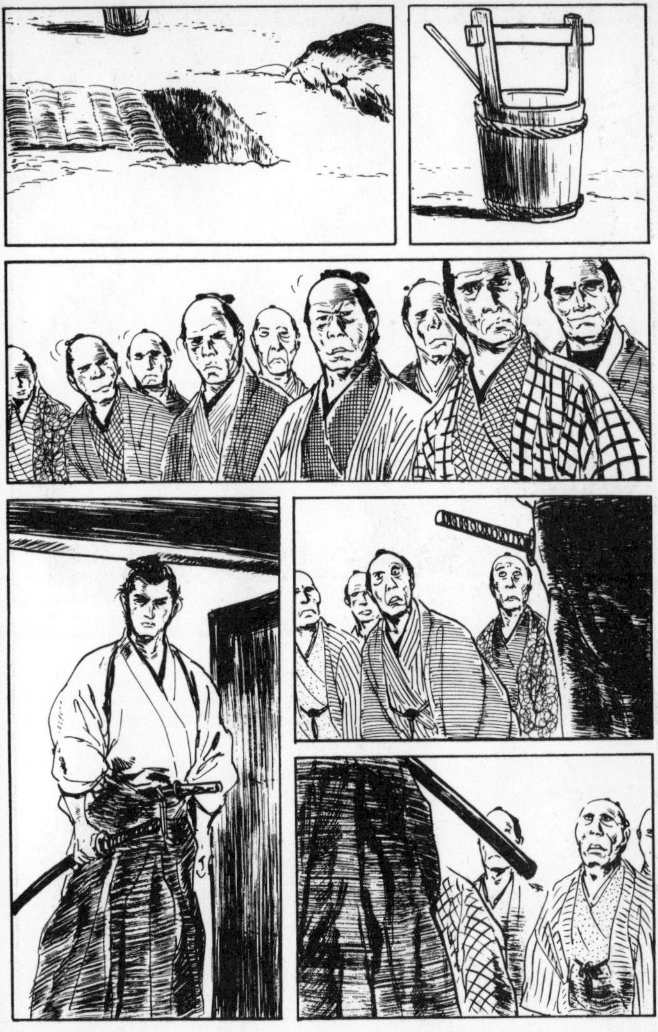

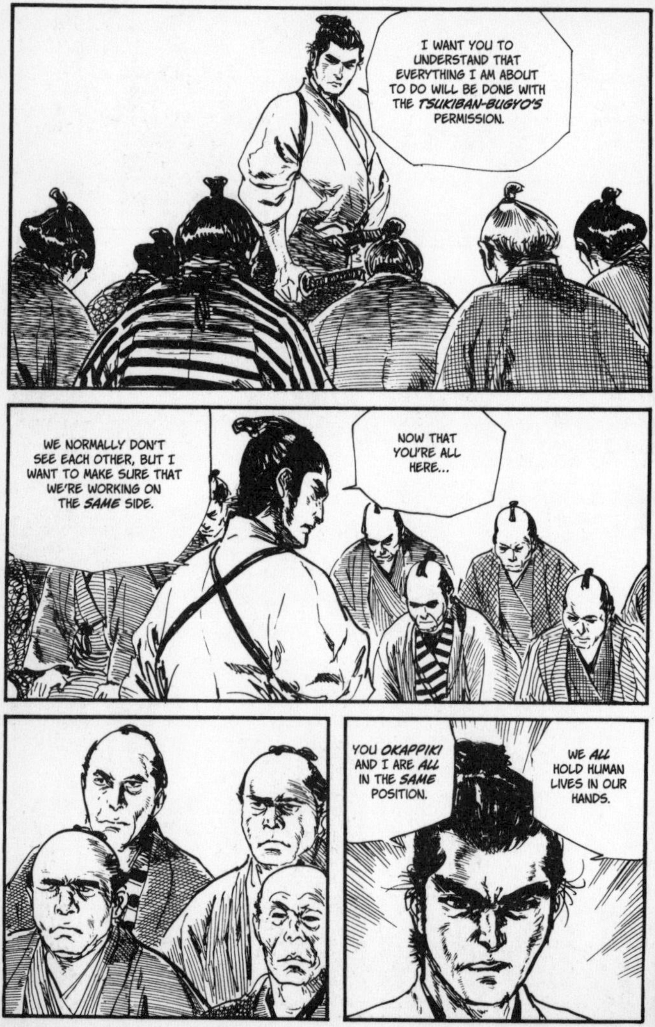
I WANT YOU TO UNDERSTAND THAT EVERYTHING I AM ABOUT TO DO WILL BE DONE WITH THE *TSUKIBAN-BUGYO'S* PERMISSION.
WE NORMALLY DON'T SEE EACH OTHER, BUT I WANT TO MAKE SURE THAT WE'RE WORKING ON THE *SAME* SIDE.
NOW THAT YOU'RE ALL HERE...
YOU *OKAPPIKI* AND I ARE *ALL* IN THE *SAME* POSITION.
WE *ALL* HOLD HUMAN LIVES IN OUR HANDS.

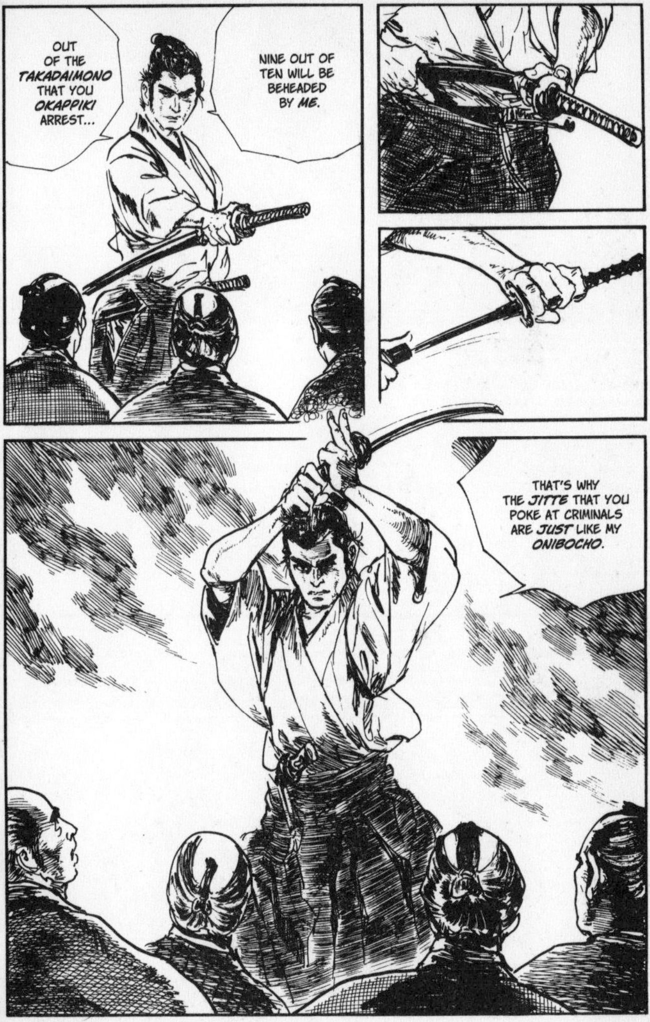
OUT OF THE TAKADAIMONO THAT YOU OKAPPIKI ARREST...
NINE OUT OF TEN WILL BE BEHEADED BY ME.
THAT'S WHY THE JITTE THAT YOU POKE AT CRIMINALS ARE JUST LIKE MY ONIBOCHO.

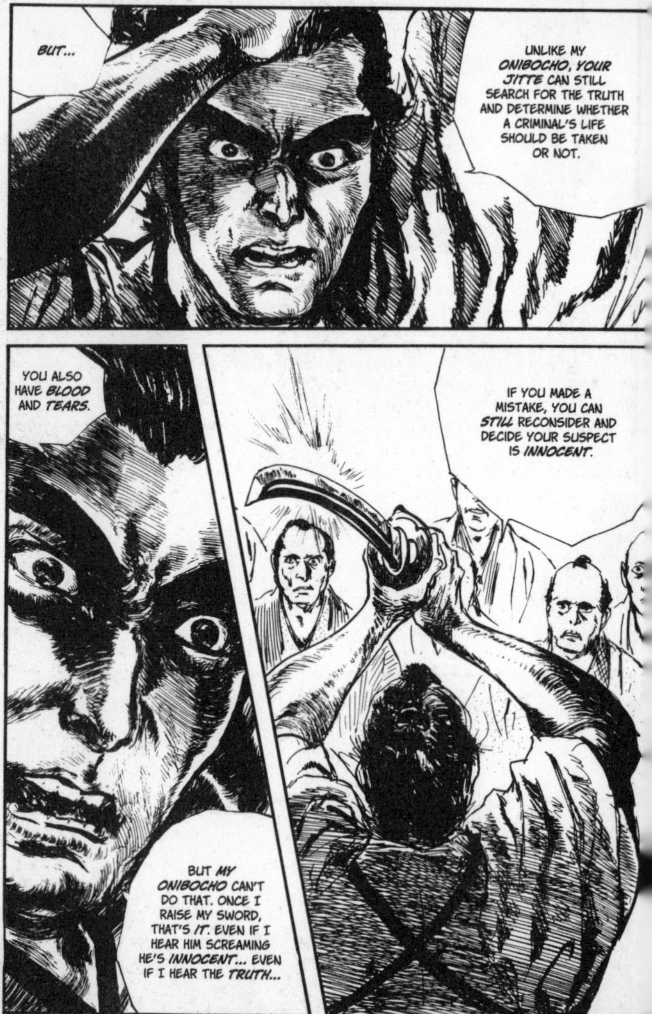
BUT...
UNLIKE MY ONIBOCHO, YOUR JITTE CAN STILL SEARCH FOR THE TRUTH AND DETERMINE WHETHER A CRIMINAL'S LIFE SHOULD BE TAKEN OR NOT.
YOU ALSO HAVE BLOOD AND TEARS.
BUT MY ONIBOCHO CAN'T DO THAT. ONCE I RAISE MY SWORD, THAT'S IT. EVEN IF I HEAR HIM SCREAMING HE'S INNOCENT... EVEN IF I HEAR THE TRUTH...
IF YOU MADE A MISTAKE, YOU CAN STILL RECONSIDER AND DECIDE YOUR SUSPECT IS INNOCENT.

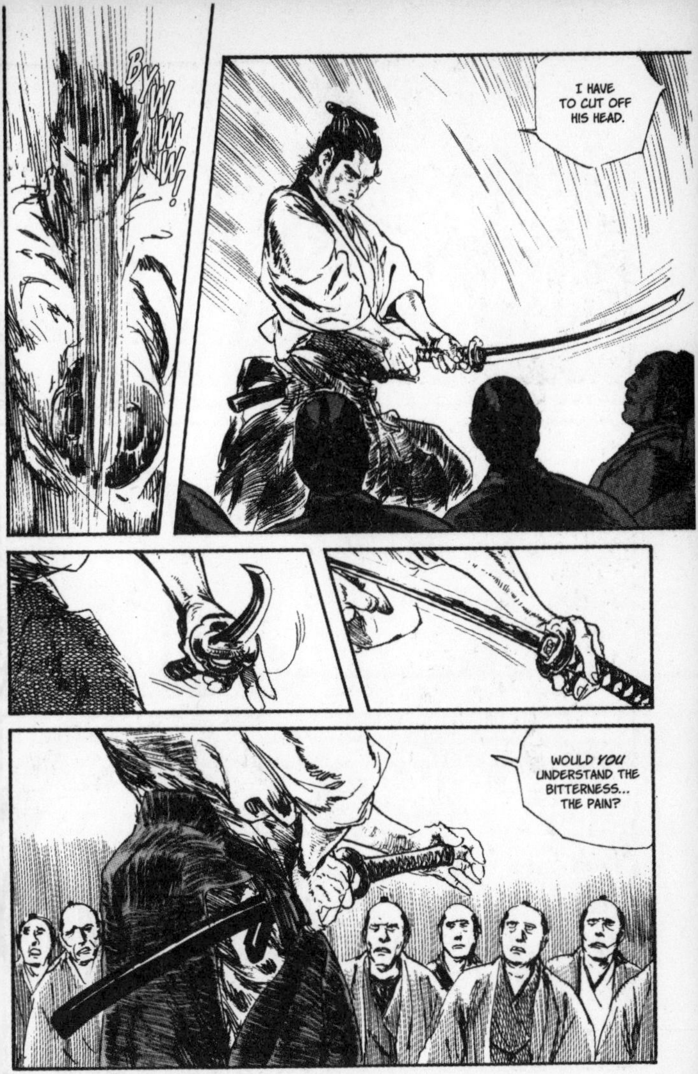
BYWWWW!
I HAVE TO CUT OFF HIS HEAD.
WOULD YOU UNDERSTAND THE BITTERNESS... THE PAIN?

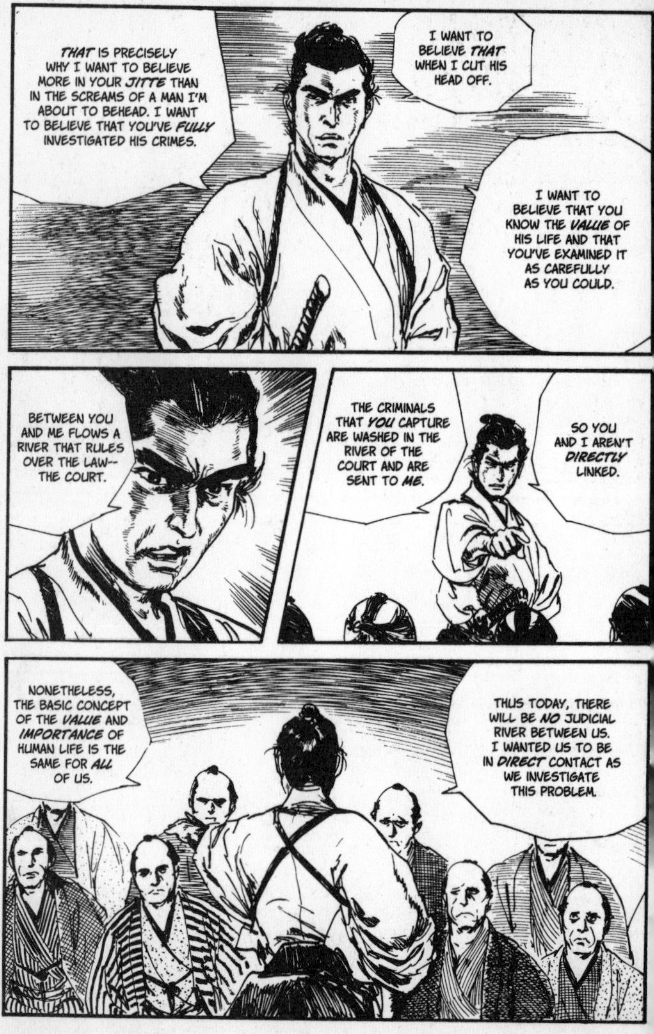
THAT IS PRECISELY WHY I WANT TO BELIEVE MORE IN YOUR JITTE THAN IN THE SCREAMS OF A MAN I'M ABOUT TO BEHEAD. I WANT TO BELIEVE THAT YOU'VE FULLY INVESTIGATED HIS CRIMES.
I WANT TO BELIEVE THAT WHEN I CUT HIS HEAD OFF.
I WANT TO BELIEVE THAT YOU KNOW THE VALUE OF HIS LIFE AND THAT YOU'VE EXAMINED IT AS CAREFULLY AS YOU COULD.
BETWEEN YOU AND ME FLOWS A RIVER THAT RULES OVER THE LAW-- THE COURT.
THE CRIMINALS THAT YOU CAPTURE ARE WASHED IN THE RIVER OF THE COURT AND ARE SENT TO ME.
SO YOU AND I AREN'T DIRECTLY LINKED.
NONETHELESS, THE BASIC CONCEPT OF THE VALUE AND IMPORTANCE OF HUMAN LIFE IS THE SAME FOR ALL OF US.
THUS TODAY, THERE WILL BE NO JUDICIAL RIVER BETWEEN US. I WANTED US TO BE IN DIRECT CONTACT AS WE INVESTIGATE THIS PROBLEM.

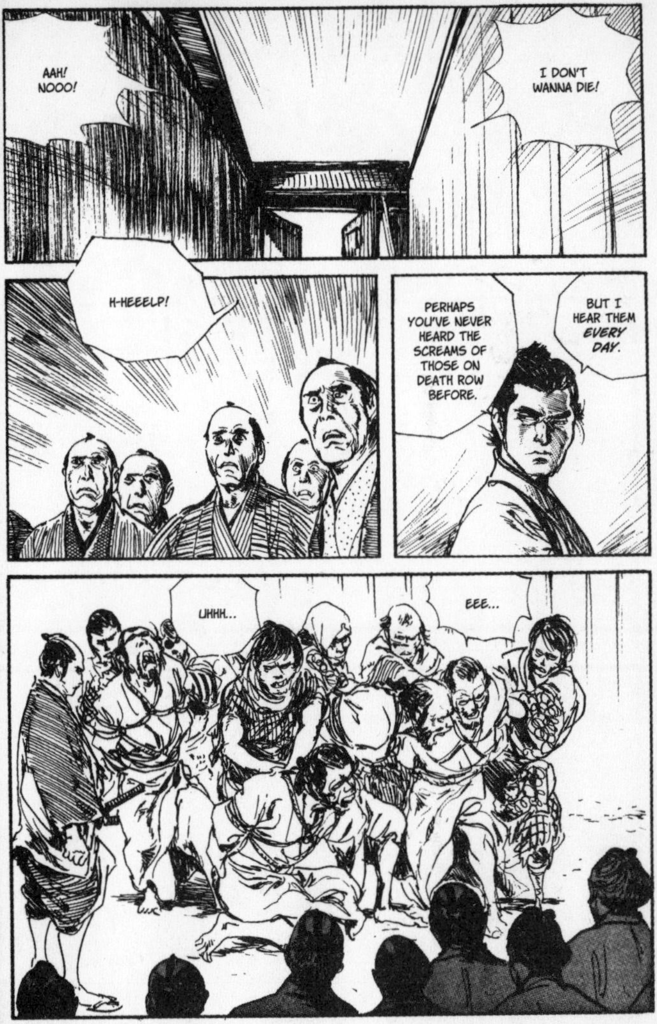
AAH! NOOO!
I DON'T WANNA DIE!
H-HEEELP!
PERHAPS YOU'VE NEVER HEARD THE SCREAMS OF THOSE ON DEATH ROW BEFORE.
BUT I HEAR THEM *EVERY DAY*.
UHHH...
EEE...

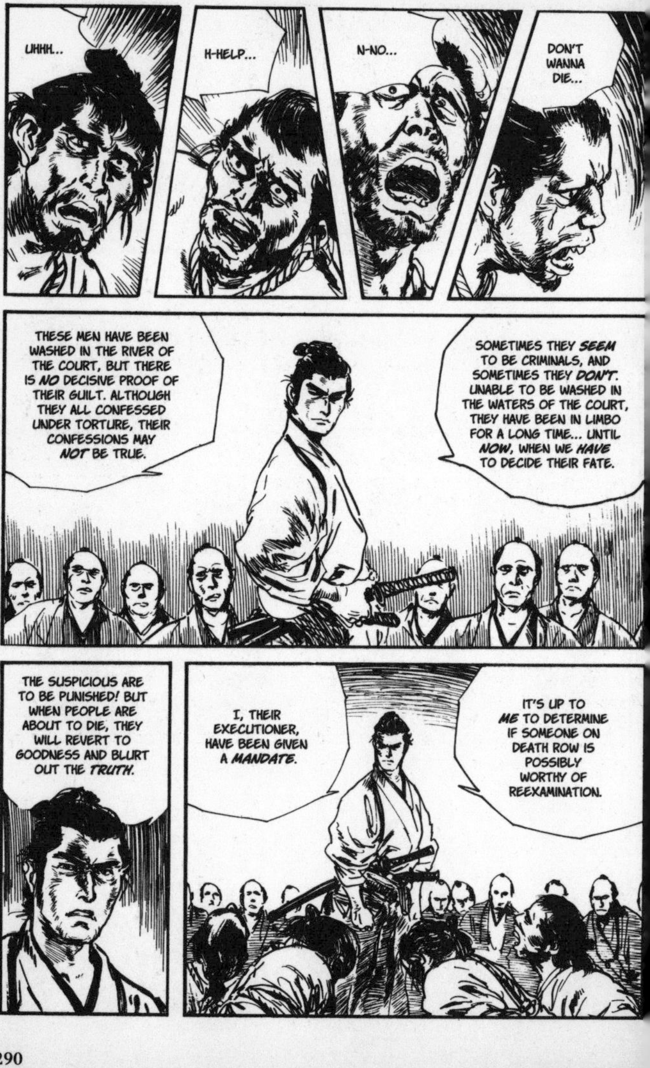
UHHH...
H-HELP...
N-NO...
DON'T WANNA DIE...
THESE MEN HAVE BEEN WASHED IN THE RIVER OF THE COURT, BUT THERE IS NO DECISIVE PROOF OF THEIR GUILT. ALTHOUGH THEY ALL CONFESSED UNDER TORTURE, THEIR CONFESSIONS MAY NOT BE TRUE.
SOMETIMES THEY SEEM TO BE CRIMINALS, AND SOMETIMES THEY DON'T. UNABLE TO BE WASHED IN THE WATERS OF THE COURT, THEY HAVE BEEN IN LIMBO FOR A LONG TIME... UNTIL NOW, WHEN WE HAVE TO DECIDE THEIR FATE.
THE SUSPICIOUS ARE TO BE PUNISHED! BUT WHEN PEOPLE ARE ABOUT TO DIE, THEY WILL REVERT TO GOODNESS AND BLURT OUT THE TRUTH.
I, THEIR EXECUTIONER, HAVE BEEN GIVEN A MANDATE.
IT'S UP TO ME TO DETERMINE IF SOMEONE ON DEATH ROW IS POSSIBLY WORTHY OF REEXAMINATION.

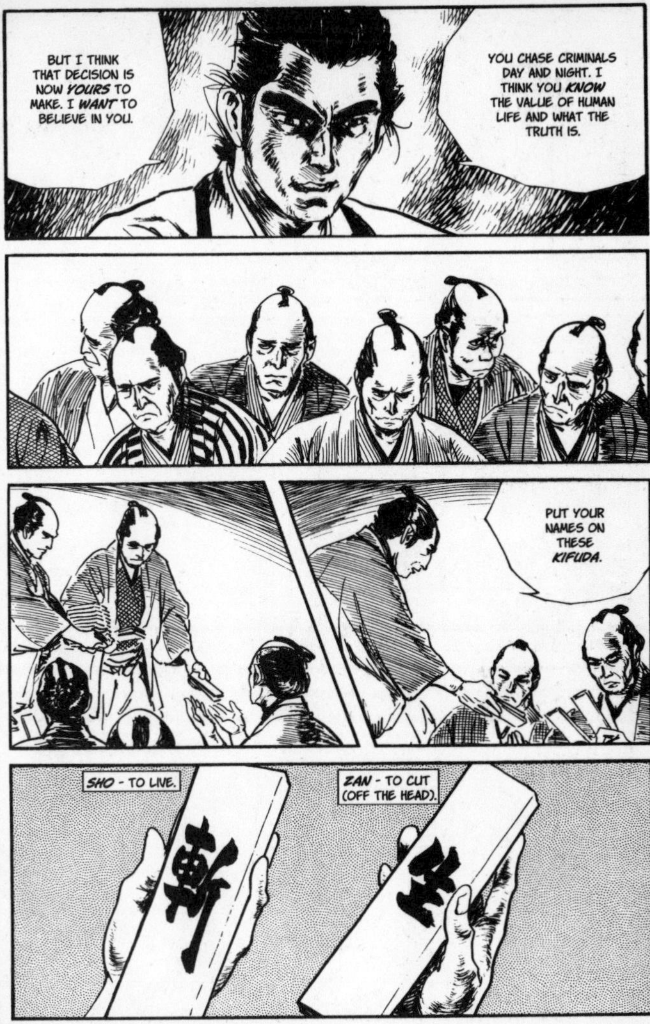
BUT I THINK THAT DECISION IS NOW *YOURS* TO MAKE. I *WANT* TO BELIEVE IN YOU.
YOU CHASE CRIMINALS DAY AND NIGHT. I THINK YOU *KNOW* THE VALUE OF HUMAN LIFE AND WHAT THE TRUTH IS.
PUT YOUR NAMES ON THESE *KIFUDA*.
SHO - TO LIVE.
ZAN - TO CUT (OFF THE HEAD).

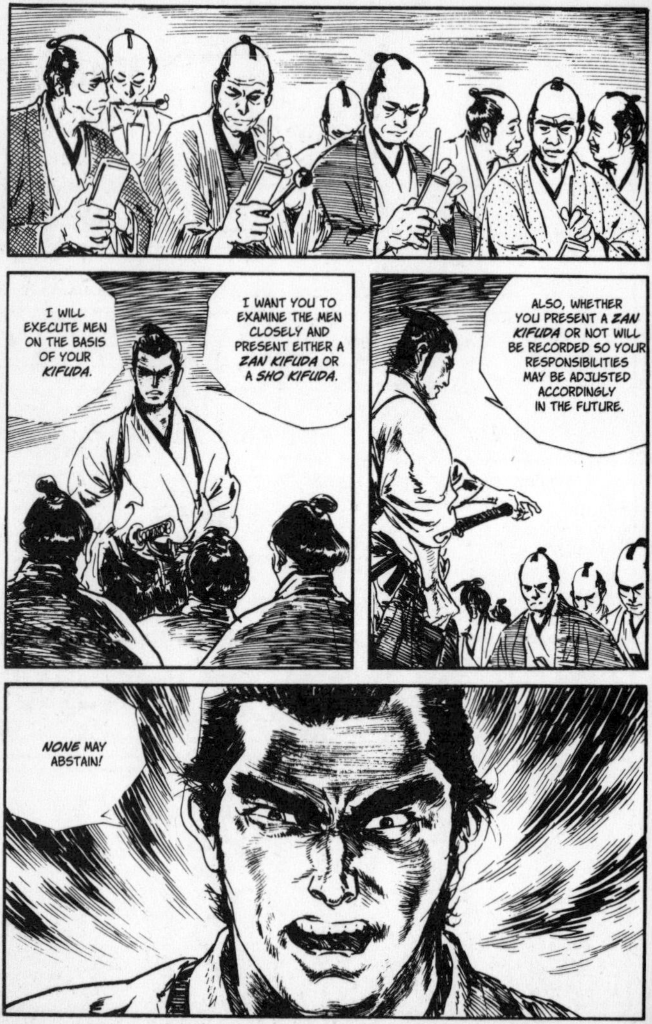
I WILL EXECUTE MEN ON THE BASIS OF YOUR *KIFUDA*.
I WANT YOU TO EXAMINE THE MEN CLOSELY AND PRESENT EITHER A *ZAN KIFUDA* OR A *SHO KIFUDA*.
ALSO, WHETHER YOU PRESENT A *ZAN KIFUDA* OR NOT WILL BE RECORDED SO YOUR RESPONSIBILITIES MAY BE ADJUSTED ACCORDINGLY IN THE FUTURE.
NONE MAY ABSTAIN!

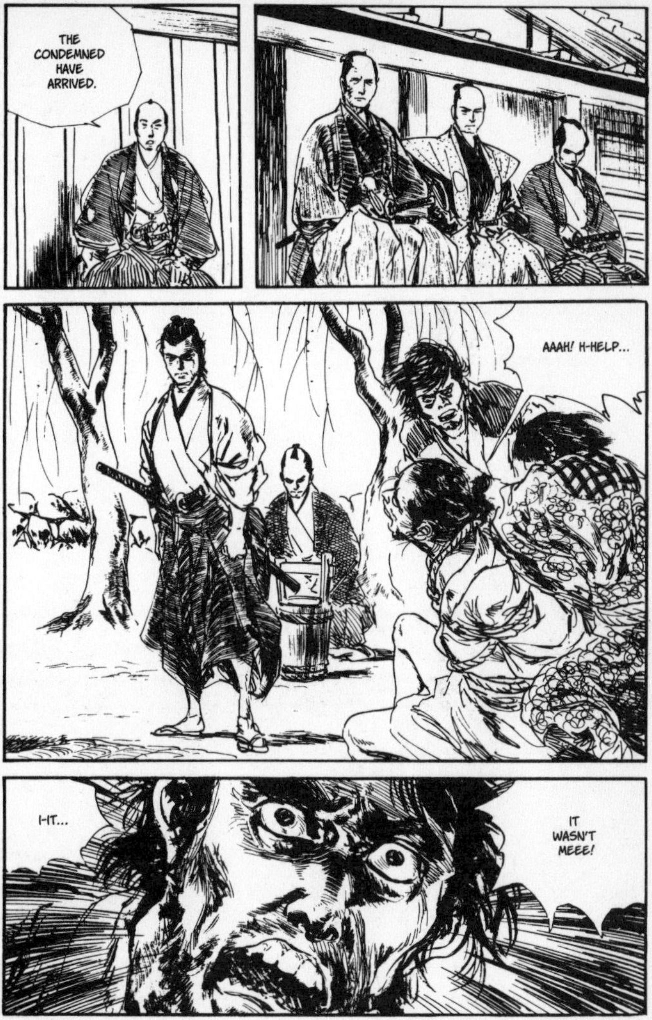
THE CONDEMNED HAVE ARRIVED.
AAAH! H-HELP...
I-IT...
IT WASN'T MEEE!

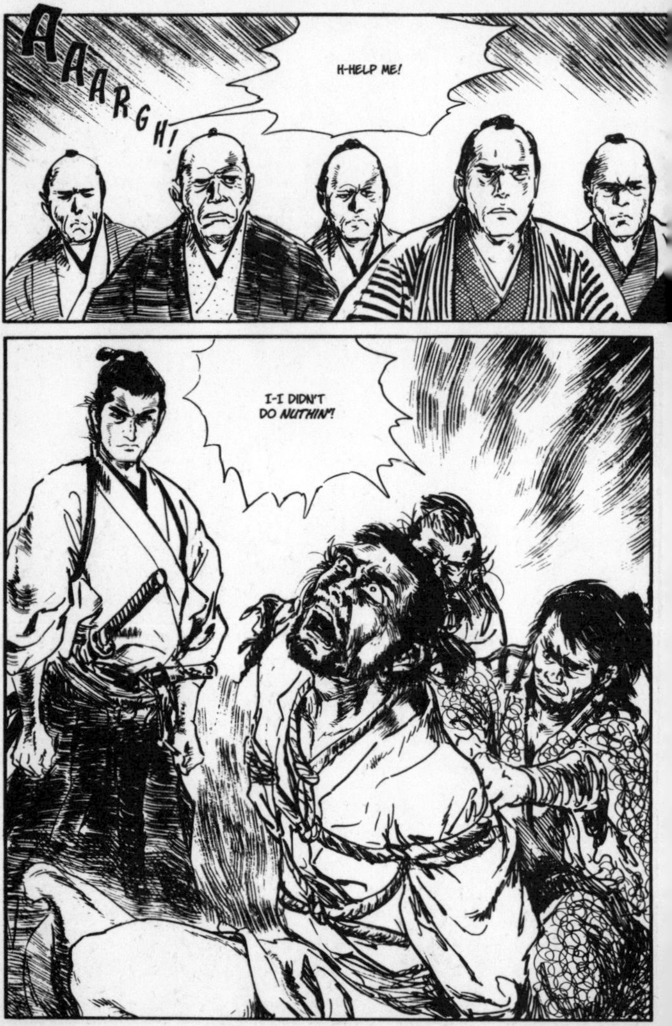
AAAARGH!
H-HELP ME!
I-I DIDN'T DO *NUTHIN'*!

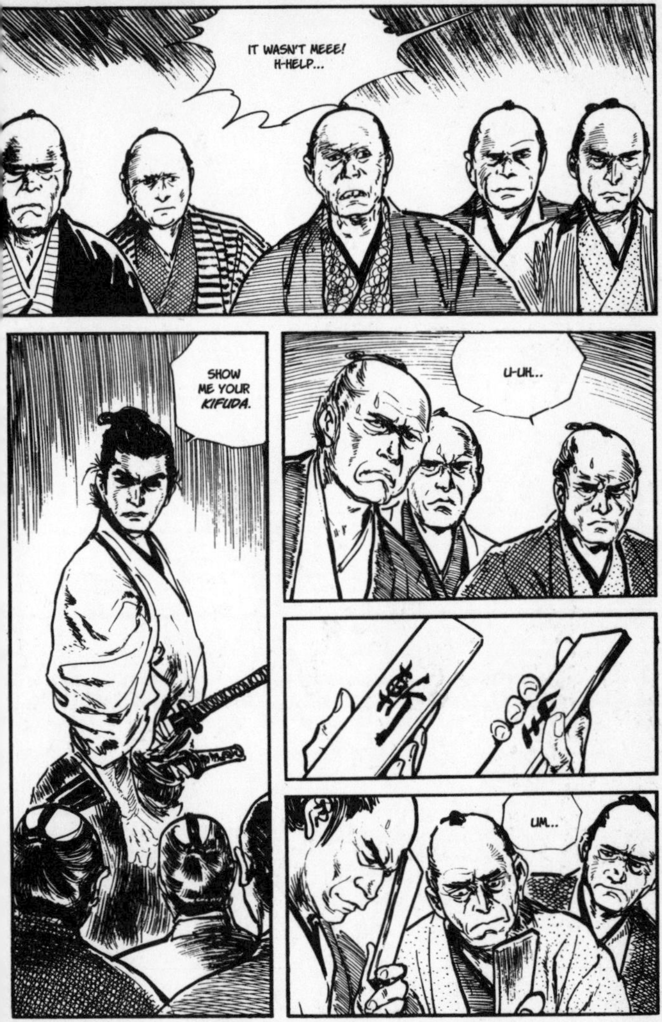
IT WASN'T MEEE! H-HELP...
SHOW ME YOUR KIFUDA.
U-UH...
UM...

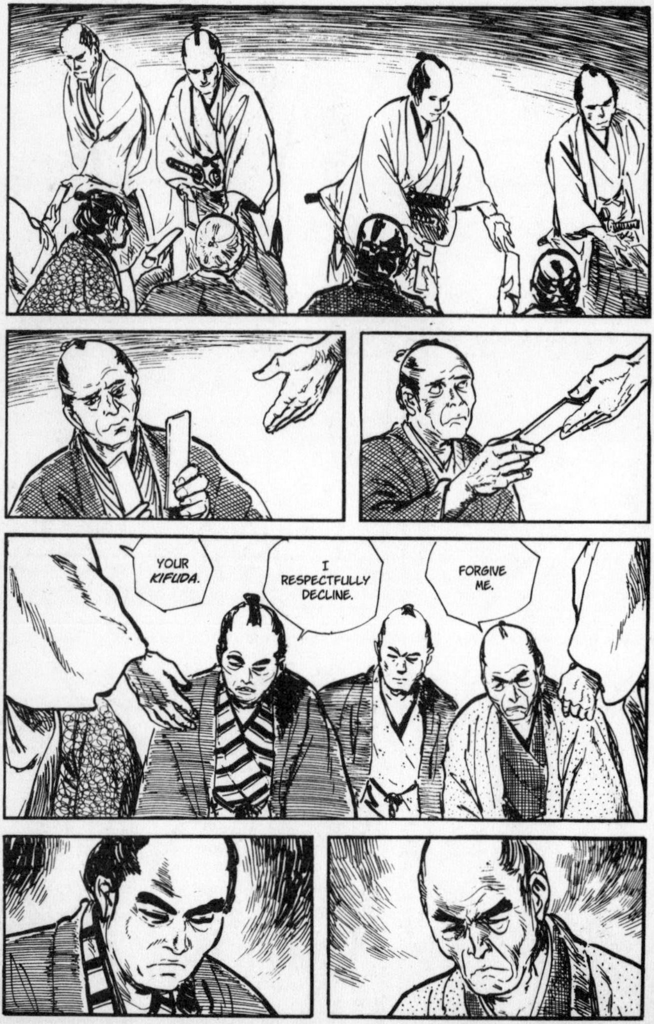
YOUR *KIFUDA*.
I RESPECTFULLY DECLINE.
FORGIVE ME.

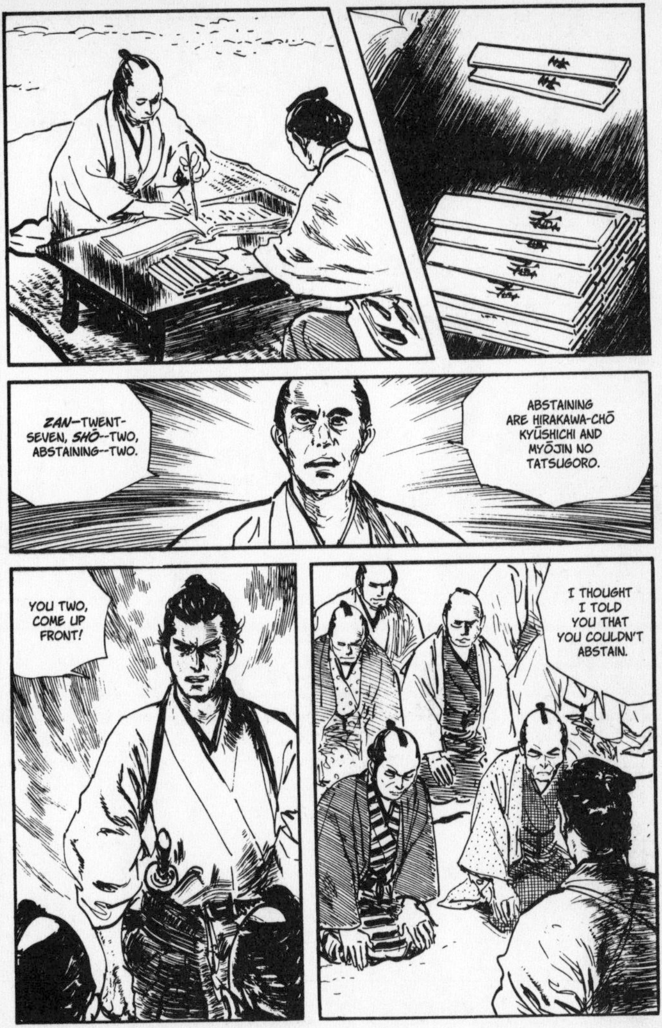
ZAN—TWENT-SEVEN, SHŌ--TWO, ABSTAINING--TWO.
ABSTAINING ARE HIRAKAWA-CHŌ KYŪSHICHI AND MYŌJIN NO TATSUGORO.
YOU TWO, COME UP FRONT!
I THOUGHT I TOLD YOU THAT YOU COULDN'T ABSTAIN.

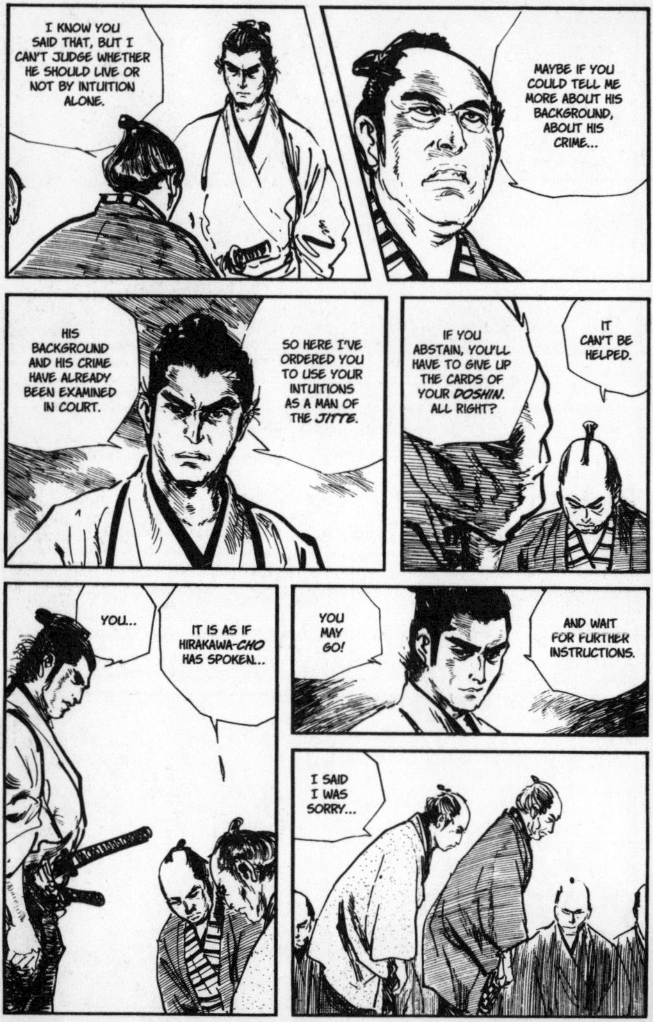
I KNOW YOU SAID THAT, BUT I CAN'T JUDGE WHETHER HE SHOULD LIVE OR NOT BY INTUITION ALONE.
MAYBE IF YOU COULD TELL ME MORE ABOUT HIS BACKGROUND, ABOUT HIS CRIME...
HIS BACKGROUND AND HIS CRIME HAVE ALREADY BEEN EXAMINED IN COURT.
SO HERE I'VE ORDERED YOU TO USE YOUR INTUITIONS AS A MAN OF THE *JITTE*.
IF YOU ABSTAIN, YOU'LL HAVE TO GIVE UP THE CARDS OF YOUR *DOSHIN*. ALL RIGHT?
IT CAN'T BE HELPED.
YOU...
IT IS AS IF HIRAKAWA-*CHO* HAS SPOKEN...
YOU MAY GO!
AND WAIT FOR FURTHER INSTRUCTIONS.
I SAID I WAS SORRY...

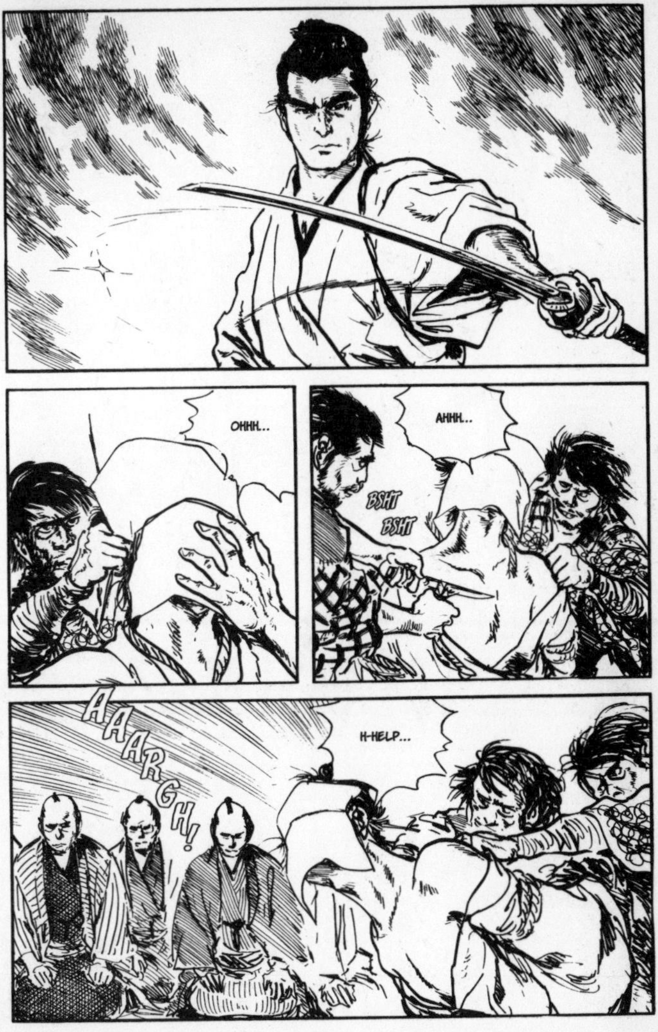
OHHH...
AHHH...
BSHT
BSHT
AAAARGH!
H-HELP...

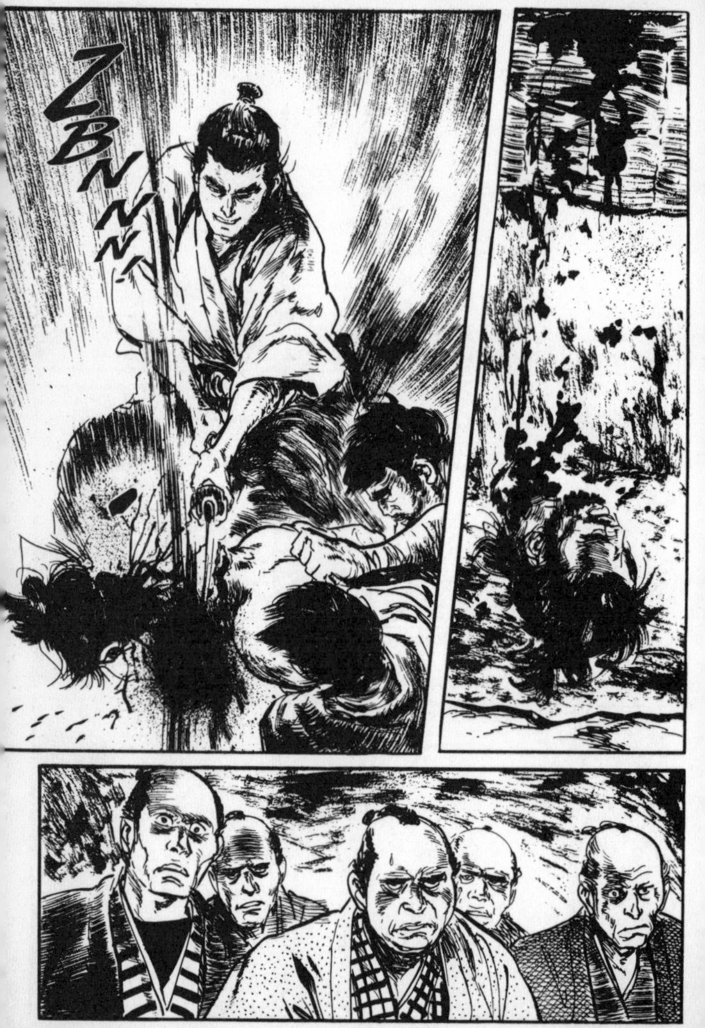
ZBNNNN

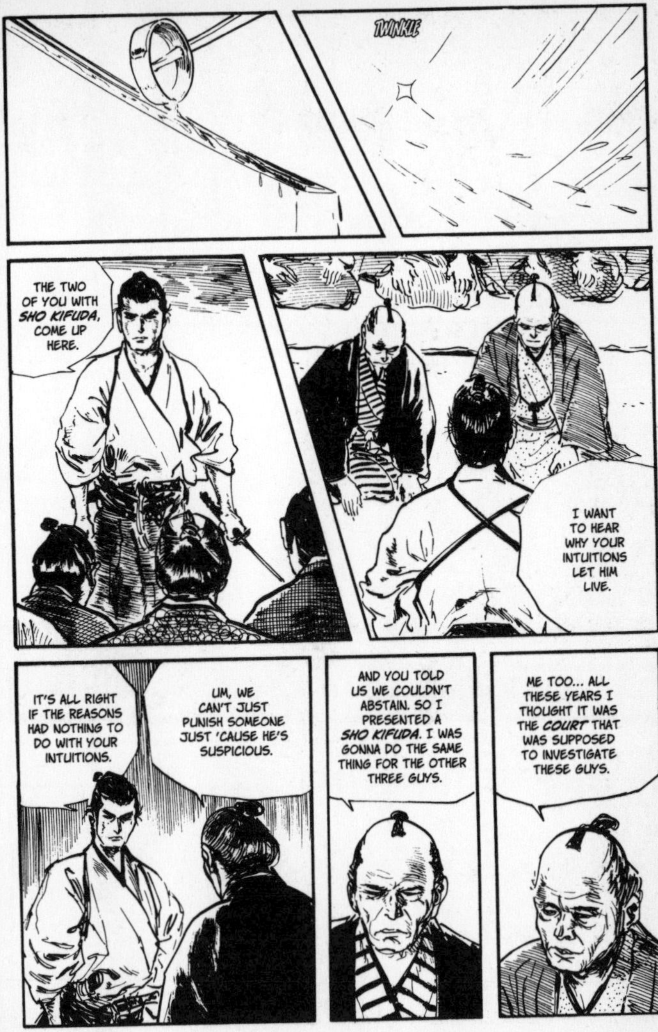
TWINKLE
THE TWO OF YOU WITH SHO KIFUDA, COME UP HERE.
I WANT TO HEAR WHY YOUR INTUITIONS LET HIM LIVE.
IT'S ALL RIGHT IF THE REASONS HAD NOTHING TO DO WITH YOUR INTUITIONS.
UM, WE CAN'T JUST PUNISH SOMEONE JUST 'CAUSE HE'S SUSPICIOUS.
AND YOU TOLD US WE COULDN'T ABSTAIN. SO I PRESENTED A SHO KIFUDA. I WAS GONNA DO THE SAME THING FOR THE OTHER THREE GUYS.
ME TOO... ALL THESE YEARS I THOUGHT IT WAS THE COURT THAT WAS SUPPOSED TO INVESTIGATE THESE GUYS.

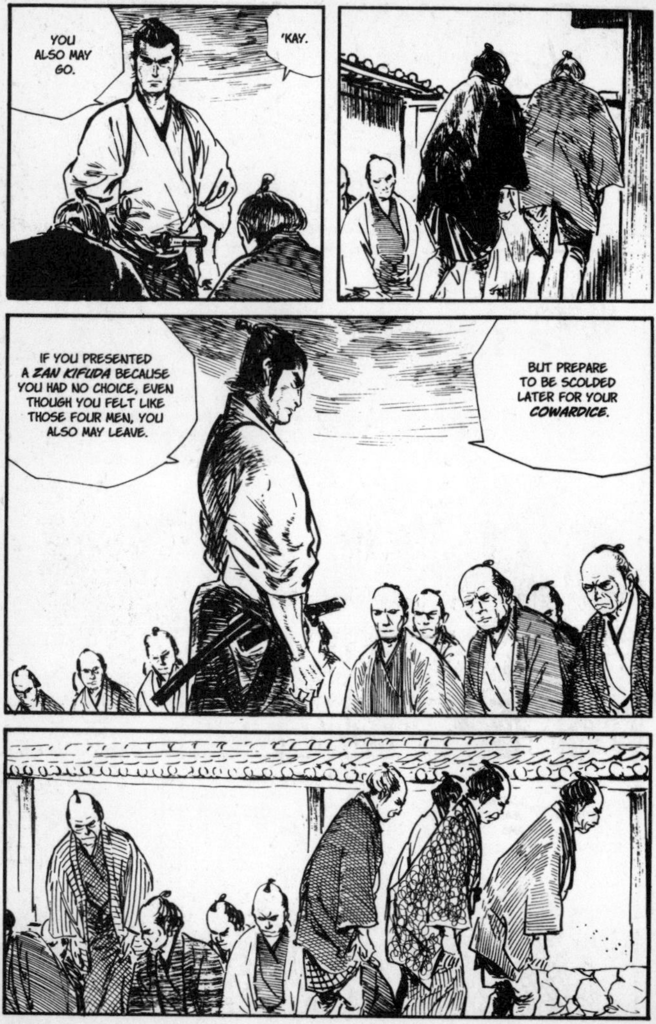
YOU ALSO MAY GO.
'KAY.
IF YOU PRESENTED A ZAN KIFUDA BECAUSE YOU HAD NO CHOICE, EVEN THOUGH YOU FELT LIKE THOSE FOUR MEN, YOU ALSO MAY LEAVE.
BUT PREPARE TO BE SCOLDED LATER FOR YOUR COWARDICE.

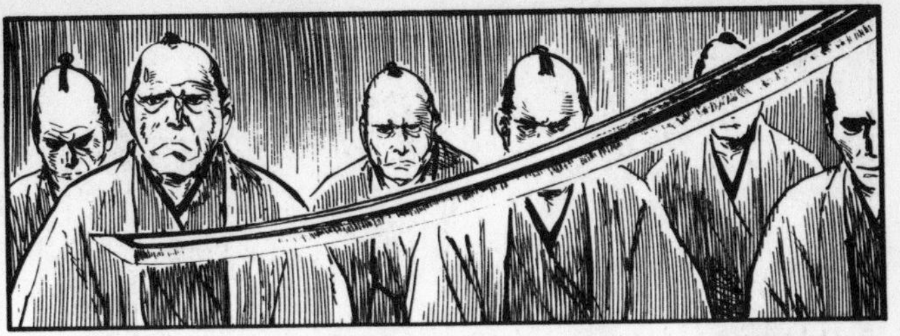

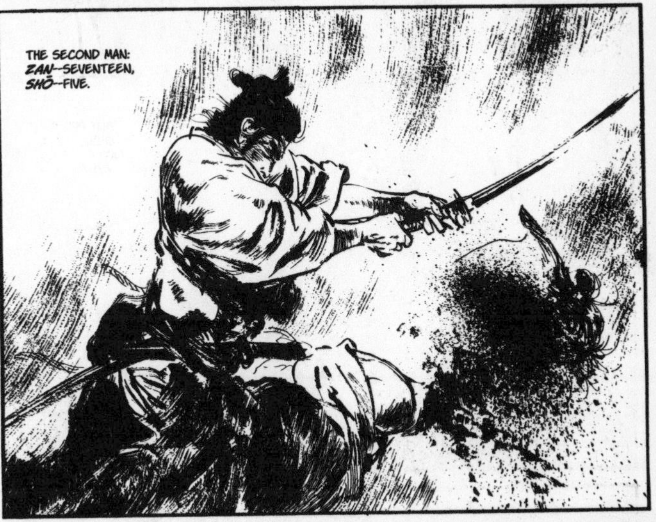
THE SECOND MAN:
ZAN--SEVENTEEN,
SHŌ--FIVE.

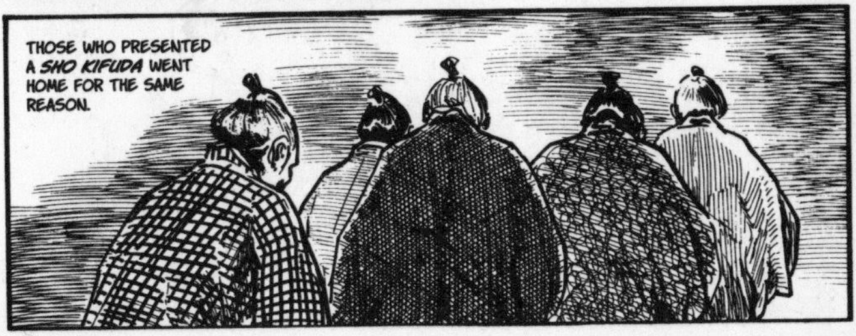
THOSE WHO PRESENTED A SHO KIFUDA WENT HOME FOR THE SAME REASON.

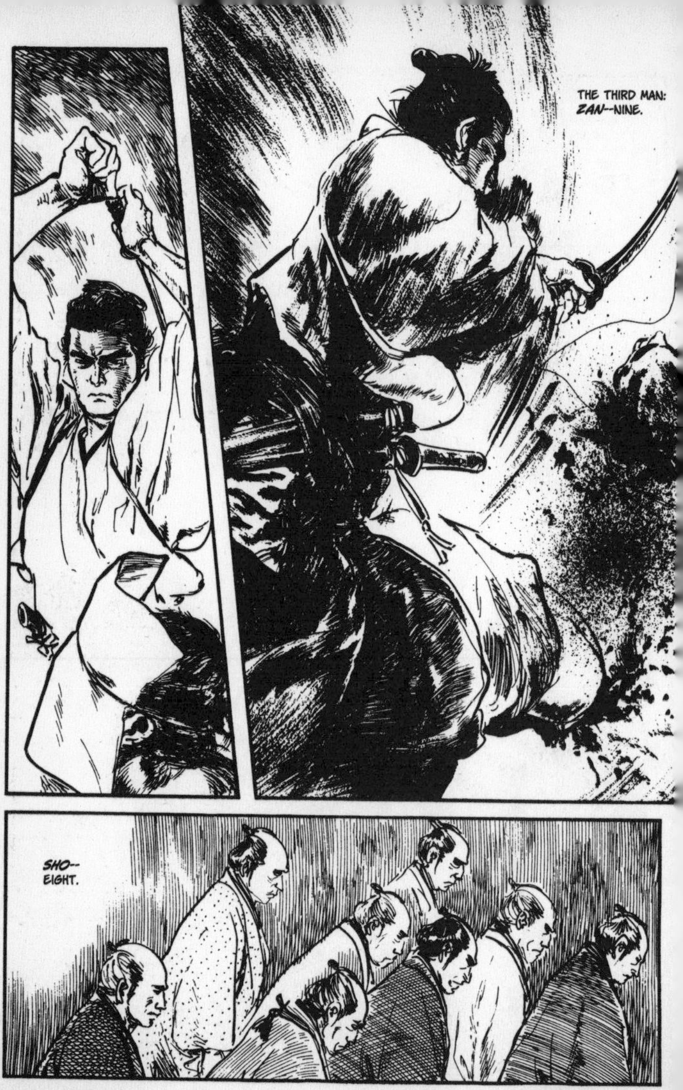
THE THIRD MAN: ZAN--NINE.
SHO-- EIGHT.

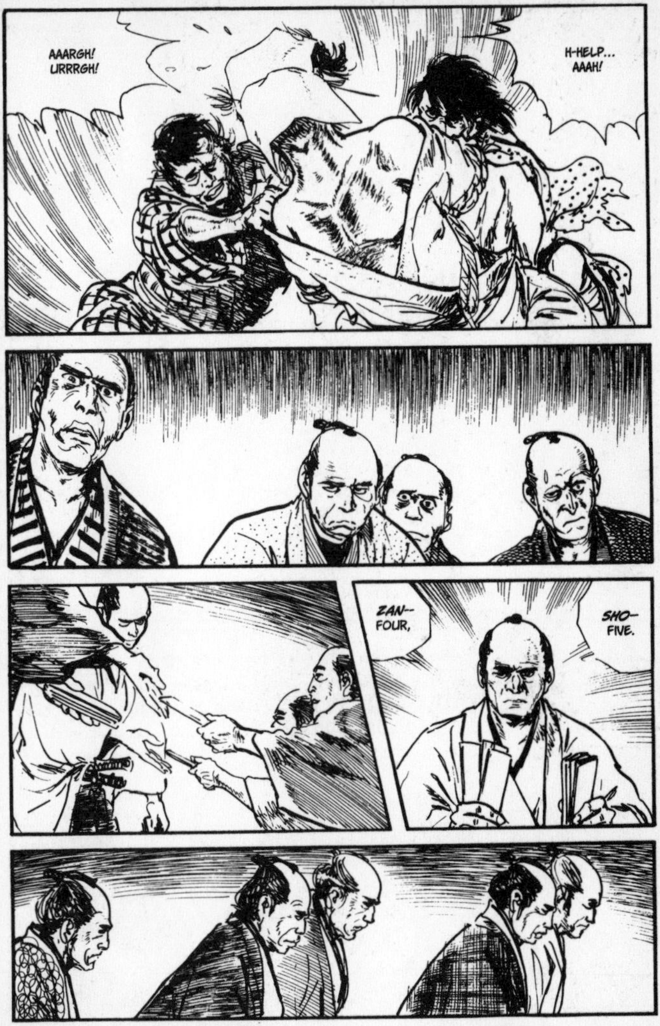
AAARGH! URRRGH!
H-HELP... AAAH!
ZAN-- FOUR,
SHO- FIVE.

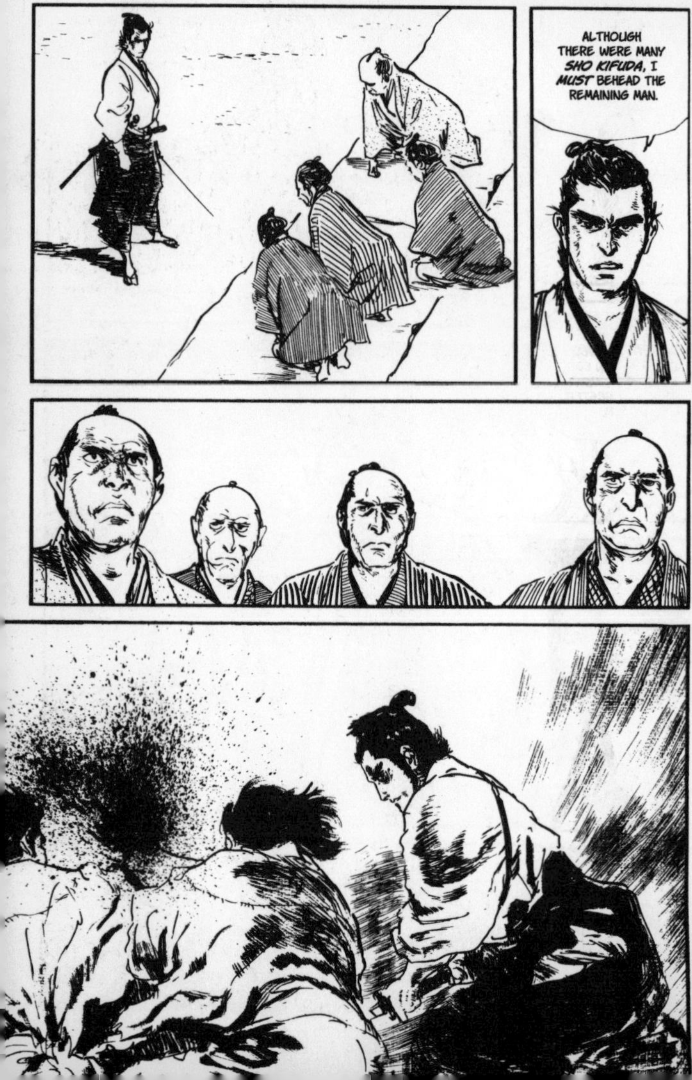
ALTHOUGH THERE WERE MANY *SHO KIFUDA*, I *MUST* BEHEAD THE REMAINING MAN.

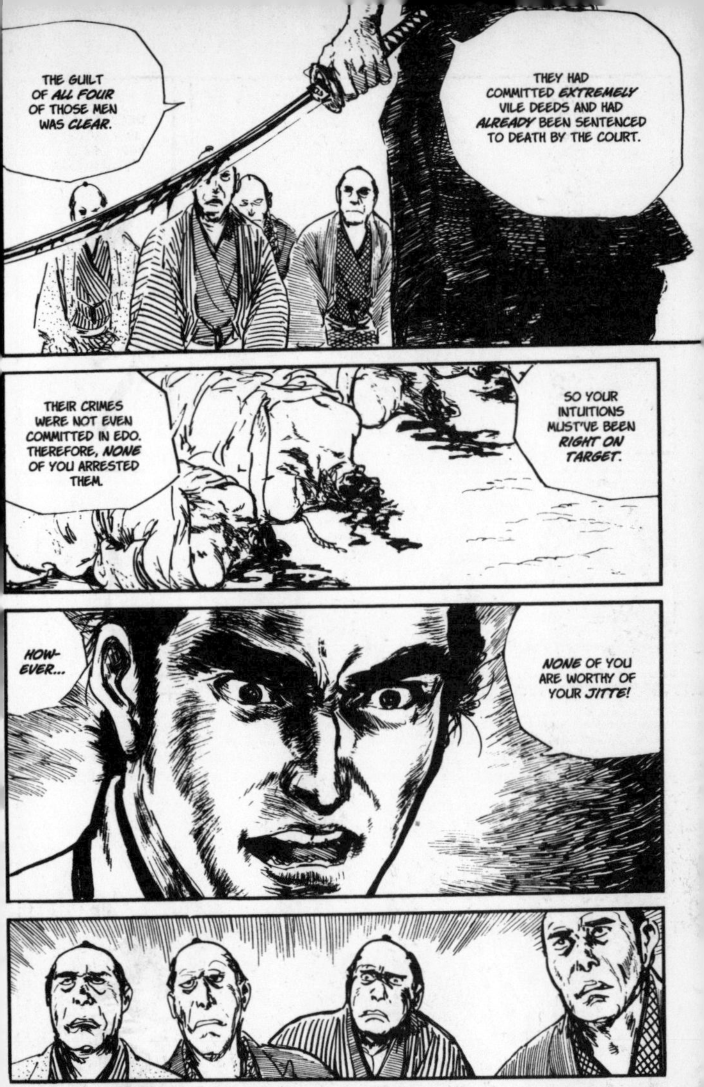
THE GUILT OF ALL FOUR OF THOSE MEN WAS CLEAR.
THEY HAD COMMITTED EXTREMELY VILE DEEDS AND HAD ALREADY BEEN SENTENCED TO DEATH BY THE COURT.
THEIR CRIMES WERE NOT EVEN COMMITTED IN EDO. THEREFORE, NONE OF YOU ARRESTED THEM.
SO YOUR INTUITIONS MUST'VE BEEN RIGHT ON TARGET.
HOW-EVER...
NONE OF YOU ARE WORTHY OF YOUR JITTE!

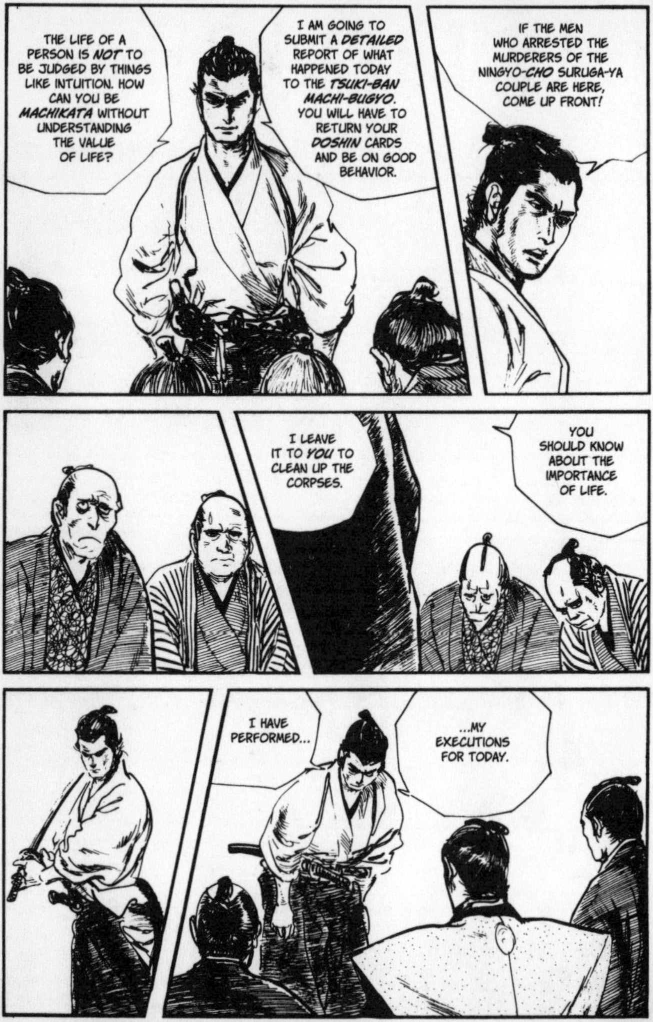
THE LIFE OF A PERSON IS *NOT* TO BE JUDGED BY THINGS LIKE INTUITION. HOW CAN YOU BE *MACHIKATA* WITHOUT UNDERSTANDING THE VALUE OF LIFE?
I AM GOING TO SUBMIT A *DETAILED* REPORT OF WHAT HAPPENED TODAY TO THE *TSUKI-BAN MACHI-BUGYO*. YOU WILL HAVE TO RETURN YOUR *DOSHIN* CARDS AND BE ON GOOD BEHAVIOR.
IF THE MEN WHO ARRESTED THE MURDERERS OF THE NINGYO-*CHO* SURUGA-YA COUPLE ARE HERE, COME UP FRONT!
I LEAVE IT TO *YOU* TO CLEAN UP THE CORPSES.
YOU SHOULD KNOW ABOUT THE IMPORTANCE OF LIFE.
I HAVE PERFORMED...
...MY EXECUTIONS FOR TODAY.

GLOSSARY

asobinin
Literally, "players." Men living in the fast lane.

bantō
The chief clerk in charge at inns, bathhouses, and other establishments, similar to today's hotel managers.

bugyōsho
Office of the commissioner (bugyō).

burei-uchi
Literally, "striking down the impolite." A samurai had the right to execute commoners for rudeness.

chō
Section of a city.

daikansho
The office of the daikan, the primary local representative of the shōgunate in territories outside of Edo. The daikan and his staff collected taxes owed to Edo and oversaw public works, agriculture, and other projects administered by the central government.

dōshin
Constable.

ebi-zume
The 'shrimp torture.' Edo police were brutal in their interrogations.

goyō
Literally, "official business." Police and posses carried "go-yo" lanterns when searching for criminals, identifying themselves as law enforcers. A shouted "Go-yo!" could be the Edo equivalent of "Halt! Police!"

for a metsuke, or "Make way!" for an official procession.

irezōmotsu
Literally, "enter bribe thing." Someone framed as a takadaimono at the end of the year by okappiki desperate for rewards.

jisha bugyō
The commissioner of shrines and temples.

jitte
A specialized weapon carried by street cops. About eighteen inches long, with no cutting edge—just two prongs designed to catch and snap off an opponent's sword blade.

jutsu
Martial arts skills, especially the techniques of the ninja.

kan
6 shaku, approximately 1.8 meters.

kifuda
Wooden slips.

kobun
Literally, "child status." Denotes junior membership in a gang.

machi-bugyō
The Edo city commissioner, combining the post of mayor and chief of police. A post held in monthly rotation by two senior Tokugawa vassals, in charge of administration, maintaining the peace, and enforcing the law in Edo. Their rule extended only to commoners; samurai in Edo were

309

controlled by their own daimyō and his officers. The machi-bugyō had an administrative staff and a small force of armed policemen at his disposal.

machikata
Town policemen.

mu
Nothingness. A crucial concept in Zen Buddhism, and a goal of all the martial arts. Clearing the mind of all extraneous thoughts and connections, to exist wholly in the moment, freed of all attachment to life and the world around you.

okappiki
Unofficial policemen who were usually former criminals.

Onibōchō
Demon Knife.

o-shirasu
Interrogation center, and often a torture chamber.

o-tameshiyaku
The swordmaster who performed o-tameshi, the testing of the shōgun's swords. The "o-" signifies respect for the shōgun.

oyabun
Literally, "father status." The boss or senior member of a yakuza gang. His underlings were known as kobun, or children.

rōjū
Inner circle of councilors directly advising the shōgun.

ryo
A gold piece.

ryū
Often translated as "school." The many variations of swordsmanship and other martial arts were passed down from generation to generation to the offspring of the originator of the technique or set of techniques, and to any deishi students that sought to learn from the master. The largest schools had their own dōjō training centers and scores of students. An effective swordsman had to study the different techniques of the various schools to know how to block them in combat. Many ryū also had a set of special, secret techniques that were only taught to school initiates.

shō
To live.

suemono-giri
Cutting through a stationary object.

takadaimono
Literally, "high platform thing." A criminal sentenced to death by crucifixion, decapitation, or burning.

tsukiban-bugyō
The commissioner on duty for a month. The northern and southern bugyōsho took turns on alternating months.

uwazumi
The sake that rises to the top in the brewing process, with the fewest impurities.

yakuza
Japan's criminal syndicates. In the Edo period, yakuza were a common part of the landscape, running houses of gambling and prostitution. As long as they did not overstep their bounds, they were tolerated by the authorities, a tradition little changed in modern Japan.

yoriki
Police lieutenant.

zan
To cut, as in cut off the head.

KAZUO KOIKE

Though widely respected as a powerful writer of graphic fiction, Kazuo Koike has spent a lifetime reaching beyond the bounds of the comics medium. Aside from co-creating and writing such classic manga as *Lone Wolf and Cub* and *Crying Freeman*, Koike has hosted the popular *Shibi Golf Weekly* instructional television program; founded the *Albatross View* golf magazine; produced movies; written popular fiction, poetry, and screenplays; and mentored some of Japan's best manga talent.

Koike started *the Gekiga Sonjuku*, a college course aimed at helping talented writers and artists—such as *Ranma* 1/2 creator Rumiko Takahashi—break into the comics field. His methods and teachings continue to influence new generations of manga creators, not to mention artists and writers around the world. Examples of Koike's influence range from the comics works of Frank Miller and Stan Sakai to the films of Quentin Tarantino.

The driving focus of Koike's narrative is character development, and his commitment to the character is clear: "Comics are carried by characters. If a character is well-created, the comic becomes a hit." Kazuo Koike's continued success in comics and literature has proven this philosophy true.

Kazuo Koike continues to work in the entertainment media to this very day, consistently diversifying his work and forging new paths across the rough roads of Edo-period history and the green swaths of today's golfing world.

GOSEKI KOJIMA

Goseki Kojima was born on November 3, 1928, the very same day as the godfather of Japanese comics, Osamu Tezuka. Art was a Kojima family tradition, his own father an amateur portrait artist and his great-great-grandfather a sculptor.

In 1950, Kojima moved to Tokyo, where the postwar devastation had given rise to special manga forms for audiences too poor to buy the new manga magazines just starting to reach the newsstands. Kojima created art for *kami-shibai*, or "paper-play" narrators, who would use manga story sheets to present narrated street plays, and later moved on to creating works for the *kashi-bon* market, bookstores that rented out books, magazines, and manga to mostly low-income readers.

In 1967, Kojima broke into the magazine market with his ninja adventure, *Dojinki*. As the manga magazine market grew and diversified, he turned out a steady stream of popular samurai manga series.

In 1970, in collaboration with Kazuo Koike, Kojima began the work that would seal his reputation, *Kozure Okami (Lone Wolf and Cub)*. Many additional series would follow, including this related series, *Samurai Executioner*.

In his final years, Kojima turned to creating original graphic novels based on the movies of his favorite director, the great Akira Kurosawa. Kojima passed away on January 5, 2000 at the age of 71.